D1569484

On the Corner

On the Corner

African American Intellectuals and the Urban Crisis

DANIEL MATLIN

HARVARD UNIVERSITY PRESS
Cambridge, Massachusetts
London, England
2013

Library of Congress Cataloging-in-Publication Data
Matlin, Daniel.
    On the corner : African American intellectuals and the urban crisis /
Daniel Matlin.
        pages   cm
    Includes bibliographical references and index.
    ISBN 978-0-674-72528-7
    1. African American intellectuals—History—20th century.   2. Clark,
Kenneth Bancroft, 1914–2005—Political and social views.   3. Baraka, Amiri,
1934– —Political and social views.   4. Bearden, Romare, 1911–1988—Political
and social views.   5. African American intellectuals—Biography.   6. African
Americans—Social conditions—1964–1975.   7. Inner cities—United States—
History—20th century.   8. Urban policy—United States—History—20th
century.   9. Harlem (New York, N.Y.)—Social conditions—20th century.
10. New York (N.Y.)—Social conditions—20th century.   I. Title.

    E185.615.M333   2013
    305.896'073—dc23   2013009716

In memory of Fergus Read
Musician, teacher, friend

Contents

Note: Illustrations follow page 198.

On the Corner

Introduction

The front page of the *New York Herald Tribune* on July 20, 1964, featured "Two Views" on the rioting in Harlem, which was then entering its third day. One was a statement from Police Commissioner Michael J. Murphy, which Harlem's ministers had been asked to read from their pulpits the previous day. The "unfortunate shooting of a Negro boy by Lieutenant Gilligan of this police department"—the killing of the unarmed, fifteen-year-old James Powell, which had sparked the rioting—would be investigated by a civilian review board, Murphy announced. However, the "looting" and the "vicious, unprovoked attacks against police" that had ensued on the streets of Harlem must, he insisted, be treated as "a crime problem and not a social problem." Appearing alongside Murphy's photograph was that of Dr. Kenneth B. Clark, who was introduced to readers of the newspaper as an academic psychologist, the director of a Harlem youth organization, and "a respected spokesman for the Negro community." Clark's article, written "exclusively for the *Herald Tribune*," was a stark rebuttal of Murphy's statement. It was a "serious mistake," Clark argued, to regard the violence in Harlem as simply the "lawlessness of criminal elements." Instead, "one must understand that Harlem is a product of violence," a "ghetto wherein human beings are confined and are exploited because they cannot escape." The rioting, Clark wrote, was a response to "the chronic day-to-day quiet violence against the human spirit which exists and is accepted as normal."[1]

The Harlem riot of 1964 abruptly cast a spotlight on black urban life in the North. In doing so, it prompted a radical and enduring shift in perceptions of black America, and of the nature and location of America's racial divisions and conflicts. For much of the preceding decade, the American media and public had been absorbed with the boycotts, sit-ins, and freedom rides staged by civil rights protesters in the Jim Crow South. The main locus of black life for centuries, it was the South that had wielded the crudest instruments of racial oppression, from plantation slavery to legally mandated segregation and disenfranchisement. Yet even as the dramatic confrontations in Mississippi and Alabama dominated news headlines during the peak years of southern protest, a demographic revolution had been quietly remaking black America. Between 1940 and 1970, in one of the most rapid and extensive internal migrations ever to occur outside a theater of war, some five million African Americans left the South for the cities of the North. Many had been forced from the land by the mechanization of southern agriculture. Like their predecessors in the early years of the twentieth century, those who journeyed north in this second phase of the "Great Migration" hoped for high-wage industrial jobs, decent housing, and relief from the dangers and demeaning rituals of Jim Crow. Yet all too often their expectations were confounded by the realities of deindustrializing "Rust Belt" cities. Job opportunities were circumscribed by the racist practices of employers and unions, while real estate agencies and city housing authorities enforced the North's own, mostly unwritten, laws of residential segregation. Moreover, vast structural changes in the nation's economy were placing the new arrivals at even greater disadvantage.[2]

Postwar America's surging economic growth concealed the uneven spread of prosperity and the disappearance of hundreds of thousands of manufacturing jobs from traditional industrial centers in the cities of the Northeast and Midwest. Aided by tax relief and federal highway construction, automated plants sprang up in the rapidly expanding suburbs where, despite the efforts of open housing activists, African Americans were systematically denied mortgages and tenancies. The skilled jobs on offer in the new suburban factories were both geographically and educationally out of reach of most African Americans, who had few options other than to crowd into deteriorating inner-city neighborhoods. The white middle and working classes abandoned the cities in droves, transferring their valuable tax dollars to the burgeoning suburbs as they searched for new employment opportunities and racially homogeneous neighborhoods and schools. As municipal tax bases collapsed, it was African Americans who disproportionately felt the force of the "urban crisis" proclaimed by city politicians and commentators.[3]

The conditions that defined that crisis—high unemployment, poverty, segregation, inadequate services, crumbling infrastructure, and dilapidated housing—combined with resentment of racially exclusive suburban prosperity to yield deep frustrations, which major incidents of police brutality were liable to ignite. The riots of the mid- and late 1960s, which commenced in Harlem in 1964 and spread over successive "long, hot summers" to Watts, Newark, Detroit, and hundreds of other urban locations across the northern states, loudly interrupted the climax of the southern protest movement and confronted many white Americans for the first time with a new demographic reality. Blacks were becoming a majority northern, urban people. Moreover, many of America's largest cities looked set to become majority black. In 1940, more than three-quarters of African Americans had lived in the South, and fully half in the rural South. By 1965, as Kenneth Clark reported that year in his book *Dark Ghetto: Dilemmas of Social Power,* virtually half of America's black population lived in northern cities. The "problem of the American Negro," Clark wrote, had become "predominantly a Northern problem."[4]

Clark's views were much sought after following the outbreak of violence in Harlem. *Newsweek*'s cover story on the riot included a lengthy quotation from the "Negro psychologist," who "angrily" described the "horrible living conditions" in the neighborhood. The nation's major television networks (ABC, CBS, and NBC) all featured Clark as a commentator in special, extended reports on the Harlem riot. The following year, *Dark Ghetto,* Clark's psychological and sociological portrait of the

Harlem community, was partially serialized in the *New York Post*. Indeed, it was in the mid-1960s that his visibility peaked. Today, Clark is widely remembered as the "scholar of the 1954 *Brown v. Board of Education* decision," whose expert testimony helped persuade the U.S. Supreme Court to outlaw segregated schooling. Yet Clark had remained a fairly obscure figure throughout the 1950s, and only in the following decade would his role in *Brown* elicit much comment in the media. By then, Clark's profile had been greatly enhanced by the rising public interest in black urban communities in the North.[5]

As the 1960s began, racial frictions in northern cities periodically diverted attention from the civil rights campaigns in the South. In July 1959, the five-part television documentary *The Hate That Hate Produced* brought Malcolm X, the Nation of Islam's acerbic Harlem minister, into the public eye for the first time, and prompted panicked editorials about "black racists" dwelling in America's cities. In the summer of 1963, as demonstrators' commitment to nonviolence was being stretched to its limit in Birmingham, Alabama, skirmishes between black youths and police in a number of northern cities, including New York and Philadelphia, were also reported in the press. Against this backdrop, Clark hosted three broadcasts on the National Education Television network in which he conducted interviews with Martin Luther King Jr., Malcolm X, and the novelist James Baldwin. Clark probed their views on the aims of black protest, the efficacy of nonviolence, and the possibility of achieving racial equality in America. A year later, however, Clark was himself enlisted by interviewers to explain why, just two weeks after President Lyndon Johnson had signed the Civil Rights Act, thousands of Harlem's residents had taken to the streets to smash windows, burn down stores, and hurl bricks and bottles at police.[6]

Clark was one of a number of African American intellectuals whose careers were transformed by the heightened attention devoted to black urban life in the North from the mid-1960s. Amid the riots and growing demands for "black power," publishers, editors, theater producers, and gallery curators all looked to black intellectuals to act as *indigenous interpreters* of black urban life to the white American public: to combine their intimate, experiential knowledge as racial "insiders" with the rigor of academic analysis, the crackle of polemic, or the poignancy of art. Identified as a "Negro psychologist," Clark was seen to be doubly qualified by his race and his profession to lay bare the emotional condition of black urban America. Accepting the role of indigenous interpreter, Clark presented *Dark Ghetto* not only as a report on years of intensive social scientific investigation, but also as an account informed by his "personal and lifelong experiences" within the Harlem community. Reporters and editors exercised little subtlety when drawing attention to his race. An article written by Clark for the *New York Post* in 1967 appeared under the title "A Negro Looks at 'Black Power.'"[7]

The aspiring poet, playwright, essayist, and activist LeRoi Jones— later Amiri Baraka—was little known beyond a few Greenwich Village cafés during the early 1960s. Yet for Jones, too, growing public interest in the discontent and violence emanating from black urban communities was to have a profound effect. As the literary elder statesman Langston Hughes would later remark, 1964 was "the Jones Year." Five of Jones's plays opened in New York theaters within the space of a few months, and his second volume of poetry, *The Dead Lecturer,* was brought out by Grove Press, a leading radical publisher. Of all his works to appear that year, it was his play *Dutchman* that garnered the most attention. Opening at the Cherry Lane Theater in the West Village on March 24, the play confronted its audience with the furious outbursts of a young black man on the New York subway who proclaims that killing whites would be a "simple act" of "sanity." *Dutchman* was greeted by critics as a lens onto the enraged black psyche. In the *New York Times,* Howard Taubman called it "an explosion of hatred, rather than a play," and ventured: "If this is the way the Negroes really feel about the white world around them there is more rancor buried in the breasts of colored conformists than any one can imagine. If this is the way even one Negro feels there is ample cause for guilt as well as alarm and for a hastening of change."[8]

Dutchman touched a raw nerve at a moment when incidents of vandalism on the New York subway were provoking fearful discussion about violent black youth in the city. Jones appeared alongside Kenneth Clark in June on a panel assembled by the *New York Herald Tribune* to discuss the outlook for the "summer ahead." Clark spoke in urgent but measured tones about the injustices facing young people in Harlem and about his own efforts, as the founder of Harlem Youth Opportunities Unlimited (HARYOU) to "direct their energy toward changing the social conditions which now exist." Jones, who at twenty-nine was two decades Clark's junior, stated by contrast that his only advice to the young African Americans who had been smashing windows on subway trains would be to "do it every night." *Dutchman*'s run at Cherry Lane was extended into 1965, and invitations abounded for Jones to contribute articles to newspapers and magazines, speak at public debates, and teach college courses. As tensions mounted in New York and finally combusted in the Harlem riot, Jones, too, began to be promoted as an indigenous interpreter of black urban life to an alarmed and fascinated white public. His wish, however, was not merely to interpret but to embody the swelling rebellion. In 1965, he left his home and his interracial marriage in bohemian Greenwich Village and moved first to Harlem and then back to his birthplace of Newark, New Jersey, where he would fashion a new identity as Amiri Baraka. Yet even this turn away from his white audience was a public performance freighted with symbolism amid the surge of black nationalist militancy. Following his arrest on weapons charges during the Newark riot in 1967, *Time* magazine dubbed him "the snarling laureate of Negro revolt."[9]

For the fifty-three-year-old artist Romare Bearden, 1964 was also a pivotal year. Since the late 1940s, Bearden's increasingly abstract canvases had won respectful comments in the New York press, but it was his full-time job as a social worker that had paid the bills. In October 1964, however, his solo exhibition *Projections* unveiled a radical shift in his artistic practice, and one that would redefine his career. Abandoning abstract painting, as readers of *ARTnews* learned, "Bearden turns to images of his native Harlem for a spectacular group of new collages." His family had arrived in Harlem from Charlotte, North Carolina, half a century earlier when he was three or four years old, and *Projections* also included images of the rural South in an allusion to the Great Migration, of which the Beardens had been a part. Exhibited just three months after the Harlem riot, however, it was Bearden's densely populated urban scenes that preoccupied reviewers. *Newsweek* discerned in the collages "tormented faces of Southern Negro women hanging upside down on the cracked stoops of Harlem tenements," and *Time* described them as "surreal cityscapes of Negro life."[10]

Bearden had arrived at a strikingly distinctive collage aesthetic. The new work reflected the tremendous breadth of his artistic influences, from the northern European genre painting of the sixteenth and seventeenth centuries to the modernist formal innovations of cubism and photomontage, to Chinese landscape painting, to the African American patchwork folk tradition. The burst of critical attention and opportunities for solo exhibitions that followed *Projections* owed much to the appeal of this engaging visual idiom. Yet, as Bearden himself observed, imagination, proficiency, and flair had seldom ensured recognition of African American artists. Like Kenneth Clark and LeRoi Jones, Bearden found his profile sharply raised by the growing appetite for intimate, "authentic" portrayals of life in black urban communities. *Newsweek* introduced him as a "husky, 50-year-old Negro," as though to underscore the decades of lived experience that imbued his depictions of "Harlem tenements." Though critics sometimes detected a surreal strain in Bearden's stark juxtapositions and variations of perspective and scale, the figurative and narrative dimensions of his collages prompted many to emphasize their documentary effect. So, too, did Bearden's use of photographic fragments culled from newspapers and magazines. To one reviewer, the Harlem collages conveyed "degrees of actuality that straightforward images could never achieve," while another experienced the "shock and impact of a swift cinematic passage." The convergence between Bearden's new figurative aesthetic and the rising public fascination with black urban life ensured that by the late 1960s he was able for the first time to earn a living from art alone. In 1968, he was commissioned by *Fortune* magazine to compose a Harlem street scene for the cover of a special issue on "Business and the Urban Crisis," and by *Time* to illustrate its cover story, "New York: The Breakdown of a City." A retrospective at the Museum of Modern Art in 1971 confirmed Bearden as a major presence in American art.[11]

Living and working in and around New York City, Clark, Jones, and Bearden all recognized the Harlem riot of 1964 as a brash announcement of black America's increasingly northern, urban presence, and as a re-inscription of Harlem's symbolic significance as a barometer of the fortunes of all black Americans. As their own careers manifest, the Harlem riot also inaugurated a new phase in the history of black intellectual life, one in which long-standing notions of racial representation and responsibility were reformulated around the task of interpreting—and transforming—black urban communities. This book explores the differing ways in which these three figures responded to the urban crisis and to their own newfound prominence as indigenous interpreters of black urban life. It asks how they conceived the dynamics of black urban communities and how they sought to communicate their insights; what they believed was at stake in representing black life to white audiences and to what extent they welcomed this role; and how they understood their own predicaments at a time when commentators spoke not only of an urban crisis but also of a "crisis of the Negro intellectual." Posing these questions raises more fundamental ones about the relationship between race and intellectual life in the United States and beyond. What role have intellectuals played in shaping the complex of meanings attached to "race"? And how has the ongoing social production and cultural reinvention of "race" affected the experience of intellectual life?[12]

The title of this book is borrowed from a Miles Davis album of 1972. Clark, Jones, and Bearden were all seen to be *On the Corner*—down on the streets of black America and so uniquely positioned to convey to white audiences the physical, social, and emotional realities of life in black urban communities.[13] This cultural recognition not only conferred status and opportunities for material rewards, but also provided a platform from which they could work to alter public perceptions of African Americans and testify to the human impact of the urban crisis. They did so from distinct disciplinary standpoints and with contrasting political convictions. Yet by the end of the 1960s, each had come to view the role of indigenous interpreter with deep skepticism. The role that had dramatically elevated their public profiles had also proved to be demeaning and confining, subject as it was to terms and conditions imposed by white audiences and cultural arbiters. Compounding the restrictive force of white expectations was the weighty sense of obligation to "the race" that had characterized black intellectual life for generations. It was at this moment during the 1960s, as the riots brought the new demography of black America into relief, that this sense of obligation attached itself primarily to the business of interpreting and ameliorating the conditions of black urban life. By the end of the twentieth century, "urban" would be widely employed as a synonym for "black." Moreover, black urban communities have continued to be regarded as the chief objects of, and proving grounds for, black intellectuals' responsibilities.[14]

The single most widely debated and controversial portrayal of urban African Americans to emerge during the postwar period was authored not by a black intellectual, but by the assistant secretary of labor in President Lyndon Johnson's administration. This was Daniel Patrick Moynihan's leaked report of 1965, *The Negro Family: The Case for National Action,* which warned that "the Negro family in the urban ghettos is crumbling." Family breakdown, Moynihan stated, was the "fundamental problem" preventing African Americans from achieving social and economic equality. Meanwhile, the social scientists Elliot Liebow and Lee Rainwater, the novelists-cum-journalists Thomas Pynchon and Tom Wolfe, and a multitude of reporters and columnists were among the many other white Americans who addressed themselves to aspects of black life in the nation's cities.[15]

Black intellectuals, however, had long claimed a privileged understanding of America and its racial illusions. W. E. B. Du Bois had written at the turn of the twentieth century of black people's "second-sight in this American world," and in 1926 he restated his belief that "we who are dark can see America in a way that white Americans can not." Ralph Ellison, an author not much given to racial mystique, would echo Du Bois when he wrote in 1969 that there were "many aspects of American life which can only be described, analyzed, and defined by black intellectuals, for no other group possesses an adequate perspective or so urgent a need." As black life in northern cities drew public fascination, black intellectuals continued to assert their privileged, experiential insight. Thus Clark drew attention to his own Harlem upbringing, while Bearden wrote of his intention "to paint the life of my people as I know it." As Carlo Rotella has observed, in texts such as Clark's *Dark Ghetto,* black authors assumed a "special authority" to define black urban life from within.[16]

Of the many black intellectuals during the 1960s who addressed themselves to questions of black urban experience, Clark, Jones, and Bearden stand out as having been raised from near obscurity by the mounting public interest in African American urban communities. Such renowned literary figures as Ellison, James Baldwin, and Lorraine Hansberry also furnished powerful images of black life in northern cities. Ellison's literary stardom had been achieved years earlier, however, when his novel *Invisible Man* (1952) had won critical plaudits and the National Book Award. Ellison was a widely published commentator and essayist by the mid-1950s. Baldwin's most searing and sustained portrait of black urban life appeared in his semiautobiographical debut novel, *Go Tell It on the Mountain* (1953). Yet his profile and creative energies waned following *Another Country* (1962) and *The Fire Next Time* (1963), and it was LeRoi Jones whom *Playboy* magazine would hail in 1965 as "the most discussed—and admired—Negro writer since James Baldwin." Hansberry's best-known play, *A Raisin in the Sun,* had opened on Broadway in 1959 and captures the strained relationships within a black family on Chicago's South Side as they prepare to integrate a white neighborhood. Warmly received by many theater critics who saw the play as an endorsement of assimilation and the "American Dream," it was later denounced by black nationalists on the same grounds. Hansberry's career was cruelly truncated in January 1965 by her death from cancer at the age of thirty-four.[17]

Fleetingly, Hansberry had intruded into a public sphere that seldom admitted black women's voices. Though Ella Baker, Fannie Lou Hamer, Elaine Brown, and many other women played important leadership roles within the civil rights and black power movements, black women were scarcely accorded the status of indigenous interpreters during the 1960s. Even Angela Davis, then a young philosophy professor at the University of California, Los Angeles, achieved notoriety not as an intellectual but as a fashion icon and a defendant in a conspiracy trial. The Chicago poet Gwendolyn Brooks, who, like Ellison and Baldwin, had made her literary reputation in the immediate postwar years, remained perhaps the most widely known black female intellectual in the mid- and late 1960s. Even so, a sympathetic commentator remarked in 1968 that the Pulitzer Prize Brooks had won in 1950 for *Annie Allen* had "guaranteed her about as much lasting attention as the Academy Award did Jane Darwell." An article on twelve prominent American intellectuals that appeared in *Life* magazine in 1967 featured not a single woman. In the eyes of the media, an authentic or representative black perspective was necessarily a male one—an assumption later mocked by the title of the black feminist anthology *All the Women Are White, All the Blacks Are Men, but Some of Us Are Brave*. Only with the upsurge of black feminist activism and scholarship from the early 1970s would black women begin to gain wide recognition as interpreters of African American experience. By the 1980s, few black male intellectuals rivaled the public profiles of the novelists Alice Walker and Toni Morrison.[18]

One purpose of *On the Corner,* then, is to reconstruct the role of indigenous interpreter and to explore the ways in which it was envisioned and experienced. Another closely related aim is to map out the boundaries of an intense, often fractious debate among black intellectuals concerning the nature of black urban life and the means and consequences of its representation. The work produced by Clark, Jones, and Bearden, which collectively spans social psychology, political polemic, fiction, poetry, drama, and the visual arts, illustrates the extent to which this debate cut across disciplines, genres, and media. This is not to suggest that disciplinary distinctions were unimportant. Indeed, rivalry between disciplines for authority to define and represent black urban life was an important element of the debate. Particularly contentious was the role of the social sciences. The 1960s marked the peak of their prestige, institutional power, and influence over policymaking in the United States. Yet the same decade witnessed a growing backlash against this influence, prompted in part by what some saw as the reductive, distorted view of black communities contained in the Moynihan Report and also by discomfort with the involvement of American social scientists as advisers to the U.S. government and military during the Vietnam War. The debate about black urban life among African American intellectuals during the 1960s illuminates the complex engagement between the social sciences and the arts at this moment of instability and tension.[19]

Clark, Jones, and Bearden rarely communicated directly with one another or commented explicitly on each other's work. Contact between them was sporadic, despite their concurrent connections to Harlem. The testy exchange between Clark and Jones in 1964 was followed by a more constructive private meeting in 1969. Clark and Bearden were on friendly terms by the late 1960s, and Bearden attended a fund-raising event in 1968 for Harlem's Northside Center for Child Development, where Clark's wife, Mamie Phipps Clark, was director and Clark himself was a board member. Bearden and Jones seem never to have met. The three men largely inhabited different social and intellectual circles and, with their contrasting disciplinary and political standpoints, approached the urban crisis and the role of indigenous interpreter in divergent ways. Yet each of them exemplifies the ways in which social scientists, literary authors, and visual artists understood themselves to be engaged in a common endeavor of representing and interpreting black urban life. Each was moved to contemplate, corroborate, or contest ideas emerging from disciplines other than his own.[20]

Dialogue and interconnections between artistic and social scientific portrayals of black life have a long history. Du Bois had authored one of the pioneering works of American urban sociology, *The Philadelphia Negro* (1899), more than a decade before the publication of his first novel, *The Quest of the Silver Fleece* (1911). During the interwar years, the novelist Zora Neale Hurston also worked as a research anthropologist, having studied with Franz Boas and Ruth Benedict. And Richard Wright in the 1940s acknowledged the influence of "Chicago School" urban sociology on his fictional evocation of Chicago's South Side. Such influences and interactions persisted during the 1960s. Clark deeply admired the urban realism of the novels of Wright and James Baldwin, while Jones's essays and poems signaled his appreciation of E. Franklin Frazier's caustic sociological portrayal of the black middle class. Not all cross-disciplinary exchanges were so complimentary, however. Some black intellectuals spoke across disciplinary boundaries chiefly to censure the work of others and to question the capacity of certain disciplines to yield valid knowledge about black life. Clark's writings, especially *Dark Ghetto,* became a prominent target for the rising critique of the social sciences.[21]

To Clark's mind, sociologists and social psychologists were uniquely placed to convey to white Americans the social "pathology" and psychological "damage" inflicted on African Americans by racism and poverty. By doing so, these disciplines would help to foster public empathy for the black urban poor and support for social reforms. Such beliefs typified the optimism of Clark's generation of postwar American social scientists, emboldened by their disciplines' enlistment into government service during World War II and by the social sciences' growing institutional power within universities during the 1950s. Clark and other "pathologist" social scientists maintained a confident expectation that social problems could be redressed through the rational application of social scientific knowledge to public policymaking, backed up by pressure from an informed public. If white Americans were made fully aware of the social and emotional harm done to African Americans by racism and poverty, and of the cost of this damage to the wider society, the federal government would be compelled to confront such inequalities. Just weeks after *Dark Ghetto* appeared in May 1965, pathologist social science reached its crest of influence when President Johnson delivered his commencement address at Howard University in Washington, D.C., and explained his Great Society programs as remedies for the "lacerating hurt" caused to black Americans by "ancient brutality, past injustice, and present prejudice."[22]

Only a few months later, however, the leaking of the Moynihan Report engendered a storm of protest, which was to have a lasting impact on the social sciences' prestige and influence. The imagery of black social pathology and psychological damage deployed by liberal social scientists to expose the force of racial oppression, invoke empathy, and stimulate reform was now branded as erroneous, insulting, and even racist. Leading the charge were two African American literary intellectuals who broadened the critique of pathologism into an indictment of the social sciences themselves. Ralph Ellison had been arguing for several years that knowledge of black life had been "distorted through the overemphasis of the sociological approach." In many cases, Ellison claimed, African Americans had themselves "accepted a statistical interpretation of our lives, and thus much of that which makes us a source of moral strength to America goes unappreciated and undefined." Ellison's close friend Albert Murray, a fellow alumnus of Alabama's Tuskegee Institute and an essayist and aspiring novelist, similarly condemned the "so-called findings and all-too-inclusive extrapolations of social science survey technicians." Murray championed a "distinctly proliterary" approach to the representation of black life, one that was attentive to the "complexities" of lived experience rather than "terminological abstractions and categories derived from laboratory experience."[23]

Both Ellison and Murray singled out Clark for criticism as a leading pathologist. They rejected *Dark Ghetto*'s harrowing portrayal of Harlem, which they considered reductive and dehumanizing. Both men also faulted black novelists such as Wright and Baldwin for capitulating to the "sociological" perspective in their writings and so abdicating the possibilities of art. By contrast, Ellison and Murray celebrated the work of their close friend Bearden, whose collages, they believed, captured dimensions of black experience beyond hardship and misery. Bearden, Ellison suggested in 1968, had sought "to reveal a world long hidden by the clichés of sociology and rendered cloudy by the distortions of newsprint and the false continuity imposed upon our conception of Negro life by television and much documentary photography." Indeed, Bearden shared his literary friends' conviction that art could account for aspects of black urban experience neglected by the social sciences. Baldwin, he felt, had erred as a novelist in "defining the Negro sociologically, but not artistically." Yet Bearden was more willing than Ellison or Murray to take seriously the claims of social scientists and to acknowledge that they, too, grasped some of the realities of life in black urban communities. Whether participants in these debates welcomed or rejected the commingling of artistic and social scientific "definitions," each was acutely aware that images of black life emanating from all points on the disciplinary spectrum had the potential to shape public perceptions of African Americans, for better or worse.[24]

The critique of pathologism framed by Ellison and Murray during the 1960s laid much of the groundwork for recent, historical accounts of the postwar social sciences' engagement with matters of race. A number of scholars have charted the failure of postwar social scientists to predict the consequences of their use of "damage imagery" and to achieve their liberal aims. Daryl Michael Scott argues convincingly that representations of black life that were intended to invoke empathy and generate public support for social reforms all too often encouraged contempt and fatalism about the black poor and fed support for a punitive politics of law and order. Alice O'Connor also shows how an emphasis on black social and psychological dysfunction proved to be "powerfully stigmatizing" and "reinforced the imagery of a basically unassimilable black lower class." Indeed, from the mid-1960s, damage imagery was increasingly appropriated by conservatives, who argued that black social and psychological pathologies were the cause, rather than the consequence, of black poverty. Government programs, entitlements, and affirmative action policies, these commentators argued, could not provide solutions. It was these very interventions, rather than racism and economic exclusion, that had created the "damage," they claimed. Beyond recounting the political failures of the liberal pathologist project, historians have also elaborated on the ethical critique mounted by Ellison and Murray. Robin Kelley charges pathologists with obscuring the "complexity" and "humanity" of black communities by characterizing black urban life merely as a set of deviant reactions to oppression.[25]

As valuable as these insights are, the studies of Clark, Jones, and Bearden that follow depart from the dominant understanding of pathologism in a number of important respects. In exploring the representations of black urban life that these figures crafted in their role as indigenous interpreters, this book seeks to achieve a more balanced understanding of the debate between pathologists and their opponents. To begin with, while the efforts and experiences of Clark, Jones, and Bearden confirm elements of the critique of damage imagery, they also reveal pathologism to have been a more capacious intellectual formation than has previously been acknowledged. Far from being the preserve only of liberal technocrats and conservative ideologues, pathologism during the 1960s was also deeply enmeshed with radical theories of social action. Clark has been portrayed as an archetypal technocrat who set about engineering social reforms from above, whereas, Scott argues, it was ultimately "the social activism of those said to be too afflicted to stand up for their own rights" that secured the victories of the civil rights era. This not only misunderstands Clark, but also wrongly assumes that damage theory entailed a denial of the agency of the oppressed.[26]

As will be seen in Chapter 1, Clark did not regard the black urban poor as passive recipients of governmental or charitable largesse. His design for the HARYOU antipoverty project was premised on the notion that the people of Harlem possessed a rebellious energy that could be channeled into transformative social action. Historians have failed to detect Clark's highly politicized understanding of psychological health and his radical conception of the therapeutic. That Clark did not see damaged self-esteem as fatal to self-assertion aligns him with James Baldwin and with the Martinique-born psychiatrist Frantz Fanon. As the historian Richard King astutely observes, both Baldwin and Fanon envisioned the black oppressed simultaneously as "damaged victims" whose hatred was "directed against the self" and as possessors of a "rage against white society" that could spur them to become "righteous avengers."[27]

Another radical response to the urban crisis that often embraced pathologism was black power. Yet neither the burgeoning scholarship on the black power movement nor the literature on damage imagery has acknowledged that many black nationalists in the 1960s and 1970s viewed black urban life through a pathologist lens. Scott in fact associates black power with a "radical assault" on damage imagery that gathered force in the wake of the Moynihan controversy. Much evidence points to the contrary, however. Following Jones's career beyond Greenwich Village and Harlem to his emergence as a black power leader in Newark during the late 1960s, Chapter 2 demonstrates how he and other black nationalist theorists diagnosed black urban life as a morass of social, psychological, and moral pathologies. Though unconcerned with appeals to the white conscience, the black power movement's internal dialogue was often saturated with damage imagery. So-called "cultural nationalists," in particular, conceived of black power as an antidote to what they viewed as widespread black self-hatred, self-denial, and moral and cultural degeneracy. No less than Clark, they combined a belief in the damaged black psyche with an expectation that African Americans would bring about profound social change.[28]

Unlike Clark, however, they also drew on a censorious, moralizing tradition of black social thought. During the nineteenth and early twentieth centuries, this "uplift tradition" had not only faulted white racism, but had also faulted African Americans themselves for their subordinate status and their perceived social and moral pathologies. Black power has typically been designated as a departure from this tradition. However, Chapter 2 argues that uplift's insistence on self-help and self-transformation, which had characterized earlier moral panics about the pathologies of black urbanization, remained crucial in the politics of the black power movement. Moreover, notions of intellectual responsibility and utility shared by Jones and other black power theorists—specifically, the notion that resolving the urban crisis depended on instigating cultural change among the black poor—substantially reproduced the elitist dynamics of uplift within the black intellectual discourse of the post-riot era, with its increasingly restrictive focus on black urban communities. Pursuing Jones's trajectory beyond his performance to white audiences thus prompts a reevaluation of pathologism and its relation to the black power movement. Black power emerges as a set of responses to the postwar urban crisis that inherited far more from the dominant traditions of black social thought—and from the therapeutic concerns of liberal social science—than has previously been recognized.[29]

Pathologism needs also to be understood within the context of a highly polarized debate about representations of black urban life during the 1960s. Yet while historians have taken seriously the charges leveled against pathologists by authors such as Ellison and Murray, little attention has been devoted to the pathologists' countercharges against their critics. Anti-pathologists were not alone in discerning that well-intended, apparently benign imagery could serve to reinforce pernicious racial attitudes. While Murray complained that *Dark Ghetto*'s "emphasis on black wretchedness . . . easily exceeds that in most books written by *white racists to justify segregation,*" Clark was no less troubled by Murray's stated aim of "accentuating the positive and eliminating the negative" in depictions of black life. Murray believed that damage imagery would lend authority to stereotypes of black mental inferiority and social deviancy. Clark, meanwhile, worried that Murray's portrayal of black urban communities as havens of joyous recreation would resonate with a competing set of stereotypes, one that asserted black people's contentment and unique capacity for enjoyment, and which had served as an ideological prop for slavery and segregation.[30]

Romare Bearden possessed a rare ability during the 1960s to navigate between these representational extremes. As Chapter 3 argues, notwithstanding his close friendship with Murray, and contrary to scholarship that emphasizes the celebratory tenor of his own work, Bearden aspired to a "realism" that would avoid the excesses of both the pathologist and anti-pathologist positions. Though wary of the relentless "sociological" preoccupation with damage and misery, Bearden was unwilling to "eliminate the negative" from his Harlem collages. He sought instead to capture the multiplicity of "the life of my people," a life burdened by, but not reducible to, injustice and poverty.

Throughout the twentieth century, Harlem held a unique symbolic importance for many African Americans. Every northern metropolis had its black neighborhoods, born of restrictive housing covenants and enlarged by successive waves of migrants. In most cities, these neighborhoods were confined to the most dilapidated and polluted areas, where only a group deemed inferior would be expected to live. Harlem was an altogether different inheritance. Plans to extend the subway north of Central Park had prompted a frenzy of construction in the final two decades of the nineteenth century, which transformed the dwindling agricultural community that comprised the remnants of the Dutch settlement of Nieuw Haarlem. Handsome brownstone town houses sprang up, and the Polo Grounds (1876) and Harlem Opera House (1889) signaled the gentility of their intended occupants. Supply outpaced demand, however, and falling prices opened the area to moderately prosperous Italian and Jewish families. When the economic downturn of 1904–1905 compounded the problem of overzealous speculation, the black entrepreneurs Philip A. Payton Jr. and James C. Thomas made their move, snapping up buildings and ushering in thousands of black tenants eager to escape Manhattan's overcrowded San Juan Hill and Tenderloin districts. Faced with this welcome revival of the market, nonresident white owners were content to sell up, while white families fled the black influx. As World War I fueled the north-ward migration of African Americans seeking industrial jobs, and as immigration from the Caribbean increased, black churches and businesses moved uptown. Harlem became first New York City's largest black community and then the largest black urban community in the world. In 1920, one-third of Central Harlem's 216,000 residents were black. On the eve of American entry into World War II, the neighbor-hood's population stood at 222,000, some 90 percent of them African Americans.[31]

With its elegant streets and fine residences, designed by such re-nowned architects as Stanford White, creator of the Washington Square Arch, Harlem's very fabric marked it as exceptional among urban Afri-can American communities. By 1925, the author and activist James Weldon Johnson could write that "Harlem is indeed the great Mecca for the sight-seer, the pleasure-seeker, the curious, the adventurous, the enterprising, the ambitious and the talented of the whole Negro world." Harlem, Johnson proclaimed, was "a city within a city, the greatest Negro city in the world. It is not a slum or a fringe, it is located in the heart of Manhattan and occupies one of the most beautiful and healthful sections of the city." For Johnson and many other writers and artists, Harlem's central location within New York was especially at-tractive. During the late nineteenth century, New York had emerged as the United States' preeminent financial and cultural powerhouse. Harlem's proximity to leading New York publishing houses and the patronage of wealthy individuals and institutions was another attribute that drew scores of black intellectuals to the neighborhood from across the country and launched the literary and artistic outpouring of the 1920s that was later termed the "Harlem Renaissance."[32]

These intellectuals, in turn, helped shape the symbolism of Harlem as the vanguard of the race's progress and the evidence of its potential greatness. Johnson thought of Harlem as "a large scale laboratory ex-periment in the race problem," one that would prove that African Americans could live in the urban North "without any race friction."

The novels and stories of Rudolph Fisher, Nella Larsen, Claude McKay, and Jean Toomer all featured Harlem as a site of expectant arrival, where protagonists fleeing the brutalities of American racism could find refuge, reinvent themselves as "New Negroes," and seek their fortunes in America's greatest metropolis. In reality, as some of these works divulged, Harlem in the 1920s was already losing some of its "healthful" character, as overcrowding, negligent landlords, and labor market inequalities confronted residents of the "great Mecca." The Depression of the 1930s ravaged Harlem, and with outbreaks of rioting in 1935 and 1943 the optimism of the preceding decade was punctured and the neighborhood's symbolism was recast. From the focus of African Americans' hopes of a "promised land" in the North, Harlem became a byword for tarnished illusions. The nation's postwar return to prosperity bypassed Harlem, like other black urban communities; the "experiment" ground to a halt. "What happens to a dream deferred?" asked Langston Hughes in "Harlem" (1951). A decade later, LeRoi Jones would answer: "In the cities, which were once the black man's twentieth century 'Jordan,' *promise* is a dying bitch with rotting eyes. And the stink of her dying is a deadly killing fume."[33]

By this time, many of Harlem's stately buildings had been reduced to cramped, insanitary tenements. Others had been razed to make way for vast modernist projects such as the St. Nicholas Houses, thirteen drab towers, each fourteen stories high, which opened in 1954 and engulfed the blocks between 127th and 131st Streets and Seventh and Eighth Avenues. Such "urban renewal" measures displaced more than 100,000 residents from their homes and reduced Harlem's population by 27,000 during the 1950s. Even so, Harlem in the 1960s remained one of New York's most overcrowded neighborhoods, with 222 people per square acre, compared with 189 per square acre in Manhattan as a whole. Across Fifth Avenue, a large Puerto Rican community had inherited the formerly Italian neighborhood of East Harlem, now labeled "Spanish Harlem." Meanwhile, the U.S. Census of 1960 recorded 241,000 residents of "Central Harlem," of whom 98 percent were black. Preying on and exacerbating the problems of unemployment, poverty, squalid housing, inferior schools, and inadequate services was heroin. Before World War II, heroin use had been most common among working-class whites. But from the late 1940s, crime syndicates targeted the trade at the growing black and Latino inner-city neighborhoods, where economic and social dislocation encouraged demand, while lax and corrupt policing lessened potential obstacles to supply. New York was the primary American hub for the importation and re-sale of the drug, and Harlem became one of the nation's largest markets. Claude Brown, who grew up in the neighborhood, recalled in his memoir *Manchild in the Promised Land* (1965) that heroin had hit Harlem in the early 1950s "like a plague." At that time, Brown claimed, he "didn't know one family in Harlem with three or more kids between the ages of fourteen and nineteen in which at least one of them wasn't on drugs." Fatal overdoses and incarceration claimed many users, while theft, assault, and murder were among the dangers to the wider community.[34]

It was the very demise of Harlem's uniqueness, its descent into the same conditions of poverty and physical decay that typified black urban communities across the North, that ironically sustained its symbolic significance. Nothing spoke more eloquently of the mirage-like disappearance of the northern "promised land" than Harlem's gritty ordinariness. "Sometimes," wrote Jones in 1962, "walking along among the ruined shacks and lives of the worst Harlem slum, there is a feeling that just around the corner you'll find yourself in South Chicago or South Philadelphia, maybe even Newark's Third Ward. In these places life, and its possibility, has been distorted almost identically."[35]

Traces of Harlem's former grandeur and its status as a "race capital" still lingered, as when Fidel Castro relocated uptown to the famous Hotel Theresa during his visit to the United Nations General Assembly in 1960. The irreverent polemics and lavish lifestyle of Harlem's notorious congressman, the Reverend Adam Clayton Powell Jr., attracted equal measures of admiration and scorn. And the emergence of Malcolm X as the Nation of Islam's principal spokesman further strengthened Harlem's image as black America's political epicenter. When Jones in 1965 wished to signify his renewed racial allegiance, it was Harlem that he designated as "home." The Black Arts Repertory Theatre/School he founded on West 130th Street that year made Harlem the crucible of the nationalist "black arts movement," which would soon take root in cities across the United States and which came to be viewed as a "Second Renaissance." The "dream," as Hughes witnessed, had not been extinguished so much as "deferred." Nonetheless, the imagery that had attached itself to Harlem by the 1960s differed radically from the optimistic pronouncements of the 1920s. Harlem, Jones wrote, was a litany of "ghetto facts which make any honest man shudder." For Clark, Harlem was "the symbol of Negro ghettos everywhere." For *Time* magazine, it was "the archetypal Negro ghetto."[36]

By the time these words appeared, the qualifier "Negro" before "ghetto" was becoming redundant. "Ghetto" had first been used in the United States during the nineteenth century to refer to Eastern European Jewish settlements such as New York's Lower East Side. The northward migration of African Americans and the impact of the Depression on black urban communities began to alter this usage during the interwar years. Even in 1925, the special Harlem issue of the *Survey Graphic* that first carried James Weldon Johnson's paean to the "greatest Negro city in the world" also contained a short essay by Eunice Roberta Hunton that began: "Harlem is a modern ghetto. True, that is a contradiction in terms, but prejudice has ringed this group around with invisible lines and bars." The social anthropologist St. Clair Drake would recall that in Chicago, "sophisticated black leaders" and a "coterie of black graduate students," himself included, had adopted the word "ghetto" during the 1930s to refer to the city's South Side, "an eight square mile area surrounded by restrictive covenants that were as effective as barbed wire in keeping blacks hemmed in." Drake and other graduate students at the University of Chicago were greatly impressed by Louis Wirth's *The Ghetto* (1928), a sociological study of Chicago's Jewish community. When Horace Cayton and Drake published their lengthy work *Black Metropolis* (1945), they characterized the Bronzeville neighborhood as Chicago's "Black Ghetto."[37]

After World War II, the changing ethnic geography of American cities catalyzed what Eric Sundquist has called the "transference of the concept of the *ghetto* from Jews to African Americans." Jews and other white ethnics were finding a new place within the nation's rapidly expanding suburbs, while black migrants streamed into the inner cities. By the 1960s, white America's increasingly suburban profile would be reflected in the novels and stories of authors such as John Updike, Richard Yates, and John Cheever. Meanwhile, James Baldwin and other African American authors had advanced the postwar blackening of "ghetto."[38]

It was the spate of urban riots beginning in Harlem in 1964 that sealed the transference. Clark's *Dark Ghetto* was only the second book about African Americans from a major publishing house to use "ghetto" in its title, a full seventeen years after Robert Weaver's study of residential segregation, *The Negro Ghetto* (1948). Many others now followed in quick succession. One was August Meier and Elliot Rudwick's popular history of African Americans, published in 1966 as *From Plantation to Ghetto*. Illustrating the extent to which the image of black America had been urbanized, their book concluded with the statement that "the future of Negroes and of American race relations will revolve around the question of what happens in and to the ghetto." That same year, Martin Luther King Jr. spoke of the "agony of ghetto existence" as his campaigning shifted northward to Chicago. It was Clark's description of America's "ghettos" as the creations of "those who have power, both to confine those who have *no* power and to perpetuate their powerlessness" that King borrowed in 1967—without attribution—in his own final book, *Where Do We Go from Here: Chaos or Community?*[39]

Yet as prevalent as it had become, the use of "ghetto" was not without its detractors. For Bearden, Ellison, and Murray, the word encapsulated the limitations of the pathologist view of black urban communities. In an interview in 1965, Ellison insisted that any black author who gave credence to "sociological theories" about black life would fall prey to myth and distortion. "If he accepts the clichés to the effect that the Negro family is usually a broken family," Ellison warned, or "that Harlem is a 'Negro ghetto'—which means, to paraphrase one of our writers, 'piss in the halls and blood on the stairs'—he'll never see the people of whom he wishes to write."[40]

This disagreement over vocabulary illustrates the contrasting motives and commitments that animated the wider debate over representations of black urban life. Though its association with American Jewish communities was receding, "ghetto" assumed a new place in postwar American consciousness through public discussion of the

Holocaust. From the late 1950s, a brace of memoirs and journals written by Jews from Eastern Europe, particularly Warsaw, imbued the
word "ghetto" with a more ominous meaning than ever before. While
Dark Ghetto avoided mention of the wartime Jewish ghettos, Clark did
draw a direct comparison between his own position as an "involved
observer" in the "prison" that was Harlem and those of Bruno Bettelheim and Viktor Frankl, psychologists "who used their skill and training to provide us with some understanding of the nature of the horror
and the barbarity of the German concentration camps." Like his own
experience of Harlem, "the circumstances of their initial observation
were involuntary." For Clark, the word "ghetto" powerfully distilled
the imagery of exclusion, stigmatization, and suffering through which
he hoped to appeal to America's conscience. "Ghetto facts" served a
similar purpose for Jones during the early 1960s, when Harlem figured
among the charges of inhumanity that he brought against white America. Later in the decade, however, for Jones and other theorists of black
power, "ghetto" served not only as an indictment of racial oppression
but also, more positively, as a demarcation of the terrain of future black
self-determination. "They ask if we are separatists," he wrote in 1967.
"You ever hear of a ghetto? That's separate. A separate state. . . . What
we want is the power to control that separate state." For Bearden,
meanwhile, as for Ellison and Murray, "ghetto" was the signature trope
of a demeaning discourse that defined black urban communities solely
in terms of their exclusion, victimization, and deviation from white
norms, and which perpetuated African Americans' invisibility, in Ellison's sense, as conscious, creative, and unique individuals who shared
a rich, complex culture.[41]

Also refracted through these debates were impressions of black urban
life that had taken shape in the midst of contrasting childhoods and careers. Bearden's experiences as a social worker in Harlem during the Depression had undoubtedly confronted him with poverty, hunger, and despair. Yet his own upbringing had exposed him to much of what was
most dynamic and exciting about Harlem, as well as instilling in him a
proud fascination with the black expressive culture and folkloric traditions of the South. His parents, products of Charlotte's small, college-
educated black elite, had quickly found their way into the social circles of

leading figures associated with the "Renaissance" of the 1920s, and their apartment on West 131st Street hosted throngs of musicians, writers, and activists during Bearden's childhood years. As the Depression chastened Harlem's mood, Bearden nonetheless found common cause with a crowd of young, idealistic black intellectuals, including Ellison, for whom the New Deal's programs for writers, artists, and actors provided an opportunity to sustain something of the creative energy of the 1920s. Bearden's portrayals of Harlem would never entirely relinquish the sense of excitement and affirmation he had felt in the neighborhood during his youth.

For Clark, Harlem's literary and artistic renaissance had been a barely audible murmur. Born in the Panama Canal Zone in 1914 to Jamaican parents, Clark was just three years younger than Bearden and also came to Harlem as a small boy. But while Bearden grew up in relative comfort, his mother a successful journalist and his father a sanitation inspector, Clark's parents had separated, and his mother faced a daily struggle to provide for her son and his younger sister from her wages as a seamstress. Clark recalled in *Dark Ghetto* that his family had moved endlessly from one set of lodgings to the next in an attempt to evade Harlem's "creeping blight." His mother's dogged commitment to her children's education, her union activism, and the racial pride that, like many Caribbean immigrants, she expressed through support for Marcus Garvey, all encouraged Clark's devotion to his studies and his own activism. However, neither his reflections on his Harlem childhood nor his characterizations of Harlem in the 1960s conveyed much appreciation for African American culture as a resource for survival and affirmation. Black religion, social life, and recreation are treated in his writings primarily as psychic diversions rooted in fantasies of escape. Murray, a native of Alabama, believed the "Panamanian" Clark to be ignorant of African American culture, and the Oklahoman Ellison thought him detached from the "heroic" black sensibility forged in the Jim Crow South. Yet Clark's immigrant background goes only so far in explaining his disheartening view of black urban life, which, after all, he shared to a significant extent with the Harlem-born Baldwin and the Mississippian Wright.[42]

With their respective southern and Caribbean origins, Bearden and Clark were participants in the two major migrations that had transformed northern black communities during the early decades of the twentieth century. Jones, born in 1934 in Newark, New Jersey, was a generation younger than Bearden and Clark and a generation removed from his own family's northward journeys from Alabama and South Carolina. Nevertheless, on a smaller scale, Jones's own life was defined by a succession of relocations that took him, in circular fashion, across the Hudson River to Greenwich Village in 1957 and then, in 1965, to Harlem and back once more to Newark. Through all of the intellectual and political contortions that accompanied and occasioned these moves, Jones continued to wrestle with the values and aspirations of his parents, which he recognized so clearly in the pages of E. Franklin Frazier's sociological study *Black Bourgeoisie* (1957). As much as his bohemian life in the Village seemed a willful affront to those ideals, the lessons instilled in him by years of Sunday school at Newark's Bethany Baptist Church were not so readily discarded. A long tradition of elite black social thought, focused on respectability and the precarious morality of the urban poor, would echo in Jones's response to the urban crisis and his conception of black power.[43]

There is a second, related sense in which Clark, Jones, and Bearden were *On the Corner*. Like generations of African American intellectuals, they believed themselves to be faced with a stark choice of direction. At this intersection, one road led toward "responsibility" to "the race," while another pointed toward free inquiry, the pursuit of their interests wherever those might lead. African American intellectuals have encountered this divergence in varying degrees and have responded in different ways. Moreover, intellectuals of many backgrounds have grappled with questions of their political utility and social function. Noam Chomsky in 1967 urged that the "responsibility of intellectuals" everywhere was "to speak the truth and to expose lies." The first artists and scholars to be known by the initially derisive appellation "intellectuals"— Émile Zola and other defenders of Alfred Dreyfus, the Jewish army officer accused of treason in France during the 1890s—would also have recognized such a duty. What has made the experience of African American intellectuals distinctive, however, is the notion of their specific responsibility *to their race:* not simply "to speak the truth," but to speak truths about, and on behalf of, a particular people.[44]

In the nineteenth and early twentieth centuries, this notion gave rise to what St. Clair Drake once called the "vindicationist" tradition in black writing. African American intellectuals devoted themselves to refuting the dominant white view that black people were biologically inferior and lacked a history of civilization. Like the nationalist historians of Europe, black intellectuals crafted narratives of a glorious past, which in this instance centered on the ancient civilizations of Egypt and Ethiopia. Others sought to rebut the racial theories of the day by means of natural history, biology, or anatomy. It was this vindicationist tradition that the historian John Hope Franklin addressed in 1963 when he contemplated the "dilemma" that lay behind the choices these authors had made. "Imagine, if you can," Franklin wrote, "what it meant to a competent Negro student of Greek literature, W. H. Crogman, to desert his chosen field and write a book entitled *The Progress of a Race.* . . . How much poorer is the field of the biological sciences because an extremely able and well-trained Negro scientist, Julian Lewis, felt compelled to spend years of his productive life writing a book entitled *The Biology of the Negro?*"[45]

From the turn of the twentieth century, such efforts were joined by accounts of contemporary black life, which, it was hoped, would mitigate racial prejudice by fostering a more empathetic view of black Americans and their social structures, beliefs, and emotions. According to the historian and political scientist Adolph Reed Jr., it was Booker T. Washington, the founder of Alabama's Tuskegee Institute and champion of vocational training, who first assumed "the definitive role of the black public intellectual—interpreting the opaquely black heart of darkness for whites." Washington's position as, in Reed's words, the sole "trusted informant" on "what the Negro thought, felt, wanted" was quickly challenged, however. Two years after Washington's *Up from Slavery* appeared in 1901, W. E. B. Du Bois announced in the opening lines of *The Souls of Black Folk* that he would lift the "Veil" of race to reveal the "deeper recesses" of black life to his implicitly white "Gentle Reader." What changed in the 1960s, as the riots illuminated the magnitude of

African Americans' northward migration, was that the object of black intellectuals' obligations became even more precisely defined. Henceforth, it was black *urban* life in the nation's major cities that comprised the deeper recesses, or the heart of darkness, beyond the veil.[46]

The role of interpreter brought unprecedented opportunities for black intellectuals in the form of recognition, influence, and earnings. A market existed for the pronouncements of those believed to possess both intimate knowledge of black life and the ability to articulate that knowledge to a broad white public. Along with such opportunities, some scholars have argued, came the potential to exploit them by furnishing white audiences with whichever distorted views of black Americans appealed to them most. Booker T. Washington has been charged with amassing power at the end of the nineteenth century by assuring white politicians and philanthropists that African Americans were content to labor diligently and to accept segregation and disenfranchisement in the South. The poets, novelists, and painters of the Harlem Renaissance have been rebuked for catering to the primitivist tastes of "Negrotarian" white patrons, as Zora Neale Hurston liked to call them. Prominent black intellectuals of the 1990s, feted in much of the mainstream media as a golden generation, were denounced by Reed as "little more than hustlers, blending bombast, clichés, psychobabble, and lame guilt tripping in service to the 'pay me' principle." Another scholar, Madhu Dubey, endorses the novelist Ishmael Reed's complaint that many black intellectuals during the last decades of the twentieth century chose the "profitable" strategy of joining the "black-pathology industry." And the literary historian and critic Houston Baker Jr. inveighs against much of the present generation as "money-hungry reactionaries who are fully allied with the worst offices of white American power brokers." Some of these accusations carry to extremes the instrumentalist logic of the "new sociology of ideas," whose exponents, influenced by the work of Pierre Bourdieu, emphasize the role of institutional forces and individual strategies of self-advancement in shaping intellectuals' thought and practice.[47]

Were the intellectuals discussed in this book, then, "on the corner" in a third sense—hustling and plying their wares in the sordid marketplace of representations and ideas?[48] Did Clark, as Murray claimed in 1966, exploit his status as a "mass-media certified Negro Negrologist" to become a "very special kind of entertainer who uses charts, graphs, and monographs as his stage props"? Historians must be mindful of the contexts in which ideas are originated, adopted, and disseminated, and of the sources of power and visibility and the inducements and rewards that may condition the work intellectuals do. Such rewards are not exclusively material, however. More was at stake in the dispute between Washington and Du Bois than money or the mantle of race leadership. Both men believed that much else depended on how African Americans were portrayed to white audiences. For Washington, the security of blacks in the South required that whites view them as unthreatening, limited in ambition, loyal in temperament, and politically inert. For Du Bois, the recognition of their humanity demanded otherwise. Against the inducements to primitivism offered by wealthy patrons such as Charlotte Osgood Mason during the 1920s should be weighed the determined political strategies of Alain Locke, James Weldon Johnson, and Charles Johnson, who hoped that a "renaissance" in black arts and letters would engender in white Americans a new respect for the intellectual capabilities of the race.[49]

Nor do the examples of Clark, Jones, and Bearden suggest that indigenous interpreters have been peculiarly or necessarily self-serving. Clark chose to donate all royalties from *Dark Ghetto* to the Northside Center for Child Development. At the very moment in the mid-1960s when Jones was most in demand as a writer and speaker and enjoyed his greatest prospects for financial success, he turned his back on his audience of white liberals for the inevitably less lucrative task of addressing impoverished black communities. The subtle, anti-sensationalist quality of Bearden's representations of black urban life is equally difficult to ascribe to any mercenary impulse. Material considerations inevitably play a part in intellectual life, as in all forms of work. But for many indigenous interpreters, the desire to alter the terms in which African American life was discussed and understood was an earnest and powerful motive.[50]

The role of interpreter, moreover, is not one that African American intellectuals have monopolized. The sociologist Zygmunt Bauman contends that with the emergence of postmodernity, the interpreter has become the archetypal intellectual:

> The typically post-modern strategy of intellectual work is one best characterized by the metaphor of the "interpreter" role. It consists of translating statements, made within one communally based tradition, so that they can be understood within the system of knowledge based on another tradition. . . . This strategy is aimed at facilitating communication between autonomous (sovereign) participants. It is concerned with preventing the distortion of meaning in the process of communication. For this reason, it promotes the need to penetrate deeply the alien system of knowledge from which the translation is to be made (for example, Geertz's "thick description").

As Bauman's reference to Clifford Geertz signals, the postmodern tendency to credit the autonomy of multiple vantage points and belief systems calls on intellectuals to assume the essentially anthropological role of rendering one system comprehensible to another. These systems, according to Geertz, might be specialized academic disciplines with their own internal conventions and "local knowledge," or particular ethnic or national groups whose customs and beliefs derive and create meaning within a cultural whole. Seen in this larger context, the opportunities for advancement held out to black interpreters as intermediaries between black and white America appear less than exceptional.[51]

What does entail a certain exceptionalism, however, is the notion of the *indigenous* interpreter. When Margaret Mead wrote about youth in Samoa or Geertz explained the Balinese cockfight, they were not understood, nor did they understand themselves, to be interpreting cultural systems of which they were full members. Their authority as interpreters did not rely on such a claim. The method of "participant observation" adopted by cultural anthropologists from the early twentieth century underscored the voluntary and temporary nature of their cultural immersion. And while white American scholars might interpret their own national or regional culture—Constance Rourke's study of American humor being one notable example—this was understood to be a choice, not an obligation. In the case of indigenous interpreters, a different set of assumptions has applied. Recognition of their interpretative authority has depended as much on their race ("A Negro Looks at Black Power") as on their intellect. The object of their interpretation— black America—is preordained by the logic of racial authenticity, which stipulates both that black intellectuals have a particular responsibility to *represent,* in both senses of that word, "their" people, and that, as racial insiders, they are uniquely capable of doing so.[52]

This predicament is not without precedent or parallel. In a multitude of historical and geographical settings, notions of authenticity and obligation have made indigenous interpreters of women intellectuals and those belonging to minority or oppressed groups. Edward Said was one who assumed the "terribly important task of representing the collective sufferings of your own people, testifying to its travails, reasserting its enduring presence, reinforcing its memory." Yet within the history of the United States, the experience of black intellectuals has been marked by the peculiar longevity and intensity of the attitudes and expectations from which the role of indigenous interpreter arises. Jews and other "white ethnics" were, by the mid-twentieth century, more or less free of expectations that their primary mission as intellectuals must be to interpret the condition of their particular ethnic group. Women have waged a continuing struggle for recognition as intellectuals, within and outside the academy, and many have felt an obligation to direct their scholarship toward redressing the inequalities they have confronted. Yet to a greater extent than black intellectuals—male or female—white American women have found an audience for intellectual work that exceeds the remit of the indigenous interpreter. Aside from the many celebrated works of fiction and scholarship concerning African Americans and various aspects of race and civil rights, it is difficult to identify a single work by a black intellectual that has been accorded as much recognition as Rachel Carson's ecological treatise *Silent Spring* (1962) or Naomi Klein's exhortation against corporate power, *The Shock Doctrine* (2007). No category of intellectuals in the United States has so persistently been confined to the role of indigenous interpreter as have African Americans.[53]

Throughout the twentieth century, black intellectuals grappled with the implications of this predicament. The historian Jonathan Scott

Holloway has astutely identified a "small canon" of writings by African American scholars and artists whose very titles signal a chronic sense of embattlement: James Weldon Johnson asserted "The Dilemma of the Negro Author" (1928), E. Franklin Frazier proclaimed "The Failure of the Negro Intellectuals" (1962), John Hope Franklin addressed "The Dilemma of the Negro Scholar" (1963), Harold Cruse diagnosed *The Crisis of the Negro Intellectual* (1967), and Cornel West revisited "The Dilemma of the Black Intellectual" (1985), to name but a few examples. This "crisis canon," Holloway argues persuasively, arises from the reality that black intellectuals "have been and still are expected to know only 'blackness' and to care only about 'black issues.' "[54]

What must be underlined, however, is that these various authors conceived of the crises, dilemmas, and failures of black intellectuals in highly contrasting ways. For John Hope Franklin, it was "tragic indeed" that the existence of racial injustice had placed special obligations on black intellectuals that curtailed their freedom to "engage in the study of any particular field." Harold Cruse, meanwhile, acknowledged no such tragedy and did not hesitate to prescribe the exact nature of black intellectuals' responsibilities. The "crisis," so far as Cruse was concerned, was that black intellectuals had consigned themselves to irrelevance by failing in their primary duties, which were to codify a distinctive African American culture, establish independent institutions, and promote group empowerment. Franklin is a comfortable fit for the tradition of the *"antirace race man or woman"* explored by the literary scholar Ross Posnock. As Posnock demonstrates, an array of black intellectuals from Du Bois to the contemporary novelist Samuel Delany, while often accepting a responsibility to serve the race, have nonetheless worked "to lift the burden of being a group representative or exemplar" and have sought the freedom "to delete the first word or to accent the second in the phrase *black intellectual*." Yet the contrasting example of Cruse, with his uncompromising assertion of the primacy of race, highlights the need to attend to the multitude of ways in which black intellectual life has been envisioned and experienced.[55]

This variance emerges sharply in the chapters that follow. For Clark, Jones, and Bearden, the deepening urban crisis reopened questions of the responsibilities, opportunities, and limitations of black intellectual life in new and more urgent forms. The ways in which they posed these questions and adapted to the role of indigenous interpreter differed markedly. This study reveals, moreover, that a congruence existed between their respective conceptions of black intellectual life, on the one hand, and their representations of black urban life, on the other. "I didn't deliberately choose to devote my life to the problems of race," Clark told an interviewer in 1965, "and perhaps I'd like to escape it." If Clark viewed black urban communities as ghettos and prisons, black intellectual life seemed to him an equally circumscribed, constricted, even damaged terrain. Surpassing even Franklin's notion of a tragic obstruction of intellectual freedom, Clark not only believed that racial obligation had prevented him from pursuing his foremost intellectual interests, but also feared that it had limited his capacity to reason on the highest theoretical levels. Black intellectual life was, for Clark, a crisis without end. Resigned to racial obligation, he would sometimes glance over his shoulder, thinking of the road not taken.[56]

Jones, on moving to New York, had taken that other road. As a precocious young poet working his way into the Beat literary scene, he had made few concessions to any notion of racial obligation. In the early 1960s, however, as students and other young Americans reinvigorated the civil rights movement and as the Cold War entered a fraught crescendo, Jones felt a rising dissatisfaction with the political disengagement that characterized his bohemian milieu. By 1964, his poems could be divided, he said, between those composed in a "lyric" mode and those motivated by a "social or political thing." At this point, Jones was experiencing a profound sense of crisis as he found himself back on the corner, unable to choose between freedom and responsibility—or to imagine any path that would negate such a choice. At the height of this crisis, "black" and "intellectual" appeared, to Jones, entirely contradictory. His aspirations to be a writer had sundered him, he believed, from the realities of black life and had driven him to a decadent aestheticism.[57]

Yet before long, Jones had embraced a new identity as Amiri Baraka and a new confidence in the possibility, even the indispensability, of the black intellectual. Disabused of universalism and pure aestheticism, he resolved his crisis by declaring intellectual freedom to be an illusion, thereby abolishing the dilemmas of the corner. Responsibility, far from being a burden, became his lifeline: only by devoting his talents to the service of the race could he be both black and an intellectual. By the late 1960s, Baraka was utterly committed to Du Bois's notion of a "Talented Tenth," which alone could "save the race," and yet entirely dismissive of Du Bois's countervailing belief in an unraced realm of thought, the "kingdom of culture." Like Clark, he viewed both black intellectual life and black urban life as riddled with pathologies. Yet where Clark faulted the "invisible walls" that maintained black people's confinement, Baraka's remedy for the pathologies of black life was to build those walls higher. "European ways of seeing and doing things" had penetrated African Americans' minds and corrupted their culture. A hermetically sealed, racially purified domain of ideas, no less than a "separate state" composed of black cities, was needed to achieve black liberation. Relinquishing his role as an indigenous interpreter for white audiences, Baraka imagined himself instead as "a black priest interpreting / the present & future for my people."[58]

Bearden's journey from his early social realism to abstraction had embodied his own quandary on the corner. In an essay of 1946, he had decried the "pressure exerted on the Negro artist to use his art as an instrument to mirror the social injustices inflicted on his people." For much of the next two decades, Bearden turned away from the representation of black life and toward an increasingly abstract aesthetic as he sought to "find out what was in me that was common to other men." And yet, having taken first racial obligation and then aesthetic freedom to extremes, it was Bearden who, in the mid-1960s, dismissed the dilemmas of the corner as posing a false choice. Prompted in part by the escalating civil rights struggle, Bearden returned to "Negro subject matter" and to a sense of himself as a "Negro artist." By now, however, he felt able to portray "the life of my people" without losing a sense of the universality of human experience, or of artistic expression. Whereas Clark felt trapped by his predicament as a black intellectual and Baraka sought to purge black thought of racial contaminants, Bearden rejected any notion of the black mind as ghettoized. Steeped in centuries of Western, Asian, and African art, Bearden discerned a way to approach the universal through the particular. In his collages, he sought at once to render the specificities of time and place and to capture the common-alities of human experience that connected "the Harlem where I grew up" even to "the Haarlem of the Dutch masters that contributed its ele-ment to my understanding of art." If black urban life was, for Bearden, distinctive without being detached, he likewise felt able to "bring some-thing" to his art "as a Negro" without confining himself to a separate domain of "Negro art."[59]

The congruence between each of these figures' conceptions of black intellectual life and their representations of black urban life brings into relief their differing racial ideologies: Clark's militant, almost assimila-tionist integrationism; Jones's hardening separatism; and the cosmo-politan pluralism espoused by Bearden. Indeed, those racial ideologies were formed in part by their self-conception as black intellectuals and their experiences of life in black urban communities. Yet this congruence also suggests the powerful ways in which changing spatial metaphors of African American experience worked to recast American notions of race itself during this period. At the very moment when the era of le-galized segregation was ending, the spatial imagery of actually existing segregation acquired its most potent sign with the widespread adoption of "ghetto," a term that, since the 1960s, has served as the predominant symbol of blackness in the United States. Yet its dominance has not been unchallenged. Black intellectual life, no less than black urban life, has been variously imagined as a dark ghetto, a separate state, and a porous enclave. Contrasting visions of place have infused the ongoing reinven-tion of the idea we call race.[60]

Chapter 1

Ghettos of the Mind

*Kenneth B. Clark and the Psychology
of the Urban Crisis*

In June 1967, *Life* magazine called its readers' attention to a "new priesthood, unique to this country and this time, of American action-intellectuals." A "brotherhood of scholars" was now at the helm of national policymaking, "shaping our defenses, guiding our foreign policy, redesigning our cities, reorganizing our schools, deciding what our dollar is worth." Among the photographs of a dozen white men who "stalk the corridors of American power"—Walt Rostow, Daniel Patrick Moynihan, James Conant, and others—appeared one portrait of an African American. Kenneth Bancroft Clark was indeed a scholar closely entwined with postwar America's liberal establishment. A tenured professor of psychology at the City College of New York, Clark served as an expert witness before courts and congressional committees and at White House conferences, befriended politicians and their advisers, and secured federal and municipal grants to fund his research and activism. After making his "enduring contribution" to the campaign against southern segregation, *Life* noted, Clark had turned to the issues of civil rights and poverty in New York City. Remembered today principally for his testimony to the Supreme Court in *Brown v. Board of Education* (1954), Clark is for historians a "symbol of integrationism," the civil rights movement's "reigning academic," and "the epitome of the establishment social scientist" during an era of liberal reform.[1]

This prevailing view of Clark as the house scholar of the integrationist liberal establishment in fact obscures as much as it reveals. Clark was an unconventional, idiosyncratic thinker whose ideas pushed against the limits of postwar American liberalism, making his establishment credentials something of a paradox. Those credentials were underlined, as many students of Clark's career have noted, by his election in 1969 to serve as the first black president of the American Psychological Association (APA), "the highest honor that his discipline could bestow." It is surprising, then, that the controversy that engulfed Clark's presidency appears nowhere in the scholarly record. Not even the APA's own volume of essays commemorating Clark makes mention of the presidential address he delivered in Washington, D.C., on September 4, 1971, which elicited front-page coverage in the national press, a wave of condemnation from his fellow psychologists, and an angry retort from the vice president of the United States.[2]

Before the assembled ranks of the nation's psychologists, Clark made an astonishing claim. "All power-controlling leaders," he argued, should be required to "accept and use the earliest perfected form of psychotechnological, biochemical intervention which would assure their positive use of power and block the possibility of their using power destructively." Little wonder that Spiro Agnew took offense. Far from languishing in Clark's archive at the Library of Congress, or even in the pages of *American Psychologist* where it first appeared, the text of this address was included as an epilogue to his book *Pathos of Power,* published in 1974. The lack of scholarly attention to Clark's disturbing proposal for the "medication" of political leaders is indicative of historians' focus on an earlier, triumphant moment in his career, when his testimony concerning the psychological harm inflicted by segregation helped to destroy the legal standing of Jim Crow. Perhaps, too, it reflects the apparent contradiction between Clark's immoderate, heretical proposal and his establishment profile. Whatever the explanation, a reappraisal of Clark's thought is overdue.[3]

Though it would be a mistake to read earlier phases of Clark's career as leading inexorably to his embrace of psychotechnological regulation, neither did he spontaneously exchange a commonplace midcentury liberalism for madcap iconoclasm. To a degree underestimated by those who have written about him, Clark had strained against many of the conventional wisdoms of American psychology and liberal social reform throughout the postwar period. His drastic prescription of 1971 was in part the result of his own troubled encounters with liberal political leadership and its exercise of power. Amid the expansive optimism of the early 1960s, an era promising a "New Frontier" and a "Great Society," Clark had believed that fundamental changes in American society could be achieved by a reform-minded, liberal administration. Over the course of the decade, he was painfully disabused of this hope. Of the sources of his disillusionment, none was more wrenching than the disintegration of his own most ambitious undertaking of the 1960s: to make white Americans understand the nature of life in black urban communities, and to orchestrate a transformation of the Harlem "ghetto."[4]

To label Clark a "radical" would be to overstate his heterodoxy, for he shared many of the assumptions of the liberal politics and social science of the time. He accepted the existence of the capitalist market economy, and like other postwar liberals, his ideas for combating poverty privileged initiatives at neighborhood level rather than systemic interventions at the level of political economy. Yet if Clark cannot be considered a radical, there were nonetheless a number of radical elements within his thought that situate him at the outer bounds of postwar American liberalism, and which bring the paradox of his establishment credentials into sharp relief. Reexamining Clark's writings and activism reveals a highly politicized notion of the therapeutic, in which rebellion against social injustice was held to be instrumental to the attainment of psychological health. Related to this belief was Clark's forceful diagnosis of the operation of "power" within American society. While he may not have offered clear proposals for large-scale economic restructuring, the necessity of a fundamental societal transformation was implicit in his characterization of America's "ghettos" as "social, educational, and—above all—economic colonies." Clark's particular vision of "community action" was one of the boldest and most far-reaching to emerge in the planning for Lyndon Johnson's abortive

"War on Poverty," and resonated with the ideals of "participatory democracy" advanced by the young radicals of the New Left.[5]

These currents in Clark's thought converged during the early 1960s
in his design for the community organization Harlem Youth Opportunities Unlimited, known as HARYOU, and in his widely publicized
book *Dark Ghetto: Dilemmas of Social Power* (1965). Even more than his
role in *Brown v. Board of Education,* it was his engagement with the urban crisis during the 1960s that established Clark as a leading expert on
black America in the eyes of government and the media. His enduring
integrationist ideals led him to be identified as a moderate at a time
when radicalism and militancy were associated with black nationalism,
and the boldest elements of his thought were often obscured by his
professed hostility to black power. Yet it was the very boldness of his
expectations that sowed the seeds of his disenchantment with the liberal political class to which he had been so firmly attached.

Clark embraced the role of indigenous interpreter wholeheartedly.
At a moment when the riots threatened to diminish white support for
further civil rights reforms, he resolved to expose the sources of frustration and alienation that underlay the violence, and to promote the
urban crisis as the next frontier of the civil rights struggle. Interpreting
black urban life to white audiences was, for Clark, a means to the larger
end of transforming conditions in black urban communities. He sought
not only to evoke empathy, but to direct it toward support for his vision
of a massive program of government intervention that would rescue
Harlem and America's other "dark ghettos." In pressing his case for a
huge injection of money and resources into those neighborhoods, Clark
placed heavy emphasis on what he believed to be the damaging effects
of racism and poverty on the social and psychological fabric of black
urban communities. Yet he did not portray "ghetto" dwellers as helpless victims. Like Amiri Baraka and other black power radicals, of whom
he was so critical, Clark combined a pathologist view of black urban
life with a belief that the black urban poor were capable of transformative social action. Unlike the black power theorists, however, Clark
placed his trust in a liberal administration in Washington to act as a
vital partner to the black urban poor in their pursuit of social change.
His blueprint for Harlem required government to bankroll not only

vital public services, but also an infrastructure of democratic participation that would unleash the collective agency of the poor themselves.

The hostile interventions that derailed his design for HARYOU drove Clark to a mounting pessimism. As his hopes of societal transformation disintegrated, he came to believe that the failure of his mission as an indigenous interpreter had been predetermined by the destructive nature of political power. However, the disillusionment that provoked his extraordinary address in 1971 was aggravated by his increasingly negative view of the possibilities afforded by black intellectual life in America. Notwithstanding his ascent to the symbolic leadership of his profession, Clark's assessment of his predicament as a black intellectual could scarcely have been more damning. For thirty years, he had directed his talent and energy to the pursuit of racial equality. Yet he was more and more vexed by his sense that America's obdurate racism had placed such an obligation upon him, and had caused him to foreclose other intellectual opportunities along the way. Now he rued the dynamics of responsibility and expectation that had cast him in the role of indigenous interpreter. Privately, he remarked that his concentration on the pursuit of racial justice had narrowed his intellectual purview and hampered his attainment of a broad, theoretical perspective. This harsh self-appraisal plagued him in the months leading up to his presidential address and underscores the colossal force he ascribed to racism. America confined its black citizens to ghettos, Clark believed, and its black intellectuals to ghettos of the mind.

The Cry of the Ghetto

On the afternoon of May 24, 1963, Clark arrived at Robert F. Kennedy's Manhattan apartment on Central Park South. Less than three weeks earlier, the spectacle of police dogs and fire hoses unleashed against peaceful demonstrators in Birmingham, Alabama, had spurred a reluctant White House to a more assertive stance in support of the campaign for civil rights. The brutality in Birmingham also sparked protests in northern cities, which made clear that patience with the strategy of nonviolence was waning among many African Americans in the nation's largest urban centers. In Chicago, black youths pelted police with bricks and bottles and assaulted Mayor Richard J. Daley's nephew. At a Harlem rally in sympathy with the Birmingham protesters, a section of the crowd chanted their support for Malcolm X. As President John F. Kennedy ordered the preparation of a civil rights bill, his brother, the attorney general, sought to gain a deeper understanding of the causes of black disaffection. Having begun to register the volatile mood among African Americans in the urban North, Robert Kennedy turned to James Baldwin, who gathered a delegation of prominent black intellectuals and entertainers to meet the attorney general and air their views.[6]

The meeting would be widely reported as a disaster. Kennedy, it appears, had hoped that those present—who included Baldwin, Clark, Lorraine Hansberry, the attorney Clarence Jones, and the singers Lena Horne and Harry Belafonte—would credit the administration with taking a firm stand on civil rights and would offer constructive proposals as to what more could be done to assist urban African Americans. But when Kennedy opened his remarks with effusive claims about the administration's civil rights achievements, a torrent of criticism ensued. "It became one of the most violent, emotional verbal assaults and attacks that I had ever witnessed," Clark would recall a few years later. For almost three hours, Kennedy was harangued by his angry guests. Horne advised him that anyone who tried to recount the administration's "proud" achievements in a Harlem barber shop or pool hall would probably "get shot." Kennedy, according to Clark, kept "retreating and saying no, and occasionally coming back and implying that we were ungrateful; that we were insatiable." Three days after the encounter, the *New York Times* stated that a "source close to Kennedy" had acknowledged that the meeting "with Negro intellectuals had been unfortunate."[7]

Despite the lack of consensus or even cordiality, Clark did not regard the meeting as an unmitigated failure. Within a few months, in fact, he spoke of the meeting as evidence that white Americans, for all their misconceptions, could be persuaded to reevaluate their deeply held beliefs. Robert Kennedy, Clark told the editors of the glossy *Pageant* magazine that fall, "by virtue of being a privileged and quite isolated wealthy white American, found certain things difficult just to comprehend." The "emotional tone" of his guests had alarmed Kennedy,

Clark believed, and the attorney general had at first struggled to appreciate "the difference between himself and James Baldwin, who grew up in Harlem and who, from the time he was a kid, was required to deal with certain kinds of realities that the Kennedy brothers could not dream of." Yet Clark seemed to think that the president's address to the nation on civil rights on June 11 had marked a new beginning and shown firmer resolve, and that the anger conveyed to his brother at the New York meeting had ultimately served a purpose:

> I think he [Robert Kennedy] learned a little. . . . I think he learned
> that the Negro's mood of impatience is not surface; that it's deep
> enough for these people to assume the very real risks of communi-
> cating it pretty directly to him in the way they did. And I think that
> a lot of the actions of his brother and of his since then seem to show
> that—while he didn't appear to understand at the time—he really
> understood much more later than he did at the time.

What Clark had apparently concluded from the tempestuous meeting and its aftermath was that African Americans who could articulate the grievances and frustrations of black urban communities could effect a positive change in white opinion. "To me," he remarked in the *Pageant* interview, "it's a miracle that—as Baldwin said—a dialogue did emerge. That's one of the things that's fascinating about America—if you take enough risks, and aren't too afraid of the sparks, the cleavages are not that great that some contact cannot be made."[8]

When Clark laid his portrait of black urban life before the American public in *Dark Ghetto,* he did so not only as a professional social scientist, but also, self-consciously, as someone who had known the Harlem "ghetto" as home. He could "never be fully detached as a scholar or participant," he wrote in the book's introduction, for more than forty years of his life had been lived within the neighborhood:

> I started school in the Harlem public schools. I first learned about
> people, about love, about cruelty, about sacrifice, about cowardice,
> about courage, about bombast in Harlem. For many years before I

returned as an "involved observer," Harlem had been my home. My family moved from house to house, and from neighborhood to neighborhood within the walls of the ghetto in a desperate attempt to escape its creeping blight. In a very real sense, therefore, *Dark Ghetto* is a summation of my personal and lifelong experiences and observations as a prisoner within the ghetto long before I was aware that I was really a prisoner.

Reaching bookstores in May 1965, in the same year as *The Autobiography of Malcolm X* and Claude Brown's *Manchild in the Promised Land,* Clark's study was among the first of a spate of books by black male authors, in genres ranging from popular social science to memoir and fiction, that were contracted by major New York publishing houses and which fed curiosity about black urban life against the backdrop of the riots and the rise of black nationalist militancy.[9]

That Clark combined the insights of a trained psychologist with the perspective of a graduate of the ghetto helped to ensure his prominence as an interpreter of black urban life. Indeed, *Dark Ghetto* found an extensive audience eager for an intimate view of Harlem. Partially serialized across seven issues of the *New York Post* in August, the book sold just under 38,000 copies in its hardback edition and a further 136,000 following reissue as a paperback in 1967. Even prior to *Dark Ghetto*'s publication, television networks, magazines, and newspapers had looked to Clark as an authority on the causes of Harlem's violence during the summer of 1964. Noting that Clark had "helped shape the Supreme Court's 1954 school desegregation decision," *Time* magazine further cited his credentials as the originator of HARYOU, the "most ambitious project" aiming to transform conditions in the famous black neighborhood.[10]

When, in 1962, Clark had begun the research that culminated in his design for HARYOU and in the writing of *Dark Ghetto,* he had behind him sixteen years of professional involvement in Harlem as a psychologist. In 1946, he had founded the Northside Center for Child Development together with his wife, Mamie Phipps Clark, who like him had earned degrees in psychology from Howard and Columbia Universities. Beginning with a loan of $936 from Mamie's father, an African American physician in Hot Springs, Arkansas, the Clarks set up their clinic in a small office on West 150th Street. They recruited an interracial staff made up initially of volunteer mental health and education professionals who administered psychological testing, psychiatric treatment, and remedial education to children from Harlem and beyond. It was Mamie Clark who assumed the leadership of Northside. Kenneth had held a full-time faculty position in the psychology department at City College since 1942, and became a full professor in 1960 (the second African American, after the historian John Hope Franklin, to hold that rank within any of New York's five municipal colleges). However, he also served as Northside's research director and as a member of its board.[11]

As the clinic grew and attracted philanthropic support during the 1950s, Kenneth Clark nevertheless questioned the efficacy of individual treatment as a response to Harlem's mental health needs. He later recalled that the clinicians faced "overwhelming statistical odds. Every child they were able to help at Northside represented at least one thousand whom they couldn't help." The Clarks were also skeptical of the therapeutic techniques that had gained ascendancy within America's burgeoning postwar psychological professions. Both the Freudian notion of the universal, intrapsychic roots of individual mental disturbances and the medical approach of psychiatry complemented the color-blind ideals of American Cold War liberalism, and Freudian therapy in particular was championed by donors who sat on Northside's board. The Clarks, however, believed orthodox Freudian theory to be insensitive to the wider social and environmental influences on psychological development, beyond the dynamics of parent-child interaction. They considered medical interventions equally inadequate, Kenneth Clark recalled, "if one were trying to help children who were suffering from economic, social and racial deprivation." Facing opposition from board members at every turn, the Clarks attempted to broaden the range of Northside's activities to involve social workers in advocacy aimed at securing improvements in education, health care, and housing provision in the local area.[12]

In 1961, Kenneth Clark learned that the President's Committee on Juvenile Delinquency and the City of New York were seeking to fund initiatives to engage with disadvantaged youth. The issue of juvenile delinquency had been the subject of much panicked editorializing in the United States throughout the 1950s, and the Kennedy administration appeared receptive to the viewpoint of liberal scholars such as Columbia University's Richard Cloward and Lloyd Ohlin, who argued that delinquency resulted from young people's lack of access to economic "opportunity" in deprived areas. Sensing the chance to pursue a more comprehensive approach to Harlem's problems than was possible through the Northside Center, Clark worked with the Harlem Neighborhoods Association to draw up a proposal for a new organization. This was the genesis of HARYOU, the venture that would consume Clark's energies over the next three years and which marked his turn toward the systematic study of black urban life.[13]

With a planning grant of $230,000 from the President's Committee and an additional $100,000 from the city, Clark, as chief project consultant, assembled a formidable staff of researchers, social workers, and local residents to conduct a major demographic, economic, educational, and institutional survey of Harlem. Their findings, together with a detailed program design, were included in a report of 620 pages, authored largely by Clark and published in 1964 as *Youth in the Ghetto: A Study of the Consequences of Powerlessness and a Blueprint for Change.* They also formed the basis of *Dark Ghetto,* Clark's attempt to convey the injustice of conditions in black urban communities to a broader public.[14]

Dark Ghetto carried a foreword by Gunnar Myrdal, the Swedish economist and sociologist whose landmark study of race relations, *An American Dilemma* (1944), had issued a "moral exhortation" to white Americans to honor the full implications of their democratic "creed." Clark had worked as a research assistant on this earlier project, and Myrdal recognized in *Dark Ghetto* an extension of his own report's moral appeal. Clark, Myrdal wrote, was "desperately anxious that the ugly facts of life in the Negro ghetto become really known to the ruling white majority," above all "how it feels to be enclosed in segregation." Indeed, *Dark Ghetto* begins with a ten-page prologue, titled "The Cry of the Ghetto," comprising a series of quotations in which residents of Harlem spoke of their grievances and frequently of their anguish. "A lot of times, when I'm working, I become as despondent as hell," a male interviewee testified, "and I feel like crying. I'm not a man, none of us are men! I don't own anything." Heroin addicts spoke of the lack of jobs that had barred them from a legitimate lifestyle, school pupils recounted the prejudice of their teachers, and men and women decried the "sadistic" behavior of police.[15]

The inclusion of such material was one means by which Clark sought to expose the human "*truth* of the ghetto," which the quantifiable "*facts* of the ghetto"—cold statistics indexing rates of delinquency or infant mortality—might actually serve to obscure. While fact was "empirical," he wrote, truth was "interpretative" and "related to value," a formulation that rebuked what has been described as the "culture of facts" that dominated the postwar American social sciences. *Dark Ghetto* was, Clark submitted, "in a sense, no report at all, but rather the anguished cry of its author." Though "controlled in part by the concepts and language of social science," this was not the work of a scholar who pretended to "absolute objectivity," Clark wrote. Instead, the reader "should know that the author is a Negro, a social psychologist, a college professor, and that he has long been revolted by those forces in American society which make for Harlems and by the fact of Harlem itself." Indeed, Clark's distinction between truth and facts served to underscore the importance of the indigenous interpreter. "To obtain the truth of Harlem one must *interpret* the facts," he wrote. His long-standing revulsion, born of forty years as a "prisoner within the ghetto," was far from a disqualification. On the contrary, it was implied, the indignation fueled by his own imprisonment was part of what equipped him to guide his readers to the truth behind the facts.[16]

Clark thought himself well positioned to act as an intermediary between black urban communities and a white public that he believed lacked the necessary insight to empathize with black protest as it entered a new and more volatile phase. "When a bewildered white liberal asks why, in the face of the passage of the Civil Rights Bill of 1964, 'they' still revolt—and not in the dignified, respectable nonviolent way of the earlier student sitins—he betrays his own alienation from the Negroes whose cause he espouses." Notwithstanding the legislative assault on legalized segregation, a complex matrix of economic, social, and political disadvantage ensured that "in many ways the Negro's situation is deteriorating," particularly in the urban North. With the hope of bridging the chasm of empathy and rekindling liberal support for reform in the challenging context of black violence and white "alienation," Clark set out "to describe and interpret what happens to human beings who are confined to depressed areas and whose access to the normal channels of economic mobility and opportunity is blocked."[17]

Showing his readers "what happens to human beings" in the ghetto meant venturing beyond the statistical "facts" of ghetto life to evoke its emotional dynamics. Clark sought to convey the injustices of black urban poverty and disempowerment less by an appeal to abstract principles of equality than by documenting the adverse psychological effects of those injustices on their victims. In this respect, *Dark Ghetto* furthered a trend by which the postwar American social sciences had furnished ever more alarming representations of black life as a quagmire of misery and psychic dysfunction. The notion that racial subordination inflicted psychological wounds on African Americans had been evident as far back as W. E. B. Du Bois's *The Souls of Black Folk* (1903), which listed among the characteristics of "double-consciousness" an "almost morbid sense of personality and a moral hesitancy fatal to self-confidence." Yet as Daryl Michael Scott has shown, it was only in the years following World War II that the image of African Americans as "victims of severe psychological damage" became prevalent. Liberal social scientists eager to bolster the case for eradicating segregation and "prejudice" painted an increasingly drastic portrait of the damaged black psyche.[18]

Indeed, in Clark's first book, *Prejudice and Your Child* (1955), as in Abram Kardiner and Lionel Ovesey's *The Mark of Oppression* (1951) and Gordon Allport's *The Nature of Prejudice* (1955), the idea of diminished black self-esteem hardened into the notion of a pervasive "self-hatred" engendered through African Americans' internalization of their subordinate status. In *Prejudice and Your Child,* Clark sought to convince a popular audience of the substance of the social scientific testimony cited by the Supreme Court's ruling in *Brown v. Board of Education.* Segregated schooling, he argued, caused deep damage to the personalities of black children, and also produced "primitive fears and hatreds" among white children that scarred their own emotional lives and personalities. Clark credited the writings of the émigré psychologist Kurt Lewin about the existence of self-hatred among European Jews, and also referred to studies that reported "feelings of inferiority and self-hatred" among the children of Italian immigrants in New York. Yet the "barriers" to "assimilation" into the "dominant culture" were greater for African Americans, Clark maintained, not least on account of skin color.[19]

For the rapidly rising numbers of African Americans in the nation's cities, Clark would stress during the 1960s, it was the "invisible walls" of the ghetto that marked out the domain of stigma and exclusion. In *Dark Ghetto,* Clark noted the origins of the term "ghetto" in sixteenth-century Venice and its later use to designate "any section of a city to which Jews were confined." The United States, however, had "contributed to the concept of the ghetto the restriction of persons of color to a special area and the limiting of their freedom of choice on the basis of skin color." Shifting from the narrower focus on the schoolroom in *Prejudice and Your Child* to a more comprehensive picture of black urban segregation, Clark argued in *Dark Ghetto* that

> human beings who are forced to live under ghetto conditions and whose daily experience tells them that almost nowhere in society are they respected and granted the ordinary dignity and courtesy accorded to others will, as a matter of course, begin to doubt their own worth. . . . These doubts become the seeds of a pernicious self- and group-hatred, the Negro's complex and debilitating prejudice against himself.

Clark conceived *Dark Ghetto* less as a catalog of Harlem's multiple indices of deprivation and disadvantage—though it contained such a catalog—than as an "anguished cry" bearing witness to the effects of such conditions on ghetto dwellers' emotional lives.[20]

Above all, Clark was concerned with the psychology of "powerlessness," and this concern had led him to the psychodynamic theories of Alfred Adler (1870–1937). Among the early theorists of psychoanalysis, Adler had been a renegade who in 1911 broke with Freud and resigned from the Vienna Psychoanalytic Society. Where Freud asserted the primacy of sexual instincts in human psychology, Adler, who originated the concept of the "inferiority complex," understood humans to be engaged in a quest for self-esteem arising from feelings of power-lessness and dependency experienced in childhood. For Clark, the Adlerian notion of powerlessness offered a framework that could en-compass both a universal human psychology rooted in common expe-riences of childhood and also a means of understanding specific forms of damage afflicting particular disempowered groups. In a speech deliv-ered in the same year that *Dark Ghetto* was published, Clark suggested that Adler's Nietzschean conception of human beings "striving for power" had implications beyond the "personal and familial level." Two years later, Clark would write approvingly of Adler's sensitivity to the psychological consequences of "social conditions" such as unemploy-ment and racial oppression. Indeed, *Dark Ghetto* not only probed the impact of powerlessness on individuals, but placed the Adlerian notion of powerlessness within the context of group relations defined by race.[21]

The ghetto's "invisible walls," Clark wrote, "have been erected by the white society, by those who have power, both to confine those who have *no* power and to perpetuate their powerlessness." Seeking to confront readers with the emotional consequences of this powerless-ness, Clark treated the ghetto's poverty not simply as a material hard-ship, but as a corrosive psychological force. "Housing is no abstract social and political problem," he contended, "but an extension of man's personality. If the Negro has to identify with a rat-infested tenement, his sense of personal inadequacy and inferiority, already aggravated by job discrimination and other forms of humiliation, is reinforced by the physical reality around him." Clark maintained this emphasis on the psychological effects of powerlessness as he proceeded through a litany of Harlem's problems: chronic unemployment resulting from inferior edu-cation and discrimination on the part of employers and unions; disease, diminished life expectancy, and high rates of infant mortality; and fami-lies rent apart by the grinding pressures of poverty. While these were the "objective dimensions" of life in the ghetto, "the subjective dimensions are resentment, hostility, despair, apathy, self-deprecation, and its ironic companion, compensatory grandiose behavior."[22]

Compounding African Americans' sense of powerlessness was the "relative" dimension of poverty. Average black family incomes had risen since 1940, Clark stated, yet ghetto dwellers were aware that their gains were dwarfed by the rapidly expanding affluence of the wider society. "They observe that others enjoy a better life," he wrote, "and this knowledge brings a conglomerate of hostility, despair, and hope." Television and movies penetrated the ghetto's walls so that residents were "bombarded by the myths of the American middle class, often believing as literal truth their pictures of luxury and happiness." Faced with the discrepancy between such images and the realities of their own lives, "the oppressed can never be sure whether their failures reflect personal inferiority or the fact of color. This persistent and agonizing conflict dominates their lives."[23]

As he disclosed in *Dark Ghetto*'s introduction, Clark had not himself lived in Harlem "in more than fifteen years." In 1950, he and his wife had become pioneers on the frontier of suburban integration, commuting to City College and Northside from the affluent town of Hastings-on-Hudson in Westchester County, where they raised their son Hilton and daughter Kate in what was described in a newspaper report of 1954 as "a spacious, rambling, two story [*sic*] house situated near the banks of the Hudson river." Kenneth Clark would later recall that his wife, who had grown up in a large family home in Arkansas, "didn't particularly like living in an apartment," and that this had prompted them to look outside the city. The move away from Harlem was also consistent, however, with the Clarks' fervent commitment to integration and their trenchant opposition to segregated schools. Three or four other black families lived in the Pinecrest neighborhood in Hastings when the Clarks arrived, and by the late 1960s the town was home to around 250 African Americans among its population of 10,000. Kenneth Clark would speak of Hastings with fondness as a place where black families felt relatively welcome. "A white family would sell to a [N]egro family, a [N]egro family could sell to a white family," he recalled in 1990. Yet in his introduction to *Dark Ghetto*, Clark intimated that scaling the ghetto's invisible walls involved greater obstacles than simply finding a new home. "The return of a former inhabitant to the Harlem ghetto appears to be a matter of personal choice," he wrote, "but who can say how free the choice really is. Can the prisoner ever fully escape the prison?"[24]

Clark had come to Harlem in 1918 as a four-year-old boy. His Jamaican parents had met in the Panama Canal Zone, where tens of thousands of migrant laborers from the British West Indies were employed during the early years of the twentieth century, and it was there that Clark and his younger sister, Beulah, were born. When his parents' marriage broke down, his mother, Miriam, decided to take her children to the United States, where she believed they would receive a better education than was possible in the Canal Zone or in Jamaica. Clark's father, Arthur, remained in the Canal Zone for the rest of his life, working for the United Fruit Company and later for the Panama Agencies Company and the Grace Steam Ship Company. Clark was to see him only once again, and permanently broke contact after his father sent him a letter in January 1938 warning him against marrying before completing his studies. In an interview in 1976, Clark's anger toward his father—"a very arrogant, egocentric person" whom he referred to as "that guy"—was palpable, and he attributed his parents' separation to his father's infidelities. He speculated, too, that "it may be that I have been involved in so damn many of these controversies because I didn't have a father that taught me to respect authority arbitrarily."[25]

In New York, Miriam Clark found work in garment factories and a home for herself and her children in Harlem. Like many West Indian immigrants, who by the end of the 1920s would constitute a quarter of Harlem's population, she encountered considerable hostility from indigenous African Americans. As the historian Jervis Anderson has noted, West Indians were often characterized by American-born black Harlemites in much the same way that Jews were widely portrayed: as a pushy, canny, thrifty, and suspiciously successful immigrant group. Clark himself would later draw more positive comparisons between Jewish and West Indian immigrants to America, emphasizing the intense "motivations" of each group and their similar concern to instill literacy in their children from a very young age. Tensions between native-born African Americans and West Indian immigrants prompted Clark's mother and a number of other congregants to leave St. Philip's Church in 1922 and establish an alternative Episcopalian church, St. Luke's, on Edgecombe Avenue. Clark himself served reluctantly as an altar boy until the age of sixteen. He was equally indifferent, he later remembered, to the speeches by Marcus Garvey that his mother, an "ardent follower" of the Jamaican Pan-Africanist, had taken him to at Harlem's Liberty Hall. Indeed, he claimed to have fallen asleep "almost every time." Of greater interest to Clark had been his mother's activism in the International Ladies' Garment Workers' Union. He had thought her activism "terrific" in spite of her experiences of racial discrimination within the union.[26]

Clark's childhood was in many respects an unsettled one. Beyond the migration to New York and the loss of contact with his father there were frequent changes of address, as his mother sought time and again to keep the family one step ahead of Harlem's "creeping blight." He was bilingual in English and Spanish when he arrived in the United States, and was nicknamed "Spanie" and "ridiculed" by his first-grade classmates when he slipped into Spanish during conversation. Harlem was also changing rapidly around him. In his first years in elementary school, many of his classmates had been "Irish, Italian, and Jewish." His closest friend at that time was an Irish American boy, but like much of Harlem's white population, the boy's family soon left the neighborhood. By the time Clark entered junior high school, "all classes consisted of only black students," though the majority of his teachers remained white.[27]

In later years, Clark would speak highly of many of his schoolteachers, who had "respected me enough as a person to hold me to a single standard of academic achievement" regardless of his race and what he called his "broken home." Yet he also recalled that his mother had had to fight hard against a recommendation from a guidance counselor that he be enrolled in a vocational high school, despite his strong academic record. At his mother's insistence he attended the well-regarded George Washington High School, on Harlem's northern border, whose student body remained predominantly white and whose alumni would also include Henry Kissinger and New York's long-serving U.S. senator, Jacob Javits. It was at high school, however, that Clark first felt that his race had a "critical and destructive" impact on his treatment by teachers, especially when he was overlooked for an economics prize he believed was rightfully his. He would later claim that he had chosen to attend Howard University in Washington, D.C., largely on account of its all-black faculty. "One of the reasons I wanted to go to Howard," he told an interviewer in 1957, "was because, maybe unconsciously, I had gotten tired of having to protect myself against the various slights and subtle prejudices which I felt coming from my high school teachers."[28]

The university that Clark entered in 1931 was not only among the most prestigious of America's black colleges, but also, as Jonathan Scott Holloway has shown, "the leading site . . . of black intellectual radicalism in academe during the interwar era." In particular, Clark would later credit three social scientists—the political scientist Ralph Bunche, the sociologist E. Franklin Frazier, and the economist Abram Harris Jr.— with demonstrating to him "that disciplined intelligence could be an instrument for racial justice, social and economic justice." While he would ultimately place less faith than his "mentors" in interracial labor solidarity as the solution to black poverty and disempowerment, their example of socially engaged scholarship dedicated to the pursuit of racial democracy proved to be a lasting influence on Clark's own career. "They were teaching the perspective of life and race," he recalled. "This was when I really started to become concerned with racial injustices in America." Living in the nation's fiercely segregated capital also made starker than ever the disjuncture between America's professed democratic ideals and the realities of unequal citizenship. During his senior year, in 1935, Clark joined a group of other Howard students in a protest inside the Capitol building, where African Americans had been denied restaurant service. Following their arrest, only Bunche's threat to resign from his teaching post deterred the university's disciplinary committee—who were mindful of Howard's congressional funding allocation—from expelling the students.[29]

During his time as an undergraduate, Clark was keenly aware of the assertive civil rights stance of the Communist Party (CPUSA). In 1976, recalling the "intensity of my resentment of American racism" led him to wonder "why I never joined the Communist Party," as some of his closest friends had done. His answer, beyond white Communists' air of "racial condescension," was that he had disagreed with the policy of national "self-determination" for African Americans in the Deep South, which the party had adopted in 1928. "This," Clark remembered, "was my idea of segregation." Rejecting both his mother's Garveyite black nationalism and the CPUSA's view of African Americans as a "nation within a nation," Clark was attracted instead to the militant integrationism of the National Association for the Advancement of Colored People. The NAACP was already engaged in legal challenges to the "separate but equal" principle, a campaign that would culminate, with Clark's assistance, in the *Brown* ruling in 1954. Clark recalled that the NAACP's lawyers would sometimes meet on the Howard campus, and that he and other students had engaged in discussions with them. In 1934, Clark was one of fifty students who joined an antilynching protest instigated by Charles Houston, the NAACP's special counsel.[30]

Clark had entered university with the intention of becoming a doctor, but his enthusiasm for the activist social science practiced by Bunche, Frazier, and Harris prompted a change of direction. So, too, did his admiration for his psychology professor, Francis Cecil Sumner. Howard University, Clark stated during an interview for a *New Yorker* profile published in 1982, was "the beneficiary of the idiocy of racism in American higher education. People like Sumner were not invited to teach at the University of Chicago or Harvard. They were black." Sumner, Clark recalled, had triggered his fascination with psychology by revealing "the promise of getting some systematic understanding of the complexities of human behavior and human interaction." Though Clark would come to reject the positivist equation of empirical "fact" with "truth," his belief that social problems could be resolved through the application of "systematic understanding" reflected the rising self-confidence of American social scientists, who increasingly claimed an epistemic authority equal to that of natural scientists. In the same interview, Clark recalled that under Sumner's influence he had glimpsed the "possibilities" for the social sciences to afford "control" over social problems. "In the physical sciences," he elaborated, "understanding was achieving control—up to a certain point. And in the biological sciences systematic understanding was providing the ability to manipulate the environment for the advantage of human beings. I saw no reason these kinds of possibilities should not extend to the social sciences."[31]

Clark remained at Howard to receive his master's degree in psychology in 1936, and then stayed on to work as an instructor during the following academic year. Among the undergraduates whom he taught in his abnormal psychology class was Mamie Phipps, whom he would marry in 1938. They had met during his senior year, and he had been drawn to her "self-assurance," while she would reflect that his seriousness and "determination" had marked him out from the majority of Howard's male students, sons of elite black families who seemed most interested in "wasting their parents' money." While Mamie pursued her own master's studies at Howard, Kenneth moved back to New York in 1937 to begin studying for a PhD in Columbia University's psychology department.[32]

Columbia was then home to a cluster of renowned social scientists whose scholarship contested prevailing notions of racial hierarchy. They included the anthropologists Ruth Benedict and Franz Boas, who argued against the view that race determined culture, and the social psychologist Otto Klineberg, whose research attacked theories of innate black mental inferiority. Nevertheless, Clark later claimed that he had chosen not to address "problems of social justice" in his doctoral research because of his predicament as the prospective first black recipient of a Columbia PhD in psychology. The "pure scholarly part of me had to be the one that was projected," he had felt, if he was to win the approval of his dissertation committee and to spare his advisers, Klineberg and Gardner Murphy, the need "to defend the first black who was moving toward a PhD in the department." Clark therefore devised a topic—"Some Factors Influencing the Remembering of Prose Material"—that would give him a rigorous training in social psychology without advertising his "social concerns." He was impressed, however, by the socially engaged scholarship of his two advisers. Murphy was a founding member of the Society for the Psychological Study of Social Issues (SPSSI), established in 1936 to represent the activist tendency within social psychology. It was largely from the ranks of fellow SPSSI members that Clark would later recruit signatories to the "Social Science Statement" on the effects of school segregation cited by the Supreme Court in 1954.[33]

Having completed his doctorate, Clark launched himself into projects that addressed the position of African Americans in the wider society. Following eighteen months on the research staff of the Office of War Information, where he investigated black "morale" on the home front, he joined Gunnar Myrdal's research team, where his responsibilities included reviewing the psychological literature on African Americans. After joining the teaching staff at City College in 1942 he maintained his focus on racial issues. Throughout the 1940s he and Mamie, who in 1943 received her own PhD in psychology from Columbia, conducted a series of studies concerning racial identification among African American schoolchildren.[34]

Yet if Clark's "awe and respect" for his professors at Howard and Columbia had led him toward a socially committed scholarship, this was not without cost to his less engagé intellectual inclinations. In 1976, Clark reflected that his decision to pursue a doctorate in social psychology had been driven by a sense of racial obligation, which had diverted him from his deepest academic interests:

> The thing that excited me most was the neurophysiological. And that was the area that I wanted to really specialize in, except that I couldn't afford it, in terms of being black, and being concerned with problems of social and racial justice, I couldn't afford the luxury of doing what I really wanted to do in psychology—namely, know more about the brain and the nervous system, and how they affected behavior. . . . But if I had had my druthers, if I were white, I think I would have gone into neurophysiology totally.

Almost twenty years earlier he had employed similar language when explaining his involvement in the legal campaign that led to the *Brown* decision. "Given certain kinds of historical circumstances," he told an interviewer in 1957, "the Negro scholar cannot afford the luxury of isolation from the larger problems and struggles." These remarks lend weight to the meaning of Clark's suggestion, in *Dark Ghetto*'s introduction, that his "return" to Harlem as an "involved observer" was less a "free" choice than the fate of one who remained a "prisoner of the ghetto."[35]

In common with W. E. B. Du Bois, Zora Neale Hurston, Ralph Ellison, and other black literary intellectuals to whom Ross Posnock has
ascribed the persona of the *"antirace race man or woman,"* Clark had pledged
himself to "race work" even as he regretted "the psychic and intellectual constriction imposed by racial identity." Yet to a greater extent
than Posnock's subjects, Clark experienced the "tension . . . between
race champion and intellectual" as an irremediable opposition that barred
him inexorably from pursuing his most sincere interests. Du Bois,
though much of his energy was expended on racial "uplift," nevertheless believed that he was able to "dwell above the Veil" and to move
"across the color line" in a raceless "kingdom of culture." For Ellison,
art was "a form of freedom" through which the simplifying distortions
of race were negated and transcended, even in the process of evoking
black life under segregation. To Clark's mind, however, the burden of
race was all-consuming and permitted no such transcendence; invisible
walls encircled black intellectual life no less than black urban life. Noting in *Dark Ghetto* that "almost every well-known Negro writer, artist,
and performer" had elected to "leave the ghetto physically," he claimed
that "they do not do so psychologically. They are still bound to it."
James Baldwin was, he stated, "the clearest illustration of this; his writings are ghetto-bound." Baldwin, Richard Wright, Lorraine Hansberry, Sidney Poitier, and Lena Horne were all, Clark implied, fellow
prisoners.[36]

Clark seemed intent on destroying all remaining associations of Harlem with cultural vitality. Unaware that the neighborhood was on the
cusp of something of an artistic revival, which included the founding
of the Black Arts Repertory Theatre/School by LeRoi Jones in the
spring of 1965 and The Studio Museum in Harlem by Romare Bearden
and others in 1968, Clark discerned only institutions that offered psychic escape. As if to 'declare every vestige of the "Harlem Renaissance"
extinguished, he wrote:

> In all of Harlem there is no museum, no art gallery, no art school,
> no sustained "little theater" group; despite the stereotype of the
> Negro as artist, there are only five libraries—but hundreds of bars,

hundreds of churches, and scores of fortune tellers. Everywhere there are signs of fantasy, decay, abandonment, and defeat. The only constant characteristic is a sense of inadequacy.

There was little sense that ghetto dwellers—artists or otherwise—drew sustenance from a distinctive cultural inheritance, or in any way transcended their material impoverishment through creative expression. Clark was virtually silent on such aspects of black life as music and dance.[37]

Dark Ghetto thus mirrored those features of *An American Dilemma* that had caused such offense to Ralph Ellison. In a review of Myrdal's report penned in 1944 and first published in 1964, Ellison charged that Myrdal had reduced black life to a set of pathological "reactions" to oppression, and had trampled over the "richness" of "Negro culture." By the mid-1960s, Ellison bracketed Clark, with whom he had been on friendly terms during the 1950s, alongside Myrdal and Frazier as typifying a crude "sociological" caricature of black life as "a catalogue of negative definitions." Clark, Ellison told the author Robert Penn Warren, "perhaps . . . has an investment in negative propaganda as a means of raising funds with which to correct some of the injustices common to Negro slums."[38]

Ellison had not always been so averse to bleak, pathologist portrayals of black urban life. In a magazine article of 1948 he had praised the work of Harlem's Lafarge Psychiatric Clinic and had claimed that the shattering of the southern migrant's dream of Harlem on arrival in the neighborhood was "as damaging to Negro personality as the slum scenes of filth, disorder and crumbling masonry in which it flies apart." In Harlem, he wrote, "one wanders dazed in a ghetto maze." By the 1960s, however, Ellison was fiercely critical not only of "sociological" studies of black life but also of those black literary authors whom he considered captives of pathologist social scientific oversimplifications. The author from whom Ellison was now most eager to distance himself, his former mentor Richard Wright, was one whom Clark deeply admired. As Clark would recall in 1981, while he had not known Wright personally, "I read, I think, almost everything that he wrote." Wright, he said, had been in "the vanguard of the black protest movement from the literary perspective. And that's got to be a major contribution." The depiction of Chicago's South Side as an enervating, suffocating environment in Wright's novel *Native Son* (1940) would resonate in Clark's characterization of "the ghetto" as "all-encompassing, a psychological as well as a physical reality" that "consumes all its residents."[39]

Wright's own career manifests the interconnections between literary and social scientific representations of black urban life. Five years after the publication of *Native Son*, Wright had contributed an introductory essay to *Black Metropolis*, a massive study of Chicago's black community by two African American social scientists, Horace Cayton and St. Clair Drake. Referring to *Native Son*'s disturbed protagonist, Wright lauded their 800-page book for documenting "the environment out of which the Bigger Thomases of our nation come." He also paid tribute to Cayton and Drake's "Chicago School" mentors, the sociologists Robert E. Park and Louis Wirth, whose accounts of social processes "gave me my first concrete vision of the forces that molded the urban Negro's body and soul." Their writings had convinced Wright "that sincere art and honest social science were not far apart, that each could enrich the other." Though Ellison, in contrast to Wright, doubted that the social sciences had anything to offer artists, his rejoinders to Myrdal and Clark nonetheless maintained the trend by which social scientists and artists engaged in a shared conversation about the nature of black life.[40]

The novelist with whom Clark most identified, however, was Baldwin. In 1963, he described Baldwin as a "close friend" and as a writer who "has mobilized that powerful weapon of words and systematic presentation of ideas, as another weapon in the Negro's struggle for justice." Clark would later recall that Baldwin had been a guest in his home in Hastings-on-Hudson, and that Baldwin had introduced Clark to his own family. Clark found him "a fascinating conversationalist" and was "spellbound" by Baldwin's "view of American racial injustice." In a rare, if modest, expression of appreciation for African American culture, Clark wrote playfully to Baldwin in October 1963 to ask "what happened to our date for fried chicken? If integration means that we must give up fried chicken, then I wonder whether it will be worth it."[41]

As with Wright's work, however, it was the tragic view of black urban life in Baldwin's novels that appealed to Clark. Baldwin's first novel, the loosely autobiographical *Go Tell It on the Mountain* (1953), vividly evokes the psychic turmoil of a boy growing up in 1930s Harlem. John Grimes dreams of escaping the misery of his surroundings through the spiritual life of the church, and of escaping the church itself, in which his tyrannical father preaches. The HARYOU report, *Youth in the Ghetto,* cited Baldwin's novel as an authoritative source on the subject of "young persons who find an apparent release by morbid absorption in religious activities." Indeed, Baldwin's essay "The Harlem Ghetto" (1948) had described black worship as a "fairly desperate emotional business" involving a "sinister" fantasy of "revenge" in which black people would be rewarded and whites punished in the hereafter.[42]

This essay may well have been prominent in Clark's thoughts as he wrote *Dark Ghetto.* Originally published in the magazine *Commentary,* whose editor, Elliot Cohen, had first alerted Clark to Baldwin's writings during the late 1940s, "The Harlem Ghetto" examines, in succession, Harlem's political leadership, press, and religious life. The chapter of *Dark Ghetto* titled "The Power Structure of the Ghetto" surveys the same institutions in an identical order, though a discussion of Harlem's social services intervenes between press and church. Both authors treated these institutions as symptomatic of the ghetto's powerlessness and, in Baldwin's words, "innate desperation." Clark went further than Baldwin, however, in suggesting that Harlem's flamboyant, pseudo-militant political operatives, its sensationalist, scandal-obsessed newspapers, and its emotionally manipulative churches headed by cynical ministers served cathartic functions that increased the "dissipation or stagnation" of the community's energies. For Clark, these institutions and actors not only reflected but exacerbated "the maelstrom of the ghetto's pathology."[43]

"Pathology" is, indeed, *Dark Ghetto*'s most persistent refrain. Clark's medical imagery—he also wrote of "the contagious sickness of the community"—served a complex representational role in his effort to foster empathy for African Americans in the midst of the urban crisis.

The application of metaphors of pathology and disease to human behavior has been characterized by scholars as a device of representational
"othering." Sander Gilman has argued that "the very concept of pathology is a line drawn between the 'good' and the 'bad,'" by which
the "potential illness, age, and corruption of the self is projected onto
others." Moreover, from the mid-1960s onward, as will be seen, critics
of pathologist representations of black urban life charged Clark and
others with constructing derogatory images that were bound to induce
revulsion toward those portrayed as sick and damaged. It is important,
however, to identify the attraction that metaphors of pathology held
for Clark and the ends to which he sought to employ them.[44]

Clark's objective in *Dark Ghetto* was to "describe and interpret what
happens to human beings" in black urban communities in order to
dramatize the injustices of segregation and poverty. In using the language of sickness and pathology, Clark appeared to believe that he
could appeal to the compassion of his liberal readers—who would regard sickness as a form of suffering resulting from misfortune—and
simultaneously warn them of their own vulnerability under the status
quo. His diagnostic approach to the lives of the black poor was intended precisely as an alternative to what he called "hypocritical moralizing." Behaviors that so alarmed middle-class white Americans—
such as illegitimacy and delinquency—were to be conceived as
problems of public health, rather than objects of moral censure. "The
problem of controlling crime in the ghetto is primarily one of changing the conditions which tend to breed widespread violence rather
than one of reforming the individual criminal," Clark contended. "An
apt analogy here may be to compare ghetto pathology to an epidemic.
To prevent epidemics, necessary public health and sanitation measures
are taken." The adoption of such measures was both a moral necessity
and, Clark stressed, ultimately a matter of self-interest for the white
majority, for the attempt to "confine" pathology within the ghetto's
walls and "prevent the spread of its contagion to the 'larger community'" would prove to be "futile." In chronicling "the ghetto's pattern
of venereal disease, illegitimacy, and family instability," Clark did not
believe that he was entrenching harmful stereotypes of black deviance,

as critics of pathologism were to claim. Rather, he believed that he was exposing the true magnitude of racial oppression.[45]

"Family instability" was a recurrent theme of social scientific treatments of black urban life. In *The Philadelphia Negro* (1899), described by the historian Herbert Aptheker as "the first scientific study in Afro-American sociology and the pioneer study in urban sociology in the United States," Du Bois had combined socioeconomic contextualization and arch moral judgment in accounting for an "astoundingly" high incidence of male marital "desertion." Both the "difficulty of supporting a family" on low wages and a "laxity of morals" were culpable, Du Bois believed, and though he protested employment discrimination, he was insistent that black "home-life" was itself in need of urgent "regeneration." During the 1930s, Frazier brought historical contextualization to bear on black families and argued that their "matriarchal" structure was a legacy of slavery, though one that was reinforced by the inadequate economic opportunities available to black men in the present day. By the 1950s, however, Frazier viewed matriarchy not only as a consequence of disadvantage, but also as a cause of further disadvantage and pathology, especially in a harsh urban environment in which female-headed households were, he considered, ill-equipped to instill the discipline necessary to dissuade black children from delinquency.[46]

Like Du Bois and Frazier, Clark treated the structure of the black family as both consequence and cause of black disadvantage. In *Dark Ghetto,* he faulted slavery for diminishing the role of fatherhood through the use of the black male as a "stud," and argued that the "menial status" to which black men had been assigned in the American economy since emancipation had reinforced the position of the female as "the dominant person in the Negro family." Yet he, too, regarded the black family's putatively exceptional structure as exerting its own injurious impact on black urban life. *Dark Ghetto* was entirely free of Du Bois's censorious talk of the "shameless lewdness" and "shrewd laziness" of the black lower class. Instead, Clark followed the example of postwar liberal social scientists such as Kardiner and Ovesey in conjoining the discourses of matriarchy and damage, thereby interpreting the harmful effects of black "family instability" as secondary effects of racial oppression.[47]

In particular, patterns of lower-class black male behavior widely condemned as morally deviant could be explained as adaptive, if ultimately harmful, responses to disempowerment. Prevented by economic marginalization from satisfying what Clark described as the "normal" male "desire for dominance" within the family (Clark did not specify whether it was nature or culture that made such a desire "normal"), the black male suffered "doubts concerning his personal adequacy." He was thus

> *compelled* to base his self-esteem instead on a kind of behavior that tended to support a stereotyped picture of the Negro male—sexual impulsiveness, irresponsibility, verbal bombast, posturing, and compensatory achievement in entertainment and athletics. . . . The pressure to find relief from his intolerable psychological position seems directly related to the continued high incidence of desertions and broken homes in Negro ghettos.

The dominant behavior of black women, Clark added, "tended to perpetuate the weaker role of the Negro male." Again, Clark intended this not as a moral criticism but as an example of the secondary effects of racial oppression, since black women were "required" to develop a "compensatory strength" in response to black men's limited economic opportunity. All the same, the pathological black family was identified as a source of further pathologies, as the lack of a "strong male father figure" in the lives of black boys diminished their own expectations of forming stable marital partnerships and established a "Distorted Masculine Image" grounded in promiscuity and "alleged sexual prowess."[48]

Dark Ghetto thus explained black "family instability" as "one of the inevitable results of the unemployment and menial job status of urban Negroes." Responsibility for the pathologies that Clark recounted therefore rested ultimately with those whose actions sustained racial oppression; the inhabitants of America's dark ghettos were "subject peoples, victims of the greed, cruelty, insensitivity, guilt, and fear of their masters." Yet Clark's depiction of the black family as a cause—albeit a secondary one—of pathology would soon expose him to severe criticism. "Not only is the pathology of the ghetto self-perpetuating," he wrote, "but one type of pathology breeds another. The child born into the ghetto is more likely to come into a world of broken homes and illegitimacy; and this family and social instability is conducive to delinquency, drug addiction, and criminal violence." Abstracted from Clark's analysis of power and powerlessness, such claims could appear to blame poverty and delinquency on the culture of the oppressed.[49]

In fact, however, Clark's analysis differed markedly from the "culture of poverty" thesis proposed by the anthropologist Oscar Lewis. In his studies of impoverished communities in Central America and of Puerto Rican immigrants in New York, Lewis argued that the extension of economic opportunities to the poor would not necessarily enable their economic advancement, because behaviors transmitted from one generation to the next—the "culture of poverty"—presented a formidable barrier to economic mobility. In 1966, Lewis claimed that poor children were often "not psychologically geared to take full advantage of changing conditions of increased opportunities which may occur in their lifetime." By contrast, Clark was adamant that such pathologies as existed within poor black families did not present insurmountable obstacles to breaking the intergenerational cycle of poverty. In *Dark Ghetto,* he was scathing about the "recent rash of cultural deprivation theories," which, he wrote, employed reassuringly "environmentalistic" concepts to arrive at a "fatalism" no less harmful than that of earlier "biologically determined" rationalizations of African Americans' subordinate status.[50]

Rejecting the "fashionable" view that poor housing, inadequate nutrition, and "parental apathy" were the principal causes of black "educational retardation," Clark argued that "these children, by and large, do not learn because . . . those who are charged with the responsibility of teaching them do not believe that they can learn, do not expect that they can learn, and do not act toward them in ways which will help them to learn." Citing evidence from the Northside Center and other remedial education initiatives, Clark insisted that children from poor families, irrespective of their home environments, achieved dramatic

improvements in literacy when given focused attention and encouragement by their teachers. Perhaps mindful of his own education in Harlem's public schools several decades earlier, Clark viewed schooling as a
vital tool in breaking the ghetto's cycle of disadvantage.[51]

Tangle of Pathology

Dark Ghetto met with a chorus of respectful, even reverential reviews
in leading magazines and newspapers. Reviewers frequently remarked
on Clark's privileged vantage point as an indigenous interpreter, and
generally recognized his attention to black "pathology" as an element
of his indictment of racism. *Newsweek* contended that while social scientists typically "live in a cool world of dispassion," Clark, "as a Negro
psychologist studying the corrosive effects of prejudice . . . necessarily
lives in a world of passion, involvement, and truths that are strongly
held but not easily measured." Highlighting the conjuncture of professional expertise and lived experience that defined the authority of the
indigenous interpreter, the review asserted that "both as a former prisoner and now as a 'prison' psychologist, Clark knows that the psychological cruelty of ghetto life is even more damaging than the poverty,
the crime, the blight, and the rat-infested tenements." In the *New
Yorker,* the left-wing journalist Nat Hentoff emphasized that Clark
"grew up in Harlem, has spent much of his time there, shares the anger
of many of its residents, and has himself been bruised against the barriers, both inside the ghetto and outside it, of those who try to change
it." Clark's analysis of "the present pathology of this country's dark
ghettos," Hentoff judged, was "unparalleled for its knowledge and sensitivity." For Frank Cordasco, writing in the *Saturday Review,* Clark's
"impassioned and eloquent recital of the consequences of a tragic social
pathology" was "a classic which will be held as important for our day
as Jacob Riis's *How the Other Half Lives* and Jane Addams's *The Spirit of
Youth and the City Streets* were for another." The child psychiatrist Robert Coles, writing in the *Reporter,* praised *Dark Ghetto* for revealing
Harlem's "fragmented, bruised lives, riddled with fantasy and futile
postures, saturated in pathology that Dr. Clark lists and discusses with
unsparing clarity, yet with an unusual acceptance of the ambiguity of

life." Clark had done as much, Coles believed, as "any American of either race" to "expose this nation's terrible wounds." This was a view shared by Anna Kross, the commissioner of the New York City Department of Correction, who wrote in the *New York Times Book Review* that Clark had rendered a "picture that may well awaken Americans to stark miseries they have refused to face."[52]

As these reviews testified, *Dark Ghetto* caught the imagination of a certain white liberal constituency and gave weight to its claims that formal legal equalities would not be sufficient to eradicate black urban disadvantage. In his commencement address at Howard University a few weeks after *Dark Ghetto*'s publication, President Johnson himself intoned that "freedom is not enough." The lives of many urban African Americans, he stated in language that echoed Clark's, were "ringed by an invisible wall." A concerted government effort was needed to "move beyond opportunity to achievement" and to make the "Great Society" a reality for all Americans. Drawing on an as-yet unpublicized report by the assistant secretary of labor, Daniel Patrick Moynihan, Johnson's address both faulted "centuries of oppression and persecution" for conditions in black communities and also described a "seamless web" of black "infirmities"—including the "breakdown of the Negro family structure"—which "cause each other," "result from each other," and "reinforce each other."[53]

Johnson's declaration that the aims of policymaking must "move beyond opportunity to achievement" has been cited as a crucial step toward government sanction for the hotly contested principle of affirmative action. At the time, however, there was little audible controversy concerning Johnson's pathologist rhetoric of black "infirmities" and his attention to black family breakdown. The text of the address had, indeed, been enthusiastically previewed by Martin Luther King Jr., Roy Wilkins, and a number of other civil rights leaders. A few months later, however, the leaking of Moynihan's report *The Negro Family: The Case for National Action* would set in motion a rising tide of criticism of pathologist accounts of black urban life, including Clark's.[54]

While Clark treated black "family instability" alongside inferior schooling, substandard housing, and employment inequalities as factors in a "self-perpetuating" cycle of pathology, Moynihan elevated black family structure to a singular importance. Recent advances toward legal equality notwithstanding, Moynihan argued, African Americans were "not equal" to other groups "in terms of ability to win out in the competitions of American life." The "fundamental problem" holding them back was "family structure," for "the Negro family in the urban ghettos is crumbling." Yet if the Moynihan Report differed from *Dark Ghetto* in its almost exclusive focus on black family structure, its diagnosis of the black urban family nevertheless converged in many respects with Clark's. Moynihan, too, traced the deterioration of the black family structure back to slavery and subsequent "discrimination, injustice, and uprooting." The concept of the "emasculation of the Negro male," which Clark explained as the combined effect of black males' economic disadvantage and black females' dominance, was substantially mirrored in Moynihan's characterization of the black "matriarchal" family. Moreover, while both authors sought to expose the "pathologies" of black urban life in order to demonstrate the need for government interventions—hence the subtitle of Moynihan's report, *The Case for National Action*—both also furnished powerful images of the problems of black communities as self-perpetuating. The description of black urban life as a "tangle of pathology," which became a focus for criticism of the Moynihan Report, was in fact borrowed from Clark's HARYOU report.[55]

Irrespective of Clark's or Moynihan's intentions, such imagery was prone to appropriation by commentators who were less attentive to historical and present socioeconomic pressures on African American communities and who counseled self-improvement, rather than costly government programs, as the appropriate response to black poverty. In June 1965, the *Washington Star* columnist Mary McGrory cited Moynihan's claims as evidence that "the time has come for them [African Americans] to get to grips with their own worst problem, 'the breakdown of Negro family life.'" The eruption of the massive Watts riot in Los Angeles in August prompted further conservative use of pathologist imagery. The columnists Rowland Evans and Robert Novak, for example, referred to the Moynihan Report to support their assertion that the riot was the result not of poverty, unemployment, or police brutality, but of "illegitimacy, and female oriented homes."[56]

Among liberals, radicals, and civil rights leaders, initial responses to the Moynihan Report varied, and not until the late 1960s would criticism reach its height. Nevertheless, a number of attacks were quickly forthcoming. Six years earlier, the reception of Stanley Elkins's study *Slavery: A Problem in American Institutional and Intellectual Life* had given an indication of the potential for pathologist claims to cause offense. Elkins's argument that slaves had been cowed and infantilized by oppression was vigorously debated among historians. The Moynihan Report, however, was widely discussed and contested far beyond the academy, not least because its diagnosis referred to contemporary African Americans against the fraught backdrop of the riots. Moynihan himself had faulted three centuries of "almost unimaginable treatment" for the fragility of the black family. Yet in calling that fragility the "fundamental problem," he had invited charges that he was blaming the victim. The rising conservative appropriation of the report also led many civil rights activists and liberals to view pathologist imagery with suspicion or outright hostility. In the *Nation,* the Boston social worker and Congress of Racial Equality (CORE) activist William Ryan accused Moynihan of fostering "a new form of subtle racism." James Farmer, CORE's national leader, called the report "a massive academic cop-out for the white conscience."[57]

Clark was moved to defend Moynihan against such charges. "If Pat is a racist, I am," he told journalists. "He highlights the total pattern of segregation and discrimination. Is a doctor responsible for the disease simply because he diagnoses it?" Nevertheless, over subsequent years the reaction against pathologism triggered by the Moynihan Report would increasingly target Clark's own writings. In 1968, the African American anthropologist Charles Valentine denounced the "pejorative tradition" of social scientific scholarship on black urban life "established by E. Franklin Frazier" and extended by Moynihan. Valentine saw fit to distinguish Clark from what he considered the "arrogant and patronizing" tone of many other pathologists, and he found much of value in Clark's HARYOU blueprint. He was critical, however, of Clark's treatment of black urban households as "disorganized" and "unstable" simply because they deviated from white middle-class norms. *Dark Ghetto* had failed, Valentine argued, to represent Harlem "in terms of its *own* social order, cultural idiom, or life style."[58]

Indeed, rejecting the pathologism of Frazier, Elkins, Moynihan, and Clark, historians and social scientists during the late 1960s and 1970s increasingly portrayed the black psyche as resilient rather than damaged and the black family as organized and functional rather than defective and fragile. John Blassingame rebuked Elkins's characterization of slaves as quiescent "Sambos," and Herbert Gutman argued that slaves had raised their children within strong, adaptive extended kinship groups. The sociologist Andrew Billingsley argued that contemporary black urban families provided a number of supportive models of socialization, and feminist scholars such as Joyce Ladner and Carol Stack answered indictments of black "matriarchy" by documenting the strength and flexibility of resource-sharing female kinship networks. Reginald Jones stated with satisfaction that his fellow black psychologists were moving "away from pathology oriented notions about the behavior of black people." Indeed, by the mid-1970s, as Daryl Michael Scott has demonstrated, liberal social scientists had largely abandoned the discourse of damage and pathology.[59]

While Moynihan drew the most fire, Clark did not emerge unscathed from the assault on pathologism. Indeed, Clark's representations of black urban life and even his authenticity as an indigenous interpreter were subjected to increasingly hostile scrutiny. Ralph Ellison, whose objections to "negative," "sociological" accounts of black life served as an inspiration to the rising generation of revisionist, anti-pathologist social scientists, chastised Clark repeatedly in interviews during the mid-1960s, as previously mentioned. However, it was Albert Murray, Ellison's close friend and a fellow alumnus of Tuskegee Institute, who was to become Clark's chief antagonist. Born in 1916, two years after Clark, and raised in Mobile County, Alabama, Murray had spent the 1950s in the U.S. Air Force before retiring in 1962 at the rank of major. At that point he moved to Harlem, set up base in an apartment just off Lenox Avenue, and launched himself into more literary campaigns. As an essayist and aspiring novelist, Murray would never enjoy the accolades heaped on Ellison, whose National Book Award–winning *Invisible Man* (1952) ensured its author's enduring renown. Nevertheless, during the 1960s Murray steadily built a reputation as an astute literary and social critic and beginning in 1974 published a clutch of well-received novels. In time, he would be anointed by Henry Louis Gates Jr. as the "foremost cultural explicant of black modernism."[60]

In January 1966, Murray took aim at Clark in an essay titled "Social Science Fiction in Harlem," published in the *New Leader,* a liberal magazine. Reflecting the mounting controversy over pathologism, and also a degree of rivalry among African American intellectuals to claim the personal authenticity and disciplinary authority to represent black urban life, Murray's essay scorned both Clark's insider credentials as a black American and what Murray considered to be *Dark Ghetto*'s portrait of "the wretchedness of U.S. Negroes." Disregarding Clark's Harlem childhood and his professional involvement in the neighborhood, Murray labeled him a "brownskin Panamanian" who had somehow turned himself into a "mass-media certified Negro Negrologist." Regaling credulous white audiences with sensationalized accounts of black "degradation," Clark was "a very special kind of entertainer who uses charts, graphs, and monographs as his stage props." Harlem was no "ghetto," Murray insisted. Unlike historic Jewish communities in Europe, African Americans were fully part of the national culture, sharing the "same calendar, religious observances, language, food," and the same "educational, economic, and political objectives as whites."[61]

The most sustained criticism of *Dark Ghetto* appeared, however, in Murray's book of social and cultural criticism, *The Omni-Americans: New Perspectives on Black Experience and American Culture* (1970). Here, Murray charged Clark with grossly distorting the realities of black urban life by making social and psychological dysfunction appear ubiquitous while ignoring such positive black attributes as resilience, self-belief, self-reliance, humor, elegance, wit, creativity, and a capacity for enjoyment. *Dark Ghetto,* according to Murray, "represents Negroes as substandard human beings who subsist in a sick community. Its image of Harlem is, in effect, that of an urban pit writhing with derelicts." Clark, he wrote, "insists that slavery and oppression have reduced Negroes to such a tangle of pathology that all black American behavior is in effect only a pathetic manifestation of black cowardice, self-hatred, escapism, and self-destructiveness." Murray also elaborated his argument that Harlem was "no ghetto at all." Scarcely isolated from the wider world, its residents were bona fide New Yorkers and Americans. Most, he claimed, worked downtown, were "as intimately involved with Macy's" as their incomes allowed, and took pride in the role that black entertainers, lawyers, and politicians played in the life of the city and nation at large. "Segregation is bad enough," Murray conceded, "but it just ain't what it used to be."[62]

The Omni-Americans also deepened Murray's attack on Clark's credentials as a Harlemite and racial insider. *Dark Ghetto,* he claimed, "reveals very little if any meaningful, first-hand contact with any black community in the United States." Murray made no mention of Clark's upbringing in Harlem and no attempt to explain why Clark's years of personal and professional contact with the Harlem community were not "meaningful." Instead, he dismissed Clark's legitimacy as an indigenous interpreter seemingly on the basis that what Clark wrote about Harlem could only be the product of an outsider's perspective. Indeed, Murray situated Clark's ideas beyond the boundaries of an authentically black sensibility. By describing black communities in terms of their deviation from white norms, Murray claimed, *Dark Ghetto* showed "how a book by a black writer may represent a point of view toward black experience which is essentially white." Black novelists whose work reflected pathologist ideas, including Wright and Baldwin, were similarly deemed to be lacking an authentically black perspective. Even the Harlem-born Baldwin was judged by the Alabama-born Murray to have surrendered all legitimacy as an insider when he designated Harlem as a "black ghetto." In doing so, Murray wrote, Baldwin had spurned "U.S. Negro tradition" and assumed the outlook of a "New York Jewish intellectual of immigrant parents." Actual immigrants such as Clark were thus far from the only targets of Murray's allegations of inauthenticity.[63]

Beneath its hyperbole and personal gibes, *The Omni-Americans* contained a perceptive critique of *Dark Ghetto* and the wider pathologist literature. Clark's book did indeed create the impression of a community mired in misery and dysfunction, and said relatively little about the positive social and cultural resources through which urban African Americans survived in challenging circumstances. Murray was also alert to the potential for pathologist imagery to backfire on its liberal advocates. Anticipating the later arguments of historians such as Daryl

Michael Scott and Alice O'Connor, Murray warned that Clark's portrait of Harlem would only strengthen white Americans' "notions of
black inferiority." By depicting black urban life as a morass of psycho-
pathology and social deviancy, he believed, Clark risked reinforcing
"the stereotypes that Negroes have always been extremely sensitive
about." Would white parents be willing to send their children to public
schools alongside "pathological" black adolescents? Rather than convincing the American public of the need for ameliorative social interventions, Murray predicted, "one-sided featuring of black pathology
might frighten white Americans into an easier tolerance of anti-Negro
police tactics."[64]

Indeed, as Scott has demonstrated, many newspapers were quickly
drawn to conservative explanations of the riots as products of a pathology bred in the home and susceptible only to black self-help and vigorous policing. Following the Watts riot of August 1965, California's
governor, Edmund Brown, attributed the violence to "hoodlums." His
successor, Ronald Reagan, espoused an even more vehement law-and-
order approach to urban unrest. Conservative social scientists such as
Harvard's Edward Banfield gave intellectual weight to such platforms,
urging repressive responses to what they characterized as the pathological criminality of the urban lower classes. And as the historian Jennifer
Light has shown, local and federal authorities increasingly resorted to
techniques and technologies developed by the defense industry in their
attempts to manage the urban crisis.[65]

Some of Murray's criticisms, however, were little more than polemical distortions of Clark's views. Clark did not harbor an "almost wor-
shipful" attitude toward "white well being," as Murray alleged. *Dark
Ghetto* was not only strident in its condemnation of white racism but
also candid about white "divorce, abortions, adultery, and the various
forms of jaded and fashionable middle- and upper-class sexual explorations." Neither, as will be seen, did Clark characterize Harlem's residents as "derelicts" incapable of action or self-assertion. For all its
gloom, *Dark Ghetto* was not devoid of hope or of affection for the community in which Clark had himself learned of "love," "sacrifice," and
"courage" as well as "cruelty," "cowardice," and "bombast." Moreover, as sensitive as Murray was to the pitfalls of pathologism, he was

less mindful of the problematic resonances and potentially conservative implications of his own representations of black urban life.[66]

The Omni-Americans was not only a critique of pathologism. It was also a manifesto for what Murray called an "affirmative," anti-pathologist perspective on black life. As will be further discussed in Chapter 3 in the context of Murray's friendship and artistic collaboration with Romare Bearden, his characterization of Harlem was no less "one-sided" than Clark's in emphasizing the vibrant, joyous, and creative rather than the dispiriting and destructive. Indeed, Murray announced at the outset his intention of "accentuating the positive and *eliminating the negative*" in his portrayal of black urban life. Celebrating the blues-inflected expressive culture and "sartorial sophistication" of Harlem's residents, Murray claimed that "Harlem for all its liabilities generates people-to-people good times which are second to none anywhere in the world." In an unpublished manuscript that likely dates from this period, Murray noted the existence of conflicting sets of historically ingrained stereotypes of African Americans. Yet he considered the notion of black "self-hatred (or self-rejection)" to be "an infinitely more serious charge than happy-go-lucky ever was." Likewise, the term "ghetto" was "far more degrading" in Murray's view "than darktown or even *niggertown*." Murray lamented that many of those who "recoil from the comic stereotypes of niggertown . . . do not seem to mind at all that those of the ghetto are pathological (a far better justification for ostracism than shiftlessness)."[67]

Here, Murray appeared to underestimate the role that "happy-go-lucky" imagery had historically played, through minstrelsy and other channels, in rationalizing slavery and segregation. A year after the publication of *The Omni-Americans,* the historian George Fredrickson would provide a detailed exploration of that imagery and its uses. The "stereotype of the happy and contended bondsman," Fredrickson observed, had been wielded by southern slave owners in part "to counter the abolitionist image of the wretched slave." Even when stereotypes of black gaiety had appeared in the arguments of some who opposed slavery and black expatriation, such imagery of a childlike and simple people had perpetuated a view of African Americans that offended their humanity and injured their social status. The Reverend Increase

Niles Tarbox of West Newton, Massachusetts, wrote in 1864 of the "more joyous and holiday feeling" of the black race, and that year the American Freedmen's Inquiry Commission remarked how blacks' "cheerfulness and love of mirth overflow with the exuberance of childhood." Children, however lovable, have seldom been accorded full political citizenship. In the twentieth century, such "romantic racialism" resurfaced in the "jazzed-up" form of white primitivism during the 1920s (and, Fredrickson might have added, the "White Negro" primitivism of the postwar era). Yet from the 1930s onward, liberal intellectuals, black and white, had increasingly discarded romantic characterizations of the "happy Negro," not least "because it was seen that they provided a covert rationale for continued segregation, exploitation, and poverty. If blacks were seen as naturally joyous and capable of deriving aesthetic pleasure from the simplest things of life, it was pointed out, then whites had a perfect excuse for doing nothing about the fact that blacks were an exploited minority."[68]

It was this very charge that Clark leveled against *The Omni-Americans*. When "Social Science Fiction in Harlem" had appeared in 1966, Clark had struggled to formulate a coherent public response. He declined an invitation from Myron Kolatch, the editor of the *New Leader,* to respond in the magazine's pages, instead sending Kolatch a letter ("*not* for publication") in which he criticized the decision to publish Murray's essay. His letter also implied, remarkably, that Murray's refusal to confront Harlem's harsh realities was itself testimony to the psychological damage caused by racism. "My summary judgment," Clark wrote, "is that Mr. Murray's article could be seen as an appendix to *Dark Ghetto:* The ghetto and an insensitive and dehumanizing society spawn a multitude of tragic consequences. Among the more tragic, and probably the most dangerous, of its human casualties are those of potential human intelligence and imagination." When *The Omni-Americans* was published, Clark managed a more nuanced response. Addressing an audience at City College, he commented that a favorable newspaper review of Murray's book had reminded him of a passage he had read many years earlier, from which he now quoted: "a strange people, merry mid their misery, laughing through their tears like the sun shining through the rain. Yet what simple philosophers they. They tread life's path as if

it were strewn with roses devoid of thorns; and make the most of life
with natures of sunshine and song." These words, Clark revealed, were
an impression of the Irish penned by an English army officer during
the nineteenth century. Yet they seemed to Clark to resonate deeply
with Murray's affirmative view of life in Harlem and with the enthusiastic reception of Murray's book:

> The writer of the review totally bought Murray's view of urban
> ghetto experience as a positive, stimulating, invigorating thing. He
> bought it uncritically, and as I have been watching the reviews of
> Murray's essays and books, there does seem to be this trend to per-
> fume the stink of the ghetto, to make it more palatable to those
> who are not required to live and to die often prematurely in Amer-
> ica's ghettos.

If Murray considered Clark an "entertainer" who supplied his white
audiences with the images of blackness they desired, Clark thought
much the same of Murray. "As a psychologist," Clark commented, he
believed that the romanticization of black or Irish experience func-
tioned primarily "to solve [sic] the guilt of the oppressor," and reflected
little of the "reality of the predicament of the oppressed." His critique
of the excesses of anti-pathologist imagery provides an important
counterweight to scholars' recent preoccupation with the pitfalls of
pathologism.[69]

Clark had been just as scathing of the romanticization of black urban
life in 1962, when he censured two American Jewish writers, Norman
Mailer and Seymour Krim. Mailer's provocative essay "The White
Negro" (1957) had identified within black urban life the ingredients
for a hedonistic antidote to the twin threats of nuclear apocalypse and
cultural sterility. In 1961, however, in a review of Jean Genet's play *The
Blacks,* Mailer regretted that, like American Jews, African Americans
appeared to be seizing every opportunity to abandon their distinctive
way of life on the margins of society. "The real horror worked on the
Jews and Negroes since the Second War is the mass-communication of
nothingness into their personality," Mailer opined. "They were two of

the greatest peoples in America, and half of their populations sold themselves to the suburb, the center, the secure." The journalist Seymour Krim had voiced similar sentiments in an article of 1959 in which he expressed a premature nostalgia for Harlem as a distinctively black neighborhood:

> If you look at Harlem without any attempt at morality at all, from a strictly physical and blindly sensuous point of view, it is the richest kind of life one can ever see in American action as far as the fundamental staples of love, hate, joy, sorrow, street-poetry, dance and death go. . . . And within a decade (some say two) it will probably end as Negroes become increasingly integrated and sinewed into the society around them. I will truly hate to see Harlem go—where will I seek then in my time of need, O merciless life?—and yet I would obviously help light the match that blows it out of existence.

Interviewed by the *New York Post,* Clark condemned Mailer and Krim's "romantic nonsense." He vigorously denied that black people with the means to leave Harlem should remain there. "I'll be damned," Clark said, "if anyone is going to tell me that because the Negro is oppressed I must live in Harlem too." He rejected equally the suggestion that something of value would be lost if segregated black communities passed into history. "What other culture is there in America?" he asked. "I am an American. You might as well tell me that President Kennedy should have a direct connection with Irish culture. There is nothing inherently *Negro* about a Negro. There is nothing in my genes that demands that I should have a particular set of goals and attitudes."[70]

Interestingly, however, during a private conversation in 1970 Clark was moved to qualify this denial of a distinctive black culture, a denial seemingly connected to his militant brand of integrationism. A few weeks earlier, he had visited Columbia, Maryland, a planned community that had opened in 1967. Recounting his visit to a colleague, the researcher Phyllis Wallace, Clark stated that he had felt "revulsion" toward the town. Columbia was trumpeted by its developers as a planned alternative to urban decay and as a model of racial inclusivity. Yet Clark had found the town "too antiseptic, too bland, too unreal."

Its "perfectly watered, plastic" environment seemed inhospitable, because "a real community needs activity, needs ferment, needs something other than perfection." In recent days, Clark continued, he had begun to ask himself whether "some other factors" might have contributed to his acute distaste for Columbia, "including factors of my own background, of someone whose formative years were spent in Harlem—a Harlem, it is true, not quite the same as contemporary Harlem, but clearly a Harlem of ferment." Few aspects of life when he was a child had been "planned" as they were in Columbia:

> I had to make adjustments and accommodations to real people who weren't placed in a well-planned day care center, or who didn't have to play in a well thought through recreation group, but who had to make their own adjustments as to how they were going to enjoy themselves when they weren't in school, and etc. Who had to find out who was going to get the potatoes off the vegetable stand to roast in the open lot, etc. Now, I admit that this is a kind of Paul Goodman-ish nostalgic praising of the past. . . . And it's interesting that I mentioned Paul Goodman because Paul Goodman, too, came out of a minority culture—the Jewish culture of his growing up years. . . . Phyllis, it would take a peculiar and special kind of upper-middle class black to say that he is happy here at Columbia. . . . I think he would have a hell of a lot more difficult time being happy there than a white of similar education. Now I didn't think I'd ever say this, but I *understand* now more clearly what the young people [mean] when they tell me something about *soul*. *Soul* is a kind of chaos which those of us who've been required to cope with it have not only coped with, but it has become an integral part of what we consider life [to be]. . . . And I don't know of any black, no matter where he *is,* including Andrew Brimmer [a governor of the Federal Reserve], who doesn't have some residue of soul which a community has to be somehow compatible with.

Clark went so far as to say that he "couldn't conceive of blacks not turning up their stereos and having their parties" and thereby disturbing the town's "well-planned" tranquillity. He made a clear distinction between Columbia and his own integrated suburban community of Hastings-on-Hudson, where he felt *"comfortable . . . because it seems to me to be real."* Nevertheless, as Clark seemed only too aware, his remarks about "soul," his "nostalgic" reminiscences about the Harlem of his youth, and even his mention of the role of music and revelry in black life amounted to a wholly uncharacteristic departure from the public persona through which, eight years earlier, he had posed the rhetorical question, "What other culture is there in America?"[71]

To Challenge the Powers That Be

Though Clark hoped to redress the "alienation" of white liberals from the black urban poor, he was not so idealistic as to believe that an appeal to white morality would in itself be sufficient to combat the urban crisis. As he observed in *Dark Ghetto,* "social change that appears on the surface to benefit a minority—as in the case of civil rights—rarely engages the commitment of the majority." Where "moral force" stood in opposition to perceived political and economic self-interest, Clark contended, "moral force may be postponed." But "where moral force and practical advantage are united, their momentum is hard to deny." For this reason, he sought to demonstrate "that the continued oppression of the Negro minority hurts the white majority too." Seeking to tap the self-interest as much as the sympathy of the wider society, Clark pointed to the "artificial reduction of the gross national product" that resulted from the underemployment and underconsumption of one-tenth of the U.S. population, a consideration he believed "may turn out to be the pivot of change." Yet he also harnessed his pathologist imagery to an appeal to white self-interest by suggesting that if left unchecked, the pent-up frustrations of the dark ghettos could erupt on a scale that would destroy America. To "those who now consider themselves privileged and immune to the ghetto's flagrant pathologies," Clark warned that the "social sickness" could not be contained within the ghetto's walls, and would prove "fatal" to the whole society if not treated. He chose as an epigraph to *Dark Ghetto* John Donne's famous meditation, "Perchance hee for whom this Bell tolls, may be so ill, as that he knowes not it tolls for him."[72]

Clark's use of damage imagery was not, then, predicated on a view of the white American public or the federal government as paragons of selfless compassion. Nor did it reflect a belief on Clark's part that the black urban poor were "derelicts" who could only be passive recipients of external largesse. Only government, Clark was certain, could provide financial resources on a scale necessary to transform conditions in black urban communities. Yet his design for HARYOU identified the people of Harlem themselves as the real agents of such a transformation. The "reservoir of energy" that had animated the southern civil rights protests also existed, Clark maintained, within the ghettos of America's northern cities, "ready to be stirred by hope." Indeed, mobilizing this latent source of power was the essence of the HARYOU proposal. To understand how Clark's view of the psychological damage wrought by racism coexisted with his notion that Harlem's residents could be agents of effective social change, it is necessary to consider how Clark's ideas of damage and of therapeutic techniques had emerged. For while damage imagery was a conventional tool of the postwar liberal social sciences, Clark's particular conception of mental health was decidedly unconventional.[73]

In recent years, historians revisiting the role of social science testimony in *Brown v. Board of Education* have subjected Clark's use of damage imagery to extensive critique. Beyond their concerns about the ethical and political hazards of representing black people as psychologically damaged, scholars have raised objections to Clark's experimental methodology and have even questioned his commitment to objective interpretation of his data. While a detailed exposition of Clark's early research and the charges against it would diverge from the aims of this study, some attention to his earliest employment of damage imagery provides a revealing perspective on his later claims about the psychopathologies of African American communities in the context of the urban crisis.[74]

In February 1951, Clark had been invited to assist the NAACP's Legal Defense Fund (LDF) in its challenge to the constitutionality of segregated schooling. Aware that the previous year, at the White House Conference on Children and Youth, Clark had argued that segregation harmed the personalities of children, the LDF's Thurgood Marshall and his legal staff believed that Clark could help them to demonstrate the "intangible" ways in which segregation might disadvantage black children even if black schools were, hypothetically, to be equally resourced. Clark agreed to coordinate the expert testimony of social scientists, and his own White House Conference paper was cited by the Supreme Court in its ruling of May 17, 1954, which held that separating black children "from others of similar age and qualifications solely because of their race generates a feeling of inferiority as to their status in the community that may affect their hearts and minds in a way unlikely ever to be undone."[75]

Clark's testimony that segregated schooling engendered a negative self-image in black children was grounded in his interpretation of data that he and his wife had produced in the early 1940s with support from the Julius Rosenwald Foundation. Applying "projective testing" methods pioneered by the psychologist Ruth Horowitz and further developed by Mamie Clark in her graduate research, the Clarks studied a sample of 253 black children between the ages of three and seven. Of these children, 134 were from segregated schools and preschools in Mamie's home state of Arkansas, while 119 came from integrated schools and preschools in Springfield, Massachusetts. In an article published in 1947, the Clarks reported that when confronted with a choice of either white or brown dolls, "approximately two thirds" of the subjects indicated a preference for the white doll, and 59 percent nominated the brown doll as the doll that "looks bad." The Clarks expressed concern about the implications of their findings for what they called, in the prevalent language of the day, "racial mental hygiene." Furthermore, while they reported that northern and southern children were "similar in the degree of their preference for the white doll," they noted a greater tendency for northern children to evaluate the brown doll negatively. The article concludes with their "qualitative" observation that when children who had rejected the brown doll were then prompted to identify the doll that "looks like you," the northern children more frequently broke down in tears or became "negativistic."[76]

A number of historians have suggested that the findings reported by the Clarks in 1947 stand in direct contradiction of the "Social Science

Statement" submitted to the Supreme Court only a few years later, which was compiled by Kenneth Clark and bore the signatures of thirty-four other eminent psychologists. In their testimony to the Court, the social scientists professed the opinion that segregated schooling was harmful to the self-esteem of black schoolchildren. But had the results of the Clarks' doll test not in fact indicated that it was black children attending *integrated* schools who exhibited a more profound self-rejection than their segregated counterparts? Such a conclusion would have been consistent with the influential "marginal man" thesis associated with the sociologists of the Chicago School. Robert Park had argued in 1928 that it was the individual who left the secure confines of the minority community and experienced closer contact with the majority population who was most susceptible to "spiritual instability, intensified self-consciousness, restlessness, and *malaise.*"[77]

Clark never offered a clear explanation of the northern children's more negative responses to the brown doll. However, in a letter of 1952 and again in his book *Prejudice and Your Child,* he did set out an unorthodox interpretation of the "qualitative data" concerning the emotional responses of the northern and southern children to which he and his wife had referred in their article of 1947. Indeed, it was substantially on the basis of this interpretation that Clark justified his contention that "children in racially segregated schools are more seriously damaged in the area of self-esteem than are children in a racially mixed school."[78]

Referring back to the doll test in *Prejudice and Your Child,* Clark recounted the ways in which some of the children who had rejected the brown doll reacted when subsequently asked to select the doll that "looks like you." One girl who had already described the brown doll as "ugly" and "dirty" broke into tears at this point. Other children displayed "terror or hostility" and had to be "coaxed" to complete the test. Clark then revealed:

> The only children who reacted with such open demonstrations of intense emotions were northern children. The southern children when confronted with this personal dilemma were much more

matter-of-fact in their ability to identify themselves with the brown doll which they had previously rejected. Some of them were able to laugh or giggle self-consciously as they did so. Others merely flatly stated: "This one. It's a nigger. I'm a nigger."

Clark then explained why he considered the ostensibly more rational responses of the southern children to be, in fact, evidence of the most harmful psychological effects of segregation:

> On the surface, these findings might suggest that northern Negro children suffer more personality damage from racial prejudice and discrimination than southern Negro children. However, this interpretation would seem to be not only superficial but incorrect. The apparent emotional stability of the southern Negro child may be indicative only of the fact that through rigid racial segregation and isolation he has accepted as normal the fact of his inferior social status. Such an acceptance is not symptomatic of a healthy personality. The emotional turmoil revealed by some of the northern children may be interpreted as an attempt on their part to assert some positive aspect of the self.

As he had put it in 1952, the southern children's "apparent adjustment" was really "an adjustment to a social pathology," namely racism. As such, it could not be considered "healthy."[79]

It is difficult to disagree with the objection raised by William Cross Jr. that Clark made sweeping generalizations on the basis of a limited set of "anecdotal data." Daryl Michael Scott goes further, however, in arguing that "Clark's reasoning was tortured" and that he resorted to "intellectual legerdemain" to "fit the findings to the cause of integration." Whether Clark's interpretation of the data was influenced by the exigencies of the campaign against school segregation is impossible to determine. However, to dismiss his reasoning as "tortured" and illogical is to continue to obscure a vital and enduring element of Clark's thought. In treating "emotional turmoil" and "assertion" as preferable to "adjustment to a social pathology," Clark had articulated a radical conception of mental health that would remain crucial to his approach to psychology during the 1960s and would profoundly affect his response to the urban crisis.[80]

The concept of "adjustment" occupied a prominent position within the postwar American social sciences. The prevailing "functionalist" paradigm in sociology held that a society's cohesion and stability depended on the "adjustment" of individuals to their position within a necessarily stratified social order. The Ford Foundation's influential behavioral sciences program, launched in 1951, placed the problem of "individual adjustment" at the heart of its research agenda. This was emblematic, Alice O'Connor observes, of liberal social scientists' "embrace of an individualized, psychologically oriented behavioral science" that located the obstacles to social stability and prosperity primarily in the maladjustments of individuals rather than in the shortcomings of the existing social structure or economic system. The demand for individual adjustment "grew out of and in turn reinforced the postwar 'consensus' that major social problems could be resolved without recourse to political mobilization or conflict and without significant institutional or economic reform."[81]

This was not a consensus to which Clark subscribed. At a symposium in March 1962, at around the time when he was beginning work on the HARYOU design, Clark argued the need for a "dynamic definition of mental health." This "might require in the first instance that it be differentiated as clearly as possible from mere 'adjustment' or accommodation to existing social norms." To meet this definition of mental health, an individual would need "to live creatively rather than merely passively" and to demonstrate the "strength of personality required to evaluate and select from his society those forces to which he will respond affirmatively, those which he would seek to modify, and those which he would reject as being inconsistent with his individuality and inimical to his concept of the fundamental values of humanity." There was, Clark believed, a widespread and "misleading tendency to equate mental health with the mere absence of disease," or with "the concepts of norm and adjustment." On the contrary, he claimed, "mental health requires the constructive use of inner turbulence."[82]

Here, Clark's ideas overlapped in a number of respects with those of "Gestalt" and other forms of "humanistic" psychology. The emphasis on personal "growth" and "excitement" in the work of Frederick Perls, Ralph Hefferline, and Paul Goodman found echoes in Clark's emphasis on "the need to live creatively." The Brandeis University psychologist Abraham Maslow, with his concept of "self-actualization," also contributed to a "positive psychology" of human growth that defined mental health as something other than "adjustment" or the absence of disease. Indeed, as the historian Ellen Herman points out, Maslow's objections to the psychology of "adjustment" would be an "inspiration" to young American radicals and social activists during the 1960s, including Maslow's former student Abbie Hoffman, a cofounder of the Youth International Party (the "Yippies"). Maslow's most celebrated critique of the therapeutics of "adjustment" appeared in *Toward a Psychology of Being* (1962). "Adjusted to what?" he asked. "To a bad culture? To a dominating parent? What shall we think of a well-adjusted slave? A well-adjusted prisoner?" It was "quite clear" to Maslow that "personality problems may sometimes be loud protests against the crushing of one's psychological bones, of one's true inner nature. What is sick then is *not* to protest while this crime is being committed."[83]

While Maslow remained aloof from the social movements of the 1960s, Clark's own rejection of "adjustment" lay at the heart of an explicitly political, activist conception of the therapeutic, one that would underlie his vision for HARYOU. In a speech delivered in Boston in 1968, Clark reflected on his and Mamie's experiences at the Northside Center since the 1940s:

> It became clear to us that we could not, given the negative realities inherent in the ghettoes of America, believe that we were really helping if we ignored these realities and attempted to get the individual children and their parents to adjust to the fact that the schools of America's ghettoes are so criminally inferior as to be dehumanizing, that the filth and degradation which this affluent society permits makes it impossible for human beings to be creative, to be constructive, that the housing to which the masses of these children and their parents were sentenced by a society which had the economic resources but seemed not to have the moral resources or

commitment to change, that we at Northside would be accessories
to the social immorality if we asked our children and their parents
to adjust to these pathologies, particularly when it was clear to us
that these were remediable.

Clark went on to outline the alternative therapeutic approach that had
emerged at Northside, and which would animate his HARYOU plan,
and "what this required in terms of the desired health of the individual":

Within the walls of the clinic, we had to try to develop in parents
and the children we saw, the personal strength, not to adjust to remediable pathology, but the personal strength to attempt to change
that pathology. Our standards of effectiveness then would have to
be the number of parents and children who joined the community
action geared to rational and effective social action and social change.

For Clark, then, the attainment of psychological health on the part of
the oppressed necessitated a refusal to adjust to the circumstances of oppression. In fact, it necessitated a commitment to resist, even to rebel.
Such rebellion might not always assume constructive forms, but even
misdirected aggression was a greater indication of psychological health
than complete submission.[84]

In *Dark Ghetto,* Clark applied this rationale in his discussion of juvenile delinquency in Harlem, boldly inviting his readers not merely to
empathize with delinquents—and, indeed, rioters—but to view their
actions as preferable to passivity. "In a curious way," he wrote, "the
delinquent's behavior is healthy; for, at the least, it asserts that he still
has sufficient strength to rebel and has not yet given in to defeat." High
rates of delinquency "show that a group is in ferment, in the process of
rejecting an inferior status and moving to a higher level." This view
was entirely consistent with Clark's commentary on the doll test more
than a decade earlier. Those southern children who, having offered a
negative judgment of a brown doll, smilingly identified it as the "doll
that looks like you," or answered, "It's a nigger, I'm a nigger," were so
profoundly damaged by racism as to have accepted the notion of their
own inferiority. The confused and dejected responses of the northern
children at least indicated that their internalization of their subordinate

status was not yet total. What has been dismissed as Clark's "tortured" reasoning remained integral to his approach to psychology during the 1960s. Moreover, while Clark regarded psychological damage as pervasive within black urban communities, he evidently did not believe that all members of these communities were damaged to a debilitating extent. Just as he had described the "emotional turmoil" of northern schoolchildren as evidence of ego resilience during the 1950s, so in *Dark Ghetto* he identified grounds for hope in unexpected places.[85]

Contrary to the historian Ben Keppel's analysis, Clark did not interpret the Harlem riot of July 1964 as the result of "pervasive resignation to the social forces that created and maintained the ghetto." Nor did *Dark Ghetto* attribute the rioting to those "bent on irrational destruction," as Keppel claims. For Clark, in fact, the reverse was true:

> The summer of 1964 brought violent protests to the ghettos of America's cities, not in mobilization of effective power, but as an outpouring of unplanned revolt. The revolts in Harlem were *not* led by a mob, for a mob is an uncontrolled social force bent on irrational destruction. The revolts in Harlem were, rather, a weird social defiance. Those involved in them were, in general, not the lowest class of Harlem residents—not primarily looters and semicriminals— but marginal Negroes who were upwardly mobile, demanding a higher status than their families had.

While rioting did not, for Clark, constitute a "mobilization of effective power," it nonetheless demonstrated that many of Harlem's residents had *not* reached the point of resignation or adjustment to their environment and subordinate status. Moreover, by presenting rioters as "upwardly mobile," Clark even encouraged his readers to identify with what he implied was their bid for inclusion in the American Dream.[86]

Back in 1945, Clark had argued that "antisocial" and "exhibitionistic" behavior on the part of the oppressed was the result of their "humiliation" by and exclusion from the wider society. In their analysis of an interview with a self-declared participant in the Harlem riot of 1943, Clark and James Barker, his colleague at City College, had concluded that "the socially accepted dehumanization of an individual or group must inevitably manifest itself in social disturbances." In June 1964, Clark went further, and seemed positively to welcome the prospect of rioting as evidence of ego resilience and the survival of some hope of social change on the part of ghetto dwellers. During a round-table discussion organized by the *New York Herald Tribune,* only weeks before the outbreak of the Harlem riot, Clark was asked whether he expected an "acting out" by black youth in New York during the summer. In remarks that were omitted from the "condensed" version of the discussion published in the newspaper, Clark replied: "We're going to have it, of course. If we don't have it, we're lost. Lost in the sense that something worse has happened, namely total stagnation."[87]

In *Dark Ghetto,* Clark drew similarly positive conclusions from the "violent protests" and "revolts" that had indeed broken out in Harlem. The "ferment" exhibited with "spasmodic ferocity" in northern cities indicated to Clark "that the past cycle, in which personal and community powerlessness reinforces [*sic*] each other, is being supplanted by a more forceful pattern of personal and community action." The outbursts were "proof," indeed, that the inhabitants of America's dark ghettos had not succumbed to resignation or acceptance of their predicament. The "reservoir of energy was there, ready to be stirred by hope, for effective or even sporadic protest could never have emerged out of total stagnation." Far from viewing Harlem's rioters as "bent on irrational destruction," Clark detected in their actions a number of essentially rational motives:

> Even those Negroes who threw bottles and bricks from the roofs were not in the grip of a wild abandon, but seemed deliberately to be prodding the police to behave openly as the barbarians that the Negroes felt they actually were. . . . [There was] a calm within the chaos, a deliberateness within the hysteria. The Negro seemed to feel nothing could happen to him that had not happened already; he behaved as if he had nothing to lose. His was an oddly controlled rage that seemed to say, during those days of social despair, "We have had enough. The only weapon you have is bullets. The only thing you can do is kill us." Paradoxically, his apparent lawlessness was a protest against the lawlessness directed against *him.* His acts were a desperate assertion of his desire to be treated as a man. He

was affirmative up to the point of inviting death; he insisted upon being visible and understood. If this was the only way to relate to society at large, he would rather die than be misunderstood.

The Watts riot of August 1965 would elicit a more pessimistic response from Clark. In Harlem, he had noted in *Dark Ghetto,* "most of the stores broken into and looted belonged to white men" who were perceived by residents as exploiters of the ghetto community. In an article written for the *New York Times Magazine,* however, Clark was evidently disturbed that "it was the Negro ghetto in Los Angeles which Negroes looted and burned, not the white community," and that black "snipers" had barred firemen from containing the blazes. He now wondered "whether a desire for self-destruction was not a subconscious factor," and characterized the rioting as a product of "unreason" and "despair."[88]

Nevertheless, in *Dark Ghetto* Clark had offered the Harlem riots as evidence of resilience and aspiration on the part of urban African Americans. "Unrest *is* a characteristic of civilization," he wrote, "and to fight against oppression—even unwisely—is a sign that men have begun to hope." Clark also warned white "'friends' of the Negro" that they must not "admonish the Negro not to engage in disruptive and lawless demonstrations lest he incite racism and reverse the progress made in his behalf." The concept of a "white backlash," he submitted, was a convenient displacement of responsibility onto the oppressed. It was "a new name for an old phenomenon, white resistance to the acceptance of the Negro as a human being." Those who placed a requirement on African Americans to prove themselves "worthy" of full equality through exemplary displays of virtue and forbearance only underlined their own lack of understanding and empathy. This in turn was evidence that the ghetto's "invisible wall is opaque from outside in."[89]

By the time that the National Advisory Commission on Civil Disorders (the "Kerner Commission") was holding its inquiry in the aftermath of the Newark and Detroit riots of 1967, a number of psychologists and other social scientists were expressing similar views to Clark's. Ellen Herman has noted that "interpreting rioting in quasi-sympathetic terms—as a bid to recoup emotional or political self-esteem—was new in the late 1960s." Indeed, many experts, including some of the Kerner

Commission's consultants and witnesses, continued to regard the riots as manifestations of the irrational tendencies of "crowds," or as the aggregate behavior of "social misfits" or those afflicted with a "brain disease." Clark, however, testified to the commission on September 13, 1967, that the rioters were "grasping an opportunity to defy a system and a society which has sentenced them to human degradation." Two months later, Elliot Liebow, the author of a sympathetic but firmly pathologist anthropological study of black "streetcorner men" in Washington, D.C., advised the commission that rioting constituted a form of self-assertion motivated by a desire to refute the notion of black passivity. The commission also received written testimony from Matthew Dumont of the National Institute of Mental Health, who suggested: "One may have to conclude that the rioter is a more mentally healthy person than the non-rioter. He is a person who believes that action means something, that things can improve." Such views strongly echoed Clark's contention in *Dark Ghetto* that the "healthy" residents of Harlem were those who had the "strength to rebel."[90]

For all its emphasis on psychological damage, *Dark Ghetto* discerned "a surprising human resilience" within black urban communities subjected to exclusion and confinement. Such resilience was, indeed, axiomatic to Clark's design for HARYOU. As he explained at a conference on "urban affairs" in 1964, "the HARYOU programs have at their core the attempt to mobilize the potential power of the people themselves for social action. The HARYOU program seeks to exploit and harness the positives and momentums of the civil rights movement." *Youth in the Ghetto,* HARYOU's planning document, noted the "crucial" role of black youth in "precipitating the present direct action approach" of the southern sit-ins and freedom rides, and stated that among HARYOU's objectives was to "prepare" Harlem's youth "to play a more effective role in the present social revolution."[91]

As these words suggest, Clark tended to downplay the extent of existing civil rights mobilization in Harlem. Neither *Youth in the Ghetto* nor *Dark Ghetto* devoted much attention to the ongoing campaigns of grassroots activists in local chapters of CORE or other neighborhood organizations. *Youth in the Ghetto* made only brief reference to the highly effective rent strikes of 1963 and 1964 waged by Harlem's tenants' rights movement, led by the charismatic organizer Jesse Gray. *Dark Ghetto* made no mention of the strikes at all. Clark's aim of securing massive government investment in the social infrastructure of Harlem and other black urban neighborhoods perhaps encouraged him to present a stark picture in which rioting was the only present outlet for the energies and frustrations of northern black communities. Yet at no point did he seek to win government favor by presenting HARYOU as a program of pacification. Nor did he envisage HARYOU as an exercise in riot prevention, one that would simply keep Harlem's youth occupied and divert their attention from the injustices of black urban life. To the contrary, *Youth in the Ghetto* insisted that there was "harnessable power to effect profound social change in the rage of the disesteemed," and that "HARYOU must give it new and more constructive expression."[92]

The HARYOU design included a series of proposals for the expansion and improvement of Harlem's social and educational services: preschool academies (a concept that would influence the Johnson administration's Head Start program); remedial education centers; a "reading mobilization year" across Harlem's schools to tackle illiteracy; youth academies to reintegrate juvenile offenders into the community; an Institute for Narcotics Research offering experimental methods of rehabilitation to addicts; and an array of job-training and work placement schemes. To Ben Keppel, such programs signify that "what HARYOU envisioned as its goal was not far outside the mainstream of American reform (except perhaps its estimated cost of $110 million to be spent in Harlem alone)." Yet Clark stated explicitly that such services and programs were, in themselves, of secondary importance to another goal that was more remote from mainstream traditions of social reform, namely "community action" on the part of Harlem's residents themselves. As *Youth in the Ghetto* put it, "these programs are subsidiary and ancillary to the basic concern with the stimulation of the type of initiative essential for social action." In 1963, Clark had written in a press release:

> HARYOU is *not* wedded to the "saturation of services" approach as
> a solution to the problems of youth in Harlem. Rather HARYOU,
> backed by facts and relevant social action programs, is seeking to

determine whether it is possible to discourage dependency and increase initiative through the systematic identification, stimulation
and use of the power and resources of the community.

Clark did not suggest that social services intrinsically fostered dependency in individuals. Rather, he believed that the treatment of Harlem's
residents as passive recipients of services designed and implemented
without their involvement was a function of the "colonial" powers
wielded by existing social service agencies, which consigned the community as a whole to a state of "powerlessness and dependency."[93]

"Community action" had become a fashionable term in liberal policy circles during the early 1960s. It emerged from a number of initiatives targeting urban poverty and juvenile delinquency, including the
Ford Foundation's "Grey Areas" program addressing urban decline;
the Mobilization for Youth project on Manhattan's Lower East Side,
whose originators included Richard Cloward; and Clark's design for
HARYOU. From the outset, the phrase "community action" was employed rather loosely to denote a variety of attempts to involve poor
people themselves in antipoverty initiatives, and the term's slipperiness
would ultimately cause serious political embarrassment to the Johnson
administration after community action was enlisted into the federal
War on Poverty. As Alice O'Connor observes, over the course of the
1960s the "community action" label would be applied to "a range of
sometimes conflicting reform visions, alternating between resident uplift to promote assimilation and community empowerment to agitate
for change." Clark's vision for HARYOU was very much one of empowerment and agitation, rather than moral exhortations to self-help.[94]

In one sense, the HARYOU proposal constituted a technocratic intervention in the Harlem community by social scientists, policy elites,
and government resources. Paradoxically, however, the purpose of this
intervention was to establish an infrastructure that would catalyze
democratic participation and galvanize the collective power of the
Harlem community. *Youth in the Ghetto* defined community action as a
"process of grass roots critical involvement with neighborhood level
programs." Without this grassroots involvement, programs would
succumb to "bureaucratic dry rot" and "organizational irrelevance."

Arguing that the problems confronting Harlem's youth were insepara-
ble from the conditions of deprivation endured by the community at
large, Clark perceived a need for both youth and adults to engage in
concerted action aimed at alleviating the oppressive conditions of
which juvenile delinquency was only a "symptom." Local residents
would play an active role in the design and implementation of programs and services to be funded through HARYOU. More important,
from Clark's perspective, they would use the infrastructure and resources provided by HARYOU to agitate more widely for social
change and greater economic opportunity. The key components of this
infrastructure were to be five "neighborhood boards," composed of
youth and adults, which would each represent a distinct locality within
Harlem; a separate, Harlem-wide youth organization, Harlem Youth
Unlimited (HYU); and a Community Action Institute, which would
"train indigenous leaders" (including the members of the neighborhood boards and HYU) and other interested residents in "techniques
for intelligent and planned social action." The success of HARYOU
would depend on "the mobilization of a large group of citizens, both
youth and adults, who are disciplined, political savants."[95]

Youth in the Ghetto did not explicitly specify elections as the means of
determining membership of the neighborhood boards. It was deemed
"essential," however, that each board should represent a "cross-section"
of its neighborhood's "occupations and educational and age levels" and
that particular care should be taken to include "working-class individuals and youth." It was evident, moreover, that Clark regarded
community action not as a politically inert vehicle for self-help, but
rather as a process that would, as he wrote in an article of 1963 published in the radical black journal *Freedomways,* involve the "risk inherent
in conflict with vested interests and those forces which have accommo-
dated to the status quo." Neighborhood boards, according to *Youth in
the Ghetto,* must have "the guts to challenge the powers that be whenever said powers are seen as shortchanging the children and families of
the community."[96]

HYU was to play "a major role in insuring that the local Boards do
not begin to 'play it safe,'" since "young people have less to lose by a

radical stance and have fewer vested interests in the system than do most adults." Indeed, Clark was encouraged by the involvement of some 200 local youths in HARYOU's research and planning phases. These "HARYOU Associates" had not only conducted surveys but had been "involved in the initial action stages of the rent strikes, which began to spread through Harlem in early 1964," and had also joined voter registration drives. *Youth in the Ghetto* expressed hope that HYU, as HARYOU's "youth movement," would "be motivated by the same community action orientation" shown by these associates. The neighborhood boards, too, would lead "drives and campaigns calculated to sensitize local residents to issues of community concern, e.g. health problems, school problems, housing, police protection, and political activity." As will be seen, such challenges to "the powers that be," emanating from the more radical among the community action organizations, would soon plunge the Johnson administration's War on Poverty into political turmoil.[97]

Beyond community action, Clark tied his HARYOU design to another rising trend when he called the program "an experiment in community psychiatry." A reflection of the enhanced status and self-confidence that America's psychological professions enjoyed by the early 1960s, the idea underpinning community psychiatry was that entire communities, not just disturbed individuals, were fitting objects of therapeutic intervention. Buoyed by President Johnson's vision of a "Great Society," advocates of community psychiatry such as Robert Reiff and Matthew Dumont looked to an expanded welfare state to promote the mental health of all citizens by transforming social environments that damaged mental health and by involving entire communities in therapeutic initiatives. What imparted a radical edge to Clark's variation on this theme was his highly politicized conception of the therapeutic. An improvement in the psychological health of the Harlem community, he wrote in 1963, would depend not only on "bringing about desirable social change," but on stimulating residents' own capacities to bring such change into being through "social action." The "HARYOU therapy," he wrote, "assumes that as the individual sees the possibility of being a part of meaningful social action, he not only develops a more positive self-image, supported by the reality of his social action, but he also contributes to the movement of the society toward greater stability and justice."[98]

Clark's rejection of the therapeutics of adjustment and his insistence on the therapeutic necessity of rebellion against injustice intersected with the views of many young radicals during the 1960s. So, too, did his concern with stimulating grassroots activism and overcoming the "powerlessness" of the oppressed. The "Port Huron Statement" issued in 1962 by the New Left group Students for a Democratic Society (SDS) sounded a number of themes that would reverberate in *Youth in the Ghetto* and *Dark Ghetto*. Among these were the statement's contentions—illustrative of the saturation of postwar American political discourse with therapeutic language—that "apathy" and a sense of "powerlessness" were major obstacles to social change and that ordinary people possessed an "unrealized potential for self-cultivation, self-direction, self-understanding, and creativity." The statement's famous advocacy of "participatory democracy," in part as a "means of finding meaning in personal life," overlapped substantially with Clark's emerging notions of community action and community psychiatry, wherein the individual "develops a more positive self-image" through "meaningful social action." Despite being at one level a technocratic intervention, Clark's blueprint for HARYOU, in proposing an infrastructure that would involve Harlem's residents in the design and administration of services and would facilitate organized protest against "the powers that be," embodied the "two central aims" of participatory democracy as envisioned by the authors of the "Port Huron Statement." These were "that the individual share in those social decisions determining the quality and direction of his life" and "that society be organized to encourage independence in men and provide the media for their common participation."[99]

This emphasis on grassroots mobilization and participation formed part of a wider reaction within the social movements of the 1960s against the enervated political culture of postwar America. As Richard King has demonstrated, many theorists and activists within the civil rights movement contested the narrow conception of politics that had come to typify American liberalism. Reaching beyond the pluralist notion of politics as the "pursuit of rights and assertion of interests," King argues, figures such as Robert Moses of the Student Nonviolent Coordinating Committee (SNCC) viewed political action as "a way of creating a new sense of self and community" and a "feeling of empowerment." They helped to reinfuse American politics with a broadly republican vision "in which political debate and action were assumed to be central to community- and self-determination." For Moses, the role of SNCC activists was to train indigenous organizers in southern black communities to catalyze grassroots political action. Translated to a northern, urban context, it was a role markedly similar to that which Clark envisaged for HARYOU.[100]

Civil rights and New Left activists derived their notions of community empowerment and participation in part from two veteran independent radicals whose own ideas of political action had been forged in opposition to the authoritarianism of the 1930s sectarian left. They were the author Paul Goodman, whose communitarian anarchism reached the younger generation through his book *Growing Up Absurd* (1960), and the Chicago-based community organizer Saul Alinsky. Clark's model of community mobilization in Harlem also bore significant similarities to the neighborhood project begun by Alinsky on Chicago's South Side in 1960, The Woodlawn Organization. As the admiring journalist Charles Silberman observed in 1964, Alinsky believed that an external stimulus, provided by sympathetic community organizers, could release untapped energies within marginalized, impoverished, apathetic urban communities. For democracy to survive, Alinsky had written, the "ordinary citizen" must be empowered "to influence the political, social and economic structures surrounding him," rather than accept a passive, dependent relationship to government and social service agencies. Describing himself as an "agitator" whose goal was to bring the community "to the point of conflict," Alinsky anticipated key elements of the HARYOU proposal, most notably the cultivation of an indigenous leadership capable of mobilizing the wider community "to challenge the powers that be."[101]

If Clark's blueprint for HARYOU exhibits a kinship with radical ideas of political action circulating within the New Left and the civil rights movement during the early 1960s, it also converges, perhaps unexpectedly, with some of the core concerns of the black power movement that coalesced later in the decade. This was not a convergence that Clark was eager to acknowledge. In *Dark Ghetto,* he caricatured black nationalists as extremists who were tragic products of a pathological environment, fanatics who abjured meaningful social activism and sought refuge in delusions of racial supremacy. In an article in the *New York Post* in 1967, Clark characterized black power as a "shoddy moral product" and denounced the "fanaticism, dogmatism, rigidity and self-destructive cruelty of black separatists." This was in stark contrast to the more sympathetic terms in which he would recall his mother's Garveyism in 1976, when he claimed that black nationalism had been, for her, "primarily a psychological boost, a basis for pride and assertion, on the part of blacks, that they did not have to accept inferior status."[102]

Clark's intense animosity toward the black power movement can best be understood as a product of his own involvement in the campaign against legalized segregation. In his article in the *New York Post,* he likened black power to Booker T. Washington's "accommodation" to white supremacy, and called it "an attempt to make a verbal virtue of involuntary racial segregation." Clark's scholarship and activism had consistently been motivated by a passionate belief in the moral and intellectual bankruptcy of notions of racial difference and a powerful commitment to integration. *Prejudice and Your Child* had been devoted in large part to exposing the fictions involved in ideas of racial difference and the harmful impact of these ideas on children as they learned discriminatory attitudes and behaviors. Having lent his energies to the legal campaign against segregation, for Clark the Nation of Islam's characterization of whites as "devils," the growing idealization of "blackness" within African American communities, and the antiwhite rhetoric of prominent black power figures such as LeRoi Jones were all painful to behold. Black power, he believed, was "a bitter retreat from the possibility of the attainment of the goals of any serious racial integration in America."[103]

Yet as much as Clark's commitment to the ideal of integration and his aversion to racial dogma led him to denounce black power, his own trajectory during the 1960s also involved something of a "retreat" from the demand for immediate integration. In a speech delivered in 1968, Clark was moved to "confess" that he and Mamie had themselves "de-emphasized our concern for desegregation." At the Northside Center, he explained, they had "postponed the pursuit of the goals for the deseg-regation of the schools and put in its place concern with building the strength, the ego strengths of our families, parents and children, so that they could grapple, hopefully successfully, with the injustices which surrounded them." In *Prejudice and Your Child,* Clark had criticized gradualist approaches to school desegregation and dismissed the notion of achieving excellence within "gilded educational ghettos" as inher-ently "undemocratic" and "incompatible with the goals of education." A decade later, however, in *Dark Ghetto,* Clark argued that "immediate integration" of public schools was an "impossibility." Given the "intran-sigence of the white community," white flight would continue for as long as areas with substantial black populations were associated with failing schools. This meant that the inferior quality of education in "ghetto schools" must be raised as the first step toward making integra-tion viable. "Inflexible" idealists, Clark wrote, would consider this a form of "camouflage for acquiescence in segregation." Nevertheless, achiev-ing "excellence in ghetto schools" would have to be the immediate priority.[104]

While Clark merely "postponed" the goal of integration, some black power theorists, including Jones/Baraka, rejected integration outright. Nevertheless, in seeking to transform the conditions of life within America's dark ghettos rather than working for immediate integration, Clark arrived at a vision of community mobilization that bore impor-tant similarities to the ideas and methods of black power activists. For Clark, no less than for the Black Panther Party in Oakland or Baraka's Committee for Unified Newark, the urgent task was to ensure that black urban communities acquired the "power" to exercise authority over their environment and to control services and resources—to "en-hance the ghetto community *as* a community," as Clark put it in *Dark Ghetto.* Notwithstanding his distaste for the rhetoric of racial separat-ism and cultural nationalism, Clark saw fit in 1969 to channel some

$10,000 toward Baraka's voter registration and education drive in Newark, which aimed to mobilize the city's black majority to ensure the election, for the first time, of a black mayor.[105]

Clark's own vision for HARYOU meshed substantially with the views of black power theorists for whom the most pressing need of African Americans in the urban North was not integration but empowerment and control over the resources and institutions that affected their lives. Indeed, the centrality of power and powerlessness in Clark's thinking highlights the significant convergence between his ideas and those of black power theorists. In *The Negro American* (1966), a volume of essays he coedited with the renowned sociologist Talcott Parsons, Clark expressed his belief that African Americans must accumulate and exercise power as a group. He did so, moreover, in terms that resonated with the critique of mainstream civil rights organizations voiced by the emerging black power movement. Martin Luther King, he argued, had been too willing to accept "minimal concessions" in Birmingham, Alabama, and "does not insist upon total change in the status of Negroes in a community but considers partial change temporarily satisfactory." The NAACP and National Urban League, he claimed, had "staked their strategies . . . perhaps in a pathetic sense, upon acceptance and identification with the articulated American concept of democracy. They took literally the ideology and promises of the system and shared unquestioningly American democratic optimism." Clark appeared to fault these organizations and to welcome the increasing focus on group empowerment when he wrote that "the Negro must now be aware that no fundamental change in his status can come through deference to or patronage from whites. . . . He is using the fuel of protest, formerly directed to demonstrations, to win inclusion in the power system itself." Clark cited as examples of this bid for power the political education and voter registration campaigns mounted by SNCC in 1964 and the formation of the Mississippi Freedom Democratic Party.[106]

Clark's characterization of America's "ghettos" as institutions designed to maintain black "powerlessness" in fact struck a chord with Stokely Carmichael and Charles Hamilton, the authors of one of the canonical texts of the black power movement. *Black Power: The Politics of Liberation in America* (1967) begins with an epigraph taken from *Dark*

Ghetto: "The dark ghettoes are social, political, educational and—above all—economic colonies. Their inhabitants are subject peoples, victims of the greed, cruelty, insensitivity, guilt, and fear of their masters." While Clark never offered a detailed or systematic explanation of his notion of the ghetto-as-colony, Carmichael and Hamilton quoted a further passage from *Dark Ghetto* that highlighted the extraction of profit from Harlem by white-owned businesses and the lack of reinvestment of that profit within the neighborhood. In appropriating a language of internal colonialism associated primarily with Communists and with black nationalists such as Malcolm X and Harold Cruse, Clark had issued a forceful institutional indictment of American society that impressed the authors of *Black Power.* Indeed, in his use of this language Clark implicitly framed his vision of social transformation in Harlem as a politics of decolonization.[107]

The points of convergence between Clark and proponents of black power extend beyond the concepts of community empowerment and internal colonialism. As will be seen in Chapter 2, Baraka and other leading theorists of black power frequently reiterated the pathologist claim that racism and social subordination inflicted psychological damage on African Americans. Contrary to scholarship that associates black power with an anti-pathologist impulse to "vindicate black culture and personality," the movement's efforts to promote a positive black self-image were often grounded in explicitly pathologist premises. Carmichael and Hamilton's *Black Power* in fact cited Clark as an authority on the "psychological effects" of black Americans' "degrading experiences," and incorporated a seventeen-line quotation from *Dark Ghetto* concerning black "self- and group-hatred." In 1972, the Republic of New Africa, a black power group formed in Detroit four years earlier, quoted *Dark Ghetto* repeatedly in a petition to the U.S. Congress demanding reparations to compensate African Americans for the "psychological disintegration" and social and economic disadvantages resulting from racism.[108]

Also overlooked have been similarities between Clark's thought and that of the Martinique-born psychiatrist and radical theorist of anticolonialism Frantz Fanon. The esteem in which Fanon was held within American black power circles has often been remarked by historians.

That Fanon's renowned advocacy of violence against the colonizer proceeded from an explicit diagnosis of the colonized as psychologically damaged has scarcely prompted any recognition of the pathologist elements within black power discourse. Indeed, Scott contends that "racial pride" led proponents of black power to "reject" Fanon's damage imagery even as they championed his "political analysis and goals." In fact, however, an Adlerian notion of a black "inferiority complex" was a common element in the thinking of Fanon, black power theorists such as Baraka, and Clark. Fanon's endorsement of a therapeutic violence against the colonizer—which, he wrote in *The Wretched of the Earth* (1963), "frees the native from his inferiority complex"—doubtless appealed to black power advocates far more than to Clark. Nevertheless, Fanon's belief that those who bore the psychological scars of oppression could themselves be incited to action against that oppression—and that such action would itself be therapeutic—had close parallels in Clark's vision of the "HARYOU therapy," in which "social action" on the part of the oppressed would result in "a more positive self-image." Clark, Fanon, and theorists of black power espoused strikingly similar pathologist understandings of the consequences of oppression, and substantially overlapping therapeutics of rebellion.[109]

As the Kennedy administration's initiatives on juvenile delinquency were absorbed into the planning for President Johnson's War on Poverty, Clark had reason to believe that his ideas about mobilizing the latent power of deprived communities were being taken seriously in Washington. He would later recall holding several conversations with Sargent Shriver, the head of Johnson's antipoverty staff, in which it was clear that Shriver and his team had read *Youth in the Ghetto* and looked on it favorably. "Community action" programs, to be "developed and conducted with maximum feasible participation of residents" of poor communities, featured in Title II of the Economic Opportunity Act, which Johnson signed on August 20, 1964. Clark would later exaggerate when he claimed in interviews that the HARYOU report had been the main inspiration for these legislative provisions. Still, alongside the Mobilization for Youth initiative on Manhattan's Lower East Side, HARYOU was one of a small number of government-aided programs that enjoyed enthusiastic support from a coterie of administration officials involved in drafting the antipoverty legislation, especially Richard Boone and David Hackett of the Office of Economic Opportunity (OEO).[110]

Yet if the legislation gave the impression that grassroots mobilization and community empowerment would have the full force of federal support, this quickly proved to be an illusion. City mayors and other municipal power brokers made clear their opposition to community action programs that involved decision making or agitation on the part of poor communities, and the "OEO radicals" who had drafted the "maximum feasible participation" clause, including Boone and Hackett, were soon marginalized. How the potentially disruptive implications of "maximum feasible participation" of the poor had escaped the attention of senior antipoverty bureaucrats, White House officials, and members of Congress has been a matter of disagreement. The historian James Patterson claims that most of the antipoverty officials who worked on the legislation "paid no attention" to the "maximum feasible participation" phrase, or assumed that it meant that black communities must be included among the beneficiaries of the antipoverty initiatives, or that existing social service agencies could be bypassed. Daniel Immerwahr, however, presents a compelling alternative explanation. Many of the officials responsible for drafting the legislation had previously been involved in designing policy for U.S. aid agencies, particularly the Peace Corps. In rural areas in India and other newly independent nations, U.S. agencies had pursued an antipoverty strategy known as "community development," which aimed to stimulate cohesion, cooperation, and active citizenship within village communities. In these locations, the authority of indigenous social elites had ensured that community development had assumed fairly conservative forms, rather than triggering agitation for radical measures such as land reform. These same policy officials used "community development" as the model for domestic "community action" programs, and failed to predict how the shift from rural settings in the developing world to American urban communities beset by racism and devoid of traditional rural structures of social hierarchy would alter the policy's outcome. The adoption of community action by the urban poor as a vehicle for radical mobilization against existing urban authorities thus took the policy's own authors by surprise. Moreover, as Thomas Jackson observes, once urban power holders made their opposition known, the War on Poverty quickly reverted to a "tradition of top-down hierarchical reform" that left "control of social policy in the hands of local elites" and continued "the exclusion of minorities and the poor from decisions affecting their lives."[111]

An early casualty of this process was Clark's vision for HARYOU. By the time HARYOU became operational in the summer of 1964, Clark's ties to the program he had initiated had been severed, and he was convinced that it had been irreversibly compromised. He would later rue the "adolescent optimism" and "romantic naivete" that had led him to believe that national and local political elites would support a program designed to place power in the hands of Harlem's residents and encourage them to confront existing authorities. Some observers had, indeed, spotted the implausibility inherent in government-sponsored community action programs at the time. In *Crisis in Black and White* (1964), Charles Silberman predicted that the antipoverty legislation's superficially radical commitment to "maximum feasible participation" would turn out to be hollow. "No government," he wrote, "no matter how liberal, is going to stimulate creation of a power organization that is sure to make its life uncomfortable."[112]

Clark had not, in fact, been unaware of what in 1963 he called "the risk of confrontation between those forces which seek change and those which resist it." Nonetheless, he had placed great faith in the liberal, reformist administrations of Kennedy and Johnson to ameliorate the "powerlessness" of the black urban poor. In his essay in *Freedomways,* he remarked:

> Already a fundamental question, first asked by one of the young people with whom HARYOU seeks to work and since by many sophisticated social analysts, is: "How can you seriously expect to impose the drastic therapy inherent in a design for social change when the sources of your support come from governmental agencies which are not ordinarily associated with significant movements

for change[?]" The only answer which can be given to this question is that the rationale, philosophy, and the total commitment that is HARYOU has not been hidden from our present, nor will be from any of our future, sources of support.

One interested onlooker was Harlem's enigmatic congressman, the Reverend Adam Clayton Powell Jr. In the event, it would be Powell's determination to control his political bailiwick, coupled with his influence in Washington, that would drive Clark out of HARYOU. Clark would later reflect that Powell "very directly and explicitly thought to give me lessons in the realities of power." Those lessons were to shake Clark profoundly, leading him to despair of his mission to interpret and transform black urban life.[113]

As chair of the House Committee on Education and Labor, through which the antipoverty legislation and any appropriations to HARYOU would have to pass, Powell had considerable means to complicate matters for Clark. In 1976, Clark recalled the close attention Powell and his staff devoted to the HARYOU proposal:

> Adam, rightly, saw that if the document were permitted to be fully implemented, that it would mean a major modification in the political and social structure of the community. He rightly saw that his vested interest in power depended upon control modifications rather than radical modifications. And as [NAACP Executive Director] Roy Wilkins said to me, "Kenneth, how could you have been so naive as to believe that a major and powerful Congressman would not want to take over . . . something of that scope and implications?"

Indeed, Powell would be far from alone among established urban politicians in viewing community action as a threat to existing electoral coalitions and patronage systems. By early 1965, the U.S. Conference of Mayors was already successfully pressuring administration officials in Washington to rein in those community action programs that engaged in voter registration drives and other forms of political mobilization.

Boone and other "radicals" were purged from the OEO, "maximum feasible participation" was revoked by congressional amendment, and authority over local antipoverty programs was entrusted to urban political machines, which opted, in Jackson's phrase, for "traditional client-bureaucrat forms of service provision."[114]

In 1962, Powell had made his first move toward ensuring his influence over government-funded youth initiatives in Harlem by encouraging political allies such as Livingstone Wingate to establish Associated Community Teams (ACT), a youth employment program that, like HARYOU, received a planning grant from the President's Committee on Juvenile Delinquency. By 1964, Powell was pressuring Clark to accept a merger of the two organizations and to grant Wingate, his former congressional aide, a prominent role directing the new entity's daily operations. This was anathema to Clark, who was convinced that the merger would reduce HARYOU to an extension of Powell's political machine and neutralize any prospects for effective grassroots mobilization. Clark later recalled his belief that Powell was determined "to be in control, not only in terms of the pork barrel aspect, but in terms of the social and political implications of having people organize to fight for their own destiny, etc. It was clear to Adam that the people had to be dependent upon him, to have him fight for their destiny, so that he would be re-elected over and over again."[115]

With Clark refusing to assent to the merger, Powell used his substantial influence and acumen to force it through. Clark believed that he would have his own allies in Washington, including not only David Hackett but also Robert Kennedy, who had chaired the President's Committee on Juvenile Delinquency. However, Kennedy was at that point planning his candidacy for election as a U.S. senator from New York, and would have wanted to keep Powell on side. Moreover, with Powell's congressional committee able to stall antipoverty legislation and appropriations, it was widely accepted in Washington, in the words of Powell's biographer, that he was "key to many of the most important measures on the President's program." While much of the New York press looked sympathetically on Clark's efforts to keep HARYOU out of Powell's hands, he could muster little support among politicians and antipoverty bureaucrats. Shriver's public statements made clear that only a joint proposal from HARYOU and ACT would be acceptable, and civil rights leaders such as the National Urban League's Whitney Young urged Clark to reach a compromise with Powell. Clark lost the support of HARYOU's board members, who were no longer prepared to resist the merger. After being excluded from the newly formed board of HARYOU-ACT, Clark submitted a letter of "resignation" on July 28, 1964. It was Wingate who became HARYOU-ACT's executive director.[116]

Dark Ghetto, though written in the aftermath of these events, only mentioned in passing that Clark had "resigned" from HARYOU following the completion of its planning phase. Yet despite skirting the issue of the merger, the book included a blistering profile of Powell. Across seven pages, Clark depicted Powell's successful political career as symptomatic of the essential powerlessness of the Harlem community. He acknowledged that Powell had established his political credentials through a series of civil rights campaigns stretching back to the 1930s. Yet he portrayed Powell as a "narcissistic" and cynical exploiter of Harlem's residents. Powell's flaunting of his luxuriant lifestyle, subsidized by his use of "public funds for personal junkets," Clark contended, was by now a major element in his appeal to his constituents. To many in Harlem, Powell's extravagance and indifference to criticism from white politicians and the media made him seem a "hero" who "defies and taunts the white enemy." In his "flamboyant" behavior, Clark suggested, Powell "has been to the Negroes a symbol of all that life has denied them. The Negro can in fantasy journey with Adam to the Riviera, enjoy a home in Puerto Rico, have beautiful girls at his beck and call, change wives 'like rich white folks.'" Undoubtedly simplifying the basis of Powell's popularity, Clark charged that the congressman's militant rhetoric and glamorous image appealed to "a powerless people" who "seek a concrete hero who will fight the battles they cannot fight for themselves." He characterized Powell's support as indicative of the dependency and illusions that any meaningful assertion of grassroots agency would need to overcome. "Those who oppose Powell," Clark wrote, "must oppose the ghetto first, for

Powell is a creature of the ghetto; and for Powell to survive, the ghetto itself must survive. To transform the ghetto would lead to Powell's political destruction."[117]

"It is difficult to find a more knowledgeable and practical expert on the problems of the nation's ghettos than Dr. Kenneth B. Clark," professed an article in the *Saturday Review* in 1968. *Dark Ghetto* had cemented Clark's reputation as an authority on black urban life and raised his public profile to new heights. Yet the fate of HARYOU and the direction of the wider federal antipoverty program shattered his faith in America's liberal governing elite. In his new position—which he maintained alongside his teaching at City College—as president of the Metropolitan Applied Research Center (MARC), a think tank devoted to urban problems, Clark observed the summers of rioting and the retreat from "maximum feasible participation" in community action programs with growing pessimism.[118]

At a MARC colloquium in December 1967, Clark vented his frustration in a paper titled "*Dark Ghetto* Revisited." It seemed to him by this time that "America has no intention" of dealing seriously with the problems of black urban communities. Believing that government and the public were now intent on forceful repression of the riots and containment of the ghettos' "pathology," rather than efforts to alleviate their suffering, Clark resorted to increasingly extreme denunciations of American racism. Noting Harlem's rising suicide rate, he suggested:

> It seems as if America has found the trick to get Negroes to kill themselves so that they can stand before the world as superior to the German Nazis. One of the ways, I suppose, is to encourage them to riot so that, under the guise of law and order, the suicide can be total and collective; Negroes have always been known to be sociable and social.

"If I sound bitter," he added, "it is only because I am."[119]

In the same paper, Clark drew an even starker parallel between American racism and Nazism: the "dark ghettos" were "America's concentration camps." He was not the first to make such comparisons.

Ellison, in his early, pathologist phase, had in 1945 likened conditions in the American South to those in "Nazi prisons," drawing, as Richard King observes, on Bruno Bettelheim's accounts of Dachau and Buchenwald. In 1959, Elkins had compared the psyches of African American slaves to those of concentration camp inmates. What is striking about Clark's comments on this and other occasions in 1967 is his implication of a deliberate, calculated strategy of militarized incarceration and even extermination (at least through provocation to "suicide"). Following the bloody suppression of the Newark and Detroit riots by police and National Guard in July, he had told a journalist that the United States was beginning to resemble "the old colonial powers" who "had to keep troops in their colonies" in order to "maintain both injustice and order. If we intend to preserve the injustices that affect both white and black, we must be prepared to use military force to maintain order. This means racial compounds that actually and psychologically are concentration camps."[120]

In September, Clark made similar claims in his testimony to the Kerner Commission. America's "ghettos" were deliberate creations of "urban planning," he said, "Just as concentration camps were planned." He had been reluctant to address the commission, he stated, given that previous investigations following the Chicago riot of 1919, the Harlem riots of 1935 and 1943, and the Watts riot of 1965 had all produced recommendations that had met with "inaction." The problem, Clark stated, was not ultimately one of knowledge:

> This society knows, I believe—and certainly the leaders of the society must know—that if human beings are confined in ghetto compounds of our cities and are subjected to criminally inferior education, pervasive economic and job discrimination, committed to houses unfit for human habitation, subjected to unspeakable conditions of municipal services, such as sanitation, that such human beings are not likely to be responsive to appeals to be lawful, to be respectful, to be concerned with the property of others.

Only a few years earlier, Clark had embraced the role of indigenous interpreter in the belief that the "invisible wall" of the "ghetto" was "opaque from outside in," and that by making both the "subjective" and "objective" dimensions of black urban life known to the American public and political leadership he could help to foster a renewed commitment to eradicate racial injustice. Now, he suggested that it was not a lack of knowledge but a "pervasive immorality" that sustained such injustice. It was "fascinating," he added, that "there was never a Presidential Commission to investigate the inner destruction of human beings in the ghetto, but there is a Presidential Commission to investigate the destruction of material things and property in the ghetto."[121]

His testimony lasted for almost three hours, and when the commission's report was released in March 1968, it was Clark who was deemed by the *Washington Post* to have been the "witness who had the most impact." Indeed, the report echoed Clark in offering what many considered a surprisingly radical verdict, that "white society is deeply implicated in the ghetto. White institutions created it, white institutions maintain it, and white society condones it." It also echoed Clark in calling for a massive program of additional investment in urban centers. President Johnson, however, was incensed that the commission found his civil rights and antipoverty measures inadequate, and refused to acknowledge its report. As Clark had gloomily predicted, the report was buried.[122]

Clark's faith in American liberalism had sunk to depths from which it would never fully rebound. He was appalled by the "barbarous form of violence" unleashed by Johnson's escalation of the war in Vietnam and by the concomitant de-escalation of the War on Poverty. In 1968, Clark and Jeanette Hopkins, his close friend and *Dark Ghetto*'s editor, published a damning verdict on the retreat from "maximum feasible participation" and empowerment through community action. *A Relevant War against Poverty* anticipated later critiques of the federal antipoverty program's reversion to traditional models of social service provision controlled by urban political machines. Analyzing more than fifty government-sponsored community action programs across the United States, Clark and Hopkins reported that in almost all cases the commitment to "social action" and decision making on the part of the poor was primarily verbal, and that "community action" was being used as a new label for the "traditional social service approach." This, they claimed, was precisely the approach that had been adopted by HARYOU-ACT. Indeed, the *New York Times* had reported in October 1965, more than a year into the program's operation, that the neighborhood boards that had been central to Clark's vision of grassroots mobilization had still not been constituted.[123]

Beneath the Johnson administration's "rhetoric" of "daring innovative liberalism," Clark and Hopkins concluded, was a fundamental reluctance to empower the poor:

> The campaign for massive [*sic*] feasible participation by the poor in the anti-poverty program must now be seen as a charade, an exhilarating intellectual game whose players never really understood the nature of power and the reluctance of those who have it to share it. It seems apparent that canny political leadership—national and city—never intended fundamental social reorganization. The political participation of the poor in their own affairs was not to be a serious sharing of power after all.

Yet there were signs that the authors' own democratic faith in the capacity of the poor to act effectively had somewhat diminished. Where residents had in fact been incorporated onto the boards of local anti-poverty programs, Clark and Hopkins contended, they had often succumbed to the illusion that they were sharing in power when in fact their involvement was mere "window dressing." The poor, they suggested, were all too easily exploited or co-opted under pretence of inclusion and empowerment. In light of this vulnerability, "it may be more relevant and forthright for a community action program to concentrate on the empathic relationship of professionals who will serve as surrogates to the poor and who have the training and skills to identify with and to help the poor." Why the involvement of such professionals would be tolerated by the same power holders who had manipulated and deceived the poor was not explained.[124]

Richard Nixon's arrival in the White House further darkened Clark's mood. In a new preface to *A Relevant War against Poverty* dated May 1969, he and Hopkins interpreted the administration's advocacy of "black capitalism" as a cynical ploy to legitimate federal inaction against poverty. Particularly galling to Clark were Moynihan's new role as Nixon's chief adviser on urban affairs and Moynihan's leaked memorandum of January 1970 suggesting that "the time may have come when the issue of race could benefit from a period of 'benign neglect.'" During an angry exchange of letters in November 1974, by which time Moynihan was serving as U.S. ambassador in New Delhi, Clark wrote: "Your famous 'benign neglect' memorandum was one of the most disturbing and dangerous public statements in a totally disturbing pattern of Nixon Administration regression on racial matters." Clark viewed the memorandum as "a calm and well-articulated rationalization for the continuation of economic and racial American inequities." That same year, Moynihan was excoriated in *Pathos of Power,* a book that wove together essays and speeches from across Clark's career. The social scientists whose research had been cited in the *Brown* ruling, Clark wrote, had "dared to be social critics." Moynihan and his fellow "neo-conservatives," however, were "mercenaries" who employed their "training and trappings and jargon" to defend an unjust status quo.[125]

A Unifying Theory

In September 1969, Clark was elected to serve as president of the American Psychological Association. He was both surprised and gratified, he later recalled, not so much because of his "color" but because his colleagues had elected "one of the people who believed that psychology, and particularly social psychology, should be harnessed to social policy, social change, etc." Almost immediately, Clark began to worry about the presidential address he would deliver at the end of his term in September 1971. The opportunity to set out his vision for the discipline before a large audience of his peers seemed at once exciting and intimidating. "And it was a disturbing thing. I was full of anxiety about it," he remembered in 1976. "I didn't have a single vacation or free moment, from the time I was president-elect up until the time I delivered the address, that was not in some way dominated by what I was going to talk about, you know, as being just a—well, it was a mess. I mean, it was really a mess."[126]

Clark's election was indicative of a broad cultural shift taking place within the United States' second-largest professional association. The APA's annual convention in 1969 had also witnessed the founding of the Association of Women Psychologists and a series of protests staged by other recently established groups, including Psychologists for a Democratic Society and the Association of Black Psychologists. Clark's initial surprise at his election gave way to recognition that the discipline had itself become "caught in the tide of social change and social activism" and that his election held a certain symbolic value within this context. During his presidency, the APA's board would vote to accept Clark's recommendation that a separate Board of Social and Ethical Responsibility for Psychology be created within the organization. However, with his presidential address looming large, he became increasingly preoccupied with thoughts about his colleagues' expectations of him and about his predicament as a black intellectual.[127]

He would recall in 1976 that even before his presidency began he had decided, in "general" terms, that he would use his address to "talk about psychology as an instrument for social change." He believed "that almost everyone wanted me, or was expecting me to talk about that subject in terms of race. And I knew I was *not* going to talk about it in terms of race, because, to me, race was merely one manifestation of a much deeper set of problems that confront human beings." Yet the transcript of a conversation between Clark and Hopkins just seven months before his address was delivered suggests the anxiety Clark felt about his ability to speak beyond the subject of race and to theorize about an underlying, universal, or general "set of problems." In the course of a discussion about public education, Hopkins prompted Clark to elucidate "your philosophy as a whole."

> *Dr. Clark:* But I don't have any philosophy as a whole.
> *Miss Hopkins:* That's not true.
> *Dr. Clark:* I can't afford it. I'm black.
> *Miss Hopkins:* Well, you've got at least to admit it.
> *Dr. Clark:* I don't have any. A black man in America cannot afford
>   the large perspective.
> *Miss Hopkins:* Who are you quoting[?]

Dr. Clark: Me.

Miss Hopkins: Why?

Dr. Clark: He can only afford to fight just one struggle at a time
and settle for small victories. . . .

Miss Hopkins: Well, at some point you have to *not* be a strategist
and help people see the coherence of your thought as a whole.

Dr. Clark: I have no thought as a whole.

And yet, as fatalistic as he sounded, Clark battled to resist this notion.
Only months later he would introduce his presidential address as an
attempt to give "theoretical coherence and unity" to the conclusions
he had drawn over the course of his career about "the dynamics of man
and society."[128]

Confirming his reluctance to dwell on the subject of race, Clark's
presidential address offered only a brief summary of his major research
projects, from the doll test to *A Relevant War against Poverty,* before entering into a broad theoretical discussion of psychology and social change.
This began with an acknowledgment of his debt to the psychodynamic
theories of Alfred Adler, and specifically to Adler's notion of a universal
but socially mediated struggle for self-esteem, grounded in a deep-rooted
anxiety of powerlessness. Clark's tribute to Adler also highlighted
Clark's own long-standing commitment to social explanations of human behavior and social remedies for psychological problems. Yet this
was quickly followed by the remark that "one finds oneself going beyond Adler even as he remains dependent upon fundamental Adlerian
insights."[129]

At this point, Clark's focus shifted abruptly to the somatic determinants of human behavior:

> The concrete base of human consciousness is the mysterious sub-
> stances and the quality of interactions among the cortical cells. All
> we seem to know about these cells is that they are unique among all
> the combinations of matter and energy which are known to exist in
> the universe. They make possible perception, awareness, evaluation,
> self-reflection, anxiety, reflection on the past, and anticipation of
> the future. . . . They create and validate humanity, and they sustain

the struggle for justice and decency in human relationships even as they provide the basis for rationalizing cruelty and inhumanities.

For more than three decades, Clark had concerned himself with the impact of the social environment on the consciousness and behavior of individuals. Suddenly, he was concerned with the "rather specific *biochemical* environment" necessary to maintain the health of the cortical cells. "They require that oxygen and nourishment be provided and regulated through an elaborate capillary system," he explained, and the "unstable equilibrium within and around these cells must be maintained within a tolerable range of variation." While social and economic deprivation had long been the subjects of his research, Clark now emphasized that "deprivation in the biochemical requirements of these cortical cells" could trigger "changes in temperament" and alter an individual's "threshold of positive and negative responses or sensitivity to external environmental forces." It was ultimately owing to these cells' "fragility" that "the human ego remains a fragile and delicate thing."[130]

In seeking to affirm their own worth against the evidence of their mortality and insignificance, Clark continued in a recognizably Adlerian vein, human beings strive to assert "social power," their capacity to influence their surroundings by bringing about or preventing some manner of change. The "dilemma of power," however, was its potential to service both the noblest and basest of instincts and to "make dominant either the primitive or the human propensities of man." Tragically, "the human brain can provide intellectual and moral rationalizations for a nonadaptive, ultimately destructive use of social power." Clark then set out the context for the central proposition of his address:

> Contemporary man's technological mastery of matter and energy, and the related thermonuclear weaponry, confronts us with the fact that it is now possible to destroy the human species through the nonadaptive use of human intelligence and the destructive, pathetic use of social power. . . . This survival crisis requires immediate mobilization of all that is positive within man to provide us with the time necessary to prevent man from destroying the human species—and to provide man with the time required to evolve and

develop a more stable organismic base for the rational and moral exercise of social power.

The urgency of this crisis did not permit continued reliance on "traditional, prescientific" approaches to "moral education," which had proved to be of dubious efficacy. Religion, philosophy, education, and law had seemed adequate tools for controlling human destructiveness in a "prenuclear age" but were wholly inadequate to meet the "present survival urgency." Moreover, Clark argued, "verbalizations" of moral purpose had too often been "prostituted by the pathos of power; they have been perverted by the pretenses of rationality in the services of inhumanity if not barbarity." Science must now assume the task of "reducing the negatives and enhancing the positive potentials in human beings" and bring about an "era of psychotechnology."[131]

Recent research in neurophysiology, biochemistry, and psychopharmacology into direct stimulation of particular regions of the brain and the effects of drugs on the "emotional and motivational levels of the individual" indicated to Clark a tremendous potential for regulating the extremes of human behavior. "We might be on the threshold," he believed, "of that type of scientific biochemical intervention which could stabilize and make dominant the moral and ethical propensities of man and subordinate, if not eliminate, his negative and primitive behavioral tendencies." Such a psychotechnology could be available "within a few years, and with a fraction of the cost required to produce the atom bomb; and much less than the present cost of our explorations in outer space." Given that the survival or extinction of the human species now rested in the hands of "a few men," it seemed to Clark

logical that a requirement imposed on all power-controlling leaders—and those who aspire to such leadership—would be that they accept and use the earliest perfected form of psychotechnological, biochemical intervention which would assure their positive use of power and reduce or block the possibility of their using power destructively. This form of psychotechnological medication would be a type of internally imposed disarmament. It would assure that there would be no absurd or barbaric use of power.

Such drastic measures were necessary to "provide the masses of human beings with the security that their leaders would not or could not sacrifice them on the altars of their personal ego pathos, vulnerability—and instability."[132]

Clark was not oblivious to the likelihood of condemnation. Though he had discussed the content of his address with only two people prior to the convention—Hopkins and a colleague at MARC, Lawrence Plotkin—both had warned him, as he remembered in 1976, that he would be "clobbered." He concluded his address by anticipating two probable lines of attack. It might be objected on "moral" grounds that his proposed psychotechnology was "manipulative and will take away from man his natural right to make errors." Such an objection, he countered, might have been valid in an age of "clubs, bows and arrows, or even gunpowder," but it was "pathetically immoral" in an age in which human "errors" could bring about the destruction of the species. It might also be argued that psychotechnological regulation would constitute an "intolerable tampering with the natural or God-given characteristics of man," or produce a "form of utopian mechanization of human beings through drugging the masses and their leaders." Clark, however, defended psychotechnology as a form of vaccination comparable to existing medical interventions to prevent "disease." Psychotechnology, if "used affirmatively, wisely, and with compassion," promised not to destroy human integrity but precisely to "enhance that which is uniquely human in man—those positive qualities which promise a future of human grandeur."[133]

Clark was indeed "clobbered." After the *New York Times* reported the speech on its front page the following day, columnists and editorial writers across the nation leaped at the opportunity to ridicule him as an eccentric professor. Clark wished, according to New York's *Daily News,* to turn humans "into two-legged vegetables—turnips, possibly." Four prominent academics issued a joint statement that condemned Clark for seeking a "quick technological fix" for complex human problems. Among them was Herbert Kelman, professor or social ethics at Harvard University, who told the press: "You cannot eliminate the abuse of power simply by manipulating the minds of individuals. You cannot manufacture a human personality that can't go wrong so long as institutional arrangements permit these abuses of power." The Illinois Agricultural Association provided the unlikely backdrop for Vice President Spiro Agnew's response to Clark's speech. Praising his audience of midwestern farmers for their faith in American individualism, Agnew attacked Clark's proposal for the psychotechnological regulation of political leaders as dangerous "drivel." Editorial writers posed the question, "Who bells the cat?" Even if an effective "humanity drug" could be produced, the *New York Times* asked, "who could have forced Hitler or Stalin to take such a drug?"[134]

Indeed, Clark had made no attempt to explain why political leaders whom he characterized as reckless egotists would ever agree to this "internally imposed disarmament." He also ignored the inevitability that psychotechnology would itself concentrate vast power in the hands of whoever was to administer the drug to political leaders. Who or what would ensure *their* positive use of power? In stating that psychotechnology was to be "used affirmatively, wisely, and with compassion," Clark had fallen back on the very notion he had declared untenable—that human beings could trust in the morality and wisdom of "power-controlling leaders." No less than was true of nuclear technology, psychotechnology would depend upon the morality and rationality of those with the power to determine its use. The "dilemma of power" had not been solved, but displaced.[135]

As Clark acknowledged in 1976, to have dismissed social and educational approaches to the improvement of human behavior and the pursuit of social progress was "almost treasonable, for a social psychologist." It could, he reflected, "be viewed as a betrayal of my own career, my role, my activities as a social psychologist who was seeking to understand [the] relationship between man and his social environment." Why, indeed, did Clark's only remaining hope for humanity now rest on biochemical manipulation of the cortical cells? There is no reason to doubt that Clark, like many of his contemporaries, was deeply disturbed by the possibility of nuclear warfare. At least as early as 1960, he had become a sponsor of the National Committee for a Sane Nuclear Policy. Though almost a decade had passed since the Cuban missile crisis by the time of Clark's presidential address, and despite movement toward détente, the Soviet Union was rapidly enlarging its nuclear arsenal, and China had possessed nuclear weapons since 1963. The possibility of a nuclear conflict remained real. Yet there are reasons to question whether Clark's advocacy of psychotechnology stemmed solely, or even principally, from a fear of nuclear destruction.[136]

Clark's recollection in 1976 that he had decided many months in advance of his presidential address that he would talk about "psychology as an instrument for social change," but that he was "*not* going to talk about it in terms of race," suggests that he had been searching for a subject matter through which to convey his beliefs about social change and psychology's means of contributing to it. Moreover, nuclear warfare was not the only scenario that Clark viewed as an imminent threat to "survival." As will be seen, for several years he had been issuing apocalyptic warnings of impending societal "self-destruction" and "annihilation" resulting from abuses of power in contexts directly related to his own research and activism. Both his wish to confound what he believed were his colleagues' expectations of him and his drastic prescription for psychotechnological regulation of political leadership convey the profound disillusionment that took hold of Clark as the visions of societal change he had entertained in the early 1960s collapsed over the course of the decade.[137]

However, not entirely unlike the rioters he had described in *Dark Ghetto,* Clark exhibited a "weird social defiance" in the face of these disappointments. In addressing "the dynamics of man and society," Clark rebelled against his own perception that the onus of grappling with American racism denied black intellectuals "the large perspective." In speaking of the threat of nuclear annihilation, he resisted the notion that black intellectuals should concern themselves only with "black" subjects. In shifting his emphasis from the social to the somatic determinants of human behavior, he returned to the corner at which he had found himself as a student forty years earlier, and reneged on the decision he had taken to forsake neurophysiology for social psychology because of the obligations inherent in "being black." As fanciful and ill-conceived as his proposal of psychotechnology was, his address demonstrated that, like Harlem's delinquents and rioters according to his analysis, Clark had not relinquished all hope—either of his own intellectual freedom or of the possibility of human progress. Yet in the desperate form of his rebellion and in his credulous demand for a neat technological solution to an intractable human "dilemma," Clark displayed only too clearly the bruising impact of his experiences as a black intellectual and of his own encounters with power.[138]

Contrary to his bleak remark to Hopkins in February 1971 that he was unable to take a "large perspective" on human problems, Clark had for several years been formulating what he called a "unifying theory of power." It was perhaps no coincidence, however, that he had first outlined this theory shortly after his own "lessons in the realities of power" had been administered by Adam Clayton Powell. Early in 1965, only months after his disengagement from HARYOU and weeks before the publication of *Dark Ghetto,* Clark delivered the annual Kurt Lewin Memorial Award Address, upon being honored by SPSSI for advancing "the integration of psychological research and social action." He took as his point of departure the British philosopher Bertrand Russell's book *Power: A New Social Analysis* (1938). Russell had asserted that "the fundamental concept in social science is Power, in the same sense in which Energy is the fundamental concept in physics." The task of the social scientist, according to Russell, was to understand social dynamics as the operation of laws of power, with power defined as "the production of intended effects" by means of influence, incentives, deterrents, or coercion. Clark proceeded to offer an elaboration of Russell's theory in the form of a more specific definition of "social power" as "the force or energy required to bring about, to sustain, or to prevent social, political, or economic change."[139]

In his address to the APA in 1971, Clark repeated these lines from his earlier speech and presented his definition of "social power" as the basis of his "unifying conceptual framework." The desire to exercise power derives, Clark contended, from a universal impulse to give meaning to a transient existence. With power comes the possibility of improving the conditions of human life. Yet an established "power system" might become "self-directing" and insensitive to the "adaptive needs" of the "organism and social system." Clark then advanced his argument for psychotechnological regulation of "all power-controlling leaders" on the grounds that the threat of nuclear warfare constituted an imminent "survival crisis." Why, though, should "*all* power-controlling leaders—and those who aspire to such leadership" be required to submit to psychotechnological medication when only "a few men" in a handful of countries possessed the means to threaten human survival in this way? Clark in fact told journalists that the medication, when perfected, should be made compulsory for everyone from "the man aspiring to be a city councilman in Ward 8 right on up to the incumbent or aspiring President of the United States."[140]

Nuclear annihilation was not, it seems, the only destructive use of power Clark had in mind when advocating psychotechnological control of political leaders. In *Dark Ghetto,* a book addressed to "hee for whom this Bell tolls," Clark had insisted that the devastation wrought by America's neglect and confinement of the black urban poor could not be contained within the ghetto's walls. In an article published in *Playboy* in 1969, Clark reiterated this warning in striking terms that anticipated the urgent, apocalyptic rhetoric of his presidential address. White Americans remained blind, he believed, to the threat that racial injustice posed not only to its immediate victims but to the entire society. The nation was storing up "the tinder of a social holocaust," Clark wrote. "As long as the War on Poverty is seen in racial terms, there will be no triumph. The society must know," he urged, "that its own economic, social, and political well-being—its own *survival*—depends on the survival of American cities." The question on which all else depended was:

> Can America find leadership wise enough and strong enough to subdue this emerging, socially condoned evil and generate new compassion, a new commitment to democracy and equality, transcending race? If it does not, the nation is doomed to *self-destruction,* either by mounting waves of violence or, like the Roman Empire, to decay from within.

The previous year, Clark had told an audience of psychiatrists that the pattern of riots and violent repression of those riots was "no longer consistent with human survival."[141]

An even more explicit connection between the theme of Clark's presidential address and his sense of the severity of the urban crisis can be found in an article he published in the *New York Times Magazine* in September 1965. There, he had employed a highly revealing metaphor: "The dark ghettos now represent a *nuclear stock pile* which can annihilate the very foundations of America." In likening the threat posed by urban deprivation to that of a nuclear attack, Clark had sought to fulfill his purpose as an indigenous interpreter by convincing his readers of the urgency with which conditions in the ghettos must be redressed. By 1971, however, he seemed to despair of convincing white Americans either that there was a moral imperative to ameliorate the urban crisis or that the health of the wider society demanded it. In the brief summation of his career with which Clark began his presidential address in 1971, he restated his belief that the federal antipoverty initiatives had "reflected a total lack of commitment to eliminate poverty, to share power with the powerless. Above all, they reflected the inability of the decision makers and the society as a whole to change the set [*sic*] of perceiving and treating the poor and dark-skin minorities as justifiably rejected inferior human beings." Clark perhaps reasoned that if white Americans could not be made to understand that the neglect of the black urban poor posed a "nuclear" threat to their society's "survival," the literal threat of nuclear annihilation might yet convince them of the need to prevent all destructive uses of power.[142]

Clark's motivation for advocating psychotechnology may not have been limited to a single existential threat, whether of nuclear annihilation or of "self-destruction" through a submerging tide of urban violence. The "dilemma of power" was rooted, he believed, in the universal fragility of the human ego, and psychotechnology promised to eliminate all manner of injustices if it could, as he hoped, "assure that there would be no absurd or barbaric use of power." Yet it is striking to consider that less than a decade earlier, when the threat of nuclear conflict had been at least as great, Clark had nonetheless placed extraordinary faith in America's liberal political leadership to use power for positive ends and even to "share power" with the oppressed. Above all, what had shattered Clark's optimism was the disintegration of his vision for a solution to America's urban crisis and his perception that he had been drawn into a "charade." As he remarked in his address to the APA, *A*

Relevant War against Poverty had attributed the failure of the federal antipoverty program to the "inhibiting fact that those human beings
with power are deeply unwilling to share even a modicum of real
power with those who have been powerless."[143]

Clark's optimism of the early 1960s had given way to an equally
pronounced pessimism about the prospects for achieving significant
social change by any means short of direct intervention in the workings
of the human brain. He would continue during the 1970s and 1980s, in
his role on the New York State Board of Regents, to agitate for improvements in the public education provided to black schoolchildren.
He would also maintain, in the pages of newspapers and magazines, his
indictments of American racism. Yet he never recovered the optimism
that had suffused his HARYOU proposal, and the rising force of con-
servatism and of law-and-order approaches to urban problems during
the final decades of the twentieth century left him dejected. "Reluctantly, I am forced to face the likely possibility that the United States
will never rid itself of racism and reach true integration," he wrote in a
short memoir published in 1993, "and while I hope very much for the
emergence of a revived civil rights movement with innovative programs and dedicated leaders, I am forced to recognize that my life has,
in fact, been a series of glorious defeats."[144]

That Clark grounded his argument for psychotechnology in the
threat of nuclear annihilation stemmed in part from his sense that he
had failed in his task, as an indigenous interpreter, of making the realities of black urban life known to white Americans. His increasingly
extreme characterizations of the "dark ghettos" as "concentration
camps" and as a "nuclear stockpile" had failed, he concluded, to account for the indifference of America's citizens and leaders. Yet he was
also seizing a chance to break free, at least momentarily, from that role.
In remarks both before and after his presidential address, Clark portrayed black intellectual life, no less than black urban life, as painfully
constricted and circumscribed by the pervasive, deep-rooted force of
American racism. The role of indigenous interpreter was one that he
had accepted, and yet one in which he had come to feel cornered and
confined. When, in 1976, he reflected on the reaction to his presidential

address, it was not the aberrant nature of his proposals so much as his predicament as a black intellectual that remained foremost in his mind:

> I think that part of the shock and surprise, on the part of my colleagues, and maybe a good deal of their criticism, stems from the fact that I did not use the occasion of the presidential address to re-hash the *Brown* decision, or to talk about race, or civil rights. I think that many of my colleagues, consciously or not, were shocked and disturbed, that the first black president of the American Psychological Association broke the expectations, you know, of the topic that is reserved for blacks. The—Namely, racial justice. And maybe didn't have the insight to see that I was talking about justice, but in a much broader context.[145]

Chapter 2

Be Even Blacker

Amiri Baraka's Names and Places

Everett Leroy Jones was born in Newark, New Jersey, on October 7, 1934. Around 1953, LeRoi Jones came into existence in Washington, D.C., later to appear in New York City's Greenwich Village and Harlem. Back in Newark, in 1967, Ameer Barakat received his name from a Sunni Muslim cleric, and a few months later, Imamu Amiri Baraka emerged on the same site. By 1975, the subject of this chapter was plain Amiri Baraka—or, alternatively, "the Chairman." Whether these names can be said to designate a single "individual" is a question best left to philosophers, but historians and other students of the twentieth-century United States have reasons of their own to be concerned with Amiri Baraka's names and places. In 1968, a majority of the thirty-eight prominent African American writers polled by *Negro Digest* magazine nominated Baraka as the "most important living black poet," "most important black playwright," and "most important black writer" in America. More recently, the literary scholar Arnold Rampersad has called him "one of the eight figures" who have "significantly affected the course of African-American literary culture." Political scientists and scholars of social movements, as well as literary historians and cultural critics, rank Baraka as one of the foremost theorists and practitioners of the black power and black arts movements.[1]

The successive names adopted by Baraka linger as eloquent markers of his geographical and ideological itinerancy. Changes of name and place not only signified, but in part constituted Baraka's rituals of self-invention. Intertwined with his desire to make himself anew was a wish to remake the cities surrounding him, and somehow to become more definitely himself in the process. Baraka's repositioning of himself—from Newark to Greenwich Village to Harlem and back to Newark—corralled the attention of many Americans because it appeared so neatly to tally the waxing and waning of liberal optimism about racial conciliation during the peak years of the civil rights and black power movements. From segregation to integration to self-imposed "separation," liberalism's great black hope had turned *enfant terrible*.

Baraka shared much of this idea of himself, albeit from a position that exalted, rather than lamented, his and much of black America's retreat from integrationist ideals. From early in his career he, too, understood his life's trajectory as archetypal, not only in its seeming embodiment of the fluctuating fortunes of the civil rights movement but also in its apparent adherence to an archetypal narrative. "The romance plot," Dorothy Ross explains, is written "from the standpoint of the human actor engaged in a mythic quest for identity. The hero embarks on a quest to achieve or recover an identity that is prefigured at the beginning and at the end enters an Edenic world." This process, Ross observes, "often takes the form of exile. The search for identity begins in the exile from home." Even in his early thirties, Baraka portrayed his own journeying as a return from strange lands to origins and a rediscovery of self; as an often "unconscious" sequence of steps "toward the thing I had coming into the world, with no sweat: my blackness." As he wrote in Harlem in 1965, by way of introducing his first collection of essays, aptly titled *Home:*

> I have been a lot of places in my time, and done a lot of things. And there is a sense of the Prodigal about my life that begs to be resolved. But one truth that anyone reading these pieces ought to get

is the sense of movement—the struggle, in myself, to understand
where and who I am, and to move with that understanding.

This movement was intellectual as well as spatial. "The Village," "Harlem," and "Newark" were mindscapes as much as landscapes for
Baraka, and his transitions between them map his intellectual and political journeying, his sense of "where *and who* I am."[2]

No less than Kenneth Clark, LeRoi Jones—as he then was—at first
reveled in the possibilities of interpreting black urban life to white
Americans. Among his early essays were earnest pieces deploring Harlem's squalor and suffering. By the time rioting convulsed the neighborhood in July 1964, his mode of address to white audiences was
shifting. Wishing to exchange his image as a downtown bohemian for
that of a black militant, Jones now sought to terrorize the white imagination with graphic evocations of black urban rage and prophecies of
imminent race war. Yet the contradictions inherent in his relationship
with white audiences became overwhelming. By the end of 1965 he
had abandoned the role that had raised him from obscurity and that
had opened New York's prestigious theaters, publishing houses, newspapers, and magazines to his work. Sooner than Clark, Jones found
that the role of indigenous interpreter trapped him in dependency on
white appetites and expectations. But while Clark's anguish was fed by
resentment of the intellectual ghettoization he felt the role imposed,
Jones embraced a strident racial separatism as his means of release from
the problematic dynamics of black performance to white audiences. In
sharp divergence from the paths taken by Clark and Romare Bearden,
Jones looked to resolve his sense of crisis as a black intellectual through
a deepening commitment to race as an absolute principle governing intellectual practice.

Though it is Jones's defection from bohemian Greenwich Village to
Harlem in 1965 that appears most dramatic—for one critic, this was
"possibly the most momentous getaway in Afro-American or American
letters"—his return to his more literal "home" in Newark, less than a
year after his move to Harlem, proved no less consequential. It was
back in his birthplace that, as Amiri Baraka, he made his first sustained

response to the two problems that came to dominate much of his career: the "crisis of the Negro intellectual," as Harold Cruse titled his hefty book of 1967, and the urban crisis engulfing African Americans in northern cities. While he regarded neither of these problems as novel, like many of his generation he viewed the 1960s as their historical apex. Moreover, Baraka came to envisage a single resolution to these two crises: the black intellectual's struggle for social legitimacy found its culmination in leadership of the struggle for black cities.[3]

Departing the Village, he renounced what he had come to view as the decadent individualism of Western intellectuals, and devoted his work henceforth to the cause of the black nation. Later, in an autobiography penned during the mid-1970s, by which time he had changed tack once again and embraced Marxism, Baraka would appeal to Frantz Fanon to explain what he now conceived as the misguided, restless years of his youth: "Fanon laid it out how the pathological intellectuals will rush headlong, unknowing, into love of their oppressors, trying not to kill them but to be them. And discovering the trap, how they have been used, they rush again headlong, or heartlong now, into Africa of their mind." It was indeed in the Africa of his mind that Baraka, once returned to Newark, had discerned a vision of black life that promised to reconcile the intellectual to the urban community, purifying both of Western contaminants. "I grew up in this ghetto," he told an interviewer in 1968, "right around the corner from where I am living now." Baraka's return to the bricks and mortar of Newark's "ghetto" was matched by an audacious bid for intellectual self-ghettoization, an attempt to delimit a sphere of exclusively black thought and action. Ironically, though inevitably, the Africa of his mind was a thoroughly Western construct, a product of peculiarly Western discontents.[4]

With his turn to black nationalism, Baraka radically repositioned himself within the debates over racial representation and responsibility. Tracking his journey from the Village to Harlem to Newark, this chapter offers a new perspective on Baraka's changing conception of black urban life and his developing notions of obligation and social engagement as a black intellectual. Beyond reconstructing his performance to white audiences, it presents a reinterpretation of Baraka's thought and activism as a nationalist intent on reconstituting black urban life in the late 1960s and early 1970s. In the process, it argues for a new understanding of black power, a movement deeply implicated in the debates among African American intellectuals concerning the nature of black urban communities, the means and ends of their transformation, and the function and utility of black intellectuals in the midst of the urban crisis. Above all, this chapter reveals the extent to which black power was a movement for self-transformation, and one grounded in a sharp moral indictment and pathologist diagnosis of black urban communities. Far from a straightforward celebration of urban African American culture, the black power movement, and particularly its "cultural nationalist" contingent, often articulated a critical, even derogatory view of the existing lifestyles, values, and beliefs of lower-class urban African Americans.

Issues of gender and sexuality have figured prominently in scholarly and popular evaluations of black power. The overwhelmingly hostile assessment that until recently dominated discussion of the movement focused particular attention on black power's supposedly predatory ideal of masculinity. Baraka, together with Eldridge Cleaver of the Black Panther Party, was singled out by black feminist authors of the 1970s and 1980s as an iconic exponent of an essentially anarchic masculine code that elevated hedonistic indulgence in violence and sexual rapacity above traditional notions of social responsibility. For Michele Wallace, Baraka typified the black power movement's masculine ideal, which she termed "Black Macho":

> Black males who stressed a traditionally patriarchal responsibility to their women and children, to their communities—to black people— were to be considered almost sissified. The black man's sexuality and the physical fact of his penis were the major evidence of his manhood and the purpose of it. LeRoi Jones was the Black Movement's leading intellectual convert, having deserted success in the white world for the uncertainty of the Black Revolution.

For the author and activist bell hooks, too, Baraka and Cleaver epitomized a black power sensibility that discarded "chivalrous codes of manhood" and "earlier romanticized versions of the male hero as a strong knight, protecting and providing for the damsel in distress," and "replaced" these with "worship of the rapist, the macho man, the brute who uses force to get his demands met."[5]

This view of black power was sustained in broader historical narratives, which typically glossed the movement as an "anarchist impulse" or an expression of "the *machismo* of leather-jacketed young men, armed to the teeth, rising out of the urban ghetto." Significantly, it was a view that located black power beyond the boundaries of the dominant traditions of African American social thought and activism. Among the most important of those traditions is that chronicled by Kevin Gaines in *Uplifting the Race: Black Leadership, Politics, and Culture in the Twentieth Century* (1996). As Gaines skillfully demonstrates, a "self-help ideology of racial uplift" had long animated the challenges to black subordination mounted by educated African Americans, from the collapse of Reconstruction in the last decades of the nineteenth century to the burgeoning civil rights movement of the mid-twentieth. The paradigm of racial uplift propelled integrationist campaigns that appealed to white America for citizenship through exemplary displays of black worthiness, as well as nationalist movements such as Marcus Garvey's Universal Negro Improvement Association, which aimed to raise the black masses to the level of "civilization." At its core was the belief that liberation would be achieved through a politics of self-help, moral transformation, and respectability.[6]

Insofar as it emphasized the transformative potential of black agency, uplift ideology could be empowering for African Americans. Yet as Gaines argues, the insistence on self-help and self-transformation was simultaneously problematic, for it engendered a "tendency to locate the problem in the bodies and behavior of African Americans, rather than in their lack of citizenship, political rights, and ultimately, in social inequities." Notions of respectability, absorbed into uplift ideology from the prevailing ideals of white middle-class America, became the yardsticks by which the "progress" of the race was measured. All too often, blame for the lack of progress toward equal citizenship was assigned to lower-class African Americans themselves, whose values and behavior were judged to be unworthy of freedom. Above all, uplift promoted the ideal of the patriarchal family and an ethos of godliness, service, and sexual restraint that would visibly refute allegations of innate black immorality. For Gaines, however, the black power movement jettisoned this tradition in its entirety. Uplift's ideals of "decorous, chaste self-restraint" gave way to "phallocentric self-assertion" and a "hyper-masculinist view" in which "black women existed not as exemplars of female chastity but as sex objects, and in Cleaver's case, as targets of a vengeful misogyny."[7]

The past decade has witnessed a surge of new scholarship that challenges the familiar "declension narrative" of black power as a descent into self-indulgent posturing and violent anarchy. Historians have uncovered a more politically and ideologically sophisticated movement, one in which local activists confronted urban poverty and police brutality and devised new strategies, such as free breakfast programs, health checks, and medical treatment, to address the disadvantages faced by black urban communities that had benefited little from civil rights legislation. By illuminating the historical antecedents of black power's insistence on self-determination and self-defense, and by exposing continuities of method and ideology, a host of recent studies have drawn attention to black power's inheritance from earlier forms of black activism, as well as its innovations. Yet the association of black power with a predatory masculinity has escaped sustained scrutiny, and the question of black power's relation to the uplift tradition awaits reconsideration.

One reason for this may be that something akin to Wallace's "Black Macho" leaps out from the pages of some of the most notorious—because most sensational—texts associated with the black nationalism of the 1960s. Nowhere is this more the case than in LeRoi Jones's verses of 1964:

A cult of death

need of the simple striking arm under
the streetlamp. The cutters, from under
their rented earth. Come up, black dada

nihilismus. Rape the white girls. Rape
their fathers. Cut the mothers' throats

or in Eldridge Cleaver's sinister declaration in *Soul on Ice* (1968): "I have lived those lines." To such texts might be added news footage of blazing city blocks reduced to rubble by the riots of the mid- and late 1960s; iconic photographs of leather-clad Black Panthers flaunting shotguns; and the sexual and criminal antics celebrated by the "blaxploitation" films of the 1970s. Moreover, few would question the contention underlying the concept of "Black Macho," that the black power movement was marred by sexism. Yet blunt terms such as "sexism" and "chauvinism" reveal little about the specific gender identities, roles, and relationships envisioned and enacted within the movement.[8]

Searching beyond black power's familiar icons and reinterpreting some of those same texts and images reveal that traditional patriarchal ideals of male responsibility toward family and community exerted a far stronger influence on the movement than the notion of "Black Macho" allows. Within the movement's discourse, black urban communities were frequently imagined as sites of moral, social, and psychological pathology, and as such were regarded as objects of remedy and reform. A convicted rapist, Eldridge Cleaver in *Soul on Ice* recalled "practicing on black girls in the ghetto" before he had "crossed the tracks and sought out white prey." A prominent obituary in 1998 stated that *Soul on Ice* "became the philosophical foundation for the black power movement. In one essay, Cleaver described his rape of white women as an 'insurrectionary act.'" Typically, it neglected to mention that Cleaver's book recounted his realization, while in prison, that he had been "wrong" to justify rape as an act of political assertion: "I had gone astray—astray not so much from the white man's law as from being human, civilized." Like other canonical black power texts, including *The Autobiography of Malcolm X* (1965) and George Jackson's *Soledad Brother* (1971), *Soul on Ice* presents a narrative of political awakening and moral self-transformation.[9]

When the name "LeRoi Jones" first peppered the pages of American newspapers and popular magazines in 1964, it was in no small part the provocative, sexually transgressive racial imagery of works such as "BLACK DADA NIHILISMUS" that drew public attention toward him. To portray Jones as a relentless exponent of "Black Macho," however, is to obscure the commitment to self-transformation that, at the height of the black power movement, engendered "Amiri Baraka." Rediscovering this commitment underscores black power's appropriation of the ethos of self-improvement that had long characterized the uplift tradition. By the late 1960s, when Baraka's influence within the black power movement was nearing its peak, the ideals of uplift were as evident in the title of his monthly column in the newspaper *Black NewArk*—"Raise!"—as they had been in Garvey's rallying cry of the 1920s, "Up you mighty Race! You can accomplish what you will!"[10]

Despite taking the form of a "retreat to the ghetto," black power was emphatically a movement to transform the "ghetto" and its inhabitants. Virtually overlooked in the scholarship on black power is the movement's pathologist diagnosis of black urban life, forged through the meeting of two distinct discourses. The first is the tradition of racial uplift ideology, which had long regarded urban communities of lower-class black migrants as incubators of pathological social structures and behaviors. The second is the postwar discourse of psychological "damage" that extended pathologist imagery inward, from social structures to the psyche. Ironically, black separatism shared in the "romance of psychology" and "triumph of the therapeutic" that characterized the wider American culture from which the movement dissented. However, in conjoining the "damage thesis" with racial uplift, the black power movement's pathologism often displayed a morally censorious tone quite at odds with the rhetoric of liberal social scientists. Baraka's most avowedly "African" remedies for the urban crisis in fact bore the hallmarks of an uplift tradition that was characteristically American in the longevity of its ethic of self-improvement as an antidote to urban deprivation.[11]

For Baraka, each element in the matrix of social and psychological pathology was a matter for both personal and collective redemption. Subject and subject matter became almost indistinguishable as the intellectual glimpsed the solution to his own crisis in the act of reckoning with the urban crisis. Equally blurred were distinctions between art and life as he enjoined black people to "dig the idea of buildings that look like John Coltrane's solos or automobiles that look like James

Brown's singing or work like that, you understand? Or cities that vibrate the way the prose of Claude McKay and Chester Himes vibrate or the poetry of Margaret Walker if you can understand that."[12]

A Sense of the Prodigal

If 1964 was "the Jones Year," the public attention focused on the young writer and his new poems and plays was in large measure a product of unease—his own, and that of the wider American society. He sensed, he would recall years later, that the New York media were making him "some kind of spokesman" on account of his "social attachments with white folks." Yet it was the troubled, increasingly fragile nature of those "attachments" that furnished much of Jones's dramatic material, and which forced the drama of his own life into the metropolitan and national gaze. As fissures developed within the civil rights movement, and as its nonviolent, interracial ethos came under strain, LeRoi Jones, as much as any of the texts he produced, commanded attention as the embodiment of an apparent groundswell of black resentment and retribution. While Kenneth Clark's public role involved interpretation in a sense roughly equivalent to analysis, Jones's writings of 1964 were received as interpretations in a somewhat distinct sense: as translations rendering comprehensible to one party the otherwise unintelligible sentiments of another. His play *Dutchman* was understood, in this manner, to verbalize for downtown audiences such nonverbal phenomena as subway vandalism and street violence. As much as his recognized artistic talent was what equipped him to assume this role, Jones, much more than Clark, was regarded not merely as a well-placed analyst of the rising tide of black anger, but as its personification. Indeed, he wished not only to reflect but positively to enact a process of black disengagement from the liberal ideal of a racially integrated society. As a thirty-year-old black man with two children by his white wife, and as a black artist closely associated with such "Beat Generation" writers as Jack Kerouac and Allen Ginsberg, Jones, in his schism with white America, appeared to capture in microcosm the latest turn of the nation's racial saga.[13]

"I'm shitting out my educated Middlewest background once and for all," William Burroughs had told Kerouac in 1957, the year Jones had arrived in New York City. The Beats' literary revolt against middle-class, middle-American, and middlebrow horizons instantly appealed to the young migrant from Newark, who regarded his own family's social milieu as no more than a black variant of America's cultural sterility and spiritual enervation. Everett Leroy, as his parents had named him, grew up in a family that clung determinedly to its precarious middle-class identity through the testing years of Depression and war. Later, in the autobiography that was steeped in his newfound Marxism, he would situate his family within an African American social spectrum extending from a tiny "yellow" elite through a respectable "brown" middle class to a teeming "black" residuum. Jones's father, Coyette Leroy, who had come to Newark from South Carolina as a young man, worked as a barber and later as a postal supervisor (two characteristically "brown" occupations), while his mother, née Anna Lois Russ, had a conspicuously "yellow" pedigree as a graduate of the prestigious Fisk University and a professional social worker. Distanced somewhat from the poorer black sections of Newark's Central/Third Ward, the house on Dey Street where Jones spent much of his childhood was in the West Ward, where black families were interspersed among Italian and Irish Americans. Jones was an unusually gifted student from an early age, and his high grades encouraged his parents' vision of continuing upward mobility. With his younger sister Elaine, he attended Sunday school at the status-conscious Bethany Baptist Church and local cotillions at which "brown and yellow ladies" were "presented to society."[14]

At Howard University in the early 1950s, however, Jones's progress faltered. Though he enrolled with ambitions to become a minister or doctor, Jones quickly tired of the careerist ethos and social pretensions of the self-declared "Capstone of Negro Education." Alain Locke had retired, E. Franklin Frazier was on leave, and only Nathan Scott's classes on Dante and Sterling Brown's unofficial sessions on the history of black music relieved the tedium. Perplexed and bored by his science classes, Jones fell behind. In 1954, after two years at Howard, he dropped out. In an effort to salvage something from his family's deflated expectations, Jones enlisted in the U.S. Air Force and spent an even unhappier period as a weatherman and air gunner in Puerto Rico before his discharge in February 1957. Yet it was also at Howard and in the air force that Jones began to immerse himself in literature and to cultivate a poetic melancholy ("the isolation, the aloneness, sometimes it was almost sweet," he would remember) in his retreat from aspirations to the respectable professions. After his first year at Howard, Jones began to spell his name "LeRoi," offering the explanation that his father's name, Coyette, was French. Poring over Eliot, Joyce, Hemingway, and Dostoevsky, Jones found in literature a sense of freedom and a possibility of self-reinvention.[15]

New York, and specifically its avant-garde cultural hot spot, Greenwich Village, seemed the most fitting place for Jones to inscribe his new identity, and his earliest writings are suffused with a belief in the transcendent potential of art. "MY POETRY is whatever I think I am," he wrote in a short essay of 1959. "(Can I be light and weightless as a sail?? Heavy & clunking like 8 black boots). I CAN BE ANYTHING I CAN." He had answered an advertisement in the *New York Times* to work at the Gotham Book Mart on Forty-Seventh Street, and began there on $50 per week. His menial responsibilities bored and irritated him, and he soon quit. Huddled over books in his chilly apartment on East Third Street, he thought of becoming a painter or a writer. But the need to pay his rent led him to a job as a clerk at a jazz journal, the *Record Changer,* where his knowledge of the music impressed his employers. It was there that he encountered a young secretary, Hettie Cohen, a Jewish woman reveling in her own freedom from her family in Queens. As she recalls in her memoir, she and the shy clerk quickly began dating. Within a year, she had fallen pregnant. "I guess we'll have to get married then," he responded, which they did, at a Buddhist temple on Ninety-Fifth Street in October 1958 (to which her father's response was "Get a divorce!"). While the Village was comparatively hospitable to such relationships, it bordered more hostile neighborhoods where signs of interracial intimacy could provoke physical attacks. The "stares from people on the street" that Baraka recalls and the "tension that rose in my own self in certain situations" resonate with the mood captured by James Baldwin's novel of interracial romance in New York, *Another Country* (1962).[16]

By the time his first collection of poems appeared in 1961 as *Preface to a Twenty Volume Suicide Note. . . . ,* Jones's bid to reinvent himself beyond the confines of the black middle class seemed assured. Finding his bearings amid the Village's poetry readings and literary hangouts, Jones had impressed Allen Ginsberg as a precocious talent and, with Ginsberg's help, entered the Beats' inner social and artistic circle. Together with Hettie, Jones took the bold step of publishing a new magazine, *Yugen,* which soon numbered Ginsberg, Kerouac, Gregory Corso, Robert Creeley, and Diane di Prima among its contributors. Yet by the turn of the 1960s, as a new wave of student protests reanimated the civil rights movement and reenergized America's political culture, Jones's belief that art would allow him to "BE ANYTHING I CAN" was already subsiding. Increasingly, he viewed the notion of artistic transcendence that had first attracted him to the Beats as a self-indulgent evasion of the political. His poetry of the early 1960s mocked the Beats' "God of Ego . . . God of Alone / in the penthouse smoking and drinking while some folks fall dead / in the street," and parodied himself as "die schwartze Bohemien" crying out "Man lookatthatblonde."[17]

An invitation to tour revolutionary Cuba in 1960 proved a turning point in Jones's attitude toward New York's downtown avant-garde. In "Cuba Libre," an essay that appeared in the Beat-oriented *Evergreen Review* and won the Longview Award for journalism, Jones chastised his friends in the Village for the "knowing cynicism" with which they had responded to his decision to visit Cuba. Anticipating later critics who labeled the Beats as "nonpolitical rebels," Jones responded fiercely to the poet Gilbert Sorrentino's purported remark that "guys in uniforms" were not to be trusted. The Beats' "so-called rebellion against what is most crass and ugly in our society," Jones contended, was devoid of "any kind of direction or purpose." Their self-conscious nonconformity merely reproduced America's "social degeneracy" and "moral disintegration" in new forms. Ascending the Sierra Maestra to witness the celebrations marking the first anniversary of Fidel Castro's revolution, Jones was impressed by militia detachments "marching, route step" with their rifles, and by the "unbelievable joy and excitement" of the crowd.[18]

Back in New York, Jones resolved no longer to be counted among those "who grow beards and will not participate in politics." He joined the Fair Play for Cuba Committee and the protests over the assassination of the Congolese leader Patrice Lumumba early in 1961. A few months later, Jones established a political group of his own, named An Organization of Young Men (OYM). Its one accessible document—an appeal to "young American Negro men"—demonstrates Jones's radicalizing stance on racial politics as well as his continuing hostility toward the black middle class. Ridiculing "the NAACP, URBAN LEAGUE, and like organizations" as "gigantic factories for the manufacture of handkerchiefs to put on our heads," Jones called for "some kind of organized militancy" to challenge black people's "continual servitude" and affirm their "brotherhood" with the "newly independent peoples of Asia and Latin America." What form of militancy Jones envisaged was unclear, but a sense of the OYM's character can be discerned from his later remark that most of the group's members—who included the jazz musicians Archie Shepp and Walter Bowe, the poet and music critic A. B. Spellman, the journalist Calvin Hicks, and the veteran commentator Harold Cruse—were young black men with "white wives or lovers," and that they "talked vaguely about going 'uptown' to work."[19]

"Uptown" was acquiring a new prominence in Jones's writings during the early 1960s. In a letter published in *Partisan Review* in 1958, he had dubbed Harlem "the veritable capital city of the Black Bourgeoisie," a bastion of the same American philistinism from which "bohemians" of all races sought refuge. His letter was provoked by Norman Podhoretz's essay "The Know-Nothing Bohemians," an attack on the Beat writers that Jones rebuffed as an "ill-considered rant." Jones took particular exception to Podhoretz's claim that "Bohemianism, after all, is for the Negro a means of entry into the world of the whites, and no Negro bohemian is going to cooperate in the attempt to identify him with Harlem or Dixieland." The "flight from Harlem," Jones retorted, was a flight not "from color" but from the vapidity of bourgeois America. Indeed, his hostility toward the black middle class reflected not only his self-conscious bohemianism, but also his reverence for E. Franklin Frazier's sociological study *Black Bourgeoisie,* published the previous year. Hettie would recall that in one of their earliest conversations Jones had mentioned Frazier's book approvingly and pronounced that "The Negro middle class is a bunch of imitation ofays." Memories of Newark cotillions could not have been far from Jones's mind as he

read of the black middle class's "society" of "make-believe" and its attempt to refashion itself "in the image of the white man."[20]

However, a sequence of short pieces written in 1962 and first published in his collection *Home* saw Jones adopt a radically different
stance by intimating a strong sense of identification with Harlem. In
"City of Harlem," the neighborhood was no longer dismissed as the
"capital of the Black Bourgeoisie," but heeded as "in a very real sense"
the "capital of Black America." Remarking on the multilayered and
contradictory "mythology of Harlem," a place widely depicted as both
the "pleasure-happy center of the universe" and a quagmire of "every human vice" and misery, Jones assumed the authority to describe Harlem
"as it is, as it exists for its people, as an actual place where actual humans
live":

> People line the streets in summer—on the corners or hanging out
> the windows—or head for other streets in winter. . . . Young girls,
> doctors, pimps, detectives, preachers, drummers, accountants, gam-
> blers, labor organizers, postmen, wives, Muslims, junkies, the em-
> ployed, and the unemployed: all going someplace—an endless stream
> of Americans, whose singularity is that they are black and can never
> honestly enter into the lunatic asylum of white America.

Yet Jones's grounds for identification with Harlem, in this essay, seemed
as much bohemian as black. Effacing the gulf between Harlem and the
Village that his letter to Podhoretz had implied, Harlem became "a
community of nonconformists, since any black American, simply by
virtue of his blackness, is weird, a nonconformist in this society."[21]

"Soul Food" burnished his insider credentials in snappy prose exult-
ing Harlem's earthy culinary delights: "Maws are things ofays seldom
get to peck, nor are you likely ever to hear about Charlie eating a chit-
terling." By contrast, "Cold, Hurt, and Sorrow (Streets of Despair)"
evokes earlier essays by James Baldwin and Ralph Ellison, who had
plumbed the depths of Harlem's misery in short pieces crammed with
personal observation. Here, Jones located himself "walking along
among the ruined shacks and lives of the worst Harlem slum" and recounted the bitter "ghetto facts" of destitution and anguish, "waste

products" of a dream of Harlem as "the black man's twentieth century 'Jordan.'" Not unlike Kenneth Clark in *Dark Ghetto,* Jones portrayed a community reduced to acts of escapism and self-delusion:

> You can stand in doorways late nights and hit people in the head. You can go to church Saturday nights and Sundays and three or four times during the week. You can stick a needle in your arm four or five times a day and bolster the economy. You can buy charms and herbs and roots, or wear your hat backwards to keep things from getting worse. You can drink till screaming is not loud enough, and the coldest night is alright to sleep outside in.

Where Jones had formerly invoked bohemianism to legitimate his indifference toward "bourgeois" Harlem, he now brandished Harlem's "Streets of Despair" to make plain the inadequacy of the Beats' shallow rebellion. White friends, he told an interviewer, were urging him not to "get involved in politics" but to "stick to poetry," and yet "I'm black. I have to be involved." In "Street Protest," another essay of 1962, Jones flaunted his familiarity with Harlem's black nationalist landmarks and icons, such as Lewis Michaux's Bookstore (the "House of Proper Propaganda"), the soapbox orators outside the Hotel Theresa, and the neighborhood's various "social prophets," including the Nation of Islam's Harlem minister, Malcolm X.[22]

In his essays of the early 1960s, Jones was an acerbic critic of the philosophy and strategy of "moderate" civil rights leaders and their liberal allies. Organizations such as the NAACP were "completely out of touch with the great masses of blacks," he alleged, and he ridiculed as "tokenism" the granting of "meager privilege to some few 'selected' Negroes" to create the illusion of progress. Nor did integrated bus terminals in Alabama "help reduce the 25 percent unemployment figure that besets Negroes in Harlem." "Integration" was becoming a dirty word in Jones's lexicon, while "nationalism," which he associated with the Cuban Revolution and defined as "acting in one's own best interests," became central to his increasingly polarized racial rhetoric. "The black man has been separated and made to live in his own country of color," he wrote in 1962. "If you are black the only roads into the mainland of American life are through subservience, cowardice, and loss of manhood. Those are the white man's roads. It is time we built our own."[23]

The following year Jones extended this racial analysis in *Blues People: Negro Music in White America*. A deeply researched book examining "the sociological significance of the changes in Negro music" through emancipation, segregation, and urbanization, *Blues People* was instantly hailed by Langston Hughes and the jazz critic Nat Hentoff and remains perhaps the most celebrated of all his writings. For Ralph Ellison, however, Jones had reduced jazz to a "hermetic expression of Negro sensibility" that obscured the "intricate network of connections which binds Negroes to the larger society." Jones indeed perceived the blues and jazz as emanating "from the depths of the black man's soul" and as manifesting an ethic of resistance, on the part of "the 'lowest classes' of Negroes," to "the constant and willful dilutions of the black middle class and the persistent calls to oblivion made by the mainstream society." A lingering bohemian sensibility was evident in his distaste for the "mainstream" and "mainland of American life," and Beat writers such as Kerouac had also valorized jazz musicians as archetypal nonconformists. Yet *Blues People* attests clearly to Jones's incipient black nationalism in its straining to define the boundaries of authentic black expression and in its concluding warning that many "poor blacks" and "young Negro intellectuals" were losing patience with "the American system," to the advantage of "groups such as the Black Muslims."[24]

"The Screamers" (1963), a short story also concerning black music, provides further insight into both the continuities and ruptures attending Jones's embrace of black nationalism. In common with Beat writers such as Kerouac, who styled himself as "a jazz poet / blowing long blues in an afternoon jam / session on Sunday," Jones looked to the spontaneity of jazz improvisation as a model for the "kinetic" verse envisioned by Charles Olson, which would liberate poetry from the page and transmit "energy" directly from performer to audience. Yet it was Jones, more than any of his contemporaries, who invested the energy of black musical performance—and poetic performance—with an avowedly political charge. The narrator in "The Screamers" recounts how, one Sunday evening in a Newark dance hall, the turbaned saxophonist

Lynn Hope had unleashed a "screamed riff" so potent that it incited his audience "to destroy the ghetto." Hope was "trying to move us," and eventually "five or six hundred hopped-up woogies" burst out onto Belmont Avenue. The "Biggers" drew knives and razors as trucks unloaded police onto the scene.[25]

This vision of urban violence prefigured the poems and plays that would thrust Jones into the media spotlight in 1964, no less than it foreshadowed the wave of riots that began to break out across America's cities that year. Yet Jones was no Lynn Hope galvanizing black crowds in "the ghetto." Uptown excursions and militant polemics notwithstanding, Jones was painfully cognizant that he remained separated from the "great masses of blacks" by his middle-class upbringing, privileged education, and literary career, and by his interracial household in cosmopolitan Greenwich Village. His identity as "die schwartze Bohemien" became a subject of mounting anxiety. A poem Jones had written in Cuba, dedicated to a young revolutionary who had derided him as a cowardly aesthete, transmuted his own political passivity into graphic images of impotence, while the starkly gendered rhetoric of the Organization of Young Men suggests a compensatory bid to assert his masculinity.[26]

A self-incriminating conflation of aestheticism, compromised masculinity, and racial apostasy pervades *The System of Dante's Hell* (1965), a long prose poem that Jones worked on throughout the early 1960s. Its final section, as he would later hint, draws on his own experiences in Shreveport, Louisiana, while absent without leave from the air force, to demonstrate that "heresy, against one's own sources" is "the basest evil." The protagonist, "Roi," is a precocious black aesthete versed in "Thomas, Joyce, Eliot, Pound," who keeps "making the queer scene" during weekend excursions from his air base. Finding himself on one occasion in "the Bottom," a poor, black section of Shreveport, Roi encounters "Peaches," a homely female prostitute who undertakes to bring this "lousy fag" to his senses. Roi pleads with her to respect his "pure white soul" and his "mind, here where there is only steel." Eventually, Peaches coaxes Roi to her bed, and he rediscovers a "real world of flesh, of smells, of soft black harmonies and color." Yet he loses his nerve and flees back to his base and his "reading," unable to recognize the "Hell" of the Bottom as his only salvation.[27]

Literary scholars concerned with Jones's work have, almost without exception, treated the theme of homosexuality in *The System of Dante's Hell* and in *The Toilet*—a play written in 1961 and first staged in 1964— as wholly symbolic, a signifier of self-gratifying aestheticism that adds an insinuation of racial disloyalty to the familiar trope of bookish effeminacy. There is evidence, however, to suggest that homosexuality was more than a literary motif for Jones. His autobiography refers to a "high-powered New York City homosexual scene in the arts" that included many of his closest friends of the period, such as fellow poets Ginsberg, Peter Orlovsky (Ginsberg's lover), and Frank O'Hara. Hettie claims that her husband "once confessed to me some homosexual feelings, though never any specific experiences." The poet Diane di Prima, with whom Jones had begun an affair in 1960 that resulted in the birth of a daughter a year or so later, "assumed" that his other partners included "both men and women" and would recall that O'Hara had made advances toward him. And in a letter to Ginsberg in September 1963, Orlovsky wrote, conceivably referring to Jones: "I hope Leroy is happy and alright. Sorry I didn't make love to him when he wanted me to." Homosexuality or bisexuality may, then, have seemed to Jones a literal aspect of his "heresy" rather than merely a literary device for its representation.[28]

Jones had arrived at his own notion of a crisis of the black intellectual. Fearing that his literary aspirations had severed his connections with any black community, Jones verged on positing an incontrovertible opposition between "black" and "intellectual," captured in the disjuncture between Roi's "mind" and the "steel" reality of the Bottom. As Ross Posnock has noted, *The System of Dante's Hell* constitutes "the intellectual" as "a category that violates black manhood" and effectively renders "black intellectual" an "oxymoron." In the works that fashioned Jones's public persona in "the Jones Year," violence would figure as the means by which the black intellectual might atone for heresies and return to racial sources. The menacing images of black retribution and guerrilla warfare that pervade his poetry and drama of

1964 tapped the swelling public anxiety over black urban violence to affirm their author's newfound militancy and animosity toward whites. Yet his words could scarcely bridge the chasm he envisioned between art and reality, and between himself and black communities. Instead, they offered predominantly white audiences a vicarious journey into a phantasm of black urban fury, and into the psyche of a black intellectual tearing himself apart.[29]

The Dead Lecturer, Jones's second collection of poetry, resounds with the contradictions of his limbo between interracial bohemia and the black "country of color." The poem "SHORT SPEECH TO MY FRIENDS" promises "a political art" worthy of Lynn Hope, and grimly intones: "Let the combination of morality / and inhumanity / begin." Yet Jones's scream is directed not toward a "ghetto" audience, but toward the white "FRIENDS" he professes to abjure "after so many years of trying to enter their kingdoms." In "BLACK DADA NIHIL-ISMUS," Jones does ostensibly address a black audience as he summons a predatory, hypermasculine black force to "rape the white girls. Rape / their fathers. Cut the mothers' throats." Again, however, the poet's insistence that he will slip his bohemian moorings betrays a recognition that his real audience remains New York's downtown avant-garde:

> *Black dada nihilismus, choke my friends*
>
> *in their bedrooms with their drinks spilling*
> *and restless for tilting hips or dark liver*
> *lips sucking splinters from the master's thigh.*

Many of his white friends, according to Hettie's memoir, were indeed "upset and angry" about the poem.[30]

The specter of "BLACK DADA NIHILISMUS" was, to a significant extent, a product of Jones's familiarity with a Beat sensibility that frequently fetishized black sexuality and violence. In an essay published in 1965, Jones would attribute to Kerouac and other "beatniks" a reverence for the "virtuous, mysterious, sensual black" who embodied experiences alien to the "white man." The same essay made reference to Norman Mailer's "The White Negro" (1957), which had explored the appeal of black "psychopathy"—"perversion, promiscuity, pimpery, drug addiction, rape, razor-slash, bottle-break, what-have-you"—to bohemians recoiling against social conformity. If Frantz Fanon's advocacy of "violence" against the oppressor as a "cleansing force" reverberated in Jones's invocation of "murder, the cleansed / purpose," nevertheless the transgressive primitivism of "BLACK DADA NIHILISMUS" manifests Jones's continuing reliance on an essentially bohemian conception of black life. Attempting to "choke" his "friends" on their own visions of black deviancy, Jones was in fact as likely to titillate as to terrify them.[31]

Dutchman, the play that raised Jones's profile as an artist and racial firebrand more than any other work, extends his "SPEECH TO MY FRIENDS" into dramatic form. As he grudgingly conceded, the audience at the Cherry Lane Theater in Greenwich Village, where the play opened on March 24, 1964, "would have to be" predominantly white. Such was the appetite for *Dutchman*'s incendiary evocation of interracial sexuality and violence that the play's New York run was extended into 1965, before it toured several other U.S. cities and crossed to Europe. Set beneath New York City on a sweltering subway train, the play thrusts together "Clay," a twenty-year-old, black "would-be poet," and his white nemesis, the red-haired temptress "Lula." Demure and respectable in his suit and tie, Clay is intrigued by Lula's suggestion that they attend a party together. He is appalled, however, when she begs him to join in her imitation of a sensuous black dance: "Let's rub bellies on the train. The nasty. . . . Uhh! Clay!" When he resists, she chides him as a "dirty white man" and an "Uncle Tom," and finally provokes the furious tirade that furnishes the play's abiding images, as Clay threatens to rip Lula's "lousy breasts off." To murder her and the other white passengers, he screams, would be a "simple act" of "sanity." His Tom-ish, buttoned-up demeanor is merely the "device" that prevents him from such acts and masks the "pure heart, the pumping black heart" beneath his placid exterior.[32]

Quoting Clay's "verbal violence" at length, Michele Wallace in 1978 characterized *Dutchman* as the epitome of "Black Macho," the misogynistic nihilism she attributed to 1960s black nationalists. Yet there are intimations within the play that, even as he wrote *Dutchman,* Jones was beginning to acknowledge that his lurid "SPEECH TO MY FRIENDS" catered to white primitivist expectations far more than it met the requirements of a "political art." It is Clay's loss of nerve, his decision to "stay safe with my words, and no deaths," that allows Lula to stab him fatally in the chest. However, Clay is already Lula's victim at the very peak of his rhetorical rage, for his threatening words are virtually dictated by her goading. "You're a murderer, Clay, and you know it," she teases him. "Get up and scream at these people. Like scream meaningless shit in these hopeless faces." In 1990, in a discussion of Miles Davis's icy onstage persona of the late 1950s and 1960s, Stanley Crouch identified a "shift in audience taste that harked back to the popularity of the glowering, sullen, even contemptuous nineteenth-century minstrel characters known as Jasper Jack and Zip Coon, who sassed and sometimes assaulted the plantation white folks." *Dutchman* offers an inkling that Jones was alive to this shift in taste and to its danger for a black artist. Clay's outburst, prompted by Lula's urging, itself takes place on a stage, before an audience of passengers who finally collude in his murder by dragging away his body, and then settle back into their seats as Lula's next hapless victim, another *"young Negro,"* boards the train. Clay's audience first imbibes his violent rhetoric, then consumes Clay himself, and yet remains hungry for more.[33]

There is no small irony, then, in the enthusiasm with which white audiences and commentators greeted the play. *Dutchman* received the *Village Voice*'s prestigious Obie Award for best off-Broadway production and was hailed by Norman Mailer as "the best play in America." Howard Taubman, the theater critic for the *New York Times,* called Jones a "promising, unsettling talent," and ventured: "If this is the way the Negroes really feel about the white world around them there is more rancor buried in the breasts of colored conformists than any one can imagine." The previous year, *Time* magazine had identified James Baldwin as the preeminent interpreter of the "dark realities of racial ferment in North and South." Yet as the violent conflagrations predicted in Baldwin's *The Fire Next Time* (1963) came to pass, it was Jones who was increasingly in demand for his unbridled expressions of rage. "I got offers to write for the *Herald Tribune* and the *New York Times,*" he would recall, and his "phone leaped with people calling for interviews." In 1965, *Playboy* magazine labeled Jones "the most discussed—and admired—Negro writer since James Baldwin."[34]

He approached his role as a "spokesman" by delivering bellicose, Clay-like performances of his own. In June 1964, discussing New York's mounting racial tensions on a panel alongside Kenneth Clark and the theologian Reinhold Niebuhr, Jones advised black youths who had been smashing windows on subway trains to "do it every night." In an article for the *Sunday Herald Tribune Magazine,* Jones again indulged in a vision of rebellion that owed as much to his bohemian, aesthetic idealization of nonconformity as to the racial politics of the moment:

> One way Negroes could force this institutionalized dishonesty to crumble and its apologizers to break and run even faster than they are now would be to turn crazy, to bring out a little American dada, Ornette Coleman style, and chase these perverts into the ocean, where they belong. Say, if Negroes just stopped behaving, stopped being what Charles desires, and just flip, go raving in the streets, screaming in verse an honest history of America, walk off their jobs—as they should have done in Birmingham after those children were murdered—and watch the country grind to a halt, the owners cracking their knuckles as they got out their gold guns and got ready to blow out their own legendary brains. It is a good, and practical, idea. Why don't you try it, Negroes?

When Harlemites did take to the streets during the riot of July 1964, Jones was out of town, teaching summer courses in literature at the State University of New York in Buffalo. Though he remembers rushing excitedly home and "getting a .45 automatic from where I had stashed it," his autobiography gives no account of his actions during the period of the riot, and Hettie claims that he quickly flew back to Buffalo "to teach his four days a week."[35]

The rioting did, however, spur Jones to project himself imaginatively into the scenario of an all-out urban race war. In *The Slave,* which opened at St. Mark's Playhouse in the East Village in December

1964, "Walker Vessels" has forsaken his apprenticeship in the "white" world of letters to assume command of black guerrilla forces. Venturing behind enemy lines, Walker steals into the apartment where he had once lived with "Grace," his white former wife, and their two daughters. Finding Grace in the company of "Easley," the "white liberal" professor who had been Walker's literary mentor and is now Grace's husband, Walker announces that he has come to reclaim his children. Meanwhile, he avails himself of the opportunity to shout and strut, and derides the "faggot professor" for his "high aesthetic disapproval of the political." As the guerrillas advance and shells rain down on the neighborhood, Walker threatens to rape Grace, and then shoots Easley dead. Finally, Grace is killed by an explosion. Walker flees the house and the curtain descends to the sound of the children's dying screams.[36]

Walker would appear, then, to be redeemed from the intellectual's heresy of alienation through his violent reaffirmation of the bond of race. Yet it was Grace, the audience learns, who had ended their marriage when he took up his "misdirected cause," whereas Walker continues to believe that she "could have stayed" with him. In an interview in 1966, Jones offered the following explanation of the play's title:

> [Walker] is still a slave in the sense that he's supposed to be leading this army, yet he's spending his time talking to the white man. That's why I called it *The Slave:* he had no business being there in the first place; he was supposed to be with his own people. . . . If he was really free, the only sound that professor would have heard is cannon-fire. Vessels has no real reason for being there. But at the time, writing the play was my way of getting through to that truth myself. You see, I had to get the truth out of myself to be able to see it.

Like Jones's other works of 1964, *The Slave* reveals its author's efforts to comprehend his own placelessness and paralysis. Why was Jones himself "spending his time talking to the white man"? Bitter words leveled at white audiences only underscored his dependence on them—his *enslavement* by them, as he came to regard it. Jones also showed Walker to be a slave to his oppressors' bankrupt morality, as the rebel leader eschews any ideology other than that which "the Western ofay" held "while he was ruling." Walker's newfound indifference toward "love or beauty" stands condemned by an essay of 1964 in which Jones appealed for plays that would not only make whites "cower," but would "take dreams and give them reality" by "preaching virtue and feeling" to black people.[37]

Far from comprising unambiguous assertions of "Black Macho," the poems and plays of "the Jones Year" deploy concurrent and contradictory modes of address. They are simultaneously vehicles for an enraged politics of accusation and insult and for an implicitly self-incriminating commentary on such politics. *The Dead Lecturer, Dutchman,* and *The Slave* have continued to rank among Jones's most renowned works, and no other single year rivals his output of 1964 either in quantity or in the degree of attention it garnered. These texts must be understood, however, not as representative of Jones's black nationalism, but rather as products of the transitional moment of his disengagement from bohemia, lines from a "SPEECH TO MY FRIENDS" that, as even the author recognized, could only be "SHORT."

Speaking to Black People

Hettie regarded *The Slave* as "Roi's nightmare," and he later recalled that it was "so close to our real lives." The play's producer, Leo Garen, had even asked Hettie for photographs of the Joneses' daughters to adorn the set, though she angrily refused. Meanwhile, commentators and reviewers were growing suspicious of the incongruence between Jones's militant posture and the realities of his lifestyle, and about his apparent indifference to any constructive approach to the racial crisis. In *Dissent,* Stanley Kauffmann situated Jones within a "Tradition of the Fake," as a writer who "preaches violence" against society "while he lives and works cozily within that society and profits by the continuance of the status quo." Kauffmann had lost patience with liberal indulgence of Jones, and deplored the Christian pacifist A. J. Muste's remark that Jones's "basic view of America's role in the world today should be seriously considered." After sitting through *The Slave,* George Dennison similarly "fancied that I heard an opportunistic playwright exploiting my own dilemmas for the sake of his career." Jones's interracial marriage was frequently cited as proof of his hypocrisy, and he later remembered seeing "a magazine satire about me as a great white-hating militant finishing one of my diatribes and then going back to the dutiful white wife."[38]

"I should not be speaking here," Jones admitted to another Village audience in yet another barbed discussion of racial discord early in February 1965. "I should be speaking to black people." Plans to relocate much of his work to Harlem were already under way, as Jones and a few associates had leased a brownstone on West 130th Street with the intention of opening an arts center. According to his autobiography, it was the assassination of Malcolm X on February 21 that "stunned" Jones into leaving the Village, and his family, within "a few days." Yet Hettie claims that throughout the spring of 1965 he continued to visit the apartment at 27 Cooper Square where they had lived with their children since 1962, "to read his mail, change his clothes, and make sorrowful love, comparing his situation to that of Jomo Kenyatta, who'd left an English wife to lead the Kenyan people." However fitfully he left the Village, he had divorced Hettie by the end of 1965, and it was now Harlem that he called *"Home."* Signing off on his first collection of essays that year, Jones promised that by the time it appeared in print, "I will be even blacker."[39]

West 130th Street opened its doors that summer as the Black Arts Repertory Theatre/School (BARTS), with Jones as its founding director. Immediately, it prompted an influx of radical black artists to Harlem from downtown and much farther afield. Poets including Larry Neal, Ishmael Reed, Calvin Hernton, David Henderson, and Ronald Snellings (later known as Askia Muhammad Touré) were joined by actors such as Yusef Iman and leading avant-garde jazz musicians including Albert Ayler, Archie Shepp, and Sun Ra. Though short-lived, BARTS provided one of the vital institutional models that inspired the growth of a nationalist "black arts movement" during the late 1960s in cities across the United States. Moreover, a year before Stokely Carmichael popularized the slogan "black power" and Huey Newton and Bobby Seale founded the Black Panther Party in Oakland, Jones was formulating a nationalist vision for Harlem that anticipated many aspects of the black power movement that flourished in the late 1960s primarily among young, urban African Americans.[40]

In particular, Jones insisted that the perennial black nationalist demand for "land" must now dispense with Garveyite notions of a "return" to Africa or the Nation of Islam's vague allusions to a separate homeland "either on this continent or elsewhere." A year before the Detroit auto-worker James Boggs and his wife, Grace Lee Boggs, published their classic essay, "The City Is the Black Man's Land" (1966), Jones wrote that there were "Black cities all over this white nation," and that "the Black Man" must claim "the ground upon which he stands." Indeed, "as director" of BARTS, Jones issued "a call for a Black Nation. In Harlem, where 600,000 Black People reside." The underlying perception—that black Americans were becoming a predominantly urban people, and that urban America looked set to become predominantly black—would be the basis of the movement to establish "black power" through black self-determination in America's cities.[41]

As Larry Neal later recalled, Harlem's plethora of "indigenous" black nationalists, such as Eddie "Pork Chop" Davis and the African Nationalist Pioneer Movement, considered the arrival of BARTS "an invasion." Indeed, as much as the company of his fellow black artists energized and inspired Jones, a feeling of acceptance and belonging in Harlem proved more elusive than he had perhaps anticipated. "Words," a prose fragment dated "Harlem, 1965," which was later included in a collection of his fictional writings, begins:

> Now that the old world has crashed around me, and it's raining in early summer. I live in Harlem with a baby shrew and suffer for my decadence which kept me away so long. When I walk the streets, the streets don't yet claim me, and people look at me, knowing the strangeness of my manner, and the objective stance from which I attempt to "love" them. . . . Last night in a bar a plump black girl sd, "O.K., be intellectual, go write some more of them jivey books."

Within the emerging black arts movement, Jones was far from alone in seeking a literal or metaphorical return "home" to the black community. The poet David Llorens felt compelled to atone for years spent "cringing" at his black "brothers," and Haki Madhubuti (Don L. Lee) for his "early escape / period, trying to be white." In the black nationalist magazine *Liberator,* Neal contended that "America infects Black intellectuals often with a peculiar kind of estrangement" that "makes reconciliation between the community and her 'intellectuals' a difficult affair."[42]

Notwithstanding the burst of creativity, performance, publication, and institution building that earned the black arts movement its reputation as a "Second Renaissance" in African American letters, suspicion of black artists and intellectuals persisted, and even increased, as the black power movement coalesced during the late 1960s. Every significant black power organization employed poetry, music, and visual art as propaganda. Yet disagreement over the extent of art's revolutionary utility became a focal point of tension between competing groups. Some movement leaders charged that art and theorizing might retard, rather than inspire, revolutionary action. Less than two weeks after raising the "black power" slogan in Mississippi in June 1966, Stokely Carmichael warned: "We have to say, 'Don't play jive and start writing poems after Malcolm is shot.' We have to move from the point where the man left off and stop writing poems." H. Rap Brown, of the Student Nonviolent Coordinating Committee (SNCC) and the Black Panthers, denounced those "intellectuals" who "talk the most and when it comes time for action, they won't shut up," and who "just discovered they were black, because they were working so hard all their lives to be white." Indeed, radical black artists such as Jones and Neal conceived of the black arts movement partly as an antidote to their own "estrangement" and political irrelevance. Neal famously defined "Black Art" as "the aesthetic and spiritual sister of the Black Power concept," a vital means by which black people could "define the world in their own terms." Anticipating the thrust of Harold Cruse's *The Crisis of the Negro Intellectual* (1967), Jones claimed in 1965 that the "Black artist" was "desperately needed to change the images his people identify with," and that it fell to the "Black intellectual" to "change the interpretation of facts toward the Black man's best interest." Yet the revolutionary credentials of black artists and intellectuals would not be as readily acknowledged within the black power movement as Jones and Neal hoped.[43]

Accordingly, a defensive, self-justifying tone permeates much of the black arts movement's discourse. Neal devoted the opening sentence of his renowned manifesto to an assurance that "the Black Arts Movement is radically opposed to any concept of the artist that alienates him from the community," while the playwright Ed Bullins sought to distinguish "Black Drama" from the "effete, white bourgeois" avant-garde. Philip Brian Harper has persuasively identified the "masculine anxiety" that underlay radical black artists' straining for recognition of their militancy and Gramscian "*organic* connection to the life of the folk." So entrenched was the association of political assertion with "manhood" in the United States (not to mention the association of an artistic sensibility with effeminacy) that, as Harper points out, even female black nationalist poets such as Nikki Giovanni invoked the "phallic standard of political engagement." While in Jones's case, his own possible bisexuality may have served as an additional, complicating factor, the preoccupation of much of black arts literature with what Neal called "legitimate manhood" suggests that "masculine anxiety" was indeed a component of the sense of "crisis" that prompted many radical black artists and intellectuals to reaffirm their identification with "black America."[44]

As important as this identification with the black community was to the radicals' sense of racial and political legitimacy, their claim to a unique revolutionary utility as artists and intellectuals rested, somewhat contradictorily, on their assumptions about what differentiated them from other African Americans. "Many Black People," Jones contended, had been denuded of their blackness by the "white magic" of the "Mass Media." For this reason, the black artist was "desperately needed to change the images his people identify with, by asserting Black feeling, Black mind, Black judgment." The black arts movement defined its purpose, as a revolutionary vanguard, as being not merely to energize or incite the people, but to transform them in its own (newly minted) "Black" image. There was "a definite need for a cultural revolution in the Black community," Neal insisted. The real task confronting black artists, according to the critic Addison Gayle Jr., was "the de-Americanization of black people." The value of black art was to be assessed "in terms of the transformation from ugliness to beauty that the work of art demands from its audience," so that the question the critic must answer was: "How far has the work gone in transforming an American Negro into an African-American or black man?"[45]

More than sixty years earlier, W. E. B. Du Bois had called upon a black "Talented Tenth" to act as "leaders of thought and missionaries of culture among their people." The "Negro race," Du Bois believed, could only be "saved by its exceptional men." To a striking extent, radical black artists of the 1960s grounded their claims to revolutionary leadership in a notion of themselves as "missionaries of culture" who were uniquely qualified, to quote Du Bois again, to "elevat[e] the mass" and "uplift" the people. Claiming for themselves as artists the role traditionally assigned by uplift ideology to the "better class" of African Americans, the principal figures of the black arts movement were similarly intent on remaking "the mass" in their own image. The leadership of BARTS, Jones explained, was inviting the people of Harlem "to help us to help themselves." Their purpose was to "restor[e] cultural understanding to the American black man" and to "project images of black power, to move, delight, and instruct black people."[46]

The tensions and contradictions that characterized the black arts movement's relationship to "the people" have not gone undetected. Jerry Watts, in a fiercely critical study of Jones/Baraka, has addressed the implausibility of black artists' self-appointed status as paragons of blackness. "On what grounds," he asks, "could the post-bohemian Roi and his followers tell the sisters in a Lexington Avenue beauty parlor that by straightening their hair, they had become instruments of white domination?" The literary historian James Smethurst considers Jones, Neal, and other participants in BARTS to have been the progenitors of the black arts movement's self-conception as a "populist avant-garde." This "paradoxical" formulation, as Smethurst explains, signals both the movement's iconoclastic literary experimentalism and its insistence upon its "roots" in the existing "popular culture" of the black community. Overlooked in these accounts, however, are the black arts movement's complex appropriation of racial uplift ideology and the ways in which radical black artists' relationship to "the people" was shaped by their self-image as a racial vanguard akin to Du Bois's "Talented Tenth." The paradox of the black arts movement might, indeed, be restated as the incongruence between the artists' wish to be considered *of* the people and their simultaneous efforts to *transform* the people in their own image.[47]

As a "School for the Harlem Community" that aimed to "help" black people "to help themselves," BARTS also embodied what Gaines describes as the uplift tradition's "ethos of service to the masses." Eventually, Jones would admit that the organization's brief existence was marred by hubris, incompetence, and vacillation on his own part. And yet, given that only a few months earlier his most "constructive" advice to black youth had been to vandalize subway trains, the theater/school in Harlem did mark a new stage in Jones's deepening engagement with black urban communities. Though he continued to declaim his "violent uncontainable hatred for the white man," Jones no longer regarded black urban life merely as a phantasm with which to disturb white audiences. Indeed, he was backing away from his role as an interpreter of black rage to white America. He now called on the "Black Artist" to "draw out of his soul the correct image of the world" and to show black people both their "weakness" and "their own strength."[48]

Previous accounts of BARTS have focused on the program of artistic performances that Jones hoped would radicalize the local population, while the organization's role as a "School for the Harlem Community" had scarcely been acknowledged. Watts faults Jones for relying on avant-garde jazz performances and street-corner drama to reach out to Harlem's residents when black people "needed jobs and housing," "better schools and less police brutality." However, a letter that Jones and his colleagues addressed to prospective "Friends" of BARTS, prior to its opening in the spring of 1965, stated that the theater/school would "serve the community" through "programs of remedial education." Promotional literature written by Jones reiterated that "the school will not only teach black arts but mathematics and reading and writing, as remedial courses," as well as "practical job training: e.g., clerical skills and key punch and digital computer operation." The school's general education program, meanwhile, featured such notable instructors as Harold Cruse (black history), Jones and A. B. Spellman (poetry), Felrath Hines and Vincent Smith (visual arts), and Sun Ra and Marion

Brown (music), with fees set at $1.50 per lesson for adults and 75 cents for children.[49]

During the roundtable discussion with Kenneth Clark the previous year, Jones had appeared uninterested in the plan by Harlem Youth Opportunities Unlimited (HARYOU) to engage with youth in Harlem. Now, emphasizing his own organization's "Children's Education Program" and "Youth Program," Jones applied to HARYOU and the Associated Community Teams (ACT) for support and secured $40,000 to help finance these initiatives. The contradictions inherent in the use of federal antipoverty money to fund a black nationalist institution quickly became evident, however. While the Economic Opportunity Act's insistence on "maximum feasible participation" of poor residents had encouraged Clark to believe that federal and local authorities would support the empowerment of Harlem's poor, he soon learned that those who had wrested control of HARYOU-ACT intended little more than riot prevention. The proposal from BARTS to take Harlem's youth off the streets at the height of summer and involve them in educational and artistic programs appealed, unsurprisingly, to city authorities and antipoverty bureaucrats. Indeed, HARYOU-ACT was tasked in June 1965 with administering a last-minute antiriot program, Project Uplift, by disbursing funds to occupy Harlem's youth, and BARTS was one beneficiary.[50]

Public outcry ensued, however, once the press learned that federal funds were being used to stage "racist plays." Jones barred Sargent Shriver from entering West 130th Street when the director of the Office of Economic Opportunity paid a visit, and HARYOU-ACT support for BARTS was quickly terminated, though not quickly enough to prevent a major "public-relations disaster" for the federal War on Poverty. The theater/school had sustained its program through the summer of 1965, but the withdrawal of funding now triggered the organization's collapse. Cruse later claimed that BARTS's leadership had been challenged by a "nihilistic fringe" of "dangerously irrational" "oppositional elements." Indeed, Jones was obliged to print leaflets denying that BARTS had "trained a group of muggers and murderers to menace the people of Harlem." With the organization imploding, Jones quit Harlem by the end of 1965. On March 10, 1966, Neal was

shot in the leg near West 130th Street, and several of the remaining occupants were arrested in a raid on the building a few days later.[51]

Jones's attempt to marry separatist idealism with financial realpolitik
had engendered the curious spectacle of BARTS participating in a
thinly veiled government project to pacify Harlem. The organization's
leadership was not blind to the irony of this situation. In an unpublished verse, Jones's colleague Edward Spriggs ridiculed "haryou the
pimp," which furnished cultural "rags" to "cool summer / ghetto wars,"
but not "loincloths in the winter" for "summertime guerrillas." Despite its separatist formulation, Jones's vision of self-determination for
Harlem shared more with Clark's original blueprint for HARYOU as
a vehicle for community empowerment than with the diversionary
aims of Project Uplift. Whatever the effectiveness of BARTS's attempts at artistic outreach, remedial education, and job training, Jones's
activities in Harlem demonstrate that he had ceased to view black urban people simply as razor-slashing, primitivist abstractions and had
begun to regard them as part of a resurgent black nation.[52]

The art that Jones produced during BARTS's brief lifetime also attests to the impact of his relocation to a black community. *A Black
Mass,* a play written during 1965, which became one of his most popular black nationalist works, presents a striking contrast to his poetry
and drama of a year earlier. Loosely based around the Nation of Islam's
creation mythology, the play depicts the black race as humanity's original, uncorrupted form. The metaphysical equilibrium sustained by the
black magicians Tanzil and Nasafi is suddenly disturbed by the errant
sorcerer "Jacoub," who spawns a new organism. This "Beast" emerges
"vomiting horribly" and grunting "I White. White. White. White."
The incorporation of black female characters, absent from *Dutchman*
and *The Slave,* signals the change of audience entailed by Jones's relocation from the Village to Harlem. Moreover, Tanzil and Nasafi embody
a black masculinity comprising benevolence and wisdom. Instead of
threatening white audiences with sinister images of black rapists, Jones
now appealed to the black male conscience to guard the purity of black
womanhood against the predatory instincts of the white Beast, who
"leaps" at the women, "trying to throw open their robes." The orgias-
tic frenzy of "BLACK DADA NIHILISMUS" had given way to a

crusade of the righteous: "And so Brothers and Sisters, these beasts are still loose in the world. . . . Let us find them and slay them. Let us lock them in their caves. Let us declare the Holy War. The Jihad. Or we cannot deserve to live."[53]

Code of Morality

In the dying days of 1965, Jones was back where he had started, in Newark. Rejoining his parents' household at the age of thirty-one underlined how both his interracial family and his black nationalist organization had fallen apart. "I felt that I had failed in New York," he later recalled. "The last days of the Black Arts had thoroughly disgusted me." If he had hoped to leave his troubles across the Hudson River, he was quickly disappointed. Jones had brought his African American girlfriend, named only as Vashti in his autobiography, to his parents' home "as if she were my wife." Within weeks, however, an eighteen-year-old dancer, Olabumi Osafemi, arrived from Harlem, pregnant with Jones's child and refusing his pleas that she have an abortion. Vashti took her leave. Humiliated in front of his parents, Jones moved with Olabumi to a rundown hotel. "It was the world's worst place," he later remembered, a "flophouse, full of prostitutes, hustlers, petty thieves, and some recent Southern immigrants." He drank heavily and slid into an "unbearable" depression.[54]

In May 1966, having begun to make contact with black artists in Newark, Jones directed *A Black Mass* at the Proctor's Theatre. Olabumi was given a part, but Jones's roving eye settled on another performer, a twenty-three-year-old local actress named Sylvia Robinson. Theirs quickly became an intense relationship, and in August 1967, LeRoi and Sylvia would be married. In the meantime, however, a tragic event occurred that would cast a shadow over their union and plague Jones for years to come. Midway through 1966, while he and Sylvia were together at a party, Olabumi fell into a coma from which she and her unborn child never recovered. Her family held Jones responsible for her death.[55]

At this lowest ebb of his life, Jones resolved that his second marriage and his return to Newark would mark a new beginning. After the chaos of his relationships with Vashti and Olabumi, and with the collapse of BARTS still weighing on his mind, Jones seemed to crave discipline and guidance. Malcolm X's autobiography, rushed into print a few months after his assassination in 1965, emphasized the Nation of Islam's "power to reform black men's lives." A former pimp, drug dealer, womanizer, and hustler, Malcolm attributed his own "transformation" to the teachings of Elijah Muhammad, the Nation's "Messenger." Since his conversion, Malcolm had "never touched a woman" other than his wife. In 1966, Jones told *Muhammad Speaks* that the Nation was the "only" black organization "functioning for the betterment of black people." In another interview, he credited Elijah Muhammad's "moral teachings" with offering "the Black man a chance to regenerate himself."[56]

"Poor Roi," Hettie had written to a friend back in 1962 after one of her husband's many infidelities, "he should never be a cocksman because he's directly out of the Baptist tradition and suffers more guilt and shame than anyone I know." As Jones now contemplated his string of failed relationships and his separation from his three daughters, the Moynihan Report of 1965 had propelled "the deterioration of the Negro family" in "urban ghettos" to national attention. Though Moynihan charged the federal government with alleviating the "crushing burden on the Negro male," the appropriation of his report by conservative commentators prompted angry denunciations from civil rights leaders. Floyd McKissick of the Congress of Racial Equality protested that Moynihan "emphasizes negative aspects of the Negroes and then seems to say that it's the individual's fault when it's the damn system that really needs changing."[57]

Moynihan's indictment of black "matriarchy" would later prove as unpopular with black feminist authors as his perceived criticism of black males did among African Americans of diverse political persuasions at the time. Yet however much they disliked the Moynihan Report, few black commentators in the 1960s, whether integrationist or nationalist, doubted that strengthening patriarchal authority would assist the progress of the race. Bayard Rustin maintained that the "Negro male" must be "head of the household," while in the pages of the black nationalist magazine *Liberator,* a panel of black women agreed to "reject the insidious, castrating feminist concept." Their moderator, Virginia Hughes, lamented that America had "denied" black women their "softness and femininity." One of the few black organizations explicitly to endorse the Moynihan Report, however, was the Nation of Islam, which stated that Moynihan's findings gave "substance to some of the Honorable Elijah Muhammad's contentions and claims." Indeed, E. U. Essien-Udom's study had revealed in 1962 that the Messenger regarded a "lack of masculine parental authority" as fundamental to the predicament of lower-class black urban communities. The Nation's directives prohibiting extramarital sexual relations, alcohol, tobacco, narcotics, and gambling aimed to replace a culture of "indolence and laziness" with one of diligence and thrift.[58]

If Jones believed he had hit rock bottom and needed to "regenerate" himself, he felt much the same about Newark. Even in 1956, the *Atlantic Monthly* had described the city as a "vast scrawl of Negro slums and poverty, a festering center of disease, vice, injustice, and crime." By the time Jones returned in 1965, Newark was considerably poorer and blacker. Many of the whites who had still made up 65 percent of the city's population in 1960 had moved out to suburban Essex County in pursuit of skilled employment and better housing. Meanwhile, new black arrivals streamed into Newark's already crowded Central Ward, to which they were largely confined as a result of discriminatory housing practices. By 1965, African Americans formed a majority of 51 percent in the city, of whom almost half had been born in the Deep South. But as the city lost 20,000 manufacturing jobs during the 1960s, black unemployment reached 12 percent. Newark experienced America's urban crisis in the most acute form. As its Model Cities application showed, it had the United States' worst housing and highest rates of crime, venereal disease, maternal mortality, and new cases of tuberculosis, the second-highest birth and infant mortality rates, and the seventh-largest number of drug addicts. More than half of the adult population had less than an eighth-grade education.[59]

The influence of the Nation's pejorative view of black urban life was evident in Jones's writing soon after his return to Newark. At the city courthouse in 1966, he watched as black defendants were hauled up in relentless succession before "Judge Jew" while "wopcops" maintained order. Drunkards, wife beaters, and those whose only evident crime was "being black, poor, and raggedy" were dispatched to the penitentiary with abrupt efficiency. Particularly troubling for Jones was a quarrel carried out before the judge by a husband and wife: "The Black Man versus The Black Woman. A public show of our estrangement and debasement. The loss of our black family." Yet Jones's disgust with the racism of a "system" that reduced black people to poverty and then punished them further for the consequences only deepened his condemnation of black people themselves. "Who would construct a system," he asked, that kept black people "sick and perverted"? But "more important, to us Black People, who would accept such as 'their lot,' who would accept, and *be* what such a system demanded? What people would *allow* themselves to be so debased? *We make what we are.*" Such formulations not only counseled black people to struggle to improve their lives and challenge their subordination, but charged them with ultimate moral responsibility for their supposed sickness, perversion, and debasement. Unlike Kenneth Clark, Jones thus recapitulated an ideology of racial uplift, which, as Gaines argues, was "by no means incompatible with social protest against racism," but which nonetheless "implicitly faulted African Americans for their lowly status."[60]

Newark's deterioration undoubtedly affected Jones's outlook. Yet his harsh words about relations between black men and women and the prevalence of alcoholism and "sensual compensation" in the black community were also a means of externalizing his own recent crises. "So self-critical" at that time, as he would later reflect, Jones was searching for a mechanism by which to restructure his own life, as much as the lives of those around him. While the Nation of Islam's doctrines held some appeal, the split that had developed between Malcolm X and Elijah Muhammad—and the Nation's probable involvement in Malcolm's murder—gave Jones reason enough to hold back. In fact, he began to explore the orthodox Sunni faith to which Malcolm had converted in the final year of his life. Jones had left the "flophouse" on Broad Street around the spring of 1966 when he scraped together a deposit and rental payment on a three-storey wooden building at 33 Stirling Street, where Newark's oldest black neighborhood bordered the city's downtown business district. He named the building Spirit House, as a "place to raise the soul," and lived with Sylvia on the third floor. Soliciting help from a "bunch of young boys in the neighborhood," he set about converting the ground floor into a theater space that could squeeze in an audience of up to fifty. Briefly, this would also serve as an unofficial Sunni *jamaat* (prayer house).[61]

One evening toward the end of 1966, however, a visitor called unannounced at Spirit House and offered Jones a vision of regeneration that he was finally willing to embrace. Sporting an olive-drab dashiki, the visitor introduced himself as Ron Karenga. In Los Angeles, in 1965, Karenga had founded the US Organization ("us" blacks, as opposed to "them" whites), in which he taught the doctrine he called Kawaida, or "tradition and reason." A former associate of Malcolm X, Karenga had assimilated many of the Nation of Islam's puritanical directives into the *kanuni* (rules) of the US Organization. As he stated in 1966, however, he intended US to be an "action organization" that would "take some stand politically," while "the Muslims have not done that." Jones saw merit in Karenga's belief that moral and behavioral transformation was a precondition of political transformation. While the Nation and Sunni Islam offered prescriptions for behavioral reform, it was Kawaida that seemed to embody the "will toward political power in the world for the Black man," as Jones defined the "concept of Black Power."[62]

As the foremost exponent of "cultural nationalism" within the black power movement, Karenga argued that political revolution could be waged only once black people had undergone a revolution in culture and consciousness. Kawaida comprised a black "value system," he claimed, that would establish the moral and social preconditions for political empowerment. By transforming African Americans' self-image and mores and by restoring patriarchal authority and social cohesion, Kawaida would endow black communities with the strength to overcome their subordination. Following his graduate work in politics and African affairs at UCLA during the early 1960s, Karenga had distilled what he considered to be the unifying features of all African cultural traditions into his *Nguzo Saba,* or "seven principles" of Kawaida. Expressed in Swahili, a suitably Pan-African language (though one heavily inflected by the Arabic of slave traders), these principles were

Umoja (unity), *Kujichagulia* (self-determination), *Ujima* (collective work and responsibility), *Ujamaa* (cooperative economics), *Nia* (purpose), *Kuumba* (creativity), and *Imani* (faith). Karenga's references to Nkulunkulu as the first ancestor appeared to derive from his reading of Eileen Jensen Krige's *The Social System of the Zulus* (1936). However, the name he gave himself (he had been born Ronald Everett on a poultry farm in Parsonsburg, Maryland, in 1941) was adapted from the definition of "Kareng'a" (a "pure-blooded Gikuyu, a nationalist") contained in Jomo Kenyatta's ethnography, *Facing Mount Kenya* (1938).[63]

Jones's activities in Harlem had already signaled his belief in the necessity of cultural transformation among black Americans. Yet Kawaida's Africanist prescriptions entailed a far more drastic overhaul of black urban culture than anything Jones had previously imagined, and implied an even greater differentiation between the revolutionary vanguard and the people who must follow it. Less than four years after the publication of *Blues People,* in which Jones had celebrated the blues as the purest expression of an autonomous black American sensibility, Ron Karenga sat across from him at Spirit House and condemned the blues as "reactionary." The product of a slave mentality, the blues were "invalid; for they teach resignation." Jones "politely disagreed," his autobiography relates, and he would continue to champion avant-garde jazz as an extension of the blues tradition, and rhythm-and-blues as a more populist form of black musical expression. Nevertheless, he was "impressed" by Karenga's visit. By 1968, he would fully embrace Kawaida as the formula for Newark's regeneration, and his own. Karenga's Africanist teachings, Jones wrote in 1970, would *"re-create the life style of a free people,* evolving it from the life style of a conquered, colonized people."[64]

"Revolution," "evolution," and "reconversion" were practically synonymous in Kawaida's cyclical reading of history. In common with earlier Pan-Africanist thinkers, such as Martin Delany and Alexander Crummell in the nineteenth century, Karenga rejected the notion that the West was history's sole agent of civilization, and asserted the priority of black empires and civilizations in Egypt and sub-Saharan Africa. Karenga dispensed with the Christian providentialism of these earlier thinkers, who had regarded the painful ordeal of slavery as part of a divine plan to school a portion of the African people in Christianity so that they might return to and civilize their homeland. Yet he and Jones shared their expectation of a cyclical transition in which the mantle of civilization would return from whites to Africans. The rapid decolonization of Africa and the rise of the black power movement in the United States signaled to Jones that black people were on the cusp of recapturing the power and splendor they had enjoyed before "the decay that made our kingdoms fall." Revolution meant, quite literally, turning full circle. By attaining what Jones called a "new consciousness of the million year old African personality," submerged during centuries of colonialism and enslavement, the global black community would complete the "evolutionary movement" back to the glory of African civilizations: "Where we was we will be agin."[65]

Kawaida's demand for wholesale "cultural reconversion" was a function of the contempt in which it held African Americans' existing lifestyles and traditions. "Bloods," as Karenga referred to those black people who had not yet been reconverted to "traditional" African ways, possessed "only elements of a culture," such as "song and dance," and lacked the necessary "total structure." Whatever Jones's misgivings about Karenga's rejection of the blues, he readily endorsed the notion that black American life amounted to little more than pathological corruptions engendered by centuries of slavery and subordination. "We have been deculturized," he would claim. "Most of us are examples of Negro Colonized Culture," which had been "totally distorted and bombarded" by "European ways of seeing and doing things."[66]

Two factors, above all, help to explain Kawaida's appeal for Jones. First, its insistence on drastic cultural transformation resonated with Jones's perception that his own situation and that of Newark had reached a point of crisis. Kawaida's "programmatic restructuring of attitudes and relationships" promised to redress both his personal failings and those he had discerned in the "sick and perverted" black defendants at the city courthouse. In the spring of 1967, Jones experienced the workings of the US Organization at first hand. While visiting San Francisco State College at the invitation of its black student union, he made a detour to Los Angeles and witnessed Karenga officiating at an *Arusi,* or Kawaida marriage ceremony. Kawaida's emphasis on the marital relationship as the "microcosm, by example, of the entire black nation" was particularly attractive to Jones. He later told an interviewer that he had been "impressed by the order, the structure" at the wedding, as he "saw Karenga, [men] in their dashikis and women with the African dress." Confronting the tight-knit, strictly regimented US Organization, Jones felt "undisciplined and relatively backward." As his autobiography would recount, the "worst thing a person could be, as far as Karenga was concerned, was *Ovyo,* a Swahili word meaning 'random,' a person acting at random, disorganized and unpredictable. This was the problem with the 'basic blood.'" In 1964, Jones had urged blacks to "bring out a little American dada" and "just flip, go raving in the streets." Within a few years, however, he believed that what "the black community" needed was "Identity Purpose and Direction." Those who had not embraced Kawaida were "moving too randomly (*ovyo* is the Swahili word for that)."[67]

Secondly, just as Jones had argued in 1965 that the black artist must "change the images his people identify with," so Karenga attached great importance to art as a tool for disseminating Kawaida's value system. True African art, Karenga maintained, was "functional, collective, and committing," and the "real function of art" at the present time was "to make revolution." The revolutionary legitimacy Jones craved as an artist was thus assured by Kawaida's cultural nationalist conception of the route to black power. While it was a Sunni Muslim cleric who furnished Jones with a new name in 1967—Ameer Barakat ("Blessed Prince")—to replace his "slave" name, it was Karenga who finally provided Jones with the status and identity he sought. Under Karenga's influence, Jones "Swahilized" his Arabic name and began to call himself Amiri Baraka. In 1968, Karenga, the "Maulana" (master teacher), conferred on him the title of "Imamu," or "spiritual leader." Baraka's enthusiasm for this role was abundant:

> *Listen to the creator*
> *speak in me now. Listen, these words*
> *are part of God's thing. I am a*
> *vessel, a black priest interpreting*
> *the present & future for my people.*

It was a role that differed strikingly from that of interpreting black rage to white audiences. Indeed, the notion of the artist as priest held considerable appeal within the black arts movement. Askia Muhammad Touré, who had been teaching at San Francisco State College during Baraka's visit, announced with similar satisfaction: "I no longer shun the 'poet' in me." Touré had "at last found the kind of personal identity that I desire, as a black man," the "role of Priest, Seer, Holyman and, finally, 'Prophet.'"[68]

This integration of the roles of artist and priest was intended to circumvent the "dreadful split between life and art," and the consequent alienation of the artist, which according to *Blues People* had befallen the West since the Renaissance. As Baraka told an interviewer in September 1967:

> The word "art" is something the West has never understood. Art is supposed to be a part of a whole life of the community. Like, scholars are supposed to be a part of the community. A person who has trouble should walk across the street to a scholar, who'll be the heaviest person in that vicinity on that subject, and ask about that. . . . [Art is] supposed to be as essential as a grocery store.

Whether Kawaida in fact constituted a religion was a subject on which even Karenga was ambivalent. When asked about his religious beliefs on one occasion, he replied that he was "the founder of a religion called Kawaida." Yet theological assertions were almost entirely absent from Kawaida literature. Religion featured in Kawaida's "Seven Criteria for Culture" only within the definition of "Mythology." In frank, pragmatic terms, it was stated that that idea of a "Chosen People" was "necessary for developing a good self-concept," and that the "African myth" of Nkulunkulu "explains why the Seven Principles are the bases of all African life." So far as belief in a deity was concerned, "We are Gods ourselves. Each Black man is the God of his own house"—a similarly pragmatic affirmation of black patriarchal authority, for "house" was a Kawaida synonym for "woman."[69]

Perhaps most revealing of Kawaida's fundamental aims, however, is Baraka's statement that "the 7 principles are a religious creed, in its most *practical* application, a code of morality," which "will transform Black people and by doing this, transform yes, America." Strengthening the community's commitment to this moral code was the purpose of the weekly "soul sessions" that Karenga had instituted in Los Angeles and which Baraka, as an "imamu," now conducted at Spirit House in Newark. That these sessions took place on Sunday afternoons is a none-too-subtle indication of the similarity between Baraka's responsibilities as a "spiritual leader" and those of the Christian ministry. Just as Baraka's former bohemian stance of contempt for the black bourgeois ethic of conformity and respectability had given way to his own elaboration of racial uplift ideology, so the denunciations of Christianity as an instrument of social control that had featured in his writings of the early 1960s now yielded to a somewhat self-conscious emulation of the traditional African American preacher as organic intellectual. Baraka was capable of a formidable jeremiad:

> Black People, you are in hell! You are condemned to Hell *because of your acts*. . . . Instead of being nationalists, Black Nationalists, interested in power, black power, for black people to control our own lives, to build our own cities, & re-create the glorious civilizations of our history, you are satisfied to be in Hell smiling at Devils, letting these devils kill yr children & yrselves w/dope, w/bad housing, w/unemployment, w/crippling noeducation, w/immorality & perversion, & w/bullets.

Indeed, if Baraka coveted a respected position in the community from which to lead the "transformation" of black people, the role of minister—to which he had once aspired as a student at Howard University—was a familiar model.[70]

As the historian David Chappell has shown, Martin Luther King Jr. embraced a tradition of "prophetic Christianity" in which visionary leaders "preached to society of its corruption and insisted on total, rather than incremental, reformation." Furthermore, while King never ceased to hold white racism to account, at the height of the Montgomery bus boycott in 1956 he had heralded the birth of a "new Negro" who would no longer accept the humiliations of segregation. Baraka, in his new role as a "black priest," similarly prophesied a radically altered "future for my people" and urged them no longer to be "satisfied" with subordination. In 1963, he had denounced King's "lie" that there was "a moral requirement" (of nonviolence) to be "met by all Negroes" if they were to gain "entrance into the secular kingdom of plenty." By the late 1960s, however, moral requirements made up the crux of Baraka's own message to African Americans. Yet his indictment of what he regarded as their present immorality far exceeded any implicit charges of passivity or resignation in King's sermons. Baraka's notes for a soul session held on November 9, 1969, include the lines: "What is the *Purpose* of *your* life? Eat—Sleep—Copulate / Stomach and Genitals. . . . To be black you must change the purpose of your life to the benefit of black nation."[71]

While Baraka preferred to style himself as an African priest rather than as an African American minister, historical continuities between black religious practices in the Old and New Worlds ought not to be overlooked. Slave preachers in the United States, the historian William Banks explains, had inherited from West African "priestly tradition" the status of "intermediaries between the gods and members of the community" and the role of "moral and aesthetic compass for life within the tribe." Baraka also fashioned his role as an organic intellectual after the second of the two "intellectual types" that Banks ascribes to West African societies. Distinct from the priests were the "medicine men," who later "resurfaced as the conjurer[s]" (both male and female) on American plantations. To understand Baraka's function in the soul sessions purely as that of a "spiritual leader" would be to neglect the profusion of medical imagery in his rhetoric. A striking example is his insistence on the need to exclude whites from soul sessions partly on grounds of "SPACE—Hospital of a sort, not enough room for Blacks."[72]

The mental health of the many African Americans whom he considered "sick and perverted" was among Baraka's foremost concerns. In *Madheart: A Morality Play,* first performed at San Francisco State College in May 1967, Baraka pitted the virtuous characters "Black Man" and "Black Woman," who displayed the "African" gender roles and dress codes he had recently encountered at the *Arusi* in Los Angeles, against the "sick," brainwashed "Mother" and "Sister," who worship the image of the dying white "Devil Lady." The two tragic, "cancer-ous" characters have been "hypnotized" by "White Magic," and Black Man sees that his only means of saving them is to "turn them over to the Black Arts and get their heads relined." In an essay of 1970, Baraka elaborated: "We are schizophrenic–manic/depressive–paranoid in our everyday world, in varying degrees, to different ends, for different rea-sons, depending on where we are in the devil's frame." Addressing a black nationalist convention that same year, Baraka rearticulated Du Bois's "two warring ideals" in terms of this racial schizophrenia. "Du Bois said we always have the double consciousness," he reminded his audience. "We trying to be Black and meanwhile you got a white ghost hovering over your head," constantly "telling you to be a ghost. We hope you won't submit."[73]

In his combining the roles of priest and medicine man, Baraka's re-sponse to what he perceived as the crisis of black intellectual life was to claim leadership of the struggle to eradicate the pathologies of black urban life. "Disease is from the selves," he wrote in an unpublished work. "From bodies. From minds. From souls." Here, once again, there are similarities as well as stark differences between Baraka's self-conception as a black power leader and Martin Luther King's as a civil rights leader. As the historian Richard King observes, Martin Luther King's vocabulary was "as often a psychological/medical one as it was religious/moral." Martin Luther King referred to the black family as "scarred" and "psychopathic" and spoke of "a battle against pathology within and a battle against oppression without." Furthermore, in as-serting black political agency and demanding black uplift and self-transformation, King regarded himself, in Vincent Harding's analysis, as a "healer" who had confronted his own "wounds" and was able to show his people a path to self-respect. Baraka's amalgam of moral, medi-cal, and political language was, again, derived as much from recent Afri-can American precedents as from prior African models.[74]

Historians have scarcely registered the extent to which the black power movement, famous for pronouncing that "black is beautiful," in fact regarded black life as pathological and envisaged self-transformation, under the guidance of an exemplary black elite or vanguard, as a vital mechanism of black liberation. Just as Gaines situates black power outside the dominant uplift tradition of moral reform, so Daryl Michael Scott places black power in opposition to the belief in the "damaged black psyche" prevalent among postwar reformers. Scott amply demonstrates how civil rights leaders such as Martin Luther King, Whitney Young, James Farmer, Bayard Rustin, and even Malcolm X echoed the pathologist claims of social scientists. He asserts, however, that "racial pride and antiliberalism called for the Black Power generation to reject Fanon's and Malcolm X's damage imagery even as they embraced their political analysis and goals." Yet in treating the affirmative view of African American family structures, mores, and self-esteem offered by black social scientists such as Robert Staples and Joyce Ladner as representative of black power ideology, Scott's analysis is misleading.[75]

Uniquely, Richard King has noted that the "black militant diagnosis of African American life in the 1960s could sometimes sound like an angry reprise of the Elkins thesis." King cites the black nationalist literary critic Addison Gayle Jr., who wrote that the "damage to the [black] psyche is immeasurable." To this might be added not only the examples of Baraka and Karenga but also Stokely Carmichael and Charles Hamilton's influential *Black Power* (1967), which, as highlighted in the previous chapter, deferred to Kenneth Clark's description of a "pernicious self- and group-hatred" among African Americans. Larry Neal's manifesto for the black arts movement also included the Moynihan-like assertion that black men were so cowed by the "white power structure" and by overbearing black matriarchs that "very often, there is nothing left but a shell."[76]

What was distinctive about black nationalists' use of damage imagery was that it was intended not as a moral appeal to the white public or the federal government, but rather as the rationale for a self-directed drive to improve black self-esteem through cultural transformation and communal empowerment. Baraka explained:

> No one respects a weak people. No matter how much somebody might tell you that they really love you and feel sorry for you because you can't get a job and your house is a roachfarm and your children are junkies, yeh they feel sorry, but that is not going to

help. The only help is community ie racial unity, and the continued move to create political representation and power for black people. We don't need anybody to feel sorry for us, we need the power to do things for ourselves.

Baraka instructed fellow black artists:

> Each aspect of black life must have light shed on it, must be analyzed must make the pain of recognizing the exact place of our crucifix- ion, the exact sloth and cowardliness, the precise ugliness and igno- rance. But also, let the black beauty glow through, whether attained or desired what we are and what we all *can* be. Stress evolution, what the world can be in strong and beautiful hands.

The meaning of "black is beautiful" within the discourse of the black power movement acquires fresh significance if blackness and beauty were to be "attained or desired," rather than merely assumed.[77]

The importance that Baraka and other black power theorists attached to psychological and moral self-transformation did not preclude en- gagement with the systemic factors underlying the urban crisis. As will be seen, Baraka offered a detailed analysis of the political, economic, and demographic forces reshaping American cities and devised a con- crete strategy for political mobilization toward the goal of black self- determination in Newark. Nor was black power a homogeneous creed in which ideas of uplift or damage were uniformly held or conceived. Africanists such as Baraka and Karenga were especially harsh in their judgment of the existing cultural and psychological characteristics of black urban communities. Indeed, self-styled "revolutionary national- ists," most notably the Black Panthers, were often scathing about dashiki-wearing, Swahili-talking cultural nationalists and their de- rogatory attitudes toward the "culture of Black People here in Amer- ica." The Panthers' Marxian credo could sometimes conflict with the conservative social ethics of the uplift tradition, as when Huey Newton condemned "the bourgeois family" as "suffocating."[78]

Yet a belief that behavioral reform was a precondition of revolution-ary action was inscribed in the "Rules of the Black Panther Party," which, like the US Organization's *kanuni,* sought to curb promiscuity, drinking, and drug use. The historian Eddie Glaude Jr. rightly points to the shared conviction across the black power movement that African Americans must undertake a "revolution of the mind," a "fundamental psychological and cultural conversion from their socialization as a sub-ordinate people to a self-determining nation." And as Robin Kelley's study of the Revolutionary Action Movement (RAM) suggests, leftist black power factions' insistence on "revolutionary ethics and moral transformation" owed as much to the values of "self-restraint, order, and discipline" promoted by the black church and the Nation of Islam as to *Quotations from Chairman Mao Tse-tung.* Kelley remarks percep-tively that Robert Williams, the author of *Negroes with Guns* (1962) and a leading intellectual presence within RAM by the late 1960s, em-ployed the "idea" of Mao's Cultural Revolution more than its specific "ideology" when he envisaged "purging black culture of a 'slave mentality.' "[79]

Despite sectarian divisions, all prominent theorists of black power shared to some extent in the belief that African Americans' existing culture and consciousness bore the marks of their subordination. The meaning of "black is beautiful" within the movement is best under-stood in conjunction with the "Negro-to-Black Conversion Experi-ence" advanced by the African American psychologist William Cross Jr. as the necessary "Psychology of Black Liberation." Far more than a simple substitution of terms, the adoption of "black" (not unlike Mar-tin Luther King's "new Negro") was meant to designate a class of indi-viduals who had themselves been transformed. "Either we will be Black Men & Black Women or we will be slaves & niggers," Baraka wrote in 1968. Two years later, he warned the "new nationalist" not to relapse and "become negroized" once more. If such ideas necessitated rupture with the past, they were nonetheless rooted in a long-standing tradition of African American thought in which black urban commu-nities were objects of moral concern and the progress of the race was viewed as contingent on the transformation of black people's values and lifestyles.[80]

Lift Up Yr Self!

At dusk on July 12, 1967, John Smith, an African American cab driver, encountered two white officers of the Newark Police Department. The officers dispensed a beating, which broke Smith's ribs, and then took him to the Fourth Precinct police station, where he was charged with a traffic violation. Word of Smith's injury was quickly transmitted across Newark on taxi drivers' radios, and a crowd of black protesters gathered outside the police station. From the Hayes Housing Project opposite, Molotov cocktails were thrown at the station house. Soon afterward a number of nearby shops were looted. The following evening, after police wielded batons against protesters who had reconvened outside the station, the Newark riot began in earnest with the smashing of storefronts on Springfield Avenue. Over five days, a large section of the Central Ward was gutted as rioters looted and burned white-owned properties, and the city's police, reinforced by 3,000 National Guardsmen, responded by firing into and burning down black businesses. Paranoid about nonexistent black "snipers," as an official inquiry subsequently acknowledged, guardsmen shot and killed twenty-one black civilians, including a seventy-three-year-old man, six women, and two children. "Newark: The Predictable Insurrection," read the cover of *Life* magazine on July 28. The by-now-familiar combination of high unemployment, overcrowded, infested, and dilapidated housing, and frequent acts of police brutality had indeed made the city rife for a violent outbreak far more devastating than the Harlem riot of 1964 and equal to the Watts riot of 1965.[81]

Shortly before 3:00 a.m. during the second night of violence in Newark, Baraka's Volkswagen was pulled over by policemen close to Springfield Avenue. A black police officer who witnessed the ensuing events recalled that his white colleagues dragged Baraka "out of that little truck, knocked him to the ground and began to beat him so viciously that I don't know how that little man is still living today." The three passengers (Baraka, the actor Barry Wynn, and the accountant Charles McCray) were arrested for possession of two revolvers, a charge they would deny when their case came to trial. According to Baraka's autobiography, he had spent the evening circling the riot area, "digging, checking, observing, participating," and driving an injured man to hospital. On November 6, an all-white jury convicted Baraka of unlawful possession of firearms. In handing down the unusually severe sentence of three years' imprisonment and a $1,000 fine, Judge Leon Kapp read out Baraka's poem "Black People!" which included the lines "Run up and down Broad / Street niggers, take the shit you want. Take their lives if need be." Kapp's use of this poem as incriminating evidence sparked a protest campaign by the PEN writers' organization, led, ironically, by Baraka's old friend Allen Ginsberg. After a week at the Trenton Penitentiary, Baraka was released pending appeal. He was eventually acquitted at a retrial in 1969.[82]

On the night of his arrest, with the riot raging close to the Newark Street jail where he was held in solitary confinement, Baraka penned some thoughts in his notebook, which he later included in his second collection of essays, *Raise, Race, Rays, Raze* (1972). Unlike the poem "Black People!" these reflections were notably ambivalent about the revolutionary efficacy of rioting. Though the spectacle of black violence palpably excited Baraka ("Our people dance in the street now!"), the looting only strengthened his belief that African Americans were enslaved by the decadent, materialistic values they had learned from their oppressors, which kept them "chained to illusions of Desire. . . . Young men and old men. Little girls outfitting their hovels with what they've learned to desire on television." As entire blocks were leveled to smoldering rubble, Baraka's mind was already turning to visions of reconstruction. His people, "Ancient Egyptians," were "still in chains," but "we will yet rebuild our noble cities." First, however, they must rebuild themselves: "Our knowledge stretches from the beginning of the planet. Believe this, brother, and lift up yr self!"[83]

By coincidence, a national Black Power Conference had been scheduled to open in Newark on July 20, 1967. With the riot now suppressed by overwhelming retaliation from the police and National Guard, a decision was taken for the conference to go ahead. As he appeared before more than a thousand delegates at the Mount Zion Baptist Church, with his head bandaged following twenty stitches to two different lacerations, Baraka's profile as a national black power spokesman was immediately enhanced. Speaking after SNCC's H. Rap Brown, who threatened that if America did not "come around," black people would "burn it down," Baraka told the audience that Newark had witnessed "a rebellion of black people for self-determination." Yet a note of admonishment betrayed his misgivings: "The next time, don't break into liquor stores. Go where you can get something to protect yourself!" Baraka's attitude toward rioting hardened further over subsequent months. An FBI informant noted that Baraka told an audience at a Methodist church in Baltimore on March 18, 1968, that rioting created "hysteria and mass confusion" and "only leaves black people dead in the streets." The human cost of the Newark riot had chastened Baraka, who circulated photographs of the bullet-ridden torso of a teenage boy, shot dead by police while looting. When the assassination of Martin Luther King on April 4, 1968, provoked a renewed spate of violence in Newark and other cities across the United States, Baraka appealed for calm.[84]

Rap Brown's inflammatory rhetoric aside, Baraka was far from alone among black power leaders in seeking to dissuade youths from rioting. Askia Muhammad Touré condemned those "fools bent upon getting a lot of Black people killed with their adolescent bravado," while the anthropologist and civil rights activist St. Clair Drake acknowledged in 1969 that the Black Panthers had "kept Oakland quiet all through" by warning young blacks that "undisciplined looting and burning" would result in them being "shot up." From the perspective of Kawaida, spontaneous, unorganized outbursts were *ovyo:* "random" actions uninformed by a revolutionary value system. Baraka told an interviewer in 1969 that defeating the white enemy would require "building, and training and educating and passing on. The white man ain't gonna fall off because a lot of niggers get mad at him." Indeed, shortly after the violence in Newark in April 1968, he had told the *Washington Post* that he was "in favor of black people taking power by the quickest, easiest, most successful means they can employ. Malcolm X said the ballot or the bullet. Newark is a particular situation where the ballot seems to be advantageous." The aim was now "to bring about black self-government in Newark" at the mayoral election in 1970.[85]

In an illuminating revisionist case study, the historian Robert Self places postwar America's "uneven economic development of metropolitan space" at the core of black power's political concerns. Focusing

on the Black Panther Party's reconstitution after 1971 as a local organization that aimed to make Oakland a "revolutionary demonstration
city," Self argues that the spatial dimension of the inequalities engendered by the rise of "city-suburb conglomerations" was well understood
by the Panthers, and informed Bobby Seale's mayoral campaign of 1973
and Elaine Brown's run for a city council seat that year. Oakland's postwar deindustrialization and the rapid growth of industry in the suburban periphery, combined with white flight, black in-migration, and
ill-conceived urban renewal, convinced the Panther leadership both
that the city was, in economic terms, "a colonized space," and that the
city's black voters could be mobilized by a politics of decolonization
that would redress the unequal distribution of employment, revenue,
and services.[86]

An essay that Baraka wrote soon after the Newark riot of 1967 displays a strikingly similar analysis of the urban crisis: "Newark is *a colony*. A bankrupt ugly colony, in the classic term, where white people
make their money to take away with them." As America's second-
largest insurance center, the city "is kept up only as far as its money-
making capacity, say for Prudential." Every day, Newark filled up with
white workers and then emptied out as they returned "back home to
the suburbs." Taxes in these wealthy suburbs were low, while Newark's
impoverished black residents were "the most heavily taxed in New
Jersey." Baraka's description of Newark not only presaged the Black
Panthers' anatomy of Oakland, but also echoed Kenneth Clark's characterization in 1965 of America's "dark ghettos" as "economic colonies."
Baraka's indignation at Newark's "horribly overcrowded" schools,
where black children "are not being taught anything" except possibly
"to hate themselves," sounded another of Clark's recurrent themes.
Baraka wrote of the "13-storey jails" that had been erected where old
housing had been torn down in the "beat up and junkie ridden" Central Ward. In the same year in which Clark called the ghettos "America's version of concentration camps," Baraka claimed that the "plan"
behind packing Newark's housing projects was "to get us all together.
In one place, where 50 rolls of barbed wire could solve all the social
dilemmas the owners think are crucial."[87]

Even as he painted this grim scenario, however, Baraka anticipated the Panthers' insistence that the circumstances of black people's confinement could also be the conditions of their empowerment. "You ever hear of a ghetto? That's separate. A separate state. . . . What we want is the power to control that separate state. To control its politics and its economics," he explained. "This is the only way we can provide decent education for our children, decent homes for our families, a livelihood for ourselves." He wrote these words only a few months before the election in November 1967 of the first black mayors of major American cities: Richard Hatcher of Gary, Indiana, and Carl Stokes of Cleveland, Ohio. Baraka noted that African Americans were already a majority in Newark, but that their "division" had resulted in the defeat in 1966 of Kenneth Gibson, the black challenger to the incumbency of Newark's mayor, Hugh Addonizio. Around the time of the elections in Gary and Cleveland, Baraka and two associates formed an organization in Newark called the United Brothers, with the intention of unifying the city's black civic and political leadership and mobilizing voters to ensure the victory of black candidates at the mayoral and council elections in 1970. This involved building alliances with non-nationalists, church leaders, and others whom Baraka had dismissed as retrograde "Negroes." Such a move was justifiable, however, according to Karenga's "concept of operational unity in our tactics."[88]

The United Brothers also became a forum in which Baraka could share his analysis of Newark's "colonial" dynamics and his policy prescriptions for redressing the inequitable distribution of metropolitan resources. One commentator on black urban politics later noted that the United Brothers had put forward two (unsuccessful) candidates for the city council in 1968 with "a Baraka-inspired demand for a commuter payroll tax on non-residents, and for local control of federally sponsored Model Cities housing programs."[89] Baraka thus anticipated key elements of the "systematic critique" of metropolitan "political economy and geography," which Self attributes to the Panthers' campaign in Oakland in 1973. Furthermore, as Komozi Woodard has shown, Baraka's initiative in bringing together Newark's black civic leadership and mobilizing its black and Puerto Rican voters was instrumental in the successful campaign to elect Gibson as Newark's mayor (and the first black mayor of a major northeastern city) in 1970. And as one of three leaders of the National Black Political Convention held in Gary in 1972, alongside Richard Hatcher and the Detroit congressman Charles Diggs, Baraka played a significant role in national efforts to increase black political representation.[90]

Yet Baraka viewed black urbanization and white flight to the suburbs not simply as an opportunity to ensure black control of city halls, but more grandly as confirmation that the "cycle" of white hegemony was ending. "Who inhabits the cities possesses the thrust of life to power," he wrote in 1970, and even years later as a Marxist he would cite the "ancient teaching" of the thirteenth-century Islamic scholar Ibn Arabi "that the cities are the chief repositories of culture and the highest thrust of human life." This sentiment helps to account for Baraka's otherwise paradoxical belief that the rapid migration of southern blacks into "our cities with torn down shacks full of vermin" would mark the next stage of black people's "evolution." "Pyramids will rise again in Newark," he wrote. If urbanization would set the stage for black empowerment, however, it was Kawaida that would "revive" the ancient culture and wisdom of black people and bring about their "actual renaissance," just as "the devils pulled themselves out of their 'dark ages' by re-embracing the 'classics.'" For this reason, Baraka devoted as much energy to the task of "cultural reconversion" in Newark as to electoral campaigning or national black power conventions. In 1968, with Karenga's endorsement, Baraka founded the Committee for Unified Newark (CFUN, pronounced *see-fun*). This new organization incorporated Baraka's nationalist theater company, the Spirit House Movers, and acted as a host institution for the United Brothers. Its core purpose, however, was to build a tight-knit group of Kawaida "advocates" as a nucleus for the transformation of values and culture among black people in Newark.[91]

The "full-time" membership of CFUN peaked at approximately three hundred in the early 1970s. Many of these men, women, and children lived in communal housing, and a majority of the adults were employed within various CFUN enterprises, which included a publishing house (Jihad), a nationalist bookstore (Nyumba ya Ujamaa), and the African Free School for children. Activity centered on three *hekalus* (temples) in the Central Ward, on Stirling Street, High Street, and Belmont Avenue. "We are actually a family," Baraka told an interviewer in 1972; "we don't look at ourselves as just an organization. We are a community in a sense because we share values." At the same time, Baraka began a new family of his own, fathering five children between 1967 and 1973 by his second wife, who took the new name Amina ("Faithful"). Members of CFUN were "very monogamous," Baraka insisted:

> Basically, it is revolutionary for a black woman and a black man to live together according to a black value system and raise a revolutionary family. In America, that is revolutionary, especially if you're . . . the stranger on the block because you've got a father and mother who live in the same house.

As exotic as his name, dress, and Swahili terminology had become, at the very core of Baraka's conception of black "revolution" was the uplift tradition's characteristic concern for the stability and cohesion of the black family.[92]

In an essay first published in the magazine *Black World* in 1970, Baraka provided a theoretical elaboration of the revolutionary "House System" sketched out in Kawaida's book of aphorisms, *The Quotable Karenga* (1967). Black men and women had "internalized" the ruptured relationships and degraded family life imposed by slavery, he maintained. In order to "erase" these pathological effects, black men and women must recover their respective "healthy African identities," grounded in Karenga's notions of "male supremacy" and female "submission." Treating feminism, tenuously, as a manifestation of "white" values, Baraka condemned white "devils" for their belief in the equality of the sexes. Men and women "could never be equals," he wrote, for "nature has not provided thus." The sexes were in fact "complementary," meaning "that we [men] have certain functions which are more natural to us, and you [women] have certain graces that are yours alone." Put simply, while "the brothers are to fly in the face of, and confront . . . evil," the black woman's role was "to inspire her man" and work within the sphere of "Social Development," which "means education, health, the home, the community."[93]

If this bears an uncanny resemblance to Moynihan's call for black women to be relieved of their matriarchal authority and black men to be permitted to "strut," the difference between Baraka's and Moynihan's formulations also merits consideration. For Moynihan, men and women were equal in most capacities. While it was in black people's interest to assimilate to America's cultural norms, there was in fact "no special reason why a society in which males are dominant in family relationships is to be preferred to a matriarchal arrangement." For Baraka, to the contrary, it was "nature" that had "not provided thus." Indeed, E. Frances White's attempt to distinguish between the "conservative" gender politics of "Afrocentric" nationalists and their progressive "counterattack against racism" fails to register the underlying essentialism that prevented cultural nationalists from transcending racial ideology as much as it determined their belief in "male supremacy." Baraka by now admitted to being "a racist, in the sense that I believe certain qualities that are readily observable on this planet have to do with racial types." Whereas the sexist attitudes of many male civil rights activists can be seen as contradicting their belief in equal rights for all, cultural nationalists such as Baraka were less invested in the concepts of rights and equality than in biological determinism. As he put it in 1970, "Our philosophy is *nature revealed*."[94]

The more common error, however, has been to exaggerate the divergence between the gender ideologies of the civil rights and black power movements. Thus Michele Wallace has argued that black power endorsed the violent, predatory sexuality of "Black Macho" typified by such works as *Dutchman,* rather than the traditional patriarchal responsibilities upheld by previous generations of black leaders. Similarly, bell hooks has used Baraka's play *Madheart* to claim that black power rejected "romanticized" and chivalrous masculine ideals and instead revered "the rapist, the macho man, the brute who uses force to get his demands met." *Madheart,* in which the character Black Man slaps Black Woman *"back and forth across the face"* and instructs her to "submit," would appear to lend credence to this argument. Yet in no other work of drama, verse, or prose did Baraka condone violence against black women, and Karenga's *kanuni* specifically proscribed the use of "physical force" in the "settlement of disputes" within the community.[95]

Far more typical of Baraka's writings and those of the wider black arts movement, in fact, was an effusion of chivalrous and romantic patriarchal imagery. "You don't deserve no woman," Baraka instructed black men in his agitprop play *Arm Yourself, or Harm Yourself!* "if you can't protect them." His poem "Beautiful Black Women" upbraids black men and women who "fail" each other and implores: "will you lift me up, mother, will you / let me help you, wife / lover." Askia Muhammad Touré exalted the "complete man" who could not only "write a beautiful poem" but also "don his armor and lead a thundering herd into battle," "protecting his family, picking up a gun to defend his community or nation." There is little here to suggest that the notion of men's "responsibility to their women and children" was viewed within the black power movement as "almost sissified," as Wallace has claimed. And while many black women would resist attempts to confine their activism to the sphere of "social development," others were eager to see black men fulfill their patriarchal responsibilities to protect and provide. A poem by Lethonia Gee, for example, lauds the image of the black man

> *As a Masai warrior*
> *With his Burning Spear*
> *Blessed by the Gods*
> *The epitome of man.*

Fellow poet Nikki Giovanni urged black boys to emulate "Mau Mau," and perhaps unwittingly invoked the all-American heroine Betsy Ross when she enjoined black "sisters" to "make a flag."[96]

Within CFUN, a multitude of carefully choreographed rituals reinforced the message that the corollary of "male supremacy" was men's responsibility to protect and provide for women and children. The *Arusi,* officiated by Baraka, not only affirmed the status of the husband as "head of the house" but also established his responsibility "always [to] provide emotional, economic and physical security for your wife and children." He was required to "lead but not be a burden, be strong and loving, considerate and creative, respectful, faithful and understanding." Another ceremony, the *Ahadi ya Akika* ("pledge of sacrifice"), welcomed newborn children into "the Black nation forever becoming" and affirmed their parents' familial responsibilities. Baraka also presided over the *Kuziliwa Karamu,* a monthly "birthday feast" at which each mother and father presented each child in the community with a fifty-cent piece wrapped in an African proverb, with the money to be contributed to the African Free School.[97]

In the late 1960s, Karenga briefly permitted polygamy within US, deeming it to be a legitimate "African" practice. It quickly became clear, however, that "tradition" was serving as a thinly veiled excuse for promiscuous male behavior, which Kawaida's *kanuni* outlawed as "playboyism." The rules of the Republic of New Africa, another cultural nationalist group, founded in Detroit in 1968 by Imari Obadele and Gaidi Obadele (two brothers formerly named Richard Henry and Milton Henry), suggest that multiple marriages were intended to ensure that each mother would "have every security provided for her" by the father of her child, thereby placing all sexual relationships within a framework that acknowledged men's paternal responsibilities. However, Sandra Hollin Flowers, one of the few scholars to address cultural nationalists' attitudes toward polygamy, points out that any such ideals were undermined by the reality that American law would recognize only the rights of a "first wife." Karenga quickly moved to restrict the practice when he saw that grievances arising from such relationships had the potential to fracture US.[98]

Within CFUN, meanwhile, Baraka had banned polygamy from the outset, and he expelled a group of former US members who tried to import the practice from Los Angeles. Back in 1966, he had initiated his own experiment in polygamy with Amina and Olabumi at Spirit House, but his relationships with both women had already been verging on collapse by the time of Olabumi's death. Baraka's subsequent disavowal of polygamy appears to have been a condition of his continuing relationship with Amina, as well as marking a critical moment in his own quest for self-transformation. The superficially exotic rituals of the *Arusi* and *Ahadi ya Akika* were in fact new ways of packaging the deeply conventional values of patriarchal responsibility and family cohesion central to the uplift tradition. In the same interview in which Baraka proclaimed the "revolutionary" significance of the stable family unit, he acknowledged that the revolution "will be about something that is quite normal, you know. It will be about black people achieving health . . . and normalcy in our time. That would be revolutionary."[99]

Indeed, at a moment when Americans were confronted by the un-abashedly permissive mores of the youth counterculture, black cultural nationalists offered an almost diametrically opposed definition of "rev-olution." If the counterculture grew out of the generational dynamics of an affluent postwar society—the sociologist Lewis Yablonsky re-ported in 1967 that 70 percent of hippies came from middle- or upper-middle-class families—many black nationalists considered free love and psychedelic liberation to be antithetical to the needs of black youth in impoverished urban communities. "A whole lot of long-haired white boys are singing about revolution," Baraka remarked in 1970, "so I know that can't be the same thing I'm talking about. . . . No few bloods high on marijuana and white women are going to *change the life style of Black people*." One of the short, didactic plays Baraka offered the com-munity in his role as priest and healer, *Junkies Are Full of (SHHH . . .)* (1971), presents two young black men engaged in a struggle to rid Newark of the narcotics trade, which is exposed as a conspiracy to sap the strength of black nationalism. Meanwhile, a series of articles by black nationalist authors in *Liberator* magazine deplored the "idle pur-suit of bravado and self-destruction" that was turning black youth to-ward drugs rather than black power, and cited hippie "LSD platoons" as a corrupting influence. The sexual mores of the counterculture were deemed equally harmful, with "love-ins" outlawed by Karenga as "negative to the principles" of black liberation. As with white flight from the cities, however, Baraka regarded the counterculture some-what gleefully as evidence of white America's "degeneration" and of a decadence to rival the final days of Rome. Black nationalists, he wrote in 1969, should welcome the "great deluge of nakedness and homo-sexuality" sweeping through white society, "because it weakens the hand that holds the chain that binds Black People."[100]

Yet Baraka warned that there was "no such thing as an instant revolution." Black empowerment would come about only through evolution and the embrace of a superior African value system. The scathing address he delivered to a black nationalist convention in Atlanta in 1970 in fact echoes the famous speech given by Booker T. Washington in the same city seventy-five years earlier, which had instructed an "ignorant and inexperienced" race patiently to acquire the skills and habits that would render it worthy of freedom. Baraka intoned:

> You are slaves because you want to be slaves, because you deserve to be slaves! . . . You are not free because you are not qualified to be free people. . . . If you had the skills to overthrow the white man, you could overthrow the white man. If you were efficient enough, you could do it; but you are none of these and most of you refuse to deal with the realities of becoming skilled and efficient enough to do it. . . . It is something that will have to be achieved through science and study and dedication and training.

Once again, the moral onus was on black people to "qualify" for freedom by transforming themselves.[101]

To this end, Baraka envisaged CFUN—not altogether unlike Washington's Tuskegee Institute—as an environment that would inculcate the virtues of discipline, hard work, social responsibility, self-respect, and personal hygiene, which he, like Karenga, believed to be lacking in the "basic blood." In the poverty-stricken, riot-scarred Central Ward, Baraka found a small but dedicated constituency of working-class African Americans who were sufficiently attracted to his message of self-transformation and communal uplift to become full-time Kawaida "advocates." Saidi Nguvu was in his late twenties when he joined CFUN in 1968. A native of Mississippi, he had just arrived in Newark after serving in Vietnam, and the "burned out" city blocks reminded him of the war zone he had left behind. Now working as a machinist, Nguvu attended a soul session one Sunday at CFUN's headquarters on High Street and joined the organization immediately afterward. "Imamu Baraka made a speech, I will never forget it," he would later recall. "It was dealing with morality, like cleaning up your lifestyle—drinking and smoking and all this type of stuff. The new man, an alternative value system." Nguvu found Baraka's sermon "so strong and convincing" that he threw his cigarettes away and "never smoked a day since. That was the impact it had on me."[102]

Another CFUN advocate from a working-class background was Taalamu (Tim Holiday), who joined in 1970 while in his early twenties. Having experienced "family problems, personal problems," Taalamu was attracted to Kawaida as "a moral code, an ethical code," and sought "an identification with manhood." Nettie Rogers joined CFUN in 1968 at the age of twenty, and was given the name "Salimu," Swahili for "to submit," which encapsulated Kawaida's ideal of femininity. She became the organization's full-time secretary and claims that women were "the backbone" of CFUN, responsible for "all the secretarial work" as well as sharing in the work of "promoting our ideologies" in local colleges and community associations. Yet she does not charge the organization's men with laxness. Indeed, Nguvu recalls that his first assignment in CFUN was "to go out and organize tenant groups to alleviate the conditions in the housing projects. To get better service, elevators, all that kind of stuff."[103]

Baraka's intention to restore "healthy African identities" to the black men and women of Newark determined CFUN's highly regimented organizational structure. The female contingent, known as *Mumininas* ("Believers") and *Malaikas* ("Good Spirits") formed their own division under Amina's leadership. In 1971 they published a handbook for nationalist women, which claimed, obscurely, that a "German named Bachkofen" had "imagined and imposed the idea of the Black matriarchy." This idea persisted "within the enslaved minds of Black people" and served "to emasculate our men" and produce "broken Black homes." In other respects, the handbook closely adhered to Baraka's and Karenga's writings and maintained that the role given to the black woman "by nature" was "to be inspirational to the man, educational for the children, and participate in the social development of the nation." The women of CFUN had established the African Free School in 1969 to offer day care to young children and an after-school program for students ages seven to seventeen, which incorporated Swahili and "hieroglyphics" alongside a curriculum of sciences and humanities oriented toward African themes. Women also provided communal meals for CFUN members.[104]

The men's division comprised an elaborate hierarchy intended to acculturate black males to "African" values of generational authority and a quasi-military code of rank and discipline. The potentially wayward *(ovyo)* energies of young males were to be contained and channeled to constructive ends within a system that privileged seniority and maturity. Boys ages seven to fifteen joined the "Super Simba" program, which, according to CFUN's monthly newspaper, *Black NewArk,* was "designed to create a new way of life for our young and to serve as an alternative to all the negative things in our community that kill our strong Black youth of today." Instructed in *yangumi* (martial arts) and *tabura* (a "form of Afrikan drills"), the boys were expected to maintain a "high level of discipline" and to "respect their elders and their family." At sixteen, boys progressed to the *Simba Wachunga* ("Young Lions"), a youth organization committed to "the upliftment of the Black Nation" through community organizing and training in political ideology and self-defense. On reaching maturity in their twenties, males were "promoted" to the level of *Mwanafunzi* ("Apprentice Teachers"). Higher authority lay with Baraka and the *Wazee* ("Circle of Elders"). Nguvu remembers one of these senior advocates, Baba Mshauri, who had been born in 1898, as a "wise man who really gave us a lot of guidance" and commanded respect "because of his age and his mind."[105]

CFUN was, for Baraka, the kernel from which postindustrial Newark would reemerge, transformed in the image of the perennial African village. Work by Terence Ranger and other historians suggests that the very notion of traditional African communities as subject to the strict patriarchal authority of a council of elders was, in reality, a twentieth-century "invented tradition," devised by colonial anthropologists and African elders themselves. Yet as fanciful as Baraka's image of a timeless, unitary Africa may have been, of greater importance here is the resonance of his idealized Africa with less geographically remote conceptions of social order. His message, that "we gotta get a betta structure," was the message of successive generations of American reformers who, in Gaines's words, "viewed the presence of poor blacks in the city . . . as a moral peril" and sought to fortify personal discipline and family life. Swahili terminology aside, CFUN's internal organization owes much to the "normalcy" of Baraka's social vision and to the uplift tradition's incorporation of the dominant American (and, in many respects, European) ideals of orderliness, respectability, and patriarchy. The Super Simba corps was, in effect, a thinly Africanized version of the Boy Scouts. At a time when the American youth and student movements were challenging the institutional authority of families and schools, Baraka upheld the duty "to believe with all our hearts in our parents, our teachers, our leaders." His "revolutionary" social ethics share more with the New Right's subsequent denunciations of "the 1960s" than with the antiauthoritarian attitudes of the New Left.[106]

Undoubtedly, CFUN became a vehicle for Baraka's own increasingly authoritarian tendencies. In September 1969, he circulated a memorandum requiring men in the organization to "salute" when he entered meetings, and women to "cross hands on breast, bow." Moreover, Baraka's ambition and profile began to trouble Karenga, much as Malcolm X had incurred Elijah Muhammad's suspicion and envy. Karenga's attentions were consumed by a turf war (probably stoked by the FBI) between US and the Black Panthers in California, which had claimed the lives of two Panthers during a shoot-out in January 1969. Baraka received reports from Los Angeles that Karenga was panicked by the threat of police subversion within US and was behaving abusively toward some advocates. Meanwhile, Baraka was thinking expansively and planning to create an umbrella organization, the Congress of African People (CAP), to coordinate existing nationalist groups across the United States and export the CFUN model to other cities. Karenga refused to sanction the plan and even sent a handful of armed men to disrupt the Atlanta convention that inaugurated CAP in September 1970. In response, Baraka swiftly terminated CFUN's connection with US. The following year, Karenga was convicted of "torturing" a woman who had recently left his organization. With Karenga imprisoned and marginalized, Baraka became Kawaida's foremost exponent. The formation of CAP, which soon claimed twenty-five affiliate branches from Brooklyn to San Diego, further enhanced Baraka's national stature. Acknowledging his rising credentials as a black power figurehead, J. Edgar Hoover resolved that the

FBI's ongoing "investigation" into Baraka's activities would receive more "aggressive, imaginative attention."[107]

On the rare occasions when white journalists now gained direct access to Baraka—usually through his publishers' efforts—they rendered him as the personification of black America's retreat from integrationist optimism to a sinister, embittered separatism. No longer an indigenous interpreter of black urban America to white audiences, he became instead a symbol of broken dialogue and of an impenetrable, alien blackness. Baraka was "lost to the tradition of American literature," and he and his Newark associates "have turned their back on the U.S. and have gone Swahili," wrote Thomas Collins in an article titled "From the Ghetto, the Cry of an Impassioned Poet." Michael Mok, reporting for *Publishers Weekly,* visited Baraka inside one of CFUN's *hekalus* and was evidently disoriented by his "African" surroundings. As if to evoke a Victorian explorer's uneasy encounter with a tribal chief, he recounted how he was "guided through the temple by a series of dashiki-clad functionaries, passed from one to the other with terse phrases in Swahili, and was finally shown into the presence of the playwright," who reportedly "runs Newark like a private fief."[108]

I Will Create a City!

Newark remained Baraka's primary focus, not least as "a base, an example" of black "nation building" that could be replicated across the country. "We will nationalize the city's institutions," he wrote in 1970, "as if it were liberated territory in Zimbabwe or Angola." With Kenneth Gibson's triumph in the mayoral elections that May—aided by CFUN's vigorous campaigning in the Central Ward, which impressed Kenneth Clark sufficiently to elicit his financial support—Baraka grew in confidence. Yet the change of administration did not lessen his demand for a transformation of black people's values and mores. Newark as it had existed would give way to a new city—a "New Ark," as he called it—only when its people, the "soon to be conscious city-tribe," were themselves made anew. "I will create a city!" he wrote in a moment of hubris. "A city of men. A city of Gods." "New-Ark," indeed, was the name a group of Puritans had given their settlement by the Passaic River some three hundred years earlier, when they imagined their city-on-a-hill as a cov-enanted community of the righteous in a new world.[109]

Despite his split from Karenga, Baraka continued to cultivate his identity as "Imamu." This, he believed, subsumed his artistic and intel-lectual persona within an organic social and political role. At the At-lanta convention that established CAP in September 1970, Baraka ended his keynote address by reading a new poem, "It's Nation Time." An incantatory plea for the race to "come together in unity" for "we are the same," the poem nevertheless reiterated Baraka's claim that black liberation necessitated a cultural and moral transformation: "all niggers negroes must change up." A similar message animates the book *In Our Terribleness* (1970), for which Baraka provided text to accompany Fundi's (Billy Abernathy's) photographs of African Americans on the streets of Newark. However, uncommonly among his writings of this period, Baraka's text, a mixture of verse and prose, appears at certain points to acknowledge the pitfalls of pejorative representations of black urban life. Prompted by the raw chic of Abernathy's stylized shots of young African Americans posing on stoops and street corners, Baraka tempered the criticisms he made elsewhere of the "lifestyle of a con-quered, colonized people" who "deserve to be slaves." In a particularly self-reflexive passage, Baraka warned against "trapping ourselves in screens of negative description." Claims that "a nigger aint shit" and "Ne-groes aint got no values" could easily engender defeatism, he implied. Commenting on the speech, dress, and gestures of Abernathy's subjects, Baraka saw fit to praise a people who had "survived" their American ordeal with "style."[110]

For the critic Jennifer Jordan, *In Our Terribleness* exemplifies Baraka's "romanticization of black street life" and his "vivid, almost sexual ex-hilaration in the free world of the [']niggers.[']" Yet the book is highly atypical of Baraka's writings of the late 1960s and early 1970s, and is also wracked by internal contradictions. Amid his flattering remarks about black people's "natural sweet smoothness," Baraka cannot resist instructing them to "sit for the service," to "pay attention to the preacher," and to "change up." As the text progresses, Baraka increasingly reverts to his jeremiad, warning his "dazed and imprisoned brothers" that "you are your own punishment. You and the devil." An angry black man "is angry at himself 1st. Or ought to be. The nigger he is." Eventually, Kawaida's seven principles are introduced as the "only salvation," the value system that will "lift us." Those who do not grasp his message "should be in training," and "We say don't smoke don't drink no dope blank on white women." If Baraka was concerned to an unusual degree, in *In Our Terribleness,* to emphasize the resilience that had allowed black people to endure the rule of "the devil," and to demonstrate his fluency in their language and style, he nonetheless remained wedded to the belief that African Americans were morally culpable for their own subordination. Far from glorifying the life of the street, Baraka ultimately faulted black people for "standin on the stoops waitin" for change, when "it will be a value system that changes us."[111]

How little tolerance Baraka in fact had for the "romanticization of black street life" is clear from his vehement denunciation of the "blaxploitation" films that emerged in the early 1970s. In "Raise!" (his monthly column in *Black NewArk*), Baraka lambasted Gordon Parks Jr.'s *Super Fly* (1972), in which the martial artist Ron O'Neal starred as a black drug dealer romping through a series of criminal antics and sexual conquests en route to a final, triumphant cocaine deal. "The various Superflies," Baraka wrote, "glorify our weakness and make heroes out of traitors. Crossing a longhaired hippywhite with a pathological negro, get a name like (Rononeil)." Baraka excoriated "Soul radio" stations, as well as "poisonous flicks," for inundating black audiences with harmful images that glamorized dissolute and self-destructive behavior: "We have niggers makin rimes about women's backsides! And all that jive and anti-free ideology, all that wine and cigarettes and grease shoot daily through our minds in white serving confusion." A white-owned film industry, he wrote, had a vested interest in marketing images of "flashy niggers" to black viewers to maintain "control of Black minds." African Americans must establish independent communications networks in order to broadcast "self-help programs" and "anti-drug programs," and must promote "criticism and self criticism, discipline and self discipline as life style."[112]

Works such as the agitprop play *Junkies Are Full of (SHHH . . .)* testify to Baraka's persistent belief in the black artist's utility as educator and image maker. Yet his desire to elevate the artist to the role of revolutionary leader entailed an even more inflated—indeed, limitless—conception of artistic instrumentality. "The Black Artist is a creator," he insisted. "The Creator. He must become as the creative function of the universe." No longer content with words and images, Baraka aspired to be an architect of social and material reality. "THE LARGEST WORK OF ART IS THE WORLD ITSELF," he proclaimed in 1969. "The potential is unlimited. . . . The creation of Cities. Of Institutions. Governments. Treaties. Ceremonies. Public Rituals of The Actual World. The Nation." Such were the masterworks of "Garvey the artist," "Malcolm the artist," and "Nyerere the artist." With CFUN and CAP already among his own artistic accomplishments, Baraka's attention turned toward the physical environment and the literal construction of the "New Ark."[113]

In 1970, CFUN began drawing up plans for "the nationalization of land" in Newark and "the Africanization of any type of 'urban renewal' on land where Black people live." Baraka devised two projects with these aims in mind. The first was a blueprint for the redevelopment of a hundred-acre site known as NJR-32, a tract earmarked by city authorities for new housing construction in the desperately overcrowded Central Ward. For Baraka, the site presented an opportunity not simply to establish black control over urban redevelopment, but to found a new nationalist community in a built environment conducive to nationalist values. Together with Earl Coombs, an African American architect whom he had known in New York, Baraka mapped out a comprehensive vision of residential, commercial, and recreational land use. Apartments in low-rise buildings would accommodate "large African families" on low and middle incomes, "with as many as five and six bedrooms" and "all the amenities available to encourage our people to work and study and develop themselves." A community-owned "shopping mall" would generate income and employment on the basis of "cooperative economics." Parks would have "features like African botanical gardens" and dedicated spaces for "outdoor performances." A social and medical center would provide "everything from a good size theater of some 2,500 seats, to family counseling, in order to maintain a healthy climate." Education and day-care facilities, medical clinics, employment and training services, and a cable television station would also be incorporated. Detailed plans and projections were submitted to the Newark Housing Authority and New Jersey Housing Finance Agency.[114]

Meanwhile, Baraka and Coombs formulated their second development plan, this time hoping to push the frontiers of the cramped black community into the predominantly Italian American North Ward. "Kawaida Towers" was conceived as a sixteen-storey apartment block comprising 210 housing units, a 300-seat theater, and communal recreation spaces, libraries, and craft workshops. "Housing for the new African peoples," a CFUN publication insisted, must "relate to the particular needs of African people raising themselves from centuries of humiliation." Kawaida Towers would pioneer "New-Traditional housing structures" and a neo-African aesthetic worthy of "the New African Man." Here, as one member of the United Brothers later remarked, was "the dream of cultural nationalism . . . embodied within a physical building." Indeed, Kawaida Towers took shape in Baraka's mind as a vertical African village, a place where the orderly ritual life of a cohesive, traditional community could be reborn. In this respect, Baraka's cultural nationalism would appear to fit James C. Hall's characterization of the "antimodernism" and "elegiac mode" of many African American intellectuals and artists during the civil rights and black power eras. Hall's work shows an uncommon appreciation of the extent to which black nationalists, as well as integrationists such as King and Baldwin, emphasized "personal sinfulness and the fragility of the community" as aspects of the "deteriorating social order" wrought by American modernity.[115]

Notwithstanding his reverence for tradition, however, it is striking to note Baraka's adherence to modernity's promise of unfolding human progress. "We are for world progress," he wrote in 1970. "So much so that we would begin with ourselves, in order that we are clearly in tune with the move of the world spirit for birth, new vision, as *constant change*." Though black people must receive "energy and spiritual direction from our past," Baraka's notion of the cyclical rise and fall of discrete civilizations did not preclude a belief in the ongoing evolution of mankind as a whole. "We must hold out such possibility of evolution even for George Wallace's cutbuddies and relatives. . . . Our ideology is 'give power to the bringers of positive change.'" Black people were now poised to carry forward the cause of world progress, and Baraka reveled in appropriating modernity's imagery, vowing to "rebuild a city in an image more modern than most of dying America." Thus, while Baraka's vision of Kawaida Towers was intended to counteract the disintegrative, atomizing effects of American modernity, it nevertheless moved beyond the "elegiac" in its assimilation of modernity's high-rise, bombastic, futuristic aesthetics.[116]

Determined that Kawaida Towers would gain the necessary approval of state and city authorities, Baraka also allowed pragmatic considerations to influence the project's design. His team procured and adapted the architectural plans of an award-winning housing development in Jersey City and selected a general contractor with ties to political representatives of Newark's Italian American community. The project was buoyed by the award of a $6.4 million mortgage by the New Jersey Housing Finance Authority and a tax abatement from the Newark City Council, and construction commenced in October 1972. Yet the demise of the project began within weeks, as State Assemblyman Anthony Imperiale stoked racial animosities in the North Ward by mobilizing a picket at the construction site. As Imperiale's stature within the Italian American community grew, city council members hurried to revoke their support for the development, and on November 21, the tax abatement was rescinded. Legal challenges from both sides limped on for several years until in 1975 the state of New Jersey declared the project unfeasible owing to inflationary construction costs. The CFUN plan for NJR-32, which the state had pledged to finance with $10 million, also collapsed in 1975 when the city council voted against a tax abatement.[117]

As Baraka's practical efforts to "create a city" crumbled, he began to reassess his political and ideological commitments. If Gibson's election in 1970 had promised the dawn of black urban self-determination and an opportunity to build a "New Ark," the demise of Kawaida Towers and the NJR-32 redevelopment informed Baraka's growing disillusionment with black power politics. By the mid-1970s, Baraka's characterization of Newark as an internal colony had been modified to account for what he now regarded as the complicity of the new black political elites. *"Black Power,"* he wrote in 1974, "now means for many merely black faces taking white place[s], internal *neo* colonialism." A "new class of blacks" had been carried into office by the nationalist tide, only to become "native agents" of the dominant economic interests within and beyond their cities.[118]

Ironically, Baraka's deepening engagement with contemporary African politics in the early 1970s played a significant part in undermining his faith in Karenga's "African" cultural nationalism and in the revolutionary efficacy of the American black power movement. Exposure to African socialists and Communists within the African Liberation Support Committee and to Kwame Nkrumah's and Amilcar Cabral's writings about the continuing exploitation of "independent" Africa oriented Baraka toward a new understanding of Newark's power dynamics. After paying "some lip service" to the idea of a payroll tax on suburban commuters, Gibson, in Baraka's account, "quickly got silent when Prudential let it be known that they were opposed to the tax." Baraka also felt "betrayed" by the mayor's tepid support for Kawaida Towers. Gibson "could have got it built at once," Baraka believed, but preferred to avoid confrontation with city and state bureaucracies. No less than Africa's "Mobutus & Senghors & Bandas," Baraka wrote in 1974, "the Gibsons, the Bradleys, the Stokes" of America's city halls were "neocolonial puppets" who "dance to the tune of monopoly capitalist politics." The faith Baraka had placed in a racial politics of "operational unity," both within Newark and at the national black conventions in Atlanta and Gary, disintegrated as he came to perceive an "oppressive international black bourgeois class" manipulating popular enthusiasm for self-determination:

> In Newark we got a black mayor, black . . . superintendent of schools, blk bd of ed, blk supt of city hospital, blk control of anti poverty program, marcus garvey public school, malcolm x hi, hrriet Tubman, mlking, rosa parks, paul robeson student center at Rutgers u., & next year a nat turner park. But we also hve the highest tb rate, venereal disease rate, infant mortality rate in the country, one of the highest crime rates. Yet the mayor busts the [street] *vendors* cause they take

money from woolworths & kleins & sears. Where Kawaida towers cant get built, no housing, the city looks like Hanoi, & they got a grant. We gotta black police chief with a beard a huge afro, wears dashikis, and will give you a lecture on afrikan culture.

"Nationalism," Baraka had concluded, was "not enough. We must be clearly anti capitalist" and "anti imperialist, in all our political work."[119]

Turmoil within CFUN—particularly concerning gender relations—also encouraged Baraka's turn away from Kawaida and his rapid embrace of leftist ideology in the mid-1970s. "One major problem with the organization of CFUN," an internal review stated, "has been the tragiclassic confrontation of men cadre and the women cadre," as the latter increasingly resisted their assigned roles "as semen-catcher and cook." In his autobiography, Baraka alludes to his wife's "struggle against male chauvinism," which "encouraged other women in the organization to struggle against it as well." By 1974, men in CFUN were "study[ing] Lenin's works about the 'woman question.'" Importantly, Baraka's disavowal of Kawaida was encouraged by his realization of the common essentialist underpinnings of sexism and racism. In May that year, Baraka observed that "feudalism, especially in its relationship to women, is often a fellow traveler of primitive nationalism," which "rests exclusively on a racial premise." Prompted by the rebellion of CFUN's *Mumininas* as well as by his disillusionment with the new black urban leadership, Baraka jettisoned a politics of race and gender beholden to the dictates of "nature" in favor of a materialist politics organized around the category of class. On October 7, 1974, his fortieth birthday, Baraka declared CAP to be a Leninist-Maoist organization. The following year, CAP was renamed the Revolutionary Communist League, and Baraka exchanged the title "Imamu" for "Chairman." As a writer and organizer he has clung to Marxism for almost four decades, and continues to live and work in Newark's Central Ward.[120]

As Baraka set about writing *The Autobiography of LeRoi Jones* during the second half of the 1970s, he began to characterize his former cultural nationalism as an extension of a "very yellow" tradition of elite African American responses to lower-class black life. For all its separatism and exoticism, his attempt to re-Africanize black American culture had "put the middle class again in the position of carping at the black masses to follow the *black* middle class." The claim he had made, as a "middle-class black intellectual," that he "knew how to be black when the black workers did not" had placed him within "another kind of clique or elite."[121] At one level, Baraka's Marxism allowed him to explain his previous ideological "errors"—including anti-Semitism, as well as "carping at the black masses"—as the all but inevitable results of his "petit-bourgeois" socialization. Yet his newfound materialism also served to mitigate the harshest claims he had made about black people's moral culpability for their own subordination: he ceased to tell black urban audiences that they "deserve to be slaves." And just as Baraka's embrace of Lenin signaled that he no longer wished to ghettoize intellectual life in the pursuit of a hermetic "black" ideology, so his quest to reconvert black Americans to an "African" culture unsullied by Western influence yielded to a renewed appreciation for the culture of black people as it existed in the United States. "We are Afro-*Americans*," he told an interviewer in 1976, "and we have to remain aware that a special culture has evolved in the United States which has benefited by the mingling of all the other people and cultures in this country, a uniquely Afro-American culture."[122]

Chapter 3

Harlem without Walls

Romare Bearden's Realism

Projections took New York's art critics by surprise. The solo exhibition, which opened at the Cordier & Ekstrom Gallery on Manhattan's Upper East Side on October 6, 1964, revealed a drastic change of direction by an artist in his sixth decade. In place of the abstract canvases for which he had become known, Romare Bearden presented a new collage aesthetic in compositions packed with figurative detail. The cotton fields, riverside baptisms, ragged rural shacks, urban tenements, and dense street scenes that filled the planes of these new works testified to Bearden's own itinerant upbringing and the Great Migration of which he had been a part. Depicting black figures in vividly constructed settings in the rural South and the urban North, *Projections* appeared at a moment when black America's increasingly urban profile commanded public attention as never before. Less than three months earlier, the pages of newspapers and magazines had been bursting with graphic accounts of the Harlem riot, an event that punctured the media's concentration on the campaigns of nonviolent protest in the South and belatedly brought the swelling black urban communities of the North to center stage in public discussion of America's racial crisis.

In producing the twenty-one works included in the exhibition, Bearden had begun by assembling small collages, each roughly the size of a piece of typewriter paper, from a combination of colored papers, fragments of photographic images snipped from the pages of magazines and books, and additions in paint. Each collage was then photostatically reproduced as a dramatically enlarged black-and-white print, typically measuring three by four feet, or six by eight. While the brightly colored collages soon became highly valued works in their own right—even superseding the enlarged prints as among Bearden's most recognizable compositions—it was the black-and-white prints, dubbed "projections" by the gallery's owner, Arne Ekstrom, that were first presented to the public and which struck reviewers as offering a privileged insight into places beyond the experience of most denizens of New York's art scene.[1]

Focusing chiefly on the urban compositions, and highlighting Bearden's upbringing in Harlem, reviewers perceived in the works an intimate, illuminating portrayal of "Negro life" and of conditions in "Harlem tenements." The renowned critic Dore Ashton quoted Bearden's remark that the series comprised "a consolidation of some memories, of some direct experiences, from childhood to the present." For Ashton, Bearden had delivered "a piercing, activist bill of particulars of intolerable facts," above all an unflinching view of "New York City's ghetto Harlem—site of overwhelming squalor and despair." Bearden's was a "tale of horror," Ashton surmised, relayed through "harrowing images" that were "direct responses to the groundswell of awareness that brought white Americans finally into a confrontation with their crimes." *Newsweek* reproduced one of Bearden's Harlem images in a review that carried the title "Tormented Faces." In the *New York Times,* Stuart Preston declared *Projections* to be "easily one of the best shows in town" and likened the works' effect to the "shock and impact of a swift cinematic passage." This was "knockout work of its kind," Preston pronounced, "propagandist in the best sense."[2]

In an essay published in 1969, Bearden voiced discomfort with the tenor of such praise. "I am afraid," he wrote, "despite my intentions, that in some instances commentators have tended to overemphasize what they believe to be the social elements in my work." Critics and commentators who had mined his compositions for social commentary and political protest had been insufficiently attentive to what he called their "aesthetic implications." In Bearden's view,

> a quality of artificiality must be retained in a work of art since, after all, the reality of art is not to be confused with that of the outer world. Art, it must be remembered, is artifice, or a creative undertaking, the primary function of which is to add to our existing conception of reality. Moreover, such devices of artificiality as distortion of scale and proportion, and abstract coloration, are the very means through which I try to achieve a more personal expression than I sense in the realistic or conventionally focused photograph. The initial public reaction to my work has generally been one of shock, which appears to arise out of a confrontation with subject matter unfamiliar to most persons. In spite of this, it is not my aim to paint about the Negro in America in terms of propaganda.

Since *Projections,* the confluence of Bearden's arresting new figurative aesthetic and subject matter with the surge of public interest in black urban life had inaugurated a new phase in his career. By the late 1960s, he was able to leave his full-time job with New York City's Department of Social Services and earn a living, for the first time, from art alone. Yet as his essay of 1969 intimated, the role of indigenous interpreter that had transformed his professional fortunes was not one he was wholly at ease with. Lauded as an impassioned, authentic black propagandist, Bearden felt slighted as an artist. The formal innovations and "artifice" of his work, and its wider meanings and resonances, had been underappreciated, he believed.[3]

More recently, Bearden's work in collage, which remained his primary medium for the remainder of his career, has secured his reputation as a major American artist and, in the words of the eminent critic Robert Hughes, "one of the finest collagists of the 20th century." Since Bearden's death in 1988, his importance has increasingly been recognized beyond the confines of debates about race and the nature of "black art." In the *New York Times* in 2004, Michael Kimmerman insisted that "Bearden was not a great black artist; he was a great artist, who wove his own life and the lives of other blacks into collages, a distinction that needs restating." Reacting against the initial reception of Bearden's collages as propagandist, scholars have been concerned to legitimate his works as sophisticated aesthetic statements of enduring value, rather than time-bound expressions of social protest. No longer seen as the chronicler of "squalor and despair," Bearden has been recast as an artist who, in Mary Schmidt Campbell's words, set out "not to attack the ruling forces" but "to celebrate the life and history of Black America." This reassessment has been driven in part by growing attention to Bearden's friendship and collaboration with the anti-pathologist critic and novelist Albert Murray. Bearden's biographer, Myron Schwartzman, has stressed the similarities in the two men's beliefs about the purposes of art and the nature of African American experience, and Henry Louis Gates Jr. has termed their relationship an "artistic alliance." The connection underpins an art historical literature that now emphasizes the affirmative, celebratory register of Bearden's portrayal of black life.[4]

Does Bearden's art in fact satisfy Murray's requirement of "accentuating the positive and eliminating the negative" in representations of black life? Like his literary friends Murray and Ralph Ellison, Bearden during the 1960s signaled his dissatisfaction with depictions of African American communities as overwhelmed by misery and dysfunction. Describing the origins of *Projections* at the time of its opening, Bearden stated: "I felt that the Negro was becoming too much of an abstraction, rather than the reality that art can give a subject. James Baldwin and other intellectuals were defining the Negro sociologically, but not artistically. What I've attempted to do is establish a world through art in which the validity of my Negro experience could live and make its own logic." The "sociological," pathologist perspective of authors such as Baldwin was a prominent target of Murray's and Ellison's critical pens, and the triangle of friendships between Bearden, Murray, and Ellison undoubtedly reflected a shared belief that black urban life offered more to those who lived it, and to artists who wished to portray it, than deprivation, pathology, and suffering.[5]

Yet despite such common ground, an understanding of Bearden's thought and artistic practice during the 1960s requires greater recognition of his divergence from Murray's mode of representation, political beliefs, and conception of the relationship between art and society.

Illustrations

Figure 1 Kenneth B. Clark addresses members of the press on the subject of racial tensions in Cleveland, June 14, 1967. (© Bettmann/CORBIS)

Figure 2 Amiri Baraka with his wife, Amina, and son, Obalaji, Newark, January 1968. (Photographs and Prints Division, Schomburg Center for Research in Black Culture, The New York Public Library, Astor, Lenox, and Tilden Foundations)

Figure 3 Romare Bearden in Harlem, 1952. Photo by Sam Shaw. (© Sam Shaw
Inc. Licensed by Shaw Family Archives Ltd., www.shawfamilyarchives.com)

Figure 4 Albert Murray (left) and Ralph Ellison at the American Academy of
Arts and Sciences, Cambridge, Massachusetts, May 24, 1967. (Fred W. McDarrah/
Premium Archive/Getty Images)

Figure 5 Romare Bearden, *The Visitation*, 1941, gouache with ink and graphite on brown paper, 30⅝ × 46¼ in. (77.8 × 117.5 cm). (Estate of Romare Bearden, courtesy of Romare Bearden Foundation, New York. © Romare Bearden Foundation/DACS, London/VAGA, New York 2012)

Figure 6 Romare Bearden, *At Five in the Afternoon,* 1946, oil on board, 30×38 in. (76.2×96.5 cm). (Fred Jones Jr. Museum of Art, University of Oklahoma, USA/ Purchase, U.S. State Department Collection, 1948/The Bridgeman Art Library. © Romare Bearden Foundation/DACS, London/VAGA, New York 2012)

Figure 7 Romare Bearden, *Mountains of the Moon,* 1956, oil on canvas,
40½×31¾ in. (102.9×80.6 cm). (Private collection. © Romare Bearden Foundation/
DACS, London/VAGA, New York 2012)

Figure 8 Romare Bearden, *Circus (Circus: The Artist's Center Ring)*, 1961, collage of various papers on paper. (Estate of Romare Bearden, courtesy of Romare Bearden Foundation, New York. © Romare Bearden Foundation/DACS, London/VAGA, New York 2012)

Figure 11 Palmer C. Hayden, *Midsummer Night in Harlem,* 1936, oil on canvas,
25×30 in. (63.5×76.2 cm). (The Museum of African American Art, Los Angeles. Palmer
C. Hayden Collection, gift of Miriam A. Hayden)

Figure 12 Romare Bearden, *The Dove,* 1964, cut-and-pasted printed papers, gouache, pencil, and colored pencil on board, 13⅜ × 18¾ in. (33.8 × 47.5 cm), New York, The Museum of Modern Art (MoMA). (Image copyright The Museum of Modern Art, New York/Scala, Florence. © Romare Bearden Foundation/DACS, London/ VAGA, New York 2012)

Figure 13 Romare Bearden, *Evening, 9:10, 461 Lenox Avenue,* 1964, collage of various papers with paint, ink, and graphite on cardboard, 8⅜×11 in. (21.3×27.9 cm). (Van Every/Smith Galleries, Davidson College, Davidson, North Carolina. © Romare Bearden Foundation/DACS, London/VAGA, New York 2012)

Figure 14 Romare Bearden, *Evening Meal of Prophet Peterson,* 1964, collage of various papers with graphite on cardboard, 12×15¼ in. (30.5×38.7 cm). (Elisabeth M. and William M. Landes, Chicago. © Romare Bearden Foundation/DACS, London/VAGA, New York 2012)

Figure 15 Romare Bearden, *Prevalence of Ritual: Baptism,* 1964, collage of various papers with paint, ink, and graphite on cardboard, 9⅛×12 in. (23.2×30.5 cm). (Hirshhorn Museum and Sculpture Garden, Smithsonian Institution, Gift of Joseph H. Hirshhorn, 1966. Photograph by Lee Stalsworth. © Romare Bearden Foundation/DACS, London/VAGA, New York 2012)

Figure 16 Romare Bearden, *Prevalence of Ritual: Conjur Woman,* 1964, collage of various papers with foil, ink, and graphite on cardboard, 9⅜ × 7¼ in. (23.8 × 18.4 cm). (Private collection, New York. Image courtesy National Gallery of Art, Washington, D.C. © Romare Bearden Foundation/DACS, London/VAGA, New York 2012)

Figure 17 Romare Bearden, *Cotton,* 1964, collage of various papers with paint, ink, and graphite on cardboard, 11⅛ × 14 in. (28.3 × 35.6 cm). (Hirshhorn Museum and Sculpture Garden, Smithsonian Institution, Gift of Joseph H. Hirshhorn, 1966. Photograph by Lee Stalsworth. © Romare Bearden Foundation/DACS, London/VAGA, New York 2012)

Figure 18 Romare Bearden, *Sermons: The Walls of Jericho,* 1964, collage of
various papers with paint, ink, and graphite on cardboard, 11⅞ × 9⅜ in.
(30.2 × 23.8 cm). (Hirshhorn Museum and Sculpture Garden, Smithsonian Institution,
Gift of Joseph H. Hirshhorn, 1966. Photograph by Lee Stalsworth. © Romare Bearden
Foundation/DACS, London/VAGA, New York 2012)

Figure 19 Romare Bearden, *Sermons: In That Number,* 1964, photostat print mounted on Masonite, 39½×30 in. (100.3×76.2 cm). (Photograph courtesy of Swann Auction Galleries, New York. © Romare Bearden Foundation/DACS, London/VAGA, New York 2012)

Figure 20 Detail (panels 1 and 2) of Romare Bearden, *The Block,* 1971, cut-and-pasted printed, colored, and metallic papers, photostats, pencil, ink marker, gouache, watercolor, and pen and ink on Masonite. Overall: 48×216 in. (121.9×548.6 cm). Six panels, each: 48×36 in. (121.9×91.4 cm). (Image copyright The Metropolitan Museum of Art/Art Resource/Scala, Florence. © Romare Bearden Foundation/DACS, London/VAGA, New York 2012)

Figure 21 Romare Bearden, *The Street,* 1975, collage of various papers with fabric, paint, and ink on fiberboard, 37 × 50½ in. (94 × 128.3 cm). (Private collection. Reproduced in memory of Elaine Lebenbom. © Romare Bearden Foundation/ DACS, London/VAGA, New York 2012)

Figure 22 Romare Bearden, *Wrapping It Up at the Lafayette,* 1974, collage,
acrylic, and lacquer, 48×36 in. (121.9×91.5 cm). (The Cleveland Museum of Art,
Mr. and Mrs. William H. Marlatt Fund 1985.41. Photograph © The Cleveland Museum of
Art. © Romare Bearden Foundation/DACS, London/VAGA, New York 2012)

Figure 23 Romare Bearden, *Profile/Part II, the Thirties: Midtown Sunset*, 1981, collage of various papers with paint and bleached areas on fiberboard, 14×22 in. (35.6×55.9 cm). (Private collection. © Romare Bearden Foundation/DACS, London/ VAGA, New York 2012)

Projections is testimony to Bearden's rare accomplishment in resisting not only pathologism but also its polar opposite, the romanticization of black urban life to which Murray was prone. As will be seen, Murray's commentaries on Bearden's art—in particular, his insistence that it not be read as a form of "protest"—set the tone for scholarship that amplifies the celebratory quality of Bearden's work at the expense of its social critique and political edge. Few studies make even the briefest mention of the fact that Bearden produced the urban scenes in *Projections* at the moment when tensions in Harlem were building up to and then erupting into the riot of July 1964. As much as the label "propagandist" fails to do justice to the nuance and complexity of Bearden's artistry, he was nonetheless, during the 1960s, an artist acutely concerned to reflect those tensions and, indeed, even to "attack the ruling forces."[6]

One means of uncovering Bearden's attitudes toward representation and the political functions of art is to reconstruct his sense of identification with earlier artistic schools and traditions. While his extensive study of the history of European, African, and Asian art has been frequently noted, the significance of his affinity for certain European artists has yet to be fully grasped. Perhaps unexpectedly, for an artist whose modernist collage aesthetic incorporated cubist distortions of scale and perspective and was anything but naturalistic, Bearden identified strongly with what he termed the "realism" of artists in previous centuries who had sought to render human life with "objectivity." Interrogating his collage work in conjunction with his writings and spoken remarks reveals an aspiration to "realism" and "objectivity" in Bearden's own artistic practice. Disavowing both the pathologist tendency toward "propaganda" and the romanticizing impulse, which he called "flattery," he revered Pieter Brueghel the Elder and other northern European genre painters of the sixteenth and seventeenth centuries, as well as Gustave Courbet, the pioneer of nineteenth-century French realism. The works of these European painters powerfully influenced Bearden's own approach to representing the lives of impoverished people at a time of social and political upheaval. In doing so, they shaped his sense of the possibilities and responsibilities of engagement, as an artist, with America's urban crisis.[7]

This lineage points to substantial differences between the artistic and political outlooks of Bearden and Murray, who was consistently scathing about the "genre" tradition. Yet the very self-assurance with which Bearden situated his own work in relation to the art of these European "masters" simultaneously underscores a crucial similarity between Bearden, Murray, and Ellison. In stark contrast both to Kenneth Clark's pained sense of black intellectual life as a bounded, marginal terrain and to Amiri Baraka's search for an intellectual sphere of racial purity, the confident cosmopolitanism of Bearden, Murray, and Ellison recalls the sentiments of W. E. B. Du Bois in *The Souls of Black Folk:*

> I sit with Shakespeare and he winces not. Across the color line I move arm in arm with Balzac and Dumas, where smiling men and welcoming women glide in gilded halls. From out the caves of evening that swing between the strong-limbed earth and the tracery of the stars, I summon Aristotle and Aurelius and what soul I will, and they come all graciously and with no scorn nor condescension.

Ellison would write in 1968 that Bearden's collages affirm "the irrelevance of the notion of race as a limiting force in the arts." Like Ellison and Murray, Bearden admired the writings of the French theorist, novelist, and sometime minister of culture André Malraux, and above all Malraux's conception of a "Museum without Walls," a vast array of artworks from every century and continent, now visible as never before to a mass audience through photography and print reproduction. The ease with which Bearden roamed the spaces of this museum, imbibing, referencing, and ultimately extending its contents, was mirrored in his portrayal of black urban life as distinctive without being detached; particular, and yet powerfully resonant with the great human themes of the canons of Western and non-Western art. Bearden's was a Harlem without walls.[8]

The Negro Artist's Dilemma

"The work which this Negro-American painter has been doing," wrote Charles Childs in *ARTnews* at the time of the *Projections* exhibition, "will surprise many who thought they knew Bearden from his abstractions. He suddenly has produced a brilliant proliferation of collages on Negro themes." It was, indeed, during his period of increasing abstraction in the years following World War II that Bearden had established an artistic reputation among New York's critical establishment. Reflecting on his career's trajectory in an interview in 1968, however, Bearden pointed out that his abstract period had been something of an interlude. While *Projections* had unveiled a change of medium in his use of collage (specifically, photomontage: collages incorporating photographic images), in fact the compositions were "kind of a reversion, you might say, back to my earliest work of the Negro subject matter: Negro genre, or Negro life, or whatever you might call it, that I first started with." Representations of black life had dominated Bearden's early artistic efforts, first as a political cartoonist and then as a painter. Yet, as the title of his 1946 essay "The Negro Artist's Dilemma" would suggest, his move toward abstraction had been prompted to a considerable degree by the discomfiting burdens of racial representation and the stark choices he had encountered on the corner.[9]

The rural and urban scenes in *Projections* evoked the principal settings of Bearden's own life: the countryside surrounding Charlotte, North Carolina, the city where he had been born in 1911 in the home of his great-grandfather, and where he would often pass his summers as a boy; Harlem, where he had arrived with his parents in around 1914, and where he would spend much of his youth; and Pittsburgh, where Bearden attended fourth grade in 1921 and the final two years of high school between 1927 and 1929 while living with his maternal grandparents. Through the windows of his interiors and at the edges of his landscapes appeared the trains that had carried the Beardens, like millions of other African Americans, from their birthplace in the South to the radically different environment of the nation's northern industrial cities.[10]

Bearden's upbringing furnished a privileged point of entry into the vibrant intellectual currents of Harlem in the 1920s and 1930s. His parents, Howard and Bessye, had belonged to the small, college-educated upper tier of black society in Charlotte, and his ambitious mother quickly attained prominence in Harlem as a Democratic activist before taking up a position in 1927 as a New York editor on the nation's leading African American weekly newspaper, the *Chicago Defender.* While Howard settled into his job as a sanitation inspector, the dynamic Bessye ensured that the Beardens' apartment on West 131st Street became a gathering place for many of the leading figures associated with the Harlem Renaissance. Among those who called at the Bearden residence in the late 1920s and early 1930s were the activist and educator Mary McLeod Bethune, the radical polymath Paul Robeson, the journalist George Schuyler, the writer and Garveyite activist Hubert Harrison, the musicians Duke Ellington and Fats Waller, the poets Langston Hughes and Countee Cullen, and the businesswoman, patron, and socialite A'Leilia Walker.[11]

Though the Beardens were a well-connected and relatively prosperous family, Romare's childhood was not without its difficulties. The family's departure from Charlotte had been triggered by a threatening incident in which a white mob had accused Howard of abducting Romare, whose skin color, unlike his father's, was so light that many who encountered him throughout his life would be surprised to learn that he was an African American. Soon after this incident Howard became a heavy drinker, and the periods Bearden spent away from Harlem with his maternal grandparents in Pittsburgh may have been a result of problems at home. It was in Pittsburgh, however, while staying in the boardinghouse run by Bessye's mother, Carrie Banks, that Bearden first showed signs of an interest in art. As Bearden would recall, he had befriended a boy named Eugene whose mother worked in a nearby brothel. Eugene's drawing of the brothel, "Sadie's house," with "the façade cut off, so you could see all the rooms," piqued the twelve-year-old Bearden's interest, and he "started taking drawing lessons from Eugene."[12]

Bearden later took classes in art and art education at Lincoln University (a black college near Oxford, Pennsylvania) and at Boston University, before graduating from New York University in 1935 with a bachelor's degree in education. His mother wished him to train as a doctor, but he was increasingly engrossed by drawing. In 1931, he had met Elmer Simms Campbell, the first African American cartoonist to be published in the *New Yorker* and the *Saturday Evening Post.* After contributing cartoons of his own to the New York University publication the *Medley,* with Campbell's encouragement Bearden achieved a coup in 1933 when a number of his political cartoons were printed in the *Crisis,* the magazine of the NAACP.[13]

Among the early targets of Bearden's pen and ink, in a cartoon for the *Baltimore Afro-American* in 1936, was the continuing exclusion of "Colored Labor" from the starkly rendered factories of "American Industry." His biographer, Schwartzman, asserts that Bearden was "never on-stage in the political arena" and remained merely a "curious, enlightened, and aware member of the audience." Measured against the content of Bearden's cartoons, this seems an obfuscation of Bearden's developing political consciousness. "His Master's Voice," which appeared in the *Afro-American* in 1935, ridiculed portly, cigar-chewing capitalists and the "Uncle Tom Race Leaders" who counseled the "Colored Man" to be "Submissive," and who denounced the NAACP as a "Bunch of Reds!" Indeed, as Bearden would himself relate in 1969, "When I first started to make pictures I was particularly interested in using art as an instrument of social change." He had believed, he recalled, that "art techniques were simply the means that enabled an artist to communicate a message."[14]

No less than his cartoons, Bearden's early paintings attest to his participation in the radical artistic and political circles of Depression-era New York, especially in the close-knit community of African American artists in Harlem for whom the Federal Art Project operated by the Works Progress Administration (WPA) was an economic lifeline. At "306," a studio on West 141st Street, Bearden spent time in the company of the artists Ernest Crichlow, Aaron Douglas, Jacob Lawrence, Norman Lewis, and Augusta Savage, as well as writers such as Richard Wright and Langston Hughes. It was here, too, that Bearden first met Ralph Ellison, who had recently arrived in New York, via Tuskegee Institute, from his native Oklahoma. Three decades later, Ellison would write of his friend:

> During the late thirties when I first became aware of Bearden's work, he was painting scenes of the Depression in a style strongly influenced by the Mexican muralists. This work was powerful, the scenes grim and brooding, and through his depiction of

unemployed workingmen in Harlem he was able, while evoking
the Southern past, to move beyond the usual protest painting of this
period to reveal something of the universal elements of an abiding
human condition.

The public art produced by the radical Mexican muralists Diego
Rivera, José Clemente Orozco, and David Siqueiros did exercise a
strong influence over many American artists during the 1930s, including those at "306." Yet Bearden's desire to refine his talents as a painter
and to imbue his art with a powerful message led him beyond Harlem's
artistic community and the Mexican vogue. His enrollment at the Art
Students League took him not only downtown but also back through
centuries of Western art history.[15]

Bearden's main instructor at the league, where he began to take
night classes in August 1933, was the renowned German émigré painter
George Grosz, a pioneer of Dada. Bearden remembered in 1969:

> The drawings of Grosz in the theme of the human situation in post
> World War I Germany made me realize the artistic possibilities of
> American Negro subject matter. It was also Grosz who led me to
> study composition, through the analysis of Brueghel and the great
> Dutch masters, and who in the process of redefining my draftsman-
> ship initiated me into the magic world of Ingres, Dürer, Holbein
> and Poussin.

Grosz's insistence on the refinement of craft through detailed study of
the draftsmanship of past masters had an enduring effect on Bearden.
Moreover, not only was Bearden attracted by Grosz's own politically
charged satires of Weimar corruption, but many of the earlier artists
to whom Bearden was introduced by Grosz—in particular, "Brueghel
and the great Dutch masters" of the sixteenth and seventeenth
centuries—had widened the realm of painterly subjects to include secular representations of the lives of townspeople, peasants, and the poor.
The painters held up to Bearden as models of draftsmanship were an
eclectic assortment, encompassing the neoclassicist Jean Auguste Dom-
inique Ingres, famed for his portrait of Napoleon, and Hans Holbein

the Younger, a painter at the court of Henry VIII. Yet it was the genre painters, above all, whom Bearden would name as his foremost influences: "I liked the painter Pieter Brueghel so much when I was in art school that the fellows used to call me Pete. . . . You ask me who my heroes were and from whom I learned something. They were the Dutch painters, Vermeer, Terborch, Pieter de Hooch in particular." No less than the example of Grosz's own work, the study of these northern European genre painters prompted Bearden to explore the possibilities of "Negro genre"—to which, as he would later comment, *Projections* marked a "reversion."[16]

A more contemporary influence on Bearden's early treatment of black American subjects, and one that was a strong presence at "306," was social realism. That Bearden's works participated in documenting the crisis of industrial capitalism and in capturing the nobility of urban proletarians and agricultural laborers is evident even in the titles of the first paintings he exhibited, at a show organized by the Art Committee of the Labor Club in New York in 1939. Bearden's *Soup Kitchen, Coal Yard,* and *Steel Mills* were among nine of his works to appear alongside those of Charles Alston, Norman Lewis, and others. *Soup Kitchen,* an oil completed in 1937 and also displayed in Bearden's first solo exhibition, held at "306" in May 1940, shows its subjects almost immobilized by chill and hunger as they hunch over steaming bowls of broth. In June 1942, Bearden's *Factory Workers* appeared in *Fortune* magazine to accompany an article on "The Negro's War." Bearden's three dark-skinned workers are heavily stylized in the social realist vein, with sculpted, almost monumental faces and disproportionately large, gesturing hands signifying their heroic productive capacity as they await admission to the factory pictured in the background.[17]

"Romie was never a poor kid," Charles Alston, his cousin by marriage, would remark many years later, but was "straight out of the middle class." Jacob Lawrence, Alston reflected, "grew up in the middle of the real Harlem poverty, and there's always been something very simple and direct about his approach, but Romie's approach to art is more intellectual. He's read a great deal all his life, and he's been intensely curious about all kinds of art." Bearden's family indeed weathered the Depression without great hardship, and his studies at the Art

Students League exposed him to art and artists from well beyond the boundaries of Harlem. Yet he was not as insulated from the "real Harlem poverty" as Alston's comments might imply. In the autumn of 1935, Bearden had begun a career as a caseworker with New York City's Department of Social Services that was to continue, with some interruptions, for more than thirty years. After 1952, he would be assigned to work with New York's Gypsy community, but during the 1930s his job was based in Harlem and undoubtedly involved visits to the homes of families grappling with extreme poverty and hunger. Even in 1949, when he described himself as an "abstractionist painter," he would tell a journalist: "There is richness in this social work, a store-house of things seen, that I draw upon in my painting."[18]

In the early 1940s, Bearden's paintings increasingly captured aspects of black life beyond the overt manifestations of poverty and production that were social realism's chief concerns. Prompted by his first visit to the South in fifteen years, Bearden produced compositions such as *The Visitation* (1941; Figure 5), a gouache in which the bearing of the two female figures, as much as the work's title, testifies to the intense spirituality of southern black life. As Mary Schmidt Campbell observes, Bearden's social realist impulse was now tempered by the "air of mystery" and "evocative poetry" with which he imbued his subjects. Though Bearden rarely attended church as an adult and did not describe himself as religious, his boyhood memories of the Shiloh Baptist Church in Charlotte had left him in no doubt as to the significance of African American religiosity and ritual. Meanwhile, works from the same period, such as the biblically inspired *They That Are Delivered from the Noise of the Archers* (1942), signal his incipient experimentation with the shallow space and geometric devices of cubism, whose pioneers, especially Pablo Picasso, had found inspiration in African sculpture.[19]

The intense fascination with black life manifested in Bearden's art during this period conveys the extent to which his identity as a "Negro artist" was not simply conferred, but willed. With green eyes and the light complexion of his mother (whose ancestry included a Portuguese carpenter, Francis Gosprey, who had lived in South Carolina before the Civil War), Bearden could have chosen to downplay his "Negro" identity. Indeed, as a talented student baseball pitcher in Boston he had reportedly received an offer to join the Philadelphia Athletics if he would agree to pass as white. His racially ambiguous appearance would be remarked on throughout his career by journalists, fellow artists, and friends. Comments about his "Russian-looking" appearance became commonplace, and a prematurely bald, heavyset Bearden would often be likened, humorously, to Nikita Khrushchev. Unlike the *New York Times* journalist Anatole Broyard, a similarly light-skinned man born into a New Orleans Creole family, Bearden made no attempt to disguise his black origins. As Ellison would put it, "Bearden is by self-affirmation no less than by public identification a Negro American."[20]

Yet Bearden was becoming acutely aware of the risky and contentious demands of racial "representation," a concept that, in Isaac Julien and Kobena Mercer's reading, encompasses both a "practice of depicting" and a "practice of delegation." In a letter of 1942 to his friend Walter Quirt, a surrealist painter, Bearden confided:

> One painter wrote from the South that my stuff was forced and deliberately painted to cater to what the critics think a Negro should paint like. To many of my own people, I learn, my work was very disgusting and morbid—and portrayed the type of Negro that they were trying to get away from. One man bought a painting and brought it back in three days because his wife couldn't stand to have it in the house.
>
> So I ask myself, is what I'm doing good or bad, Are my paintings an honest and valid statement. Have you ever felt like this? Recently I've gotten so I want to paint and then put the paintings away except to show them to a few people.

Bearden understood which "type of Negro" his critics wished him to absent from his canvasses. In a proposal that he wrote at around this time to undertake a documentary study of black urbanization, Bearden himself stated that "the American people must be informed" of the transformation of "the agricultural, adynamic clod existing almost in a state of peonage to the urban industrial type, entering into the activities of organized labor no longer through sufferances but as a factor to be considered." Sympathetic to the radical labor movement that hailed industrial modernization, yet frequently drawn back to fond childhood memories of the patterns of life around Charlotte in rural Mecklenburg County, Bearden appeared to be caught between his pride in the emergence of the "New Negro" and his lingering affection, evidenced by his paintings, for the old.[21]

To exacerbate matters, reviewers who praised Bearden's early work often betrayed an acutely patronizing romantic racialism. In *ARTnews* in October 1941, James W. Lane pronounced:

> The further removed the Negro artist is from the white man's style or subject matter, the better he is. . . . In Romery [*sic*] Bearden's composition, especially [*Women*] *Picking Cotton,* there is the deep, reverencing rhythm of the colored people. . . . The snakelike, abased body of the Negro, resigned to sing spirituals while he works, is echoed distantly by the background hills.

Two months later, a critic for the *New Yorker* who complimented Bearden's contribution to an exhibition by black artists wrote of an "almost barbaric profusion of bright reds, rich blues, and resounding purples" in the group's work and concluded: "There must be more truth than I'd realized in the ancient gag about Negroes loving bright colors." The anxiety conveyed by Bearden's letter to Quirt, particularly his expressed reluctance to exhibit his work in such a climate, had a crucial bearing on the direction his art was to take over the next two decades. Disturbed by the pitfalls of racial representation—both in his own role as a representative of the race and in the representation of African Americans within his works—Bearden began to turn away from all-black group exhibitions and from identifiably black subject matter.[22]

Following three years of service in the segregated U.S. Army, in a division that spent the war on home soil, Bearden returned in May 1945 to a rapidly changing New York art scene. The city was displacing Paris as the preeminent locus of modernist creativity in the visual arts and appeared increasingly hospitable to the aspirations of an African American painter weary of the burdens of racial representation. The ostensibly color-blind language of postwar critical modernism—and soon of Cold War liberalism—suggested that those burdens might be eased. A review in the *New York Times* late in 1945 of the last all-black group exhibition to which Bearden contributed during this period stated that "all American artists should be looked upon as Americans" and that their work "should be judged, first and last, as art alone." The ascendancy of abstraction within American art of the late 1940s and 1950s is often couched as an accommodation to the repressive political environment fueled by Cold War anticommunism. Indeed, Richard Powell contends that Bearden's renunciation of his "protest art" of the 1930s was in part "a political response to the conservative climate of the day." Yet while Bearden must have been dismayed by the hounding of Paul Robeson, once a frequent visitor to his parents' Harlem apartment, his own move toward painterly abstraction was motivated largely by his desire to break free from the constraints of prewar "Negro art."[23]

"The Negro Artist's Dilemma," published in the art journal *Critique* in November 1946, helps to reveal the shifting attitudes underlying the transformation that was occurring in Bearden's work. The essay presents a plea for the liberation of African American artists from entrenched expectations and notions of racial essentialism. All-black group shows, Bearden now believed, such as those sponsored by the Harmon Foundation since 1928, had depressed the quality of craft among black artists by removing them from wider spheres of comparison and imposing a patronizing dual standard that indulged inferior efforts. The appetite for these "segregated exhibits," Bearden charged, derived from "a sociological rather than aesthetic interest in the exhibitors' works." Moreover, "critical opinion" harmfully prescribed that the black artist must employ "African" aesthetics, must strive for a "unique, nationalistic, social expression, closely akin in feeling to jazz and the spirituals," and must provide "a trenchant reflection of his political and social aspirations."[24]

The extent to which this plea for artistic freedom marked a reversal of Bearden's attitudes is clear from a comparison with an earlier essay. In "The Negro Artist and Modern Art," published in the National Urban League's magazine *Opportunity* in 1934, Bearden had himself claimed that black artists were hindered by their lack of a "definite ideology or social philosophy," and that an "intense, eager devotion to present day life, to study it, to help relieve it" constituted "the calling of the Negro artist." It was in sharp contrast that Bearden in 1946 rejected the demand that the black artist should "mirror the misery of his people," a demand he now considered a threat to the "freedom of expression" that "is a prerequisite for any artist." Rather than becoming "subservient to a political ideology," the black artist rendered the "greatest service . . . in making his individual creations as strong as he possibly can." There was "only one art," Bearden declared, and "it belongs to all mankind." Published twelve years apart, his two essays staked out entirely opposing responses to the dilemmas of black intellectual life. At a moment when Kenneth Clark, his contemporary, was embarking with some reluctance down the path of racial obligation, Bearden after World War II returned to the corner and set off in pursuit of artistic freedom.[25]

Securing an affiliation in 1945 to Samuel Kootz's fashionable new gallery on East Fifty-Seventh Street, Bearden appeared well placed to chart a course away from "Negro art" and to pursue new formal and thematic concerns. Alongside his fellow artists at the Kootz Gallery— William Baziotes, George Byron Browne, Alexander Calder, Adolph Gottlieb, Carl Holty, and Robert Motherwell—and in common with the emerging "New York School" of painters, Bearden strove to incorporate mythic ideas and an increasingly abstract stylization into his art in a quest to locate the perennial and universal. Christ's Passion, Federico García Lorca's "Lament for the Death of a Bullfighter" (see Figure 6), and Homer's *Iliad* furnished raw materials for Bearden's exposition of "those universals that must be digested by the mind and cannot be seen merely with the eye." Images of contemporary life receded, and figures were increasingly subsumed by cubistic matrices and planes of vivid color. Critical responses were encouraging, and Bearden triumphed with a sale to the Museum of Modern Art. However, as Matthew Witkovsky observes, while the New York School painters moved toward complete abstraction, Bearden's canvases remained "relatively realistic" in their lingering, if muted, figuration. Seemingly outmoded, Bearden, Browne, and Holty were dropped by Kootz when he relaunched his gallery in 1949 with an exhibition showcasing the rising stars of abstract expressionism: Jackson Pollock, Mark Rothko, and Willem de Kooning.[26]

The 1950s were to be an unsettled and often unhappy decade for Bearden. The tension between figuration and abstraction in his work was mirrored by a further tension, which he recalled in an interview years later, between Harlem, where he lived and kept a small studio on 125th Street, and the downtown art scene. These were "two worlds" with "two different polarities," and neither seemed to embrace him any longer. He had lost his gallery representation, while the dynamic prewar community of artists in Harlem had dissipated with the withdrawal of WPA funding. Six months in Paris courtesy of the GI Bill in 1950 immersed him once again in the study of the European artistic tradition, and letters of introduction from Kootz allowed him to meet such modernist luminaries as Picasso, whom he traveled south to meet in Juan-les-Pins, and Constantin Brancusi, who roasted Bearden a meal in his sculptor's forge. Despite reveling in such cosmopolitan experiences, as his letters show, he produced little painting of his own and seemed uncertain of his future as an artist.[27]

Back in New York, "I just couldn't paint," he later remembered. He dabbled in songwriting, but despite his modest success with "Seabreeze," a number recorded by the popular singer Billy Eckstine, Bearden's anxieties about his direction as a painter contributed in 1956 to a nervous collapse. "I thought Lionel Hampton was playing the xylo's on my heart," he wrote in one of his letters to Holty. In October 1954, he had married Nanette Rohan, a dancer whose parents were immigrants from St. Martin in the French West Indies. In 1956, the couple moved from Harlem to a fifth-floor loft apartment, which included a studio space, at the corner of Canal and Wooster Streets in what would soon become Manhattan's downtown artistic epicenter, SoHo. When Bearden did paint, he largely fell into line with the prevailing tenets of abstract expressionism. Clearly influenced by Rothko's and Barnett Newman's blockish segments of color and by Pollock's emphasis on painterly process and gesture, Bearden began, as he later recalled, to "put down color in big marks" to animate his own larger and more categorically abstract compositions (Figure 7).[28]

As the fitful nature of his painting during the 1950s suggests, Bearden was never wholly at ease with abstraction. In their coauthored book *The Painter's Mind* (1969), Bearden and Holty would later censure the abstract expressionists for failing to acknowledge their place within a painterly tradition and for "attempting to break all ties with the past and, like the hero of E. M. Forster's novel, *Howard's End . . .* come upon art as a revivalist seeks to discover Christ." In his correspondence between 1948 and 1952 with Holty, a German émigré with whom he had formed a close friendship, Bearden had frequently expressed reservations about the trends in contemporary painting. "Haven't most painters been marking time," he asked, "substituting the 'effect,' the 'drip'—for the real[?]" On another occasion he wrote:

> I've also been wondering what actual philosophy justifies what we're doing. To know would certainly help clarify the problems— even those of structure. I mean by "the justification of philosophy" the extent to which Rembrandt was influenced by Spinoza's humanism either directly or by osmosis. . . . So when I look at [Theodoros] Stamos, Baziotes, and the rest, I wonder what point their work has, and to what end does it drive.

He was uneasy, too, about the avant-garde cult of individuality that surrounded the abstract expressionists—much as LeRoi Jones would criticize the Beat poets' willful alienation. Both men were troubled by what they saw as a growing detachment of art from society and its concerns. As Bearden put it to Holty:

> In a sense this isolation, in fact, as well as in spirit, makes our task really difficult. For we don't have the benefit of a strong group consciousness and contribution on lower levels that many great artists of former years enjoyed. . . . I feel that an artist, and his creations, are enhanced when he has the added emphasis and "vision" of his particularly society working along with him.

While Bearden took care to distinguish his meaning from the "sort of Marxian, or distorted Marxian, art of the people concept," he seemed to be hankering after "306."[29]

Even as figures departed from Bearden's canvases during the 1950s, he remained engaged in a deep study of European artistic traditions. He also began to learn principles of classical Chinese landscape painting, such as the use of empty space, from a bookseller whom he would always refer to simply as "Mr. Wu." "I spent three years copying," Bearden would remember. He ordered photographic enlargements of famous European paintings, which he then painstakingly copied by hand. Bearden and Holty would write in *The Painter's Mind:* "At no time in history has the art of all the world been so available to artists—at least through such information as reproductions can furnish, in what Malraux refers to as 'the museum without walls.'" Ruth Fine has detected that Bearden created a number of photostatic reversals from reproductions of paintings by old masters, such as de Hooch's genre scene *Figures Drinking in a Courtyard* (1658), with the result that the white faces of the composition's figures would appear, as in a photographic negative, black. This striking effect may well have cast Bearden's mind back to his own remark, in his essay of 1946, that the "abundant materials offered in Negro life" had yet to be treated with the sensitivity of the "rich genre painting" of Brueghel and "the other great Dutch and Flemish masters."[30]

A review in the *New York Herald Tribune* of Bearden's exhibition at the Michel Warren Gallery early in 1960—only his second solo show in a decade—heralded "Bearden's Return" to the art scene. It reported "major interest" in his "non-objective" works, which were described as "a sublimation of private experiences, more than realizations of communicable subject matter." Yet just when the art scene was beginning to enthuse about Bearden's move toward complete abstraction, the artist himself was occupied with experiments concealed from public view. The best estimate dates Bearden's first known work in collage to 1956. *Harlequin* and the later work *Circus (Circus: The Artist's Center Ring)* (1961; Figure 8) testify to Bearden's renewed interest in modernist styles of figuration—above all, in the "cut-outs" assembled by Henri Matisse from brightly colored papers during the 1940s. The tenement block fronts with dense rows of windows above which spindly acrobats perform in *Circus* signal new directions in Bearden's art.[31]

To Paint the Life of My People as I Know It

Reflecting back on his movement toward abstraction following World War II, Bearden claimed in an interview in 1964 that while he had held "nothing, of course, against representational images," he had "wanted at that time to discover a personal way of expression that might be called new. . . . I was trying to find out what was in me that was common to other men. If I remember, it was hard to do and realize." Many abstract expressionist painters had similarly believed that they could strip through cultural and temporal particularities and, by means of spontaneous gestures, access the subconscious and reveal universal aspects of the self. Yet while abstraction had enabled Bearden to breach the boundaries of "Negro art," he had never been comfortable with the flight from representation, and had regretted the absence of the "real" and of a bond between the artist and society.[32]

Years earlier, however, Bearden had observed that some artists had captured a universal humanity precisely through their nuanced representations of particular cultures, times, and places. "Rembrandt painted the ordinary Dutch people around him," Bearden had written in 1934, "but he presented their emotions in such a way that their appeal was universal." While the abstract expressionists had, in his view, neglected artistic tradition, Bearden's immersion in the "Museum without Walls" allowed him to perceive commonalities across a great swath of human subjects depicted by artists of different eras and nationalities. Curtailing his search for a nonobjective expression of universality, Bearden determined in the 1960s that "the Negro artist's dilemma" could be resolved. He would portray a Harlem without walls, rendering its people in a manner that would resonate with the most abiding human themes and so evade the narrow dictates of "Negro art."[33]

His intention to address a general human predicament through the use of materials from African American life had close parallels in the work of two black writers whom he had befriended. Ralph Ellison, whom Bearden had met at "306," and Albert Murray, whom he had first encountered at the Coupole Brasserie in Paris, had themselves become close intellectual companions after the war, when Murray was pursuing his master's degree in literature at New York University. Ellison, three years Murray's elder, was then engaged in writing the work that, on its publication in 1952, would enter the canon of "great American novels" as fast as any text before or since. Ellison claimed to have discerned "universal elements of an abiding human condition" even in some of Bearden's earliest paintings, and his novel *Invisible Man* famously concludes with its black protagonist, ensconced in his under-ground hovel, provocatively musing: "Who knows but that, on the lower frequencies, I speak for you?" Murray's career in letters was slower to take off, and less stellar when it did. Yet during the 1960s he became a respected critic and polemicist who expressed a fierce aversion to black nationalism and shared Ellison's belief that segregation had failed to prevent the emergence of a composite American national culture deeply indebted to black music, speech, and dance.[34]

When Murray moved permanently to New York in 1962, having retired from the air force, he sought out Bearden, whom he remem-bered from Paris as a "real hip literary guy" who would talk about Murray's beloved Thomas Mann and about art and philosophy. As Murray recalled their first encounter in Paris, "I didn't know whether he was white, Russian, this or that. . . . But then Romare started laugh-ing. And I said, 'This guy's colored.' Because [of] the idiom." In New York, Murray asked Ellison for Bearden's whereabouts, but "Ralph had given up on Romie," Murray later claimed, when Bearden had turned to songwriting during the 1950s. Murray pursued Bearden, and by the time *Projections* opened in 1964, not only had the two men rees-tablished their friendship, but Murray had begun to play a significant role in Bearden's professional life by providing titles for several of his collage works.[35]

Murray would also claim to have been substantially involved in Bearden's writings from the 1960s onward. In an interview in 1994, he claimed that Bearden "would get an invitation to write about some-thing. And then we would collaborate on it." Murray's immodesty needs, however, to be weighed against this claim to effective coauthor-ship of Bearden's writings. In the same interview, Murray not only referred to himself as Bearden's "major literary friend" (a notion that Ellison might have contested) but also claimed that Duke Ellington had said it was "because of friends like Albert Murray that I'm going to have to amount to something." For his part, Bearden admitted that he lacked confidence in his abilities as a prose stylist—he found the "rhythm of sentences . . . very difficult"—and that he relied on the help of editors such as Nick Lyons of Crown Publishers, who worked on *The Painter's Mind*. In a conversation in the 1980s, Bearden did not object to Myron Schwartzman's reference to one of his major publications, "Rectangular Structure in My Montage Paintings" (1969), as an essay "you wrote with Al." Yet a substantial section of that essay appears to be closely based on remarks made by Bearden during an interview in June 1968, which suggests a more limited authorial, or editorial, role for Murray.[36]

An appreciation of the nature of Bearden's intellectual relationship with Murray is clearly of importance to an understanding of his work from the time of *Projections* onward. Yet precisely because of their proximity in Manhattan and the informality of their friendship, the relationship is difficult to reconstruct. There is no trail of letters, and no record of conversations between the two men during the 1960s and 1970s. What remains, and deserves closer comparative analysis, is the work the two men produced. Murray's designation by Gates as the "foremost cultural explicant of black modernism" provides some sense of the appeal that Murray's intellectual companionship held for Bearden. Both men's imaginations were engaged by boyhood recollections of the South as well as by the commotion of black urban life in the North, and they shared a learned reverence for jazz and the blues. Moreover, both sought to harness the techniques of modernism, whether Faulkner's or Picasso's, to their explorations of African American life and culture. By the mid-1960s, their cosmopolitan black modernism was, in Gates's words, "besieged by the simplifying insurgence of black nationalism," yet Bearden and Murray held fast to their eclectic, syncretistic approaches to art and literature. While his brash, pugnacious manner contrasted with Bearden's genial aura, Murray's wit and irreverence, elegantly couched in black vernacular cadence, made him endearing company. Nevertheless, what Gates has called an "artistic alliance" concealed significant political and aesthetic differences that influenced their respective approaches to the representation of black urban life. These points of tension became especially salient as the domestic and international turmoil of the 1960s revived contentious discussions of the relationship between the artist and society. Recognizing the idiosyncrasy of Murray's political attitudes helps to situate not only him but also Bearden more accurately within the debates surrounding the role of black intellectuals in the civil rights movement and the problems of pathologism and romanticization.[37]

Murray had not experienced the radical political climate and black artistic solidarity of New York in the 1930s that had been critical for Bearden and Ellison as young men. His career as an air force pilot during the first decade of the Cold War further distinguished him from his two friends. While a dislike of "propaganda" was common to all three men by the 1960s, Murray's response to the radicalism of the decade bore a vitriolic, sometimes even reactionary slant distinct from the more tempered positions of Bearden and Ellison. Though his sophisticated theorization of African American aesthetics eventually earned him the respect of leading literary scholars such as Gates and Houston Baker Jr., the political hue of Murray's writings enhanced their appeal to a younger generation of conservative black commentators such as Stanley Crouch.[38]

Murray's reminiscences about the genesis of *Projections* illuminate the divergence between his and Bearden's views of the relationship between art and politics during the 1960s. By Bearden's own account, he had begun to assemble photomontages with African American subjects as part of his involvement in Spiral, a new forum for black artists in New York that began meeting in July 1963. Bearden initially proposed that the group work collectively to create a photomontage from images he had cut from the pages of magazines. When the suggestion was not taken up, he pursued the idea alone. The intentions of Spiral's approximately fifteen members were summarized in an unsigned foreword to the catalog for their group exhibition, which opened in May 1965 and to which Bearden contributed a collage:

> During the summer of 1963, at a time of crucial metamorphosis just before the now historic March on Washington, a group of Negro artists met to discuss their position in American society and to explore other common problems. One of those present, the distinguished painter Hale Woodruff, asked the question: "Why are we here?" He suggested, in answering his own question, that we, as Negroes, could not fail to be touched by the outrage of segregation,

or fail to relate to the self-reliance, hope, and courage of those persons who were marching in the interest of man's dignity.

Bearden had himself written in October 1963 that Spiral's members "feel that they have an obligation in helping to determine the cultural position of this democracy."[39]

When Murray referred to Spiral in 1994, it was as a "danger" to artistic integrity:

> The danger was when the civil rights movement . . . the painters in New York were trying to find a way to get into—on it. And they wanted to be *engagé*. And so part of that was, they finally organized a group called the Spiral Group. And they would meet. And some of those guys in there, you know, were all hyped up on . . . Negritude. You know, they could tell a black painting. . . . [But] what Romie discovered, was that . . . many of these people meeting in the group—didn't know the fundamentals of painting. . . . So that's how he got into this, because he could theorize for days. I mean, he knew the dynamics. He had all the stuff together. And so he decided that these—that what they should do is spend a certain amount of time on fundamentals of painting! Not just how they could become engaged in the civil rights movement, how they could make their work more relevant to the movement or something like that, but how they could become painters. Because there are certain guys, they just interested in having a studio and . . . having some girls come up and pull off their clothes.

Collage, Murray went on to say, occurred to Bearden as an appropriate didactic device for use in Spiral's meetings: "Not mixing paints, not holding the brush, none of that. That was too complicated."[40]

Murray insisted that Bearden himself had been innocent of any intention to reflect the climate of civil rights activism in his art: Bearden "wasn't talking about" the "march on Selma or something like that." Murray was dismayed that *Projections* had been received by critics as a commentary on black urban deprivation and political upheaval. In fact, Murray seems to have assumed an incompatibility between a concern to reflect contemporary social and political realities in art, which he termed "propaganda," and a concern for craft and the formal aspects of the painterly tradition:

> And so the main thing got to be getting him out of the civil rights context, which was only going to reduce the significance of his painting to propaganda! So he . . . look at all these guys [art critics], "All those accusing eyes on the streets of Harlem," and all that kind of junk. You know what I mean? And we would spend all this time talking about Miro, we were talking about this, we were talking about the principles of organization . . . we were talking about equalize surface tension, talking about flat painting . . . what do you learn from P[i]eter de [Hooch], what's he doing for [Vermeer].

Murray claimed to have urged Bearden to distance himself from the political art of the period: "I insisted that he get—that he not let people reduce it to a black boy hollering out for attention, or showing ugliness. These were aesthetic statement[s]. This was not a picture of ugliness, *or poverty*."[41]

Though Murray is reported to have attended Spiral's first meeting, his portrayal of Bearden as the patient instructor of a rowdy group of neophytes, short on talent and carried away by their naive politics and libidos, bears little resemblance to Bearden's remark in 1973 that "each of the members were capable artists and had their own metier." One or two younger members apparently introduced fellow artists to the group who were found wanting by some of the existing members, but this was hardly surprising within an informal gathering of artists with diverse backgrounds. The artists who participated in the group show in 1965 included several well-established figures of Bearden's own generation, including Charles Alston, Norman Lewis, Felrath Hines, and Hale Woodruff. All fifteen had received advanced training, including the younger artists, such as Emma Amos, who, at twenty-seven the group's youngest member and its lone woman, had studied at Antioch College, the London School of Arts, the Intaglio Workshop, and New York University.[42]

A group interview with Spiral's members by the art commentator Jeanne Siegel, published in 1966, revealed that their outlooks and views on the relationship between art and politics were as varied as their paintings. As Siegel observed, they were united not by any manifesto but by a mutual interest in what each considered a vital question: "What should be their attitudes and commitments as Negro artists in the present struggle for Civil Rights[?]" In 1968, Bearden would remark that "these meetings and discussing the identity of the Negro, what a Negro artist is, or if there is such a thing, all of these pro and con discussions, meant a great deal to me especially in the formulation of my present ideas and way of painting." Moreover, Bearden appears to have been among the more politically conscious of Spiral's artists, and one of the most concerned with developing a characteristically black visual idiom. While the painter Norman Lewis, whose style tended toward abstraction, announced his desire to create something more than an "illustrative statement" of "social conditions," and cast doubt on the existence of a "Negro Image" in art, Bearden stated: "I use subject matter to bring something to it as a Negro—another sensibility—give it an identity." Furthermore:

> I suggest that Western society, and particularly that of America, is gravely ill and a major symptom is the American treatment of the Negro. The artistic expression of this culture concentrates on themes of "absurdity" and "anti-art" which provide further evidence of its ill health. It is the right of everyone now to re-examine history to see if Western culture offers the only solution to man's purpose on this earth.

To this end, Bearden suggested that the group discuss the aesthetic theories of the Senegalese president and *Négritude* poet Léopold Senghor and the writings of the Afrocentrist historian Cheikh Anta Diop. Bearden had been aware of the concept of *Négritude,* which was ridiculed by Murray, at least since 1950, when, in Paris, he had encountered the literary circle around Senghor's journal *Présence Africaine.* In 1969, Bearden would remark to a critic that he had been influenced by "the African concept that runs through Senghor—the land, the beauty of a black woman, the protective presence of the dead, the acceptance of intuition." As will be seen, Bearden's willingness to look beyond "Western culture" and his interest in *Négritude* were in marked contrast to Murray's American nationalism and disdain for Africa.[43]

Murray's writings from the 1960s and 1970s also divulge ideas about art, politics, and the representation of black life that diverged substantially from Bearden's thinking, and which help to account for his desire to take Bearden "out of that civil rights context." Murray was unquestionably supportive of the aims of the civil rights movement. Yet he dissented from the tactical premise of many civil rights activists and sympathetic intellectuals, which he called "moral outcry rhetoric." Though he scarcely formulated a detailed alternative, Murray favored what he described as a more hard-headed, less emotive strategy based on political leverage and negotiation.[44]

Animating all of Murray's writings was a fervent pride in the expressive culture of the people he called "U.S. Negroes." They were for him the quintessential Americans, a resourceful, pragmatic people with the capacity to adapt creatively and stylishly to all situations. The blues, a "tradition of confrontation and improvisation . . . of 'resilience,'" was in Murray's view "indigenous to the United States, along with the Yankee tradition and that of the backwoodsman." The blues sensibility was also, for Murray, inextricable from a uniquely American embrace of freedom. Even during slavery, "that the *conception* of being a free man in America was infinitely richer than any notion of individuality in the Africa of that period goes without saying." Murray's affirmation of the values and lifestyles of "U.S. Negroes" was thus enmeshed in an American exceptionalist notion of a democratic national character. While Bearden suggested that remedies for America's "ill health" might lie beyond the American and Western traditions, Murray remained convinced that the American democratic heritage would deliver.[45]

Shame is often pride's unwanted companion, and much of the sting of Murray's polemical writing derived from his discomfort with the "moral outcry rhetoric" of black authors who promised to "spell out the 'nitty gritty' facts about black experience." While Murray celebrated the dignity, resilience, humor, and joyous social life of African

Americans, Kenneth Clark and others grounded their appeals for civil rights and social programs on what Murray viewed as derogatory images of black urban communities mired in social pathology and psychological damage. Civil rights leaders, instead of "putting on the poormouth" in the hope of extracting concessions through pity, should concentrate on asserting African Americans' rights under the Constitution, Murray believed. Their "welfare militancy" was "only an overreaction to a lot of second-rate folklore of white supremacy"—his characterization of pathologist social science.[46]

Murray's satisfaction that *Projections* did not furnish "a picture of ugliness, or poverty" was therefore vital to his endorsement of Bearden's artistic practice. So uncomfortable was Murray with the notion that poverty had adverse effects on the social, cultural, and psychological fabric of black life that he rebuked the southern historian C. Vann Woodward, of whom he generally approved, for lapsing into the language of a "social welfare polemicist" when writing "such completely un-Southern things as, 'While the small, mobile, trained middle class has been moving up, the great mass of Negro workers has been stagnating or, relative to white workers, losing ground.' Jolly good Big Daddy Moynihan non-violent war on poverty jive." Murray appeared hostile toward the War on Poverty, as though government social programs affronted African Americans' dignified, self-reliant blues sensibility. No such hostility was forthcoming from Bearden, the social worker, or Ellison, who would always credit the New Deal with his own survival and that of other poor blacks during the Depression.[47]

As was seen in Chapter 1, Murray's critique of pathologism for its resonance with stereotypes of black inferiority and deviancy extended to an embrace of an antithetical but equally problematic romanticization of black life, one that sometimes echoed the competing stereotypes of black joyousness that had been employed to justify white supremacy. His debut novel, the semiautobiographical *Train Whistle Guitar* (1974), recounts a boy's coming of age amid the sensory delights of black life in an Alabama mill town: the taste of southern home cooking; the sacred sounds of church music and the profane timbre of the blues; the "Saturday night jook joint function"; folktales and barber shop banter; and audacious encounters with buxom, older "honey brown girls." Indeed, in his work of criticism *The Omni-Americans* (1970), Murray had enjoined writers to "do justice to the enduring humanity of U.S. Negroes, people who, for instance, can say of their oppressors, 'Yeah, we got our troubles alright. But still and all, if white folks could be black for just one Saturday night they wouldn't never want to be white folks no more!' "[48]

These words, chosen by Murray to stand as the collective voice of black America, have an unexpected provenance. In 1965, Ralph Ellison had recounted an old "white Southern joke on Negroes" in which a white employer inquires why his most productive black worker never agrees to work overtime on Saturday nights. The worker replies, "If you could just be a Negro one Saturday night, you'd never want to be a white man again." To Ellison's mind, this "rather facile joke" at least recognized "an internality to Negro American life, that it possesses its own attraction and its own mystery." Yet while such recognition worked against the pathologist view of black life as reducible to its miseries, it strayed toward another, no less stereotyped view of black experience. In his sympathetic exploration of "White Negro" primitivism in 1957, Norman Mailer had also deployed the trope of black Saturday night revelry. Explaining how the "white hipster," faced with the prospect of nuclear annihilation, had "absorbed the existentialist synapses of the Negro," Mailer contended that "the Negro (all exceptions admitted) could rarely afford the sophisticated inhibitions of civilization, and so he kept for his survival the art of the primitive, he lived in the enormous present, he subsisted for his Saturday night kicks, relinquishing the pleasures of the mind for the more obligatory pleasures of the body." As the historian George Fredrickson has shown, the notion of the "happy Negro" had deep roots in the "romantic racialism" of the nineteenth century. No less than an emphasis on pain and pathology, a relentless emphasis on black pleasure could serve to reinforce longstanding racial stereotypes that helped to sustain oppression and inequality.[49]

While he shared Murray's hostility toward pathologist representations, Ellison's descriptions of black urban life achieved a degree of balance and complexity largely absent from Murray's writings. In 1963, Ellison recalled the environment in which he had spent his youth:

"There was all of the disintegration which you find among rural Negroes who are pounding themselves to death against the sharp edges of an urban environment. Yet Oklahoma City at that time was one of the most wonderful places I've ever known." The distinction between Ellison's view of black urban life as a complex admixture of disintegration and vitality and Murray's relatively one-dimensional affirmation of an enviable environment of joyous recreation was borne out in their respective writings about Bearden. While Murray sought to banish political inference from the discussion of Bearden's art, Ellison recognized in *Projections* "those powers that now surge in our land with a potentially destructive force which springs from the very fact of their having for so long gone unrecognized and unseen." Bearden, Ellison continued,

> doesn't impose these powers upon us by explicit comment, but in his ability to make them seem manifest allows us some insight into the forces which now clash and rage as Negro Americans seek self-definition in the slums of our cities. There is beauty here, a harsh beauty that asserts itself out of the horrible fragmentation which Bearden's subjects and their environment have undergone.

All of this, Ellison believed, had been achieved with "no preaching; these forces have been brought to the eye by formal art." Though his most recent biographer emphasizes the novelist's reluctance to "descend to the topical" during the 1960s and "discuss race and civil rights," Ellison was in no doubt as to the topicality of Bearden's *Projections*.[50]

Bearden's participation in Spiral signaled an abrupt change of direction by an artist who had previously called for the discontinuation of black group shows. Similarly, that he now wished to "bring something" to art "as a Negro—give it an identity" was a departure from the diminished significance he had attached to race in "The Negro Artist's Dilemma" and in his paintings of the late 1940s and 1950s. As Bearden recalled in 1968, some of the Spiral group's earliest discussions had concerned the role of black artists within the civil rights movement. The March on Washington had been approaching during the summer of 1963, and "we thought it might be interesting for a group of Negro artists maybe to hire a bus . . . and go down to represent the Negro artists." Whether or not this transpired, Bearden evidently returned to the representation of black life, and to a consciousness of himself as a black artist, while engaged in Spiral's inquiry into the relationship between the artist and society at a time of political upheaval. Despite his move away from Harlem in 1956, Bearden's identification with the African American community in New York, and particularly its artists, was strong. Emma Amos would recall Bearden as Spiral's "leading light," who often hosted the group's weekly meetings in his own studio before a storefront space was rented on Christopher Street in Greenwich Village for the purpose, and again on occasions after the storefront was lost in 1965 and the group continued to gather regularly for another year or so. Though Amos described her male colleagues as "a bunch of chauvinists, every single one of them!" she recounted Bearden's kindness toward the younger members of the group and the time he devoted to the group's business and correspondence.[51]

Bearden would not have forgotten the contestations and criticisms during the 1940s that had helped drive him away from the representation of African American life. That he was willing once more to face these challenges reflects the yearnings he had felt, during his period of abstraction, for the "real," for an engagement with some "philosophy," and for an art more rooted in society. This is not to suggest that he returned to the view of art he had taken during the 1930s, when, by his own account, he had viewed painting as "simply the means that enabled an artist to communicate a message" and to pursue "social change." Indeed, hurt by the reception of *Projections* as "propagandist," Bearden was at pains during the 1960s to clarify that "it is not my aim to paint about the Negro in America in terms of propaganda." No longer a political cartoonist or a social realist, Bearden wished his audiences to engage with his work's "aesthetic implications."[52]

Such sentiments encouraged Murray's efforts to enlist Bearden in his campaign against protest art and "social science fiction." In an essay of 1980 that reviewed Bearden's career as a collagist, Murray claimed that Bearden was "far more concerned with decorative and ornamental effect than with narrative or dramatic impact." Seeking to downplay any premeditated aspect of Bearden's artistic process that might be construed as political, Murray hailed Bearden's collages as the "Visual Equivalent of the Blues," works that were "far less a matter of considered representation" than "improvisation and impromptu response." Simultaneously, and somewhat contradictorily, Murray stated that Bearden's subject matter was never "incidental," but always rooted in "historic, geographic or idiomatic particulars of Afro-American experience." In his book *Stomping the Blues* (1976), Murray had attacked the notion that the blues was a form of "whining for sympathy over one's mean lot in life." Now he lauded Bearden as the embodiment of the blues tradition's philosophy of affirmation, a "stylishly heroic method of survival . . . in response to all disjunctures." Bearden's urban collage scenes, Murray wrote, were more akin to Duke Ellington's "tone parallels and celebrations" of Harlem life than to the "Welfare Department tear-jerk rhetoric" of "cynics and do-gooders" (an unfortunate characterization, in light of Bearden's years spent as a social worker).[53]

Yet the same essay contains, against the grain of his overall argument, perhaps Murray's only acknowledgment of Bearden's desire to use his compositions to reflect the turmoil of his times. "As is to be expected of an artist who began as a political cartoonist," Murray wrote, "and remains an enthusiastic admirer of Grosz, Goya, Daumier, Forain, and Kollwitz, Bearden sometimes, especially in his urbanscapes, creates configurations that may be taken as social commentary." Murray's discomfort with "social commentary" was evident in his dismissal of the "sentimentality and provincialism" of Jean-François Millet's "genre" scenes of "peasants," even as he defended Bearden's collages as "anything but genre." Remarkably, Murray preferred to see Bearden's collages as "radiant still lifes." In 1994, Murray would again employ "genre" as an epithet, which he applied to the work of Jacob Lawrence and defined as "reporting what it [is] like to be in a black community." Genre, for Murray, was the visual equivalent of "moral outcry rhetoric."[54]

The importance of Bearden's identification with the tradition of genre painting has continued to be understated or, more commonly, overlooked. Like Murray, Mary Schmidt Campbell establishes a dichotomy that Bearden would not have recognized when she writes:

"Instead of painting *mere genre scenes,* Bearden chose to penetrate the interior of the lives he portrayed and, having pierced the skin of those day-to-day lives, connect his people and events to larger more universal themes." The artist whose admiration for Brueghel had earned him the nickname "Pete" thirty years earlier and who described his own collages as a return to "Negro genre" also stated at the time of the *Projections* exhibition: "To the question, 'What am I?' I answer that I am a man concerned with truth, not flattery, who shares a dual culture that is unwilling to deny the Harlem where I grew up or the Haarlem of the Dutch masters that contributed its element to my understanding of art."[55]

Bearden by the 1960s had long renounced what he described as the subordination of aesthetics to political ideology in his earliest paintings. This did not, however, entail the depoliticization Murray was so eager to attribute to Bearden's new collage works. As for LeRoi Jones, so for Bearden, the surge of mass civil rights protest by the mid-1960s evoked new possibilities for engagement, as an artist, with society and its concerns, and with life in African American communities. A sense of his utility and responsibility as a black artist reentered Bearden's thinking. Unlike Jones, however, and in contrast to his own earlier, more doctrinaire notions of political engagement, Bearden now conceived of a responsibility both to affirm and to supersede the bonds of race. Renewing his commitment to the visual representation of black life, he nonetheless took a cosmopolitan satisfaction in conjoining "Harlem" with "Haarlem," thereby breaching the racial boundaries that would soon be zealously guarded by Jones and other figures in the black arts movement. If a notion of responsibility had led Bearden, via Spiral, back to the representation of life in black communities, it now contained within it a sense of responsibility to transgress the limits of race in his aesthetic idiom, and so to uphold the principles of freedom and shared humanity that were the civil rights movement's ultimate concerns.

More than ever, Bearden looked to the history of painting, and in particular to the genre tradition, to guide him toward an artistic practice that could bear witness to the social conditions and political forces of the moment while also capturing the transcultural and transhistorical human themes he discerned within the "Museum without Walls." Above all, he looked to traditions of painterly realism that had emerged in opposition to the conventions of genteel subject matter and idealized beauty, and which had opposed the treatment of art as a tribute to power and a diversion from life's harsher realities. His aim, he wrote in 1969, was not to produce "propaganda" but "to paint the life of my people as I know it—as passionately and as dispassionately as Brueghel painted the Flemish people of his day." The art historian Robert Delevoy has written of Brueghel:

> He shows us real men living out their lives. Not those who shape the destinies of nations, but men who toil and suffer and take their pleasures simply, anonymously, at the lowest social level; men without wealth or eminence. Whether young or wasted by the years, healthy or infirm, frail or stalwart, well-built or misshapen, sad or merry, good Christians or sinners—all alike are pasture to his eye.

Here, indeed, was a precedent for an artist concerned with "truth, not flattery."[56]

Another of Bearden's "heroes," as he stated in 1968, was the maverick nineteenth-century French painter Gustave Courbet. As he explained to an interviewer, Courbet was "an artist whose art doesn't influence me so much as his life and some of the things he attempted to do. . . . But the *realism,* this type of approach, his *objectivity,* interests me, too, in what I attempt to do." Linda Nochlin has written of Courbet's "extremely objective" approach to painting the people around him, and his belief that ethical truth was manifest in the unadorned representation of humanity. Courbet himself wrote in 1861 that "realism is essentially the democratic art." In *The Painter's Mind,* Bearden and Holty numbered Courbet among the artists who had "altered subject matter in its entirety by utilizing themes previously thought unfit for painting." Courbet's insistence on rendering the details of human life without concession to prudery or delicacy is powerfully evident in his description of the encounter with two laborers that had inspired his composition *The Stonebreakers* (1849):

It's rare to meet the most complete expression of poverty, so an idea for a painting came to me on the spot. . . . Over there is an old man bent over his task, sledgehammer in the air, his skin tanned by the sun, his head shaded by a straw hat; his trousers of rough material are all patched; and in his cracked sabots, stockings that were once blue show his bare heels. Here is a young man with dusty head and swarthy skin; his back and arms show through the holes in his filthy tattered shirt; one leather suspender holds up the remnant of his trousers, and his leather boots, caked with mud, gape dismally in many places.

The line of descent connecting the "realism" of Courbet's time to Bearden's genre "heroes" is well documented. As Petra Ten Doesschate Chu has shown, the "young Realist genre painters" in France who revolted against classicism and idealism after 1848 found inspiration in the Dutch genre tradition.[57]

Bearden's identification with painterly traditions of "realism" and "objectivity" underpinned an inclusive approach to the representation of black life. It was an approach that resisted the selective imperatives of both pathologism and romanticization. It was no more compatible with the "flattery" inherent in Murray's agenda of "accentuating the positive and eliminating the negative" than with the relentlessly grim "sociological" perspective Bearden attributed to writers such as James Baldwin. In contrast to Murray's writings, Ellison's commentaries possessed a rare insight into Bearden's conception of "realism" as a mode of representation capable of achieving political resonance without bearing the weight of propaganda, and as one distinct from naturalism in its capacity to accommodate modernist alterations of scale and perspective. Indeed, Ellison's characterization of his own mode of representation during an interview in 1948 is uncannily suggestive of the combination of stylistic modernism and "objectivity" for which Bearden would strive. Asked by the psychiatrist Karl Menninger whether what became the "Battle Royal" scene in *Invisible Man* was based directly on observed "facts," Ellison replied that "for all the detailed description of the prose, the aim is *not naturalism but realism*—a realism dilated to deal with the almost surreal state of our everyday American life."[58]

Projections

In 1976, after viewing a recent series of photographs of Harlem by the architect W. Joseph Black, Bearden noted: "What a contrast to see an intricate sculptured relief on a building and to realize what is often the brooding frustration and fragmentation in the lives of those inside. On the other hand, the meanest exterior cannot deny some persons their purpose in life, nor altogether s[t]ultify achievement." Twelve years earlier, Bearden's *Projections* had captured the stark, often ironic juxtapositions of the human and architectural environments of Harlem, where fine brownstones adorned with carved ornamentation had once housed individual families of prosperous white New Yorkers and now housed numerous black families as cramped, subdivided tenements. The multiplicity inherent in collage was ideally suited to Bearden's vision of a Harlem of contrasts, where "brooding frustration" existed alongside "purpose" and "achievement." That the fragments from which his compositions were assembled were themselves of diverse origins, and that an individual human figure—even a single face—was often spliced together from multiple sources, articulated the composite, shifting, and irreducible nature of the community he portrayed.[59]

Ellison observed in 1968 that "Bearden's meaning is identical with his method. His combination of technique is itself eloquent of the sharp breaks, leaps in consciousness, distortions, paradoxes, reversals, telescoping of time and surreal blending of styles, values, hopes and dreams which characterize much of Negro American history." Ellison's words implicitly connect the abrupt discontinuities of twentieth-century African American experience, particularly migration and urbanization, to a quintessentially modernist sensibility of displacement and schism. In Europe, in the first years of the century, this sensibility, itself engendered by social, technological, and demographic upheavals, had been subject to plastic exploration by Picasso, Georges Braque, and Juan Gris, whose innovations in cubism and collage remained crucial to Bearden's artistic method. Yet the cosmopolitan prehistory of

collage—from the use of foil papers to decorate twelfth-century Japa-
nese texts such as the *Ise-shu* manuscript, to European folk-art traditions such as scrapbooks, valentines, and weather-charms—may also
have appealed to Bearden as redolent of the hybridity of assemblage
itself. Furthermore, as the critic Hilton Kramer would later note, the
African American quilt-making tradition was both an important
precursor to the modernist development of collage and an evident
influence on what Kramer plausibly terms Bearden's "patchwork Cubism." While critics such as Clement Greenberg emphasized cubism's
inclination toward formalism and abstraction, Bearden's bold employment of narrative and figuration resisted modernism's most disintegrative tendencies. Indeed, it is striking to consider that in spite of his
formal debt to cubism, Bearden styled himself after the premodernist
master narrator, Brueghel.[60]

Bearden's use of photomontage—the collage technique pioneered
by his former teacher George Grosz, among others—lent a further
layer of meaning to his medium. Many of the photographic fragments
reassembled in his works had themselves migrated from the pages of
popular current affairs magazines such as *Life* and black-oriented magazines such as *Ebony*. At a moment when images of impeccably attired
civil rights marchers in the South were being displaced in magazines
by panicked accounts of the North's own "Negro problem," Bearden
signified on the representations of black urban life offered by the
American media. In procuring his materials from the store of visual
images relayed to the public and radically transforming and reconfig-
uring them into a personal aesthetic and social statement, Bearden acknowledged the impossibility of fully evading the legacy of prior
representations and stereotypes of African Americans. Just as *Projections*
paid its dues to artistic tradition, so Bearden's photomontage technique conceded that his own visual statements about black life would
meet not with a naked eye, but with a throng of preconceptions and
predispositions.[61]

If the process of assemblage embedded a sense of multiplicity within
each composition, the contrasts between the individual collages in *Projections* further extended Bearden's emphasis on the complexity and
variety of black life, as can be seen from a comparison of *The Street*

(Figures 9 and 10) and *The Dove* (Figure 12). The former provides perhaps Bearden's strongest evocation in collage of the "brooding frustration and fragmentation" of a black urban community. It seems likely that Bearden intended *The Street* as a response to a painting produced in 1936 by Palmer Hayden, an African American artist patronized by the Harmon Foundation of which Bearden had been fiercely critical in his essay of 1946. Not only does the angled perspective of Bearden's street scene, with its densely peopled stoops and window frames, recall the configuration of Hayden's *Midsummer Night in Harlem* (Figure 11) as though reversed in a mirror, but the sullen and downcast faces of many of Bearden's figures also reverse the stereotypically beaming countenances on view in Hayden's primitivist fantasia. *The Street* is no joyous assembly, and Bearden's guitarist appears not as the accompanist to a cheerful thrum of conversation, like the guitarist at the far right of Hayden's painting, but rather as a weary traveler who, together with his morose female companion, might have arrived recently in Harlem via the train tracks by which a boy kneels at the right of the image, only to find the "promised land" less congenial than expected. The posture of the male figure bent almost double in the lower left-hand corner is repeated by a second agonized male figure to the right of the two central figures. Meanwhile, the guitarist and his companion are themselves echoed by a rustic-looking couple farther down the street, close to the railway line, who amble toward the foreground and establish a pattern of arrival and continuing quest.

Whether this collage was assembled after the outbreak of the Harlem riot in July 1964 or during the preceding tense weeks, Bearden was unmistakably attuned to the escalating crisis confronting black urban communities. At the time of the exhibition, he remarked to the journalist Charles Childs: "I create social images within my work so far as the human condition is social, I create racial identities so far as the subjects are Negro, but I have not created protest images because the world within the collage, if it is authentic, retains the right to speak for itself." What he would later call "the distortions required of the polemicist" were not needed for his images to convey something of the adversity and distress that precipitated the outbreak of violence in Harlem. If Bearden intended *Projections* to furnish a broader vision of black urban life than that contained in newspapers and magazines, his pursuit of "realism" and "objectivity" nevertheless militated against any obscuration of poverty and hardship. Notwithstanding the importance he attached to "artifice," Bearden consciously pursued his own "documentary" effect through the techniques of photomontage and black-and-white photostatic enlargement. As he later recalled, "I also felt that by using photographs that way, almost cinematically, I could convey a sense of 'You are there'—a documentary feeling that would have something to do with the speed-fractured tempo of contemporary urban life." Indeed, Bearden appeared simultaneously to accept the role of indigenous interpreter, with all the particularity it entailed, and to signal his enduring interest in the perennial human themes of the "Museum without Walls" when he told Childs: "I have tried to look at anything in my encounters with the outside that might help *translate the innerness of the Negro experience.*"[62]

Some of the responses to *Projections* must have reminded Bearden of his experiences during the 1940s, when he had been criticized for producing "morbid" images of the wrong "kind of Negro." In 1968, he recalled an African American woman, the wife of a doctor, walking out of *Projections* because she found the works "disturbing," while another black woman complained that the images were "too stark; showed people in their worst or poorer circumstances." Though the critic Dore Ashton arguably extrapolated too much from *The Street* when she characterized the entire exhibition as "harrowing images" of "intolerable facts," her description of "eyes that look out at the spectator with relentless steadiness, eyes that can only be seen as accusing" at least captures an aspect of this particular composition. The symbolic dove presiding over the scene in *The Street* seems ironic in its gesture toward peace.[63]

By contrast, that which perches on a lintel in *The Dove* (Figure 12) signals more sincerely a mood of benign repose. The male figure seated on the steps at the center of the composition is likely enjoying a contemplative cigarette break, rather than agonizing over his predicament, and the upturned gaze of the woman who appears at the window of her basement apartment hints at the possibility of romance. By the post to the left-hand side, a gangly, jocular character teases a prim old maid, perhaps dressed for church (the dove also signifies the Holy Spirit). To the right, another young man cuts a stylish figure on the sidewalk, his cap pulled down over his dramatically enlarged head, his giant thumb and forefinger pinching his cigarette tip in an affected manner. The narrow, frontal stretch of buildings encompassed by *The Dove,* while no less haphazardly crowded than that of *The Street,* appears more intimate and domestic than the angled block shown in the latter, which seems to exist almost in the shadow of the imposing bridge in the background. Yet if *The Dove* illustrates more of the affectionate and humorous interaction that Bearden perceived in "the life of my people," it is no saccharine idealization of a black urban community. The piercing eyes and furrowed brow glimpsed through the window at the right of the collage and the earnest-looking child's face further toward the center unsettle the convivial atmosphere of the sidewalk below.

Following the example of earlier genre painters, Bearden's incorporation of rituals of everyday life—journeying, courtship, rest, and music making—also invests *The Street* and *The Dove* with enduring human themes that transcend the immediacies of time and place. His pun relating "Harlem" to "Haarlem" found its most direct expression in a collage not included in the *Projections* exhibition. As Charles Childs observed that year, Bearden's *Two Women in a Harlem Courtyard* gestures deliberately to Pieter de Hooch's *A Courtyard in Delft at Evening: A Woman Spinning* (c. 1658) in its placement of two female figures, one seated, against a backdrop of houses, chimneys, and treetops. Gail Gelburd discerns an additional, more geographically and temporally specific layer of meaning in Bearden's collage, as one of the women, sporting furs and high heels, raises her hand to announce "the new life of the North" to her barefooted, "shabbily dressed" companion. This juxtaposition of the Great Migration with an intimate scene of life in a seventeenth-century Dutch town epitomizes Bearden's visualization of a Harlem without walls.[64]

Two urban interiors further illustrate the dialogue between the particular and the universal at work in *Projections.* Bearden's *Evening, 9:10, 461 Lenox Avenue* (Figure 13) presents what is potentially a picture of deviance, since gambling had long been a preoccupation of moral panics about lower-class black urbanization. In *The Philadelphia Negro* (1899), W. E. B. Du Bois fretted that the "well-dressed loafers" around Locust Street and Ninth Avenue were "largely supported by prostitutes and political largesse, and spend their time in gambling. They are absolutely without home life, and form the most dangerous class in the community." Bearden's three card players, however, appear thoroughly domesticated. Moreover, by invoking the art historical tradition— referencing earlier works such as Caravaggio's *The Cardsharps* (ca. 1594), Paul Cézanne's *The Card Players* (1890–1892), and Diego Velázquez's genre scenes *The Luncheon* (ca. 1617–1618) and *Peasants at the Table* (ca. 1620)—Bearden projects his subjects beyond the confines of the racialized American discourse of urban vice. As so often in his work, ritual, in this case the rule-bound and repetitive performance of shuffling, dealing, hiding, and revealing cards, serves as the mechanism that propels the composition's significance beyond its apparent ethnocentrism and its record of a specific time and place, and imbues it with a broader human significance. The card game connotes relationships of power, secrecy, and persuasion, as well as a common human desire for play.[65]

The precision with which the title *Evening, 9:10, 461 Lenox Avenue* and the clock face in the lower right-hand corner establish a time and locale are counteracted, as Lee Stephens Glazer points out, by the transhistorical and transcultural connections implied by Bearden's allusions to the works of great European painters. Yet the very ethnic, geographic, and temporal particularity of the work should be understood not as negated or diminished by Bearden's concern with universality, but rather as substantiating in and of itself his expansive conception of the universal. "I did the new work," Bearden stated at the time of the exhibition, "out of a response and need to redefine the image of man in terms of the Negro experience I know best." Bearden thus rejected the partial, Eurocentric notions of universality derived from the Enlightenment and the ongoing characterization of black life in terms of deviation from white norms. In this respect, he allied himself with anticolonialist intellectuals such as Frantz Fanon, whose book *The Wretched of the Earth* (1963), contained in Bearden's personal library, exhorts: "Leave this Europe where they are never done talking of Man, yet murder men everywhere they find them." Yet Bearden did not reject the notion of a universal humanity in favor of racial determinism and separatism, in the manner of Jones/Baraka and other black cultural nationalists. Instead, he sought to recast "the image of man" in a more inclusive mold. He viewed this as a process of extension, rather than obliteration, akin to the enlargement of Malraux's "Museum without Walls." *Time* magazine in 1967 quoted Bearden's remark that "an artist is an art lover who finds that in all he sees, something is missing. To touch at the core of what he feels is missing, to put there what needs to be there, becomes the center of his life's work."[66]

Evening Meal of Prophet Peterson (Figure 14) further illustrates Bearden's wish to situate black urban life within larger contexts, in this case by alluding to contemporary trends in the wider American society and culture. Again, Bearden's meaning resides not only in the representations created directly through his process of assemblage and in the process itself, but also in his allusions to other works of art. The lavish, dramatically oversize images from which Bearden constructs this scene of a family meal evoke the abundant consumption that characterized the American postwar ideal of affluent domesticity and also the work of pop artists who were commenting at the time, with varying degrees of irony, on the emergence of the mass consumer society. However, neither the relationship between Bearden's black subjects and these prevailing American ideals, nor that between Bearden's artistic concerns and those of pop art, is straightforward.

On the surface, *Evening Meal of Prophet Peterson* furnishes a hopeful, integrationist message by envisioning black participation in the dominant trends of American home life, consumerism, and popular culture, signified by the television set and, indeed, the magazine pages and advertisements from which Bearden's icons of consumption were lifted. The incorporation of white facial features and limbs—a rarity in his photomontages—in the patchwork figure of Bearden's housewife appears, moreover, to align his visual statement with the particular integrationist creed shared by Ellison and Murray. Ellison's protagonist in *Invisible Man* comes to understand, after a stint working in a paint-mixing plant, that the brightest of whites contains a drop of black. Murray stated the corollary in *The Omni-Americans:* "The overwhelming majority of the residents of Harlem, along with most other native-born

U.S. Negroes, are part-white Anglo-Saxon Protestants, and Southern at that, with all the racial as well as cultural ramifications this implies." American culture, Murray insisted, *"even in its most segregated precincts"* was *"irrevocably composite"* and *"incontestably mulatto."*⁶⁷

Murray also flatly denied that the term "ghetto," with its connotations of total, enforced isolation, was a valid signifier of the social and political realities of black urban life:

> It is very curious indeed that at a time when Harlem Negroes encounter fewer restrictions, exercise more political power, earn more money, and have more involvements elsewhere than ever before, media reporters (following a writer like [Kenneth] Clark) describe them as denizens of a ghetto, who are all but completely ostracized from the mainstream of American life—which media reporters refer to as the white world. The term ghetto does not apply to Harlem, if indeed it applies to any segregated housing area in the United States. Perhaps it applies to this or that Chinatown. It *does not* and *never has* applied to segregated areas where U.S. Negroes live.

Nor was "ghetto" a word Bearden was apt to use. Asked during a discussion recorded in 1970 to describe the settings and experiences that informed his work, Bearden checked himself: "I was going to use the word 'ghetto' but I don't think that's a nice word. I would say urban community." In seeking to capture the interconnections between black urban life and the broader patterns of human existence in his enlargement of the "Museum without Walls," Bearden, too, rejected Clark's view of Harlem as a "ghetto" or even a "concentration camp." Yet, as collages such as *The Street* testify, Bearden did not join with Murray in depicting a Harlem steadily increasing in political power, wealth, and integration into the life of New York City as a whole. Thus, to return to *Evening Meal of Prophet Peterson,* it is notable that while Bearden admits the symbols of a burgeoning American consumer culture into a Harlem tenement apartment, the relationship of this black family to the ideal of affluent American domesticity remains as ambiguous as the relationship between the composition and its title. Father Christmas and a plump turkey insinuate that the abundance many Americans were experiencing habitually as an evening meal remained, for the Petersons, only a seasonal treat.[68]

Since the late 1950s, artists such as Robert Rauschenberg and Jasper Johns had, in Thomas Crow's words, challenged abstract expressionism's "promise of expressive revelation" by incorporating into their artworks "things known and seen on occasions beyond counting." The use of "found objects" such as newsprint, photographs, maps, and flags testified to a renewed interest in the material dimension of modern life and the role of the mass media in forging the public sphere. The urban environment was frequently the subject of artists including Claes Oldenburg, whose installation *The Street* (1960) evoked vagrancy in a shantytown of scavenged cardboard. Andy Warhol's *Disaster* series of 1963 comprised silk screens produced from news photographs of menacing and violent urban scenes including car crashes and, in *Red Race Riot,* the beating of civil rights protesters in Birmingham, Alabama. Pop art, in the hands of Warhol, Roy Lichtenstein, and others, further extended the preoccupation with "things known and seen" into the realm of quotidian and commercial imagery.[69]

Though Bearden's adoption of photomontage participated in this movement toward "found objects," and though *Evening Meal of Prophet Peterson* references pop art's documentation of the ubiquitous imagery of consumption, Bearden's art was substantially at odds with contemporary trends. Whereas the "new realism" of the 1960s challenged abstraction through a relentless focus on material objects, Bearden's figurative work in collage retained a traditionally humanistic character. Indeed, *Evening Meal of Prophet Peterson* establishes a forceful tension between rituals of spirituality and familial love, on the one hand, and an encroaching materialism, on the other. As a vision portending deepening integration of African Americans into the dominant patterns of American social, cultural, and economic life—as further suggested by the appearance of white faces in the window toward the left of the composition and to Prophet Peterson's right—the tone of the work is noticeably ambivalent. It echoes something of the skepticism of James Baldwin, who in 1963 had posed the question, "Do I really want to be integrated into a burning house?" As his remarks in the Spiral interview show, Bearden viewed "anti-art," as well as racism, as a product of a "gravely ill" American society. During a seminar in 1975, Bearden would describe pop art as "a kind of anti-art movement" that had found nothing more meaningful to sanctify than "the Campbell Soup can, the hamburger or the lemon meringue pie." Though Bearden loaned *Evening Meal of Prophet Peterson* to a fund-raising event for the Congress of Racial Equality in May 1964, his use of pop imagery within the work conveys a sense of anxiety about what, in the process of integration, might actually be lost.[70]

A sense of impending loss also suffuses the images of southern rural life in *Projections*. As Bearden remarked in 1968, "a lot of the life that I knew in certain rural Negro surroundings is passing." In works such as *Prevalence of Ritual: Baptism* (Figure 15), Bearden "set down some of my impressions of that life" in vivid, almost audible depictions of distinctive, intimate rituals of southern African American communities. Trains and train tracks serve to bind together the rural and urban scenes in *Projections* and to signal travel and migration as central elements of twentieth-century African American experience. Yet the familiar liberatory associations of trains and migration within African American arts and letters are tempered in *Baptism* by Bearden's growing ambivalence about the black encounter with urban industrial modernity, and by his sadness at the erosion of black southern communities that the Great Migration entailed. "In this picture," he wrote in 1969, "the train represents the encroachment of another culture."[71]

Of his *Prevalence of Ritual: Conjur Woman* (Figure 16), Bearden commented:

> A conjur woman was an important figure in a number of Southern Negro rural communities. She was called on to prepare love potions; to provide herbs to cure various illnesses; and to be consulted regarding vexing personal and family problems. Much of her knowledge had been passed on through generations from an African past, although a great deal was learned from the American Indians. A conjur woman was generally greatly feared and it was believed that she could change her appearance.

Yet "the world is without her kind of mystery now." The economic underpinning of black life in the rural South, witnessed in *Cotton* (Figure 17)—a composition that recalls the genre paintings of Millet about which Murray was so scathing—had been ravaged since the 1940s by the mechanization of agriculture, which had helped to set in motion the second wave of the Great Migration. The northern urban life that Bearden evoked in works such as *The Street* and *The Dove* grew directly from the diminution of the communities pictured in his southern scenes. Meanwhile, *Evening Meal of Prophet Peterson* questioned how the distinctive aspects of black culture might fare against the onslaught of modern commercial culture in the city.[72]

Bearden's casework among New York's Gypsies since 1952 had heightened his concerns about the impact of rapid urbanization on the fabric of traditional cultures. "I think the gypsies are going to disappear," he stated in 1968, "because the economic basis of gypsy life with the encroachment of many things of modern civilization is disappearing." Coppersmiths were redundant in an age of stainless steel, and "people don't believe" in fortune-telling any longer. "Their way of life was disintegrating," he would reflect in 1977. The young were marrying non-Gypsies, sending their children to public schools, and moving out from Manhattan's Lower East Side to Queens and Coney Island. The Gypsies had been "truly a culture within a culture," he remarked. Bearden had "good friends" among the Gypsies, and he may have perceived similarities between their female fortune-tellers and the "conjur women" of North Carolina, or between the "Foolish-Jack" stories of Gypsy folklore, in which a superficially dim-witted youth outsmarts his social betters, and the trickster tales of African American oral tradition. Bearden's own love of black folklore was captured by Ellison in a letter of 1986: "you're the Bear-den who told me about Brer Rabbit's adventure in a bear's den ('Don't a mother move, Brer Rabbit cried')."[73]

His career in social work, from which he finally retired in 1969 following three years on a part-time basis, also points toward Bearden's divergence from some of Murray's attitudes. The work, Bearden agreed with an interviewer in 1968, was "sociological" in nature, and there was little of Murray's indiscriminate hostility toward the social sciences in Bearden's comment: "It's funny that the sociologists have never touched gypsy life or their customs and, before it all disappears, it certainly would make an interesting study. Somebody like Oscar Lewis who did things about the Mexican family should investigate the gypsies." If Bearden had in mind nothing more than an affectionate portrait of Gypsy customs, then the social anthropologist Oscar Lewis, whose controversial "culture of poverty" thesis emphasized the role of behavioral pathologies in restricting the economic mobility of the poor, would seem an unlikely candidate for the task. Without overburdening Bearden's comment, it is possible to infer a less dismissive stance than Murray's toward social scientists who examined the causes and consequences of poverty. While Bearden's criticism of Baldwin for "defining the Negro sociologically but not artistically" suggests a belief that artists should strive for a fuller, more variegated representation of communal life than the aggregates offered by social scientists, his reference to Lewis suggests that Bearden recognized the legitimacy of social scientific investigations of poverty within their own province. Bearden, in other words, did not echo Murray's blanket condemnations of "war on poverty jive" and "the shortcomings of social science as an intellectual discipline."[74]

Alongside Bearden's depictions of black urban and rural life, a number of the works in *Projections* reimagine mythic or historical scenarios in ways that pointedly addressed the political context of the 1960s. While Bearden intended the vision of lived experience in his urban and rural "Negro genre" works to "speak for itself," the two compositions bearing the title *Sermons* are more direct in their invocation of moral judgment. They lent a more strident, polemical tone to the exhibition as a whole, and so cast doubt on Mary Schmidt Campbell's claim that Bearden's intention was "not to attack the ruling forces." In *Sermons: The Walls of Jericho* (Figure 18), Bearden plays on the tradition of African American identification with the Old Testament's narrative of the "chosen people." Investing his hectic composition with the energy of the "sensational thunderous sermons" remembered from his boyhood visits to North Carolina, Bearden pictures the Israelite chieftain Joshua, who conquered Canaan by circling Jericho for seven days with his army before sending up the war cry that brought the walls of the city tumbling down. Previous commentaries have failed to decipher the allegorical message of Bearden's sermon, which mirrors his remarks in the Spiral group interview that "Western society, and particularly that of America, is gravely ill," and that "Western culture" might not offer "the only solution to man's purpose on this earth." Bearden's Joshua on horseback is an African warrior, his arms raised as he calls forth his soldiers' fearsome cry. While Nnamdi Elleh reads the collage as an exercise in cultural syncretism, and Campbell perceives "the destruction of African, Egyptian, Greco-Roman structures," what is clearly tumbling in *The Walls of Jericho* is the edifice of Western power. Corinthian columns and Gothic and neoclassical arches topple, while bronze Benin heads merge with photographic fragments of dark faces to populate Bearden's army of victors. Joshua's raised hands—one constructed from traditional African statuary and the other from modern photography—further signify Bearden's allegorical interconnection of past and present.[75]

Sermons: In That Number (Figure 19), with its draining hourglass, extends Bearden's warning of imminent judgment. Murray remembers suggesting this work's title after viewing *The Walls of Jericho*. Yet if his choice of the lyric, "Lord, I want to be in that number," from "When the Saints Go Marching In," indicates his appreciation of Bearden's theme of moral judgment in the *Sermons,* the composition's imagery nonetheless underscores Bearden and Murray's political differences. In this prophecy of a divinely ordained deluge of New York City, identified by landmarks such as the Chrysler Building in the top right-hand corner, Bearden depicts a society in its death throes, one enthralled by one-hundred-dollar bills and vanity mirrors, and so oblivious to the coming judgment as to be preoccupied with sending rockets into space. White figures in GI helmets and cowboy hats are sucked down to their watery graves, while black musicians at the lower left of the composition play out the exit music from higher ground. Whereas Bearden's scenario recalls the similarly apocalyptic title of Baldwin's *The Fire Next Time* (1963), a comment by Murray in 1996 on the black militancy of the 1960s encapsulates his contrasting perspective: "Let's talk about 'the fire next time.' You know damn well they can put out the fire by Wednesday."[76]

Indeed, the implication in Bearden's *Sermons* of a crisis of Western power and of the gathering strength of non-Western societies—inspired by the rapid decolonization of Africa and Asia, and the challenge posed by the "nonaligned" nations to America's Cold War geopolitics—sits uneasily beside Murray's political attitudes. Murray's trenchant American nationalism and indifference toward Africa, already evident by 1970 in *The Omni-Americans,* were abundantly clear in later interviews in which he stated that African societies had never attained the "refinement" of "civilization," and curtly dismissed American Afrocentrists: "Who's greater than the United States[?] And we are an inextricable part of that! And you're going to give up all of that, the greatest stuff in the world, to go back and claim you don't have a pisspot on the left-handed side of the Nile? Of the Zulu River?" Bearden had expressed very different sentiments in an unpublished manuscript:

> The concept of black inferiority, the basic rationale of the slave dealer, has been so institutionalized and imbedded in American unconsciousness that Americans are often both disbelieving and skeptical when told that at a time when most Britons and Europeans were crawling around in caves with stone axes, African civilizations were advanced in agriculture, skilled in iron mining, smelting and casting, the developers of great cities and empires the size of Europe. Yet, as scores of books have made plain, especially since World War II and the emergence of "new" African nations, this is so.

Bearden's logic here, interestingly, would attribute Murray's disbelief in African civilization to an unconscious sense of racial inferiority: the very phenomenon of diminished black self-esteem that Murray censured as "pseudo-psychiatric nonsense."[77]

As a recently retired air force major who had spent much of his career teaching geopolitics in the officers' training program at Tuskegee Institute, Murray was scarcely hostile to the exercise of American power during the Cold War. While Murray, like Ellison, supported the United States' military intervention in Vietnam, Bearden chose to contribute *In That Number* to an exhibition of 1967, *Protest and Hope,* which presented "works of commentary on Civil Rights and Vietnam." In 1973, Bearden included images of student antiwar demonstrators making peace signs in his celebratory collage *Berkeley—The*

City and Its People, which he created for Berkeley's city council chamber. For Bearden, America's "treatment of the Negro" was a "symptom" of the general ill health of Western societies, and works such as *In That Number* tied the African American subjects that dominated *Projections* to the rising global challenge to Western political and cultural hegemony. For Murray, however, the United States was the world's lone champion of freedom, and the civil rights struggle essentially a local difficulty.[78]

To See How Life Can Triumph

With the critical and commercial success of *Projections,* which reopened in October 1965 at the Corcoran Gallery in Washington, D.C., Bearden's transition to collage and his return to the representation of black life reinvigorated his artistic career. Outside his studio, Bearden threw himself into curatorial and organizational roles in which he hoped to rekindle the interaction between black artists and communities that he recalled from his days at "306" during the Depression. In 1964 he was appointed as art director of the newly formed Harlem Cultural Council, a role in which he sought to connect Harlem residents with the work of contemporary African American artists and with the black artistic heritage. Together with Jim Loew, a young art enthusiast from Brooklyn, Bearden oversaw the conversion of the basement of a furniture store on 125th Street into what he considered a "very acceptable gallery" for the exhibition *Art of the American Negro,* which opened in June 1966 with works by Merton Simpson, Faith Ringgold, Bearden, and others. It was, he proudly remarked, Harlem's first major show featuring black artists since the 1930s.[79]

In an interview in 1968, Bearden explained that a further reason "why I revere Courbet," beside the "objectivity" and "realism" of his painting, was Courbet's appreciation of "the social responsibilities of the artist." While Bearden resisted the suggestion that black artists should exhibit their work "exclusively" in black communities, he felt that "a great deal of effort should be made in this direction," to ensure that artwork existed not only for "the patrons of art" but also for the community that had nurtured the artist. "I think that in time this will

make for a better artist," he commented, "because the artist can learn
something of the feelings of the community about his work. To make
an artist you need many hands and all working together can make for
something very meaningful."[80]

In calling for engagement between African American artists and
communities, Bearden shared a major concern of the black arts movement then emerging among younger, black nationalist artists. Yet he
rejected the dogmatic racialism often evident within the black arts
movement. "I don't think that the Negro community then should
be exposed just to Negro artists, but that they begin to be involved in
all of art," he stated. Moreover, in lauding Courbet's beliefs about
"the social responsibilities of the artist," Bearden implied that his own
sense of social obligation, even though mediated by the specificities of
race and the urban crisis, could derive inspiration from across the color
line. He continued, as well, to urge the wider American public to acknowledge black artists' past and present contributions. He was gratified by the attention devoted to *The Evolution of Afro-American Artists,
1800–1950,* a free-entry exhibition held in the Great Hall of the City
College of New York in the fall of 1967, which he co-curated with
Carroll Greene Jr. As reported in the *New York Times,* "By special arrangement with the Board of Education, some 2,100 children a day from
schools all over the city will be bused to visit the exhibition," which
was "said to be the most comprehensive of its kind ever assembled."
Bearden saw no need, then, to choose between community-oriented art
and exposure to a wider public. Rather, he viewed support for black
artists within their own communities as a step toward recognition by a
society in which "myriad aspects of Negro culture" remained "for the
most part ignored." To this end, Bearden served on the curatorial council of The Studio Museum in Harlem, which was founded in 1968,
and joined with Ernest Crichlow and Norman Lewis in establishing
the Cinque Gallery in 1969, with a grant of $30,000 from the Urban
Center of Columbia University, to exhibit works by talented young
minority artists.[81]

Bearden also played a prominent role during the late 1960s in pro-
testing the underrepresentation of black artists in New York's museums
and galleries, as well as what he considered to be the misrepresentation

of black subjects by these institutions. When, in November 1968, the Whitney Museum of American Art mounted the exhibition *The 1930's: Painting and Sculpture in America* without including the work of Jacob Lawrence, Hale Woodruff, or any other African American, Bearden joined other black artists on a picket line. Faith Ringgold, who had organized the picket, remembers Bearden's disappointment that only around thirty artists joined the action: "'Where are all the militants?' I heard him ask. 'Here's something for them to get involved in.'" Some of the protesters carried placards demanding a solo exhibition for Bearden, while the painter Peter Bradley told the press: "The whites are not interested in our art unless it's chauvinistic. They want us to paint the spades-in-a-cornfield type of thing."[82]

Controversy over the representation of black artists and black urban subjects reached its peak, however, with the Metropolitan Museum of Art's 1969 exhibition *Harlem on My Mind: Cultural Capital of Black America, 1900–1968.* As Henry Louis Gates Jr. has noted, the aim of Allon Schoener of the New York State Council on the Arts and Thomas Hoving, the director of the Metropolitan, was "to mount a different sort of show, a show not devoted primarily to the high art of such great artists as Romare Bearden and Jacob Lawrence, but rather a virtual documentary history." Many black artists in New York, however, believed that the exhibition's white organizers were premature in pursuing a "different" approach when major museums and galleries such as the Metropolitan had never accorded black artists significant attention. Moreover, as Schoener would later concede, the involvement of Harlem community members and African American art experts in the exhibition's planning stage was little more than "window dressing." The historian John Henrik Clarke, director of the Heritage Program of Harlem Youth Opportunities Unlimited and the Associated Community Teams (HARYOU-ACT), wrote to Bearden as the planning progressed that "the trouble with this project is that it never belonged to us and while a lot of people listened to our suggestions about the project, very few of those suggestions were ever put into effect."[83]

Particularly galling for Bearden, as he wrote to Schoener in June 1968, was the fact than an art museum would exclude the work of African American artists from its first significant exploration of black life.

As promotional material announced, the intention behind the exhibition was to use "a variety of communications techniques—including photographs, films, television, documentary recordings of sound and voices, music, and memorabilia" to "interpret a world which has been known intimately only to the black people in New York City." As Clarke's letter to Bearden indicated, the idea that white curators could "interpret" Harlem without recourse to black intermediaries from the neighborhood (the project "never belonged to us") was by this time an affront to the status of the indigenous interpreter. The stated aim of creating a "total environment" that would replicate Harlem's sights and sounds might also have struck Bearden as a kind of ghetto theme park, reconstructed at a safe distance using a "live two-way television communication channel" to connect museum visitors with the corner of Seventh Avenue and 125th Street. Certainly, Bearden seemed wary of the potential for exoticism when he wrote to Schoener that "something must be done as to the title." The exhibition's title, indeed, was borrowed from a popular song written by Irving Berlin in 1933 for a sketch about Josephine Baker, the African American dancer and singer who had appeared in grossly primitivist Parisian revues wearing little except a skirt of bananas. Berlin's lyrics have the Baker character, now the owner of a "Riviera chateau," lamenting that she has "become too damned refined" and declaring a "longing to be low-down," with "Harlem on my mind."[84]

Though Bearden continued throughout 1968 to push for a greater role for black artists and photographers in the exhibition, he had already warned Schoener in June that hostility in the Harlem community was such that "it might actually be best to phase the show out." When the exhibition did open on January 18, 1969, the adverse publicity generated by the Harlem Cultural Council's withdrawal of support for the exhibition and the protest organized by Benny Andrews's Black Emergency Cultural Coalition, in which Bearden took part, was overshadowed by allegations that an essay included in the catalog, written by a seventeen-year-old Harlem schoolgirl, was anti-Semitic. Yet the show attracted huge crowds, of whom some 15 percent (more than six times the average proportion at the Metropolitan) were African Americans. Not all found fault with the exhibition's portrayal of black urban life. William Booth, the African American chairman of the city's Human Rights Commission, stated: "We have had complaints that the show was one-sided. From what I've seen here today, I can't see the validity of that complaint. Both the up and the down of Harlem are in this exhibit. . . . It is a rounded view." By this time, however, Bearden's mind was set. "They were giving it a sort of light, sensational treatment," he later claimed. "I was so mad I never went to see the exhibition."[85]

If Bearden's activism of the late 1960s often saw him make common cause with a younger generation of radical black artists, his tolerance of the black arts movement had limits. After moderating a symposium on "The Black Artist in America," which was published in the *Metropolitan Museum of Art Bulletin* in January 1969 (presumably as part of an effort by the museum to rescue its relations with black artists), Bearden sent a copy of the transcript to Ellison along with a note that read: "I think the discussion will interest you. You will see who are the hustlers, or the hustler[s] and politician[s], and some who are really interested in artistic problems." Of the six participating artists, who included Jacob Lawrence, Hale Woodruff, and the sculptor Richard Hunt, the most vocally militant was Tom Lloyd, who urged fellow artists to produce posters venerating black heroes and expressed support for "some form of separatism" to reconnect the black artist with "the people in the ghetto." What may have particularly disturbed Bearden was Lloyd's remark, "I'm not only concerned with art, you know. With me art is a secondary thing." To Bearden, this would have seemed a regrettable echo of his own belief during the 1930s, since recanted, that artistic techniques were "simply the means" of communicating a political message. In 1971, Bearden wrote to his former Spiral colleague Reginald Gammon that too many African Americans were "painting political cartoons and badly." He was sick of "internecine" quarrels about the definition of "truly black" art, and sick of hearing that black art should not be "tricky" like "whitey abstract art." Bearden was disheartened by the intellectual self-ghettoization inherent in the black arts movement's disregard for the Western artistic tradition. In Ellison's view, an important aspect of Bearden's achievement was his refusal to surrender his "artistic freedom" to the protective myth that the history of Western painting was "irrelevant to the Negro artist."[86]

Appraising *Romare Bearden: New Collages,* which opened at Cordier & Eckstrom on October 10, 1967, John Canaday of the *New York Times* grasped more than any other critic how Bearden's realism achieved political resonance "without falling into the traps of picturesqueness, pathos and righteous indignation":

> As part of his complex subject matter—or perhaps as its sum—he shows us what has happened to the Negro but he shows it as a fact, not an accusation. The accusation is built-in, and is thus more effective than the mawkish tirade that so many painters end up with no matter how good the cause or how sincere their convictions in this difficult area.

Significant alterations in Bearden's artistic method had taken place by the time of this exhibition, as he explained in an interview in 1968. Following *Projections,* he had ceased to produce black-and-white photostatic enlargements from small collages and had begun instead to assemble larger collages, typically four by five feet, as unique works. Creating the photostatic enlargements and having them mounted and framed had been "a very expensive process," and "since they were considered as prints, they couldn't sell for too much," whereas his new collages could be exhibited and sold as "original work." Photostatically enlarged fragments of photographs continued to appear as elements within his compositions. Yet, as Ruth Fine notes, the density of photographic imagery within Bearden's collages decreased as he began to devote larger areas to colored papers. The combined effect of these changes was to lessen what Bearden would later call the "urban" and "documentary feeling" that had characterized *Projections.*[87]

Bearden's collages of the late 1960s continued, nevertheless, to register the grittier dimensions of the black urban environment, as well as to affirm expressive culture and community. *Time* magazine noted the "irony of a startlingly adult little girl licking an ice-cream cone amid hostile stares in a Harlem *Summertime* ('They grow up fast, in that part of town')." A reporter for the *Amsterdam News* also surmised that the 1967 collage "symbolizes the Harlemese that 'children grow up fast in the ghetto.'" Bearden's *Rocket to the Moon* (1967) issued an oblique commentary on the growing blight of narcotics within black urban communities as it punned on the theme of space travel to signal a metaphorical "high." And his cover art for a November 1968 issue of *Time* returned to the device of toppling buildings to illustrate the urban crisis engulfing Mayor John Lindsay during a year in which New York witnessed major strikes by teachers and sanitation workers, rioting in Harlem following the assassination of Martin Luther King Jr., and student occupations at Columbia University. Collages such as *Black Manhattan* (1969) struck a reviewer for *Arts Magazine* as "stifling" in their "dominance of architectural façade over the subjects themselves. . . . Windows and doorways are exaggerated symbols of escape, as well as implying imprisonment; the pervading imprisonment of life as a particular people."[88]

The activism in which Bearden engaged alongside younger African American artists bore personal fruit for him in 1971 in the form of a major retrospective at the Museum of Modern Art. *Romare Bearden: The Prevalence of Ritual* ran from March 25 to June 7, before touring over the following year to galleries in Washington, D.C., Berkeley, Pasadena, and Atlanta, and concluding at The Studio Museum in Harlem. Ironically, it was Tom Lloyd (the proponent of artistic "separatism") who, along with Faith Ringgold, had played a vital role in lobbying MoMA's director, John Hightower, to demonstrate his commitment to black artists by mounting a Bearden exhibition. With this prestigious retrospective, his election in 1972 to the National Institute of Arts and Letters, and a Rockefeller Fellowship in 1973 at the Metropolitan Museum, Bearden had gained entry into the heart of the American artistic establishment only a few years after leaving his job as a social worker.[89]

To what extent Bearden's new status might have contributed to the mellowing of his representations of black life during the early 1970s is difficult to gauge. From the time of the MoMA retrospective onward, however, critical discussion of Bearden's art began to employ vocabulary quite different from that which had greeted his work during the 1960s. In *Newsweek,* the same publication that in 1964 had announced *Projections* under the headline "Tormented Faces," Douglas Davis wrote in 1971:

> Though he studies the racial crisis, he ennobles everything he touches, leaving himself open to charges of sentimentality. . . . A friend of Bearden's, sitting in on his discussion, [remarks,] "He leaves out all the pain and anguish he went through. . . . He forgets that." Bearden agrees. "I don't want to cry," he says of the early, struggling years when the color barrier in art was higher than now, "and say how bad it was. I want to see how life can triumph."

Charles Allen, writing in the *New York Times,* considered Bearden's new work *The Block* (1971) to be insipid in comparison to *Projections.* A vast collage mounted on six panels with a combined width of eighteen feet, *The Block* (Figure 20, detail) was accompanied by a recording of street sounds and gospel singing, strangely echoing the "total environment" proposed for *Harlem on My Mind.* Bearden had based his panorama of a city block on the view from Murray's apartment overlooking Lenox Avenue and 133rd Street, which Bearden had sketched during the summer of 1970. For Allen, "The treatment is too decorative, the vision too serene, the color too cheerful." Given Bearden's inclusion of a rough sleeper (panel 4), a funeral service (panel 2), and a view into a family's drab living quarters (panel 1), these charges seem inflated, and perhaps speak most to Allen's preconceptions about Bearden's obligation, as an indigenous interpreter, to furnish a picture of pervasive hardship and misery.[90]

A mellower perspective and more "cheerful" use of color were indeed evident, however, in Bearden's reworking in 1975 of his earlier collage *The Street* (1964). The hunched, agonized figures in the bottom left corner of the original have disappeared from the later version (Figure 21). The mournful faces of the guitar player and his female companion have given way to mouths open in song, and a smiling figure has been added to the couple's immediate right. Windows that had revealed detached, sullen children now open onto lovemaking and, below, a mother's tender embrace of her infant. In contrast to both the black-and-white enlargement and the original collage of 1964 (Figures 9 and 10), the color tones in the 1975 composition envelop the scene in a snug luminescence. As Bearden's close friend Harry Henderson, a journalist, observed at around this time, "His work has a kind of warmth and satisfaction that's new. His paintings lack the harshness of some of the earlier ones; they seem to glow. It's something that's come out of Romie—his proud feeling about what black people have achieved."[91]

As the 1970s progressed, Bearden produced fewer collages depicting contemporary black urban life. His exhibition at Cordier & Ekstrom early in 1975, *Of the Blues,* looked back to the interwar heyday of Harlem nightspots such as the Lafayette (Figure 22) and the Savoy, and to Saturday night dances in rural North Carolina. Composed while Murray was working on his book of musical interpretation *Stomping the Blues* (1976), Bearden's new collages complement Murray's emphasis on the celebratory tenor of black communal life, the "irrepressible joyousness, the downright exhilaration, the rapturous delight in sheer physical existence" that Murray regarded as the blues' essence. Writing in the *Village Voice,* David Bourdon observed that Bearden was "becoming more painterly in his use of color, which is sometimes sprayed or splashed on in a manner that approaches Lyrical Abstraction." Now in his sixties, Bearden was preoccupied more than ever with his memories of Mecklenburg County, North Carolina, a world that he tenderly evoked in his exhibition of 1978, *Profile/Part I, the Twenties.* "The countryside is green to an almost preternatural degree," noted Hilton Kramer, "and the interior light romantic as only memory can make it." Beginning in 1973, Bearden spent several months of each year on the Caribbean island of St. Martin, where Nanette's parents had been born. By the 1980s, as he neared the end of his life, Bearden was painting watercolors and gouaches of the island's Obeah people, who "defy the rationality of the Western mind," and whose ritual practices could be "traced back to Africa." The Obeah, and other islanders who could "tell you what plants you shouldn't touch and what plants you can take home and brew for tea," must have reminded Bearden of the "conjur women" of the American South, who had dispensed "love potions" and "herbs to cure various illnesses."[92]

Bearden's collages and watercolors of the 1970s and 1980s include some of the most arresting works of his long career and were keenly welcomed by many critics and collectors. Yet images of contemporary urban life, which had been so vital in raising his profile as an artist during the mid-1960s, had largely dropped out of his oeuvre. His mode of representation was increasingly affirmative and celebratory, while his choice of subjects seemed to locate the grounds for celebration primarily in nostalgia: for childhood memories of a disappearing way of life in the rural South; for a time when the blues and jazz, rather than soul music, had furnished the pulse of black urban life; and for the rituals of the remote Obeah, whose understanding of nature Bearden related to their African ancestry. While any explanation for this must be tentative, a number of possible reasons may be discerned within the shifting, intersecting dynamics of Bearden's experiences as an artist, on the one hand, and of the urban crisis, on the other. The enthusiastic reception of his urban scenes as "propagandist," and, conversely, the complaint that they were "too serene" when critics felt them to be insufficiently "harrowing," made clear the pitfalls and limitations of the role of indigenous interpreter. For an artist who wished the "aesthetic implications" of his work to be taken seriously, social critique may have come to seem, in this context, an obstacle to the kind of recognition he sought.[93]

The changing contours of the urban crisis may also have made the role of indigenous interpreter seem to Bearden to be less worthwhile. The petering out of the riots after 1968 marked the end of a period when outbursts of frustration and anger had nonetheless conveyed a restless anticipation of change. Adjustments in police conduct following the Kerner Commission's report reduced instances of provocation that had often triggered the rioting. Yet the relative tranquillity of black urban communities during the 1970s owed less to any tangible improvements in social conditions than to diminished expectations, as inner cities sank into a period of stagnation symbolized for many by Daniel Patrick Moynihan's phrase "benign neglect." Bearden's comments in an interview in June 1968 intimate his own rapidly subsiding expectations. A registered Democrat, Bearden expressed his disillusionment with the coming presidential election: "I was extremely interested until Senator [Robert] Kennedy was shot. . . . [Martin Luther]

King was shot and now Kennedy. You know, a lot of the Negro people felt that he was one of their last hopes. And I think that he had caught something of the resonance and flavor of the Negro poor." Without hope, it was difficult for Bearden to engage with contemporary black urban life. While Kenneth Clark's response to the rightward turn in American politics from the late 1960s was to delve ever more desperately into disturbing questions of power and social control, and while Amiri Baraka's disappointment with the new black urban politics propelled him toward Marxism, Bearden seemed to retreat from the present and find comfort in his memories. When he did produce urban images in the later part of his career, for example in his exhibition of 1981, *Profile/Part II, the Thirties,* they tended to be romantic cityscapes such as *Midtown Sunset* (Figure 23), a glimmering Manhattan skyline. "Shunning heavy sociopolitical messages," *Vogue* enthused that year, "Bearden makes pictures that celebrate the everyday pleasures of being alive."[94]

Since the end of the 1960s, the American media had been turning its attention toward younger, angrier artists who seemed to embody the mood of the black power movement then reaching its peak. A feature on black artists in *Time* magazine in April 1970 dwelled on twenty-eight-year-old Dana Chandler, the "youngest and angriest," who produced paintings on black power themes and whose "scorn for the white art world is complete." Also attracting attention were the large murals that had sprung up in black inner-city neighborhoods since 1967, when the *Wall of Respect* was created on Chicago's South Side by artists associated with the Organization of Black American Culture, including Barbara Jones-Hogu and Wadsworth Jarrell. *Time* read the *Wall of Respect* as a barometer of black urban sentiments, as the original design, which featured tributes to Malcolm X, Marcus Garvey, and Nina Simone, was frequently amended "to reflect changes in ghetto feelings." By the mid-1970s, however, when the black power movement had also dissipated under the pressures of state repression and ideological schism, the American public's interest in work by black artists—reported in the *New York Times* in 1969 under the headline "Negroes' Art Is What's In Just Now"—had collapsed. As Mary Schmidt Campbell observes, "exhibitions of work by Black American artists virtually disappeared."[95]

Almost uniquely, Bearden withstood the vagaries of public interest in "black art" and continued to exhibit frequently during the 1970s and 1980s. The urban crisis had provided the context for his rise to prominence during the mid-1960s, and, as Michael Kimmerman has observed, in adopting collage Bearden had "hit upon the perfect urban medium." Yet the distinctive aesthetic that Bearden had forged from his experiments with fragments of magazine pages at the time of Spiral's meetings proved highly adaptable, and his appeal outlived his status as an indigenous interpreter of contemporary black urban life. If Murray had been intent on "getting him out of that civil rights context," by the mid-1970s he could be more or less satisfied. While Bearden had not conceived *Projections* as "propaganda," his concern during the 1960s with "realism" and "objectivity," and with "truth, not flattery," had ensured that racism, poverty, and hardship found a place within his inclusive representations. As the prospect of radical social change receded, however, so Bearden's artistic engagement with the urban crisis diminished, while his visual reminiscences increasingly conformed to Murray's celebratory intent. There is a faint indication, however, of Bearden's lingering hope that the political impetus that had inspired many black artists during the 1960s might return. Shortly before he died on March 12, 1988, Bearden made a request to the painter Richard Mayhew: "Let's reactivate Spiral."[96]

Epilogue

As widely as they differed in their backgrounds, personalities, disciplines, and beliefs, Kenneth B. Clark, Amiri Baraka, and Romare Bearden encountered a common set of dynamics through which race shaped the contours of African American intellectual life. At crucial moments in their careers, each faced the dilemmas of the corner. Like black scholars and artists before them, each visited and revisited the imagined juncture where the pathways of racial obligation and intellectual freedom diverge. Moreover, the prominence that Clark, Baraka, and Bearden attained against the backdrop of the riots of the mid- and late 1960s marked the beginning of a new era in the history of African American intellectuals. The task of explaining to white Americans the nature of the urban crisis and its consequences for black communities offered a route to greatly enhanced public recognition. And yet the very notions of racial authenticity that established that route ensured that, for black intellectuals, it would be virtually the *only* road to recognition as public figures. Though the thirst for insights into black urban life transformed their public profiles and professional fortunes, ultimately Clark, Baraka, and Bearden each came to view the role of indigenous interpreter as riddled with constraints and frustrations.

It was Clark who courted the role most assiduously, setting out to lay "the *truth* of the ghetto" before the white American public and to explain the meaning of the riots to white liberals perplexed and disturbed by this violent turn. By fusing the authority of the social scientist with that of the "prisoner of the ghetto," Clark sought to make the emotional dimensions of existence in Harlem real for those outside its "invisible walls," as a precondition for a radical mobilization against America's urban crisis. Yet it was Clark, too, who came to feel the role's limitations most profoundly. The fate of Harlem Youth Opportunities Unlimited (HARYOU) and of the federal War on Poverty signified for him the futility of the role in the face of entrenched concentrations of power chronically aligned against the black urban poor. But equally important to his disillusionment was his rising anguish at being denied a voice beyond "the topic that is reserved for blacks." Burdened no less by his own sense of obligation toward black urban America than by white expectations of black intellectual performance, Clark was himself cornered, hemmed in by the very real consequences of the fiction of race. His commitment to tether his work to the pursuit of social justice for African Americans scarcely wavered. Yet he came to regard the toll of that commitment on his own intellectual freedom and capabilities as devastating.[1]

In his tortuous self-extrication from New York's literary bohemia, LeRoi Jones's urge to identify with black rebellion spurred him to create phantasms of black urban violence at the very moment when actual outbreaks of violence in black urban communities commanded fraught attention. The incendiary imagery of "BLACK DADA NIHILISMUS," *Dutchman,* and *The Slave* found a keen reception among white liberals eager to comprehend African American rage, and among white bohemians entranced by notions of transgressive blackness. Yet in relinquishing his role as an indigenous interpreter, Jones manifested his belief that, like the characters Clay and Walker in his plays, he had become a "slave" to the primitivist fascination with his "scream." Graphic evocations of black rage and retribution were a means of recanting his "social attachments with white folks." However, the success of those plays only seemed to confirm his dependence on white audiences and white primitivism. Determined to avoid the fate of Clay,

who is consumed and destroyed by his audience, and the mental cap-
tivity that grips Walker, Jones departed for "home." In his subsequent
quest, as Amiri Baraka, to define an authentically black sensibility, he
remained trapped by the essentialism that underlay the white fascination with blackness. By the mid-1970s, however, he had discarded the
cultural nationalist ideology that policed the boundaries of black intellectual practice as rigidly as any white audience.[2]

Bearden's return to figuration and "Negro genre" was motivated in
part by his wish to "translate the innerness of the Negro experience."
Imbuing his collages with what he called a "documentary feeling,"
Bearden sought to convey, amid the multiplicity of human life captured in his compositions, something of the turmoil wrought on black
communities by the urban crisis. For Bearden, too, however, the nature of white expectation and appreciation became a source of discomfort. The *Projections* exhibition initiated a period of unprecedented
public attention and financial success in his career, as the role of indigenous interpreter finally enabled him, now in his fifties, to live solely
from his earnings as an artist. Yet while Bearden hoped that interest in
his representational "realism" would be matched by appreciation of his
imaginative achievements and techniques of "artifice," he found that
the status of indigenous interpreter greatly diminished critical consideration of his work's "aesthetic implications." He had been admitted
into the public arena of newspapers and mass-market magazines not as
an artist, but as a "propagandist." If white audiences and cultural gate-
keepers conferred the status of indigenous interpreter, they also dictated its terms.[3]

Such common dynamics and recurrent dilemmas as these have made
African American intellectual life distinctive and uniquely challenging.
However, black scholars and artists have conceived of and responded to
their predicaments in highly contrasting ways. To recognize the limitations imposed on black intellectual practice in the public sphere, or to
witness the tension between intellectual freedom and racial obligation,
is not to claim the existence of a unitary black intellectual experience.
The imperative to avoid the diametrical impulses of pathologism and
romanticization applies no less urgently to discussions of black intellectual life than to those of black urban life. To reduce the history of

African American intellectuals either to a litany of racism's damaging effects on black thought or to a triumph of the life of the mind over the divisive falsities of race is to obscure the variance between black intellectuals' experiences, and to conceal the ways in which individuals' beliefs about the possibilities and limitations of black intellectual life were mutable and contingent.

It would be simple enough to read Clark's anxiety that he had "no thought as a whole" as indicative of the very damage and pathology whose existence he asserted so strenuously. Jerry Watts, indeed, has diagnosed a "rather typical black intellectual 'disease'" that "arises out of the struggle to confront the inevitable internalization of inferiority among subjugated persons." In language redolent of Clark's own writings, Watts describes the result of this "inevitable" process as an "overbearing self-doubt." Yet to the extent that Clark did come to question his own intellectual capabilities, his self-doubt would seem to have had its basis not primarily in internalization of any notion of black inferiority, but rather in a belief that racism, and the very construct of race, had denied him the opportunity to develop the full range of talents and interests that were innately his. How the example of Romare Bearden might trouble such pathologist accounts is yet more suggestive, as there are scant grounds for detecting an internalization of inferiority at any point in his long career. What stands out, in fact, is the self-assurance with which, even as he assumed the role of indigenous interpreter, Bearden felt able to think both through and beyond race. He would "bring something" to his art "as a Negro," and at the same time "redefine the image of man."[4]

Equally mistaken, however, would be to regard as "typical" Bearden's confident cosmopolitanism, his satisfaction that his intellectual practice could simultaneously affirm and transcend the bonds of race. Bearden warrants inclusion in the lineage of black intellectuals constructed by Ross Posnock, those for whom devotion to "race work" proved no obstacle to—and was relieved by—a life of the mind lived within a Du Boisian, universal "kingdom of culture." Yet not all of those who wished for relief from the burdens of racial representation and obligation found the gates of this kingdom to be open. None was more implacably opposed to the limiting, dehumanizing force of racial essentialism than Clark; and yet to him, the life of the mind appeared but one more ghettoized domain. To romanticize as ubiquitous the possibilities of transcendence through a raceless sphere of "culture" would be no less of a distortion than the view of black intellectual life as a tangle of pathology.[5]

Similarly, while "crisis" and "dilemma" have been recurring tropes in black intellectual life, their meanings and consequences have been anything but uniform. The persistence and intensity of racism have confronted African American intellectuals with particularly acute challenges, not least those of negotiating the expectations of white and black audiences. Yet while this substantially shared predicament has frequently precipitated a sense of crisis among black intellectuals, the divergent ways in which crises have been imagined and resolved, or unresolved, are of importance. At particular moments in their careers, Clark, Baraka, and Bearden each experienced a sense of crisis on the corner, where a stark choice between racial responsibility and intellectual freedom seemed unavoidable. Clark's decision, for responsibility, did not end his sense of crisis, but launched him on a career marred by feelings of entrapment and regret. For Baraka, however, the choice of responsibility offered to resolve the crisis of alienation. The path of aesthetic freedom came to seem, to him, nothing more than a mirage, and through a notion of responsibility to the race he arrived at a sense of security in the possibility of being at once black and an intellectual. To Bearden, meanwhile, the corner itself eventually seemed an illusion, a false dichotomy that had prompted his own crises as he veered from social realism to abstraction. Resolution, for him, took the form of an artistic practice that posed no such choice between responsibility and freedom, the particularity of Harlem and the universality of the "Museum without Walls."

In confronting white Americans with the scale of the Great Migration and the depth of the urban crisis, the riots of the mid- and late 1960s marked the moment at which black urban life became the chief object of interpretation and perceived responsibility for African American intellectuals. It has remained so ever since. The equation of "black" and "urban" has become ever more flagrant in a nation in which, since the 1990s, a majority of the population has lived in suburbs. Notwith-standing the commercial regeneration of downtown areas in cities such as Philadelphia and Baltimore, and the sporadic and partial but much-discussed "gentrification" of Harlem, the terms "black" and "urban" continue to stalk public discourse as problematic, threatening signifiers bound up in intensely politicized debates about crime and welfare. As deindustrialization proceeded apace in northern cities in the final decades of the twentieth century, grim indices of urban poverty and violence—together with the sensationalized images of "welfare queens" and racially coded discussions of criminality deployed by con-servative politicians and media—stoked continued fascination with black urban communities as America's own heart of darkness. The emergence of hip-hop from the 1970s and its transformation into a major component of globalized youth culture have raised the visibility of black urban communities—or at least a notion of them—to unpre-cedented heights. In the process, the rap artist has been hailed, and decried, as the direct, authentic voice of "the ghetto," an organic intel-lectual par excellence. Yet this has scarcely diminished public interest in black intellectuals more traditionally defined: as scholars and artists whose accreditation as racial insiders is seen to be matched by academic or artistic credentials conferred by "mainstream" institutions. If 2 Live Crew were the recognized voice of the streets by 1990, it nonetheless fell to Henry Louis Gates Jr. to give *New York Times* readers "2 Live Crew, Decoded."[6]

Indeed, the raging controversy surrounding hip-hop during the 1990s was accompanied by a new surge of media attention directed at black intellectuals in the academy. Much of this attention was focused on Harvard University's Department of Afro-American Studies, and particularly on Gates and Cornel West. Their coauthored book *The Future of the Race* (1996) reasserted the responsibility of the "remnants of the Talented Tenth" to "assume a renewed leadership role for, and within, the black community." As Jonathan Scott Holloway has noted, Gates and West believed themselves to be "morally obliged to speak and act as racial representatives for black America to white America." The publishing houses, magazines, newspapers, and television networks that grant access to "white America" were eager to accommodate them in this role. The prominence of Gates, West, bell hooks, Michael Eric Dyson, and others has underscored the success of black/Afro-American/ African American studies departments and programs since the late 1960s in developing a critical mass of black intellectuals within American universities and in the public sphere—a notable achievement of civil rights and black power activism.[7]

Such success, however, has remained bounded to a significant extent by the same constraints encountered by black intellectuals during the 1960s: the sense of obligation, externally and internally imposed, to tailor intellectual work to the service of the "black community"; the logic of racial authenticity that privileges firsthand accounts of black experience; and confinement to "the topic that is reserved for blacks." The attention focused on black intellectuals as insiders privy to life behind the "Veil" has served all the while to cement their treatment as outsiders on matters not directly related to race. The very reasoning that has established authenticity and intimate experience as the grounds for public interest in what black intellectuals have to say has deemed their opinions on all other matters irrelevant. Black scholars, as Holloway observes, work in small but increasing numbers in fields unrelated to race, but are admitted into the ranks of public intellectuals only when "speaking to blackness." Even conservative black intellectuals who proclaim their support for "color-blind" public policies, such as Thomas Sowell and Shelby Steele, have won access to the media as columnists and pundits only by establishing themselves as commentators on the subject of race. And while it might be hoped that Barack Obama's presidency will translate into recognition of black intellectuals beyond discussions of race, to date it has only appeared to generate demand for firsthand perspectives on being "Black in the Age of Obama."[8]

Even as widening class divisions have strained the notion of a unitary black community, the problematic notion of authenticity has continued to percolate through recent popular and academic discussions of black urban life. One scholar has commended Albert Murray's writings as providing "an insider's view of the Black Experience that establishes, authentically, its beauty, its complexity, and all of its contradictions." Michael Eric Dyson, author of a brace of books about black urban America, is promoted by his publisher as a "former welfare father from

the ghetto of Detroit," a "critic, scholar, and ordained Baptist minister"
who "charts the progress and pain of African Americans." Such formulations scarcely acknowledge the diversity of African Americans' experiences, beliefs, and sensibilities. However, a number of African American voices in recent years have conspicuously challenged the dynamics
of obligation, expectation, and authenticity that have yoked black
intellectual practice to the role of indigenous interpreter. Percival
Everett's novel *Erasure* (2001) fiercely satirizes the ghettoization imposed on black authors by the book industry. Its protagonist, himself a
writer whose experimental fiction has suffered from limited exposure
and wholly inappropriate placement on the African American Studies
shelves of bookstores, finds himself angrily penning *My Pafology,* an
outrageously hyperbolic spoof of a ghetto novel, only for it to be accepted at face value by publishers and become a runaway commercial
success. In *Harlem Is Nowhere: A Journey to the Mecca of Black America*
(2011), Sharifa Rhodes-Pitts also critiques the notion of the authentic
or definitive insider's view. Raised in Texas and educated at Harvard,
she explores her own relationship to Harlem as a shifting, contingent,
deeply personal construct enmeshed in layers of mythology and memory imbibed from books, photographs, folklore, and hearsay. Despite
her book's subtitle, reminiscent of the genre Murray once castigated
as ghetto "safari," Rhodes-Pitts renounces "the typical obligation of
writing about Harlem—offering pronouncements that Harlem is this
or Harlem is that," and chooses instead to foreground the dynamic
subjectivity of the relationship between person and place.[9]

Clark, Baraka, and Bearden came to prominence at a moment when
black urban life erupted into public consciousness with unprecedented
force, and when the momentum of the civil rights movement raised
hopes that conditions in the nation's cities could be imminently transformed. As the federal War on Poverty, the riots, and the mass mobili-
zations of the civil rights and black power movements faded, however,
the notion of an immediate "urban crisis" capable of swift resolution
increasingly gave way to the notion of an "underclass" chronically sundered from the mainstream economy and society. Yet in many respects, the terms in which black urban life has been portrayed and

contested in recent decades attest to the longevity of the concepts and conflicts that structured the debates of the 1960s. The term "underclass" has its origins in liberal pathologist discourse, specifically in Gunnar Myrdal's 1963 study *Challenge to Affluence*. Its adoption by commentators such as Dinesh D'Souza typifies the conservative appropriation of pathologist imagery to identify cultural and moral deficiencies as the root cause of black poverty. However, liberals and radicals have increasingly fought a rearguard battle to reclaim pathologism as a progressive language of political critique.[10]

As the controversy over the Moynihan Report receded while black urban poverty persisted and deepened, variants of pathologist imagery began to regain favor by the 1980s among liberal and radical black intellectuals. No longer fixated on the supposed problems of black "matriarchy," assertions of black social and psychological damage nonetheless resurfaced in accounts of racism and economic exclusion. The novels of Toni Morrison, such as *Beloved* (1987), have frequently centered on enduring traumas engendered by slavery. Cornel West wrote in 1993 that the "white dehumanizing endeavor" had "left its toll in the psychic scars and personal wounds now inscribed in the souls of black folk." In 2001, he reiterated that through the "psychic violence" of racism, African Americans have been "taught systematically to hate themselves." Similarly, bell hooks has counted black "self-hatred" as among racism's pernicious effects.[11]

For liberals and radicals, damage imagery promises once again to dramatize social injustice and to counter conservative attacks on the morality of the black urban poor and neoconservative explanations of black poverty as the result of misguided welfare policies. Meanwhile, the language of moral condemnation and self-improvement characteristic of the uplift tradition resounded in the Million Man March instigated by the Nation of Islam's leader Louis Farrakhan in 1995 as an occasion for black men to atone for their shortcomings as partners and fathers, and more recently in Bill Cosby's well-publicized claims about a lack of personal responsibility among lower-class African Americans.[12]

The resurgence of pathologist imagery has not gone unchallenged, however. The anti-pathologist reaction set off by the Moynihan con-

troversy has echoed loudly in many responses to the pathologist revival. The sociologist William Julius Wilson was fiercely attacked for
resurrecting the phrase "tangle of pathology" in his book *The Truly
Disadvantaged* (1987). Like Clark, who had originated the phrase, and
Moynihan, who had popularized it, Wilson was charged by critics such
as Adolph Reed Jr. with undermining his own call for structural solutions to black urban poverty by portraying the behavior of the black
poor as deviant and the problem of black poverty as self-perpetuating.
Within the arts, the multi-award-winning film *Precious* (2009), based
on Sapphire's novel *Push* (1996), sparked an impassioned anti-pathologist
backlash among some reviewers. The story of an illiterate, drastically
overweight teenage girl in Harlem who has been sexually abused by
her father and fantasizes about having a light-skinned boyfriend, *Precious* was berated by the African American film critic Armond White
as an "orgy of prurience," a "sociological horror show" filled with
"brazenly racist clichés." White labeled the film's director, Lee Daniels, a "shrewd pathology pimp."[13]

How oppressed and impoverished people can be depicted in a manner that both witnesses the extent and consequences of their suffering
and simultaneously recognizes their dignity, resourcefulness, and
agency remains an intractable problem for social scientists, artists, and
indeed historians. Michael Katz has recently remarked, after thirty
years of teaching urban studies at the University of Pennsylvania, that
students who enter his classroom "eager to help change the world"
often leave it feeling demoralized and helpless. The field of urban studies needs a "new narrative," Katz proposes, one in which poor communities do not figure simply as passive victims of relentless structural
forces. This important warning recalls the most persuasive of Albert
Murray's criticisms of Clark's *Dark Ghetto*. Yet the excesses of *anti*-
pathologist imagery, exposed by Clark's countercharges against Murray, need also to be kept in mind as a new narrative is being formed.
Those excesses may, indeed, be found even in the writings of some
of the most accomplished scholars working in African American history today.[14]

Robin Kelley forcefully indicts pathologist social scientists for "playing
the dozens" with urban African Americans, and resolves "to recognize

the importance of pleasure and laughter in people's lives, to see culture and community as more than responses to, or products of, oppression." Such benign intentions become acutely problematic, however, when Kelley enjoins his readers to think of young black female prostitutes not as victims, but as creative agents reclaiming their bodies. Their turn to prostitution, he suggests, should be understood as "transgressive" and "potentially empowering since it turns labor not associated with wage work—sexual play and intercourse—into income." Readers, he urges, should consider "the extent to which anonymous sex is a source of pleasure" for these women.[15]

Beyond raising the dilemmas of "structure" and "agency" faced by any author confronting the experience of oppressed groups, such statements stray perilously (if unintentionally) close to historically ingrained stereotypes of "happy-go-lucky" African Americans and their putative aversion to work and supposedly uninhibited sensuality—no less than pathologist imagery resonates with entrenched stereotypes of black mental inferiority and criminality. The literary scholar Hazel Carby offers a rare insight into the hazards of emphasizing black "pleasure," or, as Murray requested, "accentuating the positive and eliminating the negative," when she interrogates the "rediscovery" of Zora Neale Hurston's novels since the 1980s. Echoing Clark's response to the reception of Murray's writings, Carby wonders whether Hurston's *Their Eyes Were Watching God* (1937) has become "the most frequently taught black novel because it acts as a mode of reassurance that, really, the black folk are happy and healthy."[16]

Representations of black life are not doomed to lapse into pathologism or romanticization. But to navigate between these polar extremes requires a focused awareness of the panoply of racial stereotypes embedded in culture and consciousness over centuries. Bearden's *Projections* evidenced just such awareness, and furnished a powerful and capacious vision of black life in the process. Ralph Ellison also grappled arduously but productively with this challenge in 1958, when, at a particular stage on his journey from writing *Invisible Man* (whose protagonist has been described as "horribly damaged") to leading the assault on pathologism, he remembered the jazz guitarist Charlie Christian, a childhood friend from Oklahoma City:

He spent much of his life in a slum in which all the forms of disintegration attending the urbanization of rural Negroes ran riot. Al-
though he himself was from a respectable family, the wooden tenement in which he grew up was full of poverty, crime and sickness.
It was also alive and exciting, and I enjoyed visiting there, for the
people both lived and sang the blues. Nonetheless, it was doubtless
here that he developed the tuberculosis from which he died.

The lives evoked here are neither enviable nor entirely pitiable. Ellison
witnesses the ingenuity of a culture as well as the results of an intolerable injustice. Crucially, he disavows the strategic selectivity that un-
derlies both romanticization and pathologism, neither "eliminating the
negative," which would trivialize the effects of oppression, nor reducing black lives to passive victimhood. Such strategic representations
may be motivated by the best of intentions. In the end, however, they
benefit their subjects little more than they enlighten their audiences.[17]

Notes

Introduction

1. "Behind the Harlem Riots—Two Views," *New York Herald Tribune,* July 29, 1964, 1, 7.

2. On the scale of this migration, see Nicholas Lemann, *The Promised Land: The Great Black Migration and How It Changed America* (New York: Vintage, 1992), 6. See also Ira Berlin, *The Making of African America: The Four Great Migrations* (New York: Viking, 2010), 152–200.

3. Thomas J. Sugrue, *The Origins of the Urban Crisis: Race and Inequality in Postwar Detroit* (Princeton, NJ: Princeton University Press, 1996), 5–8; Lemann, *Promised Land,* 6; David McAllister, "Realtors and Racism in Working-Class Philadelphia, 1945–1970," in *African American Urban History since World War II,* ed. Kenneth L. Kusmer and Joe W. Trotter (Chicago: University of Chicago Press, 2009), 123–141. On the open housing movement, see Thomas J. Sugrue, *Sweet Land of Liberty: The Forgotten Struggle for Civil Rights in the North* (New York: Random House, 2008), 200–250; Martha Biondi, *To Stand and Fight: The Struggle for Civil Rights in Postwar New York City* (Cambridge, MA: Harvard University Press, 2003), 223–241. For contemporary discussion of the urban crisis, see "Tax Called Cure for Urban Blight," *New York Times,* July 3, 1960, R2; Victor Gruen, *The Heart of Our Cities: The Urban Crisis: Diagnosis and Cure* (New York: Simon & Schuster, 1964); Robert B. Semple Jr., "Urban 'Crisis' Will Be Studied at Hearings Called by Ribicoff," *New York Times,* Aug. 2, 1966, 48.

4. Kenneth B. Clark, *Dark Ghetto: Dilemmas of Social Power* (New York: Harper & Row, 1965), 21–22. The concept of "urban crisis" in the context of the 1960s has been usefully explained as a "ghetto-centered social and cultural upheaval organized under the rubric of race and its semi-synonymous subtopics of poverty, crime, riots, and urban renewal." See Carlo Rotella, *October Cities: The Redevelopment of Urban Literature* (Berkeley: University of California Press, 1998), 270. On police brutality, see Marilynn S. Johnson, *Street Justice: A History of Police Violence in New York City* (Boston: Beacon Press, 2003), 229–276. On the riots in Harlem and beyond, see Shatema A. Threadcraft, "New York City Riot of 1964," in *Encyclopedia of American Race Riots,* ed. Walter Rucker and James Nathaniel Upton, vol. 2 (Westport, CT: Greenwood Press, 2007), 478–480; Janet L. Abu-Lughod, *Race, Space, and Riots: Chicago, New York, and Los Angeles* (Oxford: Oxford University Press, 2007); Jeanne Theoharis, "Alabama on Avalon: Rethinking the Watts Uprising and the Character of Black Protest in Los Angeles," in *The Black Power Movement: Rethinking the Civil Rights-Black Power Era,* ed. Peniel E. Joseph (New York: Routledge, 2006), 27–53; Joe R. Feagin and Harlan

Hahn, *Ghetto Revolts: The Politics of Violence in American Cities* (New York: Mac-millan, 1973).

5. "Harlem: Hatred in the Streets," *Newsweek,* Aug. 3, 1964, 20; "Smoldering Summer in Harlem," ABC, July 23, 1964, 22:30–23:00; "CBS News Special Report: 117th Street New York, N.Y.," CBS2, July 29, 1964, 19:30–20:30; "Harlem: Test for the North," NBC, July 26, 1964, 17:00–18:00. For descriptions of these broadcasts, see "CBS Special News Report," advertisement, *New York Times,* July 29, 1964, 67; "2 Documentaries to Examine Riots," *New York Times,* July 23, 1964, 55. Extracts from *Dark Ghetto* appeared daily in the *New York Post,* Aug. 9–15, 1965, coinciding with the riot in Watts, Los Angeles (August 11–15). See also Woody Klein, ed., *Toward Humanity and Justice: The Writings of Kenneth B. Clark, Scholar of the 1954* Brown v. Board of Education *Decision* (Westport, CT: Praeger, 2004). Ben Keppel has observed that Clark was "a figure little known outside his field" during the 1950s. See Ben Keppel, *The Work of Democracy: Ralph Bunche, Kenneth B. Clark, Lorraine Hansberry, and the Cultural Politics of Race* (Cambridge, MA: Harvard University Press, 1995), 99.

6. On *The Hate That Hate Produced* and its reception, see Manning Marable, *Malcolm X: A Life of Reinvention* (London: Allen Lane, 2011), 160–162. On urban violence in 1963, see Sugrue, *Sweet Land of Liberty,* 303–305. Clark's interviews were published as Kenneth B. Clark, *The Negro Protest: James Baldwin, Malcolm X, Martin Luther King Talk with Kenneth Clark* (Boston: Beacon Press, 1963).

7. Clark, *Dark Ghetto,* xv; Kenneth B. Clark, "A Negro Looks at 'Black Power,'" *New York Post,* Nov. 11, 1967, 30.

8. Langston Hughes, *Black Magic: A Pictorial History of the Negro in American Entertainment* (1967; repr., Englewood Cliffs, NJ: Prentice-Hall, 1971), 5, quoted in Werner Sollors, *Amiri Baraka/LeRoi Jones: The Quest for a Populist Modernism* (New York: Columbia University Press, 1978), 281 n.10; LeRoi Jones, *The Dead Lecturer* (New York: Grove Press, 1964); LeRoi Jones, *Dutchman,* in *"Dutchman" and "The Slave"* (New York: Morrow Quill Paperbacks, 1964), 2, 35; Howard Taubman, "The Theater: 'Dutchman'; Drama Opens on Triple Bill at Cherry Lane," *New York Times,* Mar. 25, 1964, 46.

9. "Six Thoughtful Men on the Summer Ahead," *New York Herald Tribune,* June 14, 1964, in *The Black Power Movement, Part I: Amiri Baraka from Black Arts to Black Radicalism,* ed. Komozi Woodard (microfilm, 9 reels) (Bethesda, MD: University Publications of America, 2000), reel 1, frame 12; "Curtains for LeRoi," *Time,* Jan. 12, 1968, 14. On the duration of *Dutchman*'s initial run, see Sollors, *Amiri Baraka/LeRoi Jones,* 284 n.1.

10. Charles Childs, "Bearden: Identification and Identity," *ARTnews,* Oct. 1964, 51; "Tormented Faces," *Newsweek,* Oct. 19, 1964, 105; "Art in New York: Uptown: Romare Bearden," *Time,* Oct. 23, 1964, NY5.

11. On the lack of recognition afforded to black artists, see Romare Bearden and Harry Henderson, *Six Black Masters of American Art* (New York: Zenith Books, 1972), 40; see also Bearden's remarks as quoted in Grace Glueck, "Negro Art from 1800 to 1950 Is on Display at City College," *New York Times,* Oct. 16, 1967, 47. "Tormented Faces," 105; Stuart Preston, "Bonnard Retrospective at

Modern Museum," *New York Times,* Oct. 10, 1964, microfilm N68–87, Romare Bearden Papers, Archives of American Art, Smithsonian Institution, Washington, DC, frame 381; [author and titled unclear], *New York Herald Tribune,* Oct. 10, 1964, ibid.; *Fortune,* Jan. 1968; *Time,* Nov. 1, 1968; *Romare Bearden: The Prevalence of Ritual,* ex. cat. (New York: Museum of Modern Art, 1971).

12. See Harold Cruse, *The Crisis of the Negro Intellectual: From Its Origins to the Present* (1967; repr., London: W. H. Allen, 1969). "Race," as intellectual historians and others have demonstrated, is a social construction first conceived in the modern world and is neither a meaningful biological or genetic categorization nor a perennial form of human identity. See, for example, Ivan Hannaford, *Race: The History of an Idea in the West* (Washington, DC, and Baltimore: Woodrow Wilson Center Press and Johns Hopkins University Press, 1996); George W. Stocking, *Victorian Anthropology* (New York: Free Press, 1987); Paul Gilroy, *Against Race: Imagining Political Culture beyond the Color Line* (Cambridge, MA: Harvard University Press, 2000).

13. Miles Davis, *On the Corner* (Columbia PC 31906), 1972.

14. See, for example, the discussion of "The Responsibility of Intellectuals in the Age of Crack" among several prominent African American intellectuals in 1992, available at www.bostonreview.net/BR19.1. Faced with the question "Do African American intellectuals have special responsibilities to address the crisis of the American inner cities?" the University of Pennsylvania law professor Regina Austin replied that she would "take that as a foregone conclusion." The Harvard Law School professor Randall Kennedy, however, argued that "all Americans" had such a responsibility. "If black intellectuals owe a higher responsibility does that mean that white intellectuals have a lesser responsibility? I don't think so." The historian Marybeth Hamilton has also noted that "urban" became "a euphemism for 'black'" by the late twentieth century. See Marybeth Hamilton, "Sexuality, Authenticity and the Making of the Blues Tradition," *Past & Present* no. 169 (Nov. 2000): 148.

15. Daniel Patrick Moynihan, *The Negro Family: The Case for National Action* (1965), in *The Moynihan Report and the Politics of Controversy: A Trans-Action Social Science and Public Policy Report,* ed. Lee Rainwater and William L. Yancey (Cambridge, MA: MIT Press, 1967), 43; Elliot Liebow, *Tally's Corner: A Study of Negro Streetcorner Men* (Boston: Little, Brown, 1967); Lee Rainwater, *Behind Ghetto Walls: Black Families in a Federal Slum* (Chicago: Aldine, 1970); Thomas Pynchon, "A Journey into the Mind of Watts," *New York Times Magazine,* June 12, 1966, 34–35, 78–84; Tom Wolfe, "Mau-Mauing the Flak Catchers" (1970), in *Radical Chic and Mau-Mauing the Flak Catchers* (London: Cardinal, 1989), 95–153.

16. W. E. B. Du Bois, *The Souls of Black Folk: Essays and Sketches* (1903; repr., London: Archibald Constable & Co., 1905), 3; W. E. B. Du Bois, "Criteria of Negro Art," *Crisis* 32 (Oct. 1926): 296; Ralph Ellison, "Haverford Statement" (1969), in *The Collected Essays of Ralph Ellison,* ed. John F. Callahan (New York: Modern Library, 1995), 429; Romare Bearden, "Rectangular Structure in My Montage Paintings," *Leonardo* 2, no. 1 (1969): 18; Rotella, *October Cities,* 273.

17. Ralph Ellison, *Invisible Man* (1952; repr., London: Penguin, 2001); James Baldwin, *Go Tell It on the Mountain* (1953; repr., London: Penguin, 2001); James Baldwin, *Another Country* (1962; repr., London: Penguin, 2001); James Baldwin, *The Fire Next Time* (1963), reprinted in James Baldwin, *Collected Essays,* ed. Toni Morrison (New York: Library of America, 1998), 287–347; Lorraine Hansberry, *A Raisin in the Sun* (1959; repr., New York: French, 1984). On Ellison's career in the 1950s, see Arnold Rampersad, *Ralph Ellison, A Biography* (New York: Alfred A. Knopf, 2007), 268–380. On the decline of Baldwin's profile after 1963, see Carol Polsgrove, *Divided Minds: Intellectuals and the Civil Rights Movement* (New York: W. W. Norton, 2001), 237. On Baldwin's thought and career more generally, see Lawrie Balfour, *The Evidence of Things Not Said: James Baldwin and the Promise of American Democracy* (Ithaca, NY: Cornell University Press, 2001); James Campbell, *Talking at the Gates: A Life of James Baldwin* (London: Faber and Faber, 1991). For *Playboy*'s comment on Jones and Baldwin, see Theodore R. Hudson, *From LeRoi Jones to Amiri Baraka: The Literary Works* (Durham, NC: Duke University Press, 1973), 19. On the reception of *A Raisin in the Sun* and on Hansberry's death, see Keppel, *Work of Democracy,* 180–187, 22. For a general account of black literary intellectuals at midcentury, see Lawrence P. Jackson, *The Indignant Generation: A Narrative History of African American Writers and Critics, 1934–1960* (Princeton, NJ: Princeton University Press, 2011).

18. Bettina Aptheker, *The Morning Breaks: The Trial of Angela Davis* (Ithaca, NY: Cornell University Press, 1997); Gwendolyn Brooks, *Annie Allen* (New York: Harper, 1949); James N. Johnson, "Blacklisting Poets" (1968), in *On Gwendolyn Brooks: Reliant Contemplation,* ed. Stephen Caldwell Wright (Ann Arbor: University of Michigan Press, 1996), 46; Theodore H. White, "The Action Intellectuals, Part I: In the Halls of Power," *Life,* June 9, 1967, 43–76; Gloria T. Hull, Patricia Bell-Scott, and Barbara Smith, eds., *All the Women Are White, All the Blacks Are Men, but Some of Us Are Brave: Black Women's Studies* (New York: Feminist Press, 1982); Kimberley Springer, *Living for the Revolution: Black Feminist Organizations, 1968–1980* (Durham, NC: Duke University Press, 2005). On black women's roles within the civil rights and black power movements, see Belinda Robnett, *How Long? How Long? African-American Women in the Struggle for Civil Rights* (New York: Oxford University Press, 1997); Bettye Collier-Thomas and V. P. Franklin, eds., *African American Women in the Civil Rights–Black Power Movement* (New York: New York University Press, 2001). On the rising visibility of black female novelists and the persistent marginalization of black female scholars and critics, see Hazel V. Carby, "African-American Intellectuals Symposium," *Journal of African American History* 88 (Winter 2003): 78–81; Michele Wallace, *Invisibility Blues: From Pop to Theory* (London: Verso, 1990), 213–240. For an overview of black feminist literature, see Patricia Hill Collins, *Black Feminist Thought: Knowledge, Consciousness, and the Politics of Empowerment* (1990; repr., London: Routledge, 2008).

19. On the power and cultural authority of the postwar social sciences, and their decline, see Dorothy Ross, "Changing Contours of the Social Science Disciplines," in *The Cambridge History of Science,* vol. 7, *The Modern Social Sciences,* ed.

Theodore M. Porter and Dorothy Ross (Cambridge: Cambridge University Press, 2003), 229–237; Joel Isaac, *Working Knowledge: Making the Human Sciences from Parsons to Kuhn* (Cambridge, MA: Harvard University Press, 2012); Walter A. Jackson, *Gunnar Myrdal and America's Conscience: Social Engineering and Racial Liberalism, 1938–1987* (Chapel Hill: University of North Carolina Press, 1990); David Milne, *America's Rasputin: Walt Rostow and the Vietnam War* (New York: Hill & Wang, 2008); Ron Robin, *The Making of the Cold War Enemy: Culture and Politics in the Military-Intellectual Complex* (Princeton, NJ: Princeton University Press, 2003).

20. The meeting between Clark and Jones is discussed below in Chapter 1. On the Northside Center, see Gerald Markowitz and David Rosner, *Children, Race, and Power: Kenneth and Mamie Clark's Northside Center* (1996; repr., New York: Routledge, 2000). The friendly acquaintance between Kenneth Clark and Romare Bearden was confirmed in an interview by the author with Clark's daughter, Kate Clark Harris, in London on May 27, 2008.

21. W. E. B. Du Bois, *The Philadelphia Negro: A Social Study* (1899; repr., Millwood, NY: Kraus-Thomson, 1973); W. E. B. Du Bois, *The Quest of the Silver Fleece: A Novel* (Chicago: A. C. McClurg & Co., 1911); Richard Wright, introduction to Horace R. Cayton and St. Clair Drake, *Black Metropolis* (1945; repr., London: Jonathan Cape, 1946), xviii; E. Franklin Frazier, *Black Bourgeoisie: The Rise of a New Middle Class* (New York: Free Press, 1957). Clark's admiration for Wright and Baldwin and Jones's appreciation of Frazier are discussed below in Chapters 1 and 2, respectively. Among the few studies that attend to the interplay between social scientific and literary representations of African American life are Richard H. King, *Race, Culture, and the Intellectuals, 1940–1970* (Washington, DC, and Baltimore: Woodrow Wilson Center Press and Johns Hopkins University Press, 2004); Rotella, *October Cities;* Jay Garcia, *Psychology Comes to Harlem: Rethinking the Race Question in Twentieth-Century America* (Baltimore: Johns Hopkins University Press, 2012). On Hurston, see Karen Jacobs, "From 'Spy Glass' to 'Horizon': Tracking the Anthropological Gaze in Zora Neale Hurston," *NOVEL: A Forum on Fiction* 30 (Spring 1997): 329–360.

22. Allan M. Winkler, *The Politics of Propaganda: The Office of War Information, 1942–1945* (New Haven, CT: Yale University Press, 1978); Christopher Simpson, ed., *Universities and Empire: Money and Politics in the Social Sciences during the Cold War* (New York: New Press, 1998); Daryl Michael Scott, *Contempt and Pity: Social Policy and the Image of the Damaged Black Psyche, 1880–1996* (Chapel Hill: University of North Carolina Press, 1997), 71–136; Lyndon B. Johnson, "Commencement Address at Howard University: 'To Fulfill These Rights,'" June 4, 1965, in *Public Papers of the Presidents of the United States: Lyndon B. Johnson, 1965,* vol. 2 (Washington, DC: Government Printing Office, 1966), 638.

23. Ralph Ellison, "That Same Pain, That Same Pleasure: An Interview" (1961), in *Collected Essays,* 75; Albert Murray, *The Omni-Americans: New Perspectives on Black Experience and American Culture* (New York: Outerbridge & Dienstfrey, 1970), 5, 147.

24. Ralph Ellison, "The Art of Romare Bearden" (1968), in *Collected Essays*, 690; Charles Childs, "Bearden: Identification and Identity," *ARTnews*, Oct. 1964, 62.

25. Scott, *Contempt and Pity*, 137–159; Alice O'Connor, *Poverty Knowledge: Social Science, Social Policy, and the Poor in Twentieth-Century U.S. History* (Princeton, NJ: Princeton University Press, 2001), 19; Robin D. G. Kelley, *Yo' Mama's Disfunktional! Fighting the Culture Wars in Urban America* (Boston: Beacon Press, 1997), 4. See also John P. Jackson Jr., *Social Scientists for Social Justice: Making the Case against Segregation* (New York: New York University Press, 2001); William E. Cross Jr., *Shades of Black: Diversity in African-American Identity* (Philadelphia: Temple University Press, 1991). On the conservative appropriation of damage imagery, see Scott, *Contempt and Pity*, 156–159.

26. Scott, *Contempt and Pity*, 138–139.

27. King, *Race, Culture, and the Intellectuals*, 149–150.

28. Scott, *Contempt and Pity*, 163–167, 172. Richard King has noted that both Malcolm X and the black nationalist literary critic Addison Gayle Jr. depicted African Americans as psychologically scarred by American racism; see King, *Race, Culture, and the Intellectuals*, 159.

29. The history and historiography of uplift are discussed in detail below in Chapter 2. For the most influential treatment, see Kevin K. Gaines, *Uplifting the Race: Black Leadership, Politics, and Culture in the Twentieth Century* (Chapel Hill: University of North Carolina Press, 1996).

30. Albert Murray, *The Omni-Americans: Black Experience and American Culture* (1970; repr., New York: Da Capo, 1990), 42, 7. Clark's critique of Murray's work is examined in detail below in Chapter 1.

31. Jonathan Gill, *Harlem: The Four Hundred Year History from Dutch Village to Capital of Black America* (New York: Grove, 2011), 121–125; David Levering Lewis, *When Harlem Was in Vogue* (1981; repr., New York: Penguin Books, 1997), 25–27; Andrew Beveridge, "An Affluent, White Harlem?" *Gotham Gazette,* Aug. 2008, www.gothamgazette.com/article/Demographics/20080827/5/2620. On earlier black communities in New York City, see Carla L. Peterson, *Black Gotham: A Family History of African Americans in Nineteenth-Century New York City* (New Haven, CT: Yale University Press, 2011).

32. David Lowe, *Stanford White's New York* (New York: Doubleday, 1992); James Weldon Johnson, "Harlem: The Culture Capital," in *The New Negro: Voices of the Harlem Renaissance,* ed. Alain Locke (1925; repr., New York: Simon & Schuster, 1992), 301; Thomas Bender, *New York Intellect: A History of Intellectual Life in New York City, from 1750 to the Beginnings of Our Own Time* (New York: Alfred A. Knopf, 1987), 169–171; Lewis, *When Harlem Was in Vogue,* 89–118. See also George Hutchinson, *The Harlem Renaissance in Black and White* (Cambridge, MA: Belknap Press of Harvard University Press, 1995); James De Jongh, *Vicious Modernism: Black Harlem and the Literary Imagination* (Cambridge: Cambridge University Press, 1990); Anne Elizabeth Carroll, *Word, Image, and the New Negro: Representation and Identity in the Harlem Renaissance* (Bloomington: Indiana University Press, 2005). On the retrospective naming of the "Harlem Renaissance,"

see Andrew M. Fearnley, "When the Harlem Renaissance Became Vogue: Peri-odization and the Organization of American Historiography" (2012, paper in the author's possession).

33. Johnson, "Harlem," 310; Rudolph Fisher, "The City of Refuge," in Locke, *New Negro,* 57–74; Nella Larsen, "Quicksand" (1928), in *Quicksand and Passing* (London: Serpent's Tail, 1989); Claude McKay, *Home to Harlem* (1928; repr., Boston: Northeastern University Press, 1987); Jean Toomer, *Cane* (1923; repr., San Francisco: Arion, 2000); Cheryl Lynn Greenberg, *Or Does It Explode? Black Harlem in the Great Depression* (New York: Oxford University Press, 1997); Langston Hughes, "Harlem" (1951), in *Selected Poems of Langston Hughes* (New York: Alfred A. Knopf, 1959), 268; LeRoi Jones, "Cold, Hurt, and Sorrow (Streets of Despair)" (1962), in *Home: Social Essays* (1966; repr., Hopewell, NJ: Ecco Press, 1998), 95.

34. W. Joseph Black, "Visions of Harlem," draft manuscript, May 10, 1971, p. 38, box 1, folder 10, W. Joseph Black Papers, Schomburg Center for Research in Black Culture, New York Public Library; W. Joseph Black, "Visions of Harlem," draft manuscript, n.d., n.p., box 1, folder 11, ibid.; Richard Hammer, "Report from a Spanish Harlem 'Fortress,'" *New York Times Magazine,* Jan. 5, 1964, 22, 32–39; Clark, *Dark Ghetto,* 25; Eric C. Schneider, *Smack: Heroin and the American City* (Philadelphia: University of Pennsylvania Press, 2008), x, xiv, 42–44; "Drugs," *Black Enterprise,* Apr. 1973, 23–26; Claude Brown, *Manchild in the Promised Land* (1965; repr., New York: Touchstone, 1999), 180. For a powerful critique of postwar "urban renewal," see Themis Chronopoulos, *Spatial Regulation in New York City* (New York: Routledge, 2011), 5–57.

35. Jones, "Cold, Hurt, and Sorrow," 94–95, 96.

36. Sondra Kathryn Wilson, *Meet Me at the Theresa: A History of Harlem's Most Famous Hotel* (New York: Atria, 2004), 204–217; Charles V. Hamilton, *Adam Clayton Powell, Jr.: The Political Biography of an American Dilemma* (New York: Atheneum, 1991); Marable, *Malcolm X,* 108–109; Jones, *Home;* James Edward Smethurst, *The Black Arts Movement: Literary Nationalism in the 1960s and 1970s* (Chapel Hill: University of North Carolina Press, 2005), 108–114; C. W. E. Bigsby, *The Second Renaissance: Essays in Black Literature* (Westport, CT: Greenwood Press, 1980); Clark, *Dark Ghetto,* 25; "No Place Like Home," *Time,* July 31, 1964, 12.

37. David Ward, *Poverty, Ethnicity, and the American City, 1840–1925: Changing Conceptions of the Slum and the Ghetto* (Cambridge: Cambridge University Press, 1989), 2, 178; Eunice Roberta Hunton, "Breaking Through," *Survey Graphic* 6 (Mar. 1925): 684; St. Clair Drake, "The 'Internal Colony': Mere Analogy or Scientific Concept?" n.d. [c. 1974], typescript, 1–2, box 23, folder 8, St. Clair Drake Papers, Schomburg Center for Research in Black Culture, New York Public Library; Louis Wirth, *The Ghetto* (Chicago: University of Chicago Press, 1928); Horace R. Cayton and St. Clair Drake, *Black Metropolis* (1945; repr., London: Jonathan Cape, 1946), 174–213.

38. Eric J. Sundquist, *Strangers in the Land: Blacks, Jews, Post-Holocaust America* (Cambridge, MA: Belknap Press of Harvard University Press, 2005), 391; Kenneth T. Jackson, *Crabgrass Frontier: The Suburbanization of the United States* (New

York: Oxford University Press, 1985), 238–245; John Updike, *Rabbit, Run* (1960; repr., London: Penguin, 2006); Richard Yates, *Revolutionary Road* (1961; repr., London: Methuen, 1986); John Cheever, "The Swimmer" (1964), in *The Stories of John Cheever* (London: Vintage, 2010), 776–788; Catherine Jurca, *White Diaspora: The Suburb and the Twentieth-Century American Novel* (Princeton, NJ: Princeton University Press, 2001); James Baldwin, "The Harlem Ghetto" (1948), in *Collected Essays,* 42–53; Ralph Ellison, "Harlem Is Nowhere" (1948), in *Collected Essays,* 324.

39. Robert C. Weaver, *The Negro Ghetto* (New York: Harcourt, Brace, 1948); August Meier and Elliot M. Rudwick, *From Plantation to Ghetto: An Interpretive History of American Negroes* (New York: Hill & Wang, 1966), 252; David J. Garrow, *Bearing the Cross: Martin Luther King Jr. and the Southern Christian Leadership Conference* (1986; repr., London: Vintage, 1993), 466; Clark, *Dark Ghetto,* 11; Martin Luther King Jr., *Where Do We Go from Here: Chaos or Community?* (New York: Harper & Row, 1967), 36. For two contrasting views of King's authorship/plagiarism, see Keith D. Miller, "Composing Martin Luther King, Jr.," *PMLA* 105 (Jan. 1990): 70–82; Richard H. King, *Civil Rights and the Idea of Freedom* (New York: Oxford University Press, 1992), 111–114. On the emergence of the "ghetto" as the "principal representative terrain" of black American life, and of American racial divisions, see Rotella, *October Cities,* 216.

40. Ralph Ellison, "A Very Stern Discipline" (1967), in *Collected Essays,* 726. Though conducted in 1965, this interview was first published in 1967 in *Harper's Magazine.*

41. Emmanuel Ringelblum, *Notes from the Warsaw Ghetto: The Journal of Emmanuel Ringelblum,* ed. Jacob Sloan (New York: McGraw-Hill, 1958); Bernard Goldstein, *Five Years in the Warsaw Ghetto* (Garden City, NY: Doubleday, 1961); Sundquist, *Strangers in the Land,* 204–205; Michael E. Staub, *Torn at the Roots: The Crisis of Jewish Liberalism in Postwar America* (New York: Columbia University Press, 2002), 8–9; Clark, *Dark Ghetto,* xvii; Jones, "Cold, Hurt, and Sorrow," 96; Imamu Amiri Baraka (LeRoi Jones), "Newark—Before Black Men Conquered" (1967), in *Raise, Race, Rays, Raze: Essays since 1965* (New York: Vintage, 1972), 71. Bearden, Ellison, and Murray's common dislike of "ghetto" is discussed below in Chapter 3.

42. Clark, *Dark Ghetto,* xv; Albert Murray, "Social Science Fiction in Harlem," *New Leader,* Jan. 17, 1966, 21; Ellison quoted in Robert Penn Warren, *Who Speaks for the Negro?* (New York: Random House, 1965), 340–341.

43. Frazier, *Black Bourgeoisie.* More detailed biographical information about Clark, Jones, and Bearden appears in the chapters that follow. On the West Indian immigrant community in New York, which constituted one-quarter of the city's black population during the 1920s, see Nancy Foner, ed., *Islands in the City: West Indian Migration to New York* (Berkeley: University of California Press, 2001).

44. Noam Chomsky, "The Responsibility of Intellectuals" (1967), in *American Power and the New Mandarins* (London: Chatto & Windus, 1969), 257; William Paulson, "Intellectuals," in *The Cambridge Companion to Modern French Culture,* ed. Nicholas Hewitt (Cambridge: Cambridge University Press, 2003), 146.

45. St. Clair Drake, *Black Folk Here and There: An Essay in History and Anthropology,* vol. 1 (Los Angeles: Center for African American Studies, University of California, Los Angeles, 1987), xvii–xix; John Hope Franklin, "The Dilemma of the American Negro Scholar" (1963), in *Race and History: Selected Essays, 1938–1988* (Baton Rouge: Louisiana State University Press, 1989), 299. On the vindicationist tradition and Afrocentric and Egyptocentric historiography, see also Wilson Jeremiah Moses, *Afrotopia: The Roots of African American Popular History* (Cambridge: Cambridge University Press, 1998).

46. Adolph Reed Jr., "'What Are the Drums Saying, Booker?' The Curious Role of the Black Public Intellectual" (1995), in *Class Notes: Posing as Politics and Other Thoughts on the American Scene* (New York: New Press, 2000), 77, 79; Booker T. Washington, *Up from Slavery,* ed. William L. Andrews (1901; repr., Oxford: Oxford University Press, 2000); Du Bois, *Souls of Black Folk,* vii–viii.

47. Manning Marable, "Booker T. Washington and the Political Economy of Black Accommodation," in *Black Leadership* (New York: Columbia University Press, 1998), 23–39; Nathan Irvin Huggins, *The Harlem Renaissance* (New York: Oxford University Press, 1971); Valerie Boyd, *Wrapped in Rainbows: The Life of Zora Neale Hurston* (New York: Simon & Schuster, 2003), 99–111; Reed, "What Are the Drums Saying, Booker?" 86; Madhu Dubey, *Signs and Cities: Black Literary Postmodernism* (Chicago: University of Chicago Press, 2003), 29; Ishmael Reed, *Airing Dirty Laundry* (Reading, MA: Addison-Wesley, 1993), 3; Houston A. Baker Jr., *Betrayal: How Black Intellectuals Have Abandoned the Ideals of the Civil Rights Era* (New York: Columbia University Press, 2008), xviii; Charles Camic and Neil Gross, "The New Sociology of Ideas," in *The Blackwell Companion to Sociology,* ed. Judith R. Blau (Malden, MA: Blackwell, 2001), 236–249; Pierre Bourdieu, *Pascalian Meditations,* trans. Richard Nice (Cambridge: Polity Press, 2000). Jerry Gafio Watts's emphasis on the role of "social marginality facilitators" in the careers of African American intellectuals also exemplifies an instrumentalist sociology of intellectual life that tends to reduce ideas to products of their authors' professional predicaments and attempts at "reproduction of themselves as intellectuals." See Jerry Gafio Watts, *Heroism and the Black Intellectual: Ralph Ellison, Politics, and Afro-American Intellectual Life* (Chapel Hill: University of North Carolina Press, 1994), quotations at 16, 14; Jerry Gafio Watts, *Amiri Baraka: The Politics and Art of a Black Intellectual* (New York: New York University Press, 2001).

48. The charge of artistic prostitution has been brought against Miles Davis in precisely these terms. See Stanley Crouch, "On the Corner: The Sellout of Miles Davis" (1990), in *Considering Genius: Writings on Jazz* (New York: Basic Civitas Books, 2006), 240–256.

49. Albert Murray, "Social Science Fiction in Harlem," *New Leader,* Jan. 17, 1966, 21, 23; Raymond Wolters, *Du Bois and His Rivals* (Columbia: University of Missouri Press, 2002), 40–76; Wilson Jeremiah Moses, *Creative Conflict in African American Thought: Frederick Douglass, Alexander Crummell, Booker T. Washington, W. E. B. Du Bois, and Marcus Garvey* (New York: Cambridge University Press, 2004), 152, 205; 216; Lewis, *When Harlem Was in Vogue,* xxii, 48.

50. Undated invitation to a book-signing event by Clark, box 187, folder 1, Kenneth B. Clark Papers, Manuscript Division, Library of Congress, Washington, DC.

51. Zygmunt Bauman, *Legislators and Interpreters: On Modernity, Post-Modernity, and Intellectuals* (Ithaca, NY: Cornell University Press, 1987), 5; Clifford Geertz, introduction to *Local Knowledge: Further Essays in Interpretative Anthropology* (New York: Basic Books, 1983), 14. For a discussion of African American intellectuals since the 1970s, which also makes reference to Bauman's notion of the postmodern interpreter, see Dubey, *Signs and Cities,* 39.

52. The notion of racial representation can usefully be understood as comprising both "representation as a practice of depicting" and "representation as a practice of delegation." See Isaac Julien and Kobena Mercer, "De Margin and De Centre" (1988), in *Black British Cultural Studies: A Reader,* ed. Houston A. Baker, Manthia Diawara, and Ruth H. Lindeborg (Chicago: University of Chicago Press, 1996), 197. Margaret Mead, *Coming of Age in Samoa: A Psychological Study of Primitive Youth for Western Civilization* (New York: William Morrow, 1928); Clifford Geertz, "Deep Play: Notes on the Balinese Cockfight," *Daedalus* 101 (Winter 1972): 1–37; Constance Rourke, *American Humor: A Study of the National Character* (New York: Harcourt, Brace and Company, 1931). On the emergence and development of "participant observation," see Henrika Kuklick, "Personal Equations: Reflections on the History of Fieldwork, with Special Reference to Sociocultural Anthropology," *Isis* 102 (Mar. 2011): 1–33.

53. Barack Obama's books *Dreams from My Father: A Story of Race and Inheritance* (New York: Three Rivers Press, 2004) and *The Audacity of Hope: Thoughts on Reclaiming the American Dream* (New York: Crown Publishers, 2006) are, at most, partial exceptions, since matters of race and the significance of Obama's own black and/or mixed-race identity have been fundamental to their reception and are, indeed, among their central themes. Edward W. Said, *Representations of the Intellectual: The 1993 Reith Lectures* (London: Vintage, 1994), 32; Marc Matera, "Colonial Subjects: Black Intellectuals and the Development of Colonial Studies in Britain," *Journal of British Studies* 49 (Apr. 2010): 388–418; Norman L. Friedman, "The Problem of the 'Runaway Jewish Intellectuals': Social Definition and Sociological Perspective," *Jewish Social Studies* 31 (Jan. 1969): 3–19; David A. Hollinger, *Science, Jews, and Secular Culture: Studies in Mid-Twentieth-Century American Intellectual History* (Princeton, NJ: Princeton University Press, 1998); Rachel Carson, *Silent Spring* (Boston: Houghton Mifflin, 1962); Mark Hamilton Lytle, *Rachel Carson, "Silent Spring," and the Rise of the Environmental Movement* (New York: Oxford University Press, 2007); Naomi Klein, *The Shock Doctrine: The Rise of Disaster Capitalism* (New York: Metropolitan Books/Henry Holt, 2007).

54. Jonathan Scott Holloway, "The Black Intellectual and the 'Crisis Canon' in the Twentieth Century," *Black Scholar* 31 (Spring 2001): 2, 5, 12. Plausible additions to Holloway's canon might include Langston Hughes, "The Negro Artist and the Racial Mountain," *Nation,* June 23, 1926, 692–694; Romare Bearden, "The Negro Artist's Dilemma," *Critique: A Review of Contemporary Art* 1 (Nov.

1946): 16–22; Saunders Redding, "The Problems of the Negro Writer," *Massachusetts Review* 6 (Autumn–Winter 1964–1965): 57–70; Sanford Pinsker, "The Black Intellectuals' Common Fate and Uncommon Problems," *Virginia Quarterly Review* 70 (Spring 1994): 220–238; Hortense J. Spillers, "*The Crisis of the Negro Intellectual:* A Post-Date," *boundary 2* 21 (Autumn 1994): 65–116.

55. Franklin, "Dilemma of the American Negro Scholar," 301–302; Cruse, *Crisis of the Negro Intellectual;* Ross Posnock, *Color and Culture: Black Writers and the Making of the Modern Intellectual* (Cambridge, MA: Harvard University Press, 1998), 5.

56. Quoted in "Light on the Ghetto," *Newsweek,* May 31, 1965, 81.

57. "LeRoi Jones Reads and Comments on His Poetry," sound recording, cassette 1, side 1, [New York?] 1964, Schomburg Center for Research in Black Culture, New York Public Library.

58. W. E. B. Du Bois, "The Talented Tenth" (1903), in *Writings by W. E. B. Du Bois in Non-Periodical Literature Edited by Others,* ed. Herbert Aptheker (Millwood, NY: Kraus-Thomson, 1982), 17–29; Du Bois, *Souls of Black Folk,* 4; Imamu Amiri Baraka, "The Art of Excellence in Black Life," address at Columbia University Law School, New York, Feb. 28, 1973, transcript, 6, box 3, "Columbia University" folder, Amiri Baraka Papers, Moorland-Spingarn Research Center, Howard University, Washington, DC; Imamu Amiri Baraka, "All in the Street," in *Spirit Reach* (Newark, NJ: Jihad Publications, 1972), 11. Posnock incorporates Jones into the tradition of the *"antirace race man or woman"* by focusing on his conflicted thoughts regarding race and artistic freedom. Yet Posnock's generalized conclusions about "Baraka" are all based on texts written during the early and mid-1960s by an author who called himself, and thought of himself as, LeRoi Jones. While Posnock reveals a good deal about Jones's thinking at that time, these texts arose from a brief, transitional moment and cannot establish that "Baraka" belongs within the "antirace race" tradition. Since 1965, Jones/Baraka has adhered to a notion of organic, politically engaged intellectual practice that admits of no "conflict between race champion and intellectual," and he has evidenced no desire to "lift the burden of being a group representative or exemplar." See Posnock, *Color and Culture,* 5, 43–45, 220–259, quotations at 5.

59. Bearden, "Negro Artist's Dilemma," 21; Childs, "Bearden," 61, 25; Romare Bearden interviewed by Henri Ghent, New York, June 29, 1968, www.aaa.si.edu/collections/interviews/oral-history-interview-romare-bearden-11481; Jeanne Siegel, "Why Spiral?" *ARTnews,* Sept. 1966, 51.

60. The relationships between space, place, identities, and social formations have been illuminated by cultural and historical geographers. See, for example, Kay J. Anderson, "The Idea of Chinatown: The Power of Place and Institutional Practice in the Making of a Racial Category," *Annals of the Association of American Geographers* 77 (1987): 580–598; Tim Cresswell, *In Place/Out of Place: Geography, Ideology, and Transgression* (Minneapolis: University of Minnesota Press, 1996); Charles W. J. Withers, "Place and the 'Spatial Turn' in Geography and in History," *Journal of the History of Ideas* 70 (Oct. 2009): 637–658.

1. Ghettos of the Mind

1. Theodore H. White, "The Action Intellectuals, Part I: In the Halls of Power," *Life,* June 9, 1967, 43–76, quotations at 44, 52; Nicholas Lemann, *The Promised Land: The Great Black Migration and How It Changed America* (New York: Vintage, 1992), 162; Taylor Branch, *Parting the Waters: America in the King Years, 1954–1963* (New York: Simon & Schuster, 1989), 809; Jonathan Scott Holloway, *Confronting the Veil: Abram Harris, Jr., E. Franklin Frazier, and Ralph Bunche, 1919–1941* (Chapel Hill: University of North Carolina Press, 2002), 216.

2. Ben Keppel, *The Work of Democracy: Ralph Bunche, Kenneth B. Clark, Lorraine Hansberry, and the Cultural Politics of Race* (Cambridge, MA: Harvard University Press, 1995), 172; Gina Philogène, ed., *Racial Identity in Context: The Legacy of Kenneth B. Clark* (Washington, DC: American Psychological Association, 2004). By 1982, when the *New Yorker* published a lengthy profile of Clark's career, his presidential address and the ensuing controversy had already been expunged from the record. See Nat Hentoff, "Profiles: The Integrationist," *New Yorker,* Aug. 23, 1982, 37–73. Other major scholarly treatments of Clark's career are Damon Freeman, "Kenneth B. Clark and the Problem of Power," *Patterns of Prejudice* 42 (2008): 413–437; Damon W. Freeman, "Not So Simple Justice: Kenneth B. Clark, Civil Rights, and the Dilemma of Power, 1940–1980" (unpublished PhD dissertation, Indiana University, 2004); Ben Keppel, "Kenneth B. Clark in the Patterns of American Culture," *American Psychologist* 57 (2002): 29–37; Gerald Markowitz and David Rosner, *Children, Race, and Power: Kenneth and Mamie Clark's Northside Center* (1996; repr., New York: Routledge, 2000); Layli Phillips, "Recontextualizing Kenneth B. Clark: An Afrocentric Perspective on the Paradoxical Legacy of a Model Psychologist-Activist," *History of Psychology* 3 (2000): 142–167.

3. Kenneth B. Clark, "The Pathos of Power: A Psychological Perspective," *American Psychologist* 26 (1971): 1056; Kenneth B. Clark, *Pathos of Power* (New York: Harper & Row, 1974), 153–179. The only partial exception to this scholarly silence is a single sentence mentioning Clark's presidential address in Markowitz and Rosner, *Children, Race, and Power,* 205. On the tendency of civil rights narratives to smooth the contours of American democracy's "triumphal moment," see Jacqueline Dowd Hall, "The Long Civil Rights Movement and the Political Uses of the Past," *Journal of American History* 91 (2005): 1234.

4. The dynamics of liberal optimism are explored in Howard Brick, *Age of Contradiction: American Thought and Culture in the 1960s* (Ithaca, NY: Cornell University Press, 1998).

5. Kenneth B. Clark, *Dark Ghetto: Dilemmas of Social Power* (New York: Harper & Row, 1965), 11.

6. Thomas J. Sugrue, *Sweet Land of Liberty: The Forgotten Struggle for Civil Rights in the North* (New York: Random House, 2008), 291–292; Carol Polsgrove, *Divided Minds: Intellectuals and the Civil Rights Movement* (New York: W. W. Norton, 2001), 176.

7. Clark quoted in Jean Stein, *American Journey: The Times of Robert Kennedy,* ed. George Plimpton (New York: Harcourt Brace Jovanovich, 1970), 120; Sugrue, *Sweet Land of Liberty,* 295; Polsgrove, *Divided Minds,* 181.

8. "Probing the Negro Revolt," *Pageant,* Oct. 1963, 151–152.

9. Clark, *Dark Ghetto,* xv; Malcolm X with the assistance of Alex Haley, *The Autobiography of Malcolm X* (New York: Grove Press, 1965); Claude Brown, *Manchild in the Promised Land* (New York: Macmillan, 1965). Further examples include LeRoi Jones, *Home: Social Essays* (New York: William Morrow, 1966); Eldridge Cleaver, *Soul on Ice* (New York: McGraw-Hill, 1968); William H. Grier and Price M. Cobbs, *Black Rage* (New York: Basic Books, 1968); H. Rap Brown, *Die, Nigger, Die!* (New York: Dial Press, 1969). On the rise of "first-person ghetto narrative" in American writing during the 1960s, especially the writings of Malcolm X and Claude Brown, see Carlo Rotella, *October Cities: The Redevelopment of Urban Literature* (Berkeley: University of California Press, 1998), 269–292, quotation at 273.

10. See *New York Post,* Aug. 9–15, 1965. On sales of *Dark Ghetto,* see Keppel, *Work of Democracy,* 297 n.29. For Clark's comments in the print media, see "No Place Like Home," *Time,* July 31, 1964, 17; "Harlem: Hatred in the Streets," *Newsweek,* Aug. 3, 1964, 20; Ernest Dunbar, "Harlem's Violent Mood," *Look,* July 28, 1964, 29–31. The psychologist Claude M. Steele recalls watching Clark's commentary on the Harlem riot on television as a child. See Claude M. Steele, "Kenneth B. Clark's Context and Mine: Toward a Context-Based Theory of Social Identity Threat," in Philogène, *Racial Identity in Context,* 61.

11. Markowitz and Rosner, *Children, Race, and Power,* 19–20; "Dr. Clark Gets Full Professorship," New York *Amsterdam News,* Jan. 14, 1961, box 220, folder 7, Kenneth B. Clark Papers, Manuscript Division, Library of Congress, Washington, DC (hereafter cited as Clark Papers).

12. The Reminiscences of Kenneth B. Clark, Feb. 4 and Mar. 19, 1976, transcript, 146, 33, 136–137, Oral History Collection of Columbia University in the City of New York (hereafter cited as Clark Reminiscences); Stella Chess, Kenneth B. Clark, and Alexander Thomas, "The Importance of Cultural Evaluation in Psychiatric Diagnosis and Treatment," *Psychiatric Quarterly* 27 (1953): 102–114; Markowitz and Rosner, *Children, Race, and Power,* 82, 85. On the rapid growth and rising prestige of psychology and psychiatry in postwar America, see Ellen Herman, *The Romance of American Psychology: Political Culture in the Age of Experts* (Berkeley: University of California Press, 1995); Martin Halliwell, *Therapeutic Revolutions: Medicine, Psychiatry, and American Culture, 1945–1970* (New Brunswick, NJ: Rutgers University Press, 2013); James H. Capshew, *Psychologists on the March: Science, Practice, and Professional Identity in America, 1929–1969* (Cambridge: Cambridge University Press, 1999). For critical historical assessments of the practice of psychoanalysis in America, see Joel Pfister and Nancy Schnog, eds., *Inventing the Psychological: Toward a Cultural History of Emotional Life in America* (New Haven, CT: Yale University Press, 1997).

13. Clark Reminiscences, Apr. 7, 1976, transcript, 151–152; Arnold H. Lubasch, "City Plans to Aid Harlem's Youth," *New York Times,* June 13, 1962,

box 48, folder 8, Clark Papers; Richard A. Cloward and Lloyd E. Ohlin, *Delinquency and Opportunity: A Theory of Delinquent Gangs* (Glencoe, IL: Free Press, 1960); Edward R. Schmitt, *President of the Other America: Robert Kennedy and the Politics of Poverty* (Amherst: University of Massachusetts Press, 2010), 68–69. See also James Gilbert, *A Cycle of Outrage: America's Reaction to the Juvenile Delinquent in the 1950s* (New York: Oxford University Press, 1986).

14. Harlem Youth Opportunities Unlimited Inc., *Youth in the Ghetto: A Study of the Consequences of Powerlessness and a Blueprint for Change* (New York: Harlem Youth Opportunities Unlimited Inc., 1964). For a description of the origins of the HARYOU report, see ibid., 21–31. On Clark's authorship of the main sections of the report, see Freeman, "Kenneth B. Clark and the Problem of Power," 414.

15. Gunnar Myrdal, *An American Dilemma: The Negro Problem and Modern Democracy,* 2 vols. (New York: Harper & Bros., 1944); Clark, *Dark Ghetto,* x, 1–10, quotations at 1, 4. On the "moral exhortation" in Myrdal's report, see Walter A. Jackson, *Gunnar Myrdal and America's Conscience: Social Engineering and Racial Liberalism, 1938–1987* (Chapel Hill: University of North Carolina Press, 1990), 187. For Clark's recollections of his collaboration with Myrdal in the early 1940s, see Clark Reminiscences, Sept. 9, 1976, transcript, 392–394.

16. Clark, *Dark Ghetto,* xxiii–xxiv, xx–xxi. On the persistent tendency for "questions of value" to be "bracketed by mainstream social science" in the United States, see James T. Kloppenberg, "The Place of Value in a Culture of Facts: Truth and Historicism," in *The Humanities and the Dynamics of Social Inclusion since World War II,* ed. David A. Hollinger (Baltimore: Johns Hopkins University Press, 2006), 126–158, quotations at 140. For Clark's conception of social science as "the science of human morality," which "must state and deal with values," see Clark, *Pathos of Power,* x.

17. Clark, *Dark Ghetto,* 17, 34, xxii.

18. Daryl Michael Scott, *Contempt and Pity: Social Policy and the Image of the Damaged Black Psyche, 1880–1996* (Chapel Hill: University of North Carolina Press, 1997), 7 (Du Bois quotation), 141.

19. Kenneth B. Clark, *Prejudice and Your Child* (Boston: Beacon Press, 1955), 9, 50; Abram Kardiner and Lionel Ovesey, *The Mark of Oppression: Explorations in the Personality of the American Negro* (New York: W. W. Norton, 1951); Gordon W. Allport, *The Nature of Prejudice* (Cambridge, MA: Addison-Wesley, 1955); Kurt Lewin, "Self-Hatred among Jews," *Contemporary Jewish Record* 4 (1941): 219–232. On Lewin's influence on the literature on black self-hatred, see William E. Cross Jr., *Shades of Black: Diversity in African-American Identity* (Philadelphia: Temple University Press, 1991), 5, 12, 33–36.

20. Clark, *Dark Ghetto,* 11, 63–64. On the Venetian ghetto, see Riccardo Calimani, *The Ghetto of Venice,* trans. Katherine Silberblatt Wolfthal (Milan: Rusconi, 1988).

21. Kenneth B. Clark, "Kurt Lewin Memorial Award Address—1965: Problems of Power and Social Change: Toward a Relevant Social Psychology," *Journal of Social Issues* 21 (1965): 13; Kenneth B. Clark, "Implications of Adlerian Theory for an Understanding of Civil Rights Problems and Action," *Journal of Individual*

Psychology 23 (1967): 183, 189. See also Alfred Adler, *Understanding Human Nature,* trans. Colin Brett (1927; repr., Oxford: Oneworld, 1992). Clark made *Understanding Human Nature* required reading for his students at a Harvard University summer school in 1965; see Kenneth B. Clark, "Social Relations 226: Common Reading List," box 54, folder 5, Clark Papers. On Adler's life and thought, see Jon Carlson and Michael Maniacci, eds., *Alfred Adler Revisited* (New York: Routledge, 2011); Loren Grey, *Alfred Adler, the Forgotten Prophet: A Vision for the 21st Century* (Westport, CT: Praeger, 1998). Neo-Freudian theorists in the United States such as Eric Fromm, Karen Horney, and Harry Stack Sullivan also viewed Freudian psychoanalysis as excessively concerned with sexual instincts and insufficiently attentive to cultural context and social interaction. See Martin Birnbach, *Neo-Freudian Social Philosophy* (Stanford, CA: Stanford University Press, 1962).

22. Clark, *Dark Ghetto,* 11, 32–33.

23. Ibid., 34–35, 12.

24. Ibid., xvii; "It's Largely a Matter of Psychology in Lives of Mamie and Kenneth Clark," *New York Age Defender,* Mar. 20, 1954, box 220, folder 6, Clark Papers; Ralph Blumenthal, "Today Is Nudging Yesterday in a Tranquil Hudson Town," *New York Times,* Feb. 26, 1968, 39. For Kenneth Clark's recollections of Hastings-on-Hudson in an interview conducted in 1990, see www.hastingshistoricalsociety.blogspot.co.uk/2010/05/house-tour-preview-kenneth-clark.html.

25. Clark Reminiscences, Feb. 4, 1976, transcript, 1, 12–14, 17; Kenneth B. Clark, "An Architect of Social Change," in *Against All Odds: Scholars Who Challenged Racism in the Twentieth Century,* ed. Benjamin P. Browser and Louis Kushnick with Paul Grant (Amherst: University of Massachusetts Press, 2002), 148; Arthur Bancroft Clark to Kenneth B. Clark, Jan. 25, 1938, box 1, folder 1, Clark Papers. On West Indian migrant laborers in the Panama Canal Zone during the early twentieth century, see Bonham C. Richardson, *The Caribbean in the Wider World, 1492–1992* (Cambridge: Cambridge University Press, 1992), 138.

26. Clark Reminiscences, Feb. 4, 1976, transcript, 37, 28–30, 33, 35; Jacob S. Dorman, "Back to Harlem: Abstract and Everyday Labor during the Harlem Renaissance," in *The Harlem Renaissance Revisited: Politics, Arts, and Letters,* ed. Jeffrey O. G. Ogbar (Baltimore: Johns Hopkins University Press, 2010), 76; Jervis Anderson, *Harlem: The Great Black Way, 1900–1950* (London: Orbis, 1982), 303. On the International Ladies' Garment Workers' Union, see David Dubinsky, *The Master of Seventh Avenue: David Dubinsky and the American Labor Movement* (New York: New York University Press, 2005). Clark offered a critique of ongoing racial discrimination within this union in *Dark Ghetto,* 43–45.

27. Clark, *Dark Ghetto,* xv; Clark Reminiscences, Feb. 4, 1976, transcript, 27–28, 10; Kenneth B. Clark, "Racial Progress and Retreat: A Personal Memoir," in *Race in America: The Struggle for Equality,* ed. Herbert Hill and James E. Jones Jr. (Madison: University of Wisconsin Press, 1993), 3–4.

28. Clark, "Racial Progress and Retreat," 5–6; Kenneth B. Clark, "A Few Remarks," address delivered at New York Civil Liberties Union Testimonial Dinner Honoring Kenneth B. Clark, Oct. 14, 1975, transcript, box 4, folder 3, Clark Papers; Clark Reminiscences, Feb. 23, 1976, transcript, 60–61; "Transcript

of Dr. Clark's conversation in unpublished doctoral dissertation [by James Moss]," 1957, 118–119, box 190, folder 4, Clark Papers.

29. Holloway, *Confronting the Veil,* 31, 62–63; Clark Reminiscences, Feb. 23, 1976, transcript, 71–72, 74–75; Clark, "Racial Progress and Retreat," 7–9.

30. Clark Reminiscences, Feb. 23, 1976, transcript, 82–83, 85; Kenneth B. Clark, lecture delivered at World Affairs Conference, Mills College, Oakland, CA, Dec. 3, 1963, transcript, 9, box 159, folder 3, Clark Papers; Patricia Sullivan, *Lift Every Voice and Sing: The NAACP and the Making of the Civil Rights Movement* (New York: New Press, 2009), 197. On the Communist "black belt thesis," see Cedric J. Robinson, *Black Marxism: The Making of the Black Radical Tradition* (Chapel Hill: University of North Carolina Press, 1993), 227; Nikhil Pal Singh, *Black Is a Country: Race and the Unfinished Struggle for Democracy* (Cambridge, MA: Harvard University Press, 2004), 110.

31. Hentoff, "Profiles," 45. On Sumner, see Thomas F. Sawyer, "Francis Cecil Sumner: His Views and Influence on African American Higher Education," *History of Psychology* 3 (2000): 122–141. On black scholars' near-total exclusion from Ivy League universities, see Bruce Kuklick, *Black Philosopher, White Academy: The Career of William Fontaine* (Philadelphia: University of Pennsylvania Press, 2008). On positivism in the American social sciences, see Dorothy Ross, *The Origins of American Social Science* (Cambridge: Cambridge University Press, 1991).

32. Hentoff, "Profiles," 46; Clark Reminiscences, Feb. 23, 1976, transcript, 72, 95.

33. Clark Reminiscences, Sept. 9, 1976, transcript, 360–361; Kenneth B. Clark, "Some Factors Influencing the Remembering of Prose Material," *Archives of Psychology,* no. 253 (July 1940), ed. R. S. Woodworth; Frances Cherry, "Kenneth B. Clark and Social Psychology's Other History," in Philogène, *Racial Identity in Context,* 28. See also Ruth Benedict, *Patterns of Culture* (Boston: Houghton Mifflin, 1934); Franz Boas, *Race, Language, and Culture* (New York: Macmillan, 1940); Otto Klineberg, *Negro Intelligence and Selective Migration* (New York: Columbia University Press, 1935); Vernon J. William, *Franz Boas and His Contemporaries* (Lexington: University Press of Kentucky, 1996).

34. Hentoff, "Profiles," 46; Clark Reminiscences, Sept. 9, 1976, transcript, 395–396; Mamie P. Clark, "Changes in Primary Mental Ability with Age," *Archives of Psychology,* no. 291 (May 1944), ed. R. S. Woodworth.

35. Clark Reminiscences, Feb. 23 and Feb. 4, 1976, transcript, 72, 55–56; "Transcript of Dr. Clark's conversation in unpublished doctoral dissertation," 137; Clark, *Dark Ghetto,* xvii.

36. Ross Posnock, *Color and Culture: Black Writers and the Making of the Modern Intellectual* (Cambridge, MA: Harvard University Press, 1998), 5, 9; W. E. B. Du Bois, *The Souls of Black Folk: Essays and Sketches* (1903; repr., London: Archibald Constable & Co., 1905), 109, 4; Ralph Ellison, "Bearden" (1988), in *The Collected Essays of Ralph Ellison,* ed. John F. Callahan (New York: Modern Library, 1995), 834; Clark, *Dark Ghetto,* 195. Clark continued: "The problem for the Negro scholar is even more acute in view of the fact that he is not permitted to escape into the subjectivity and emotion that are an expected part of the life of the artist."

37. Clark, *Dark Ghetto,* 195. On Harlem's arts scene in the second half of the 1960s, see James Edward Smethurst, *The Black Arts Movement: Literary National-ism in the 1960s and 1970s* (Chapel Hill: University of North Carolina Press, 2005).

38. Ralph Ellison, *"An American Dilemma:* A Review" (1964), in *Collected Es-says,* 339–340; Ralph Ellison, " 'A Very Stern Discipline' " (1967), in *Collected Essays,* 748; Robert Penn Warren, *Who Speaks for the Negro?* (New York: Random House, 1965), 340. The friendship between the Ellisons and the Clarks is evident in Ralph Ellison and Fanny Ellison to Kenneth B. Clark and Mamie Clark, Nov. 25, 1955, box 41, folder 8, Ralph Ellison Papers, Manuscript Division, Library of Congress, Washington, DC.

39. Ralph Ellison, "Harlem Is Nowhere" (1948), in *Collected Essays,* 324–325; Ellison, " 'A Very Stern Discipline,' " 726, 748; "Dr. Kenneth B. Clark: Inter-preter of Mankind," interview by Wendell B. Harris Jr., Mar. 30, 1981, tran-script, 45–46, box 194, folder 1, Clark Papers; Richard Wright, *Native Son* (New York: Harper & Bros., 1940); Clark, *Dark Ghetto,* 57. For Ellison's critique of Wright, see Ralph Ellison, "The World and the Jug" (1963), in *Collected Essays,* 155–188; Ralph Ellison, "That Same Pain, That Same Pleasure: An Interview" (1961), in *Collected Essays,* 63–80. That Ellison's pathologist account in "Harlem Is Nowhere" was penned four years after his anti-pathologist critique of *An Ameri-can Dilemma* is a puzzling fact that, to this author's knowledge, still awaits explanation.

40. Richard Wright, introduction to Horace R. Cayton and St. Clair Drake, *Black Metropolis* (1945; repr., London: Jonathan Cape, 1946), xviii. See also Robert E. Park, "The Nature of Race Relations," in *Race Relations and the Race Problem,* ed. Edgar T. Thompson (1939; repr., New York: Greenwood Press, 1968), 3–45; Louis Wirth, *The Ghetto* (Chicago: University of Chicago Press, 1928). Other African American literary authors of the 1940s whose work engaged with socio-logical and psychological notions of black urban pathology, and whose writings are likely to have been familiar to Clark, include Ann Petry and Chester Himes. On Petry, see Lawrence P. Jackson, *The Indignant Generation: A Narrative History of African-American Writers and Critics, 1934–1960* (Princeton, NJ: Princeton University Press, 2011), 142–146. On Himes, see Jay Garcia, *Psychology Comes to Harlem: Rethinking the Race Question in Twentieth-Century America* (Baltimore: Johns Hopkins University Press, 2012), 75–82.

41. Kenneth B. Clark, "The Negro in Contemporary America," lecture deliv-ered at Mills College, Oakland, CA, Dec. 3, 1963, transcript, 15–16, box 159, folder 3, Clark Papers; Kenneth B. Clark, "Introduction to the Wesleyan Edi-tion," *King, Malcolm, Baldwin: Three Interviews* (Middletown, CT: Wesleyan Uni-versity Press, 1985), 13; Kenneth B. Clark to James Baldwin, Oct. 14, 1963, box 23, folder 7, Clark Papers.

42. James Baldwin, *Go Tell It on the Mountain* (1953; repr., London: Penguin, 2001); HARYOU, *Youth in the Ghetto,* 572; James Baldwin, "The Harlem Ghetto" (1948), in *Collected Essays,* ed. Toni Morrison (New York: Library of America, 1998), 48.

43. Baldwin, "Harlem Ghetto," 43–49, quotation at 47–48; Clark, "Introduction to the Wesleyan Edition," 13; Clark, *Dark Ghetto*, 150–182, quotations at 150, 162.

44. Clark, *Dark Ghetto*, 81; Sander L. Gilman, *Difference and Pathology: Stereotypes of Sexuality, Race, and Madness* (Ithaca, NY: Cornell University Press, 1985), 23. See also Jonathan Gil Harris, *Foreign Bodies and the Body Politic: Discourses of Social Pathology in Early Modern England* (Cambridge: Cambridge University Press, 1998). On the history of the idea of "social pathology" and its links to progressive and radical politics, see Dorothy Porter, "John Ryle: Doctor of Revolution?" in *Doctors, Politics, and Society: Historical Essays,* ed. Dorothy Porter and Roy Porter (Amsterdam: Editions Rodopi BV, 1993), 247–274, esp. 250–252.

45. Clark, *Dark Ghetto*, xxii, 73, 109, 81, 74.

46. Herbert Aptheker, "Introduction" (1973), in W. E. B. Du Bois, *The Philadelphia Negro: A Social Study* (1899; repr., Millwood, NY: Kraus-Thomson, 1973), 30; Du Bois, *Philadelphia Negro*, 67; Scott, *Contempt and Pity*, 42–51, 74–75.

47. Clark, *Dark Ghetto*, 70; Du Bois, *Philadelphia Negro*, 311–312; Kardiner and Ovesey, *Mark of Oppression;* Scott, *Contempt and Pity*, 77–78.

48. Clark, *Dark Ghetto*, 70–71 (emphasis added).

49. Ibid., 47, 11, 81.

50. Oscar Lewis, *Five Families: Mexican Case Studies in the Culture of Poverty* (New York: Basic Books, 1959); Oscar Lewis, *La Vida: A Puerto Rican Family in the Culture of Poverty: San Juan and New York* (New York: Random House, 1966), xlix, quoted in Alice O'Connor, *Poverty Knowledge: Social Science, Social Policy, and the Poor in Twentieth-Century U.S. History* (Princeton, NJ: Princeton University Press, 2001), 119; Clark, *Dark Ghetto*, 130–131.

51. Clark, *Dark Ghetto*, 130–131, 140–148. A few years earlier, Clark had responded angrily to the former Harvard University president James Bryant Conant's book *Slums and Suburbs: A Commentary on Schools in Metropolitan Areas* (New York: McGraw-Hill, 1961). Conant's argument that vocational training should receive greater priority than algebra and foreign languages in schools in disadvantaged neighborhoods would condemn black children, Clark argued, to be "hewers of wood and drawers of water." See Peter H. Binzen, "Psychologist Says Negro Is Victim of 'Educational Inferiority' Theory," *Philadelphia Bulletin,* n.d., box 200, folder 8, Clark Papers.

52. "Light on the Ghetto," *Newsweek,* May 31, 1965, 78, 81; Nat Hentoff, "Urban Blight," *New Yorker,* July 31, 1965, 71, 75; Frank M. Cordasco, "Wanted: A World Fit to Live In," *Saturday Review,* June 5, 1965, 21; Robert Coles, "A Compelling Summons," *Reporter,* Oct. 21, 1965, 61–62; Anna M. Kross, "Wanted: Bootstraps," *New York Times Book Review,* June 20, 1965, 6.

53. Lyndon B. Johnson, "Commencement Address at Howard University: 'To Fulfil These Rights,'" June 4, 1965, *Public Papers of the Presidents of the United States: Lyndon B. Johnson, 1965,* vol. 2 (Washington, DC: Government Printing Office, 1966), 635–640; Lee Rainwater and William L. Yancey, introduction to *The Moynihan Report and the Politics of Controversy: A Trans-Action Social Science and*

Public Policy Report, ed. Lee Rainwater and William L. Yancey (Cambridge, MA: MIT Press, 1967), 3–4.

54. Guian A. McKee, *The Problem of Jobs: Liberalism, Race, and Deindustrialization in Philadelphia* (Chicago: University of Chicago Press, 2008), 216; Rainwater and Yancey, introduction to *Moynihan Report,* 3–4.

55. Daniel Patrick Moynihan, *The Negro Family: The Case for National Action* (1965), in Rainwater and Yancey, *Moynihan Report,* 43, 61, 51, 75; Clark, *Dark Ghetto,* 88; HARYOU, *Youth in the Ghetto,* 156. The phrase "tangle of community and personal pathology" also appeared in Clark, *Dark Ghetto,* 106.

56. McGrory quoted in Lee Rainwater and William L. Yancey, "The Report Becomes Public," in Rainwater and Yancey, *Moynihan Report,* 135; Evans and Novak quoted in O'Connor, *Poverty Knowledge,* 207. McGrory was responding to the summation of Moynihan's contentions in President Johnson's Howard University commencement address of June 4, 1965.

57. Stanley M. Elkins, *Slavery: A Problem in American Institutional and Intellectual Life* (Chicago: University of Chicago Press, 1959); Ann J. Lane, ed., *The Debate over Slavery: Stanley Elkins and His Critics* (Urbana: University of Illinois Press, 1971); Moynihan, *Negro Family,* 43; Ryan and Farmer quoted in Daniel Geary, "Tangled Ideologies: Reconsidering the Reception of the Moynihan Report," paper delivered at the annual convention of the Organization of American Historians, Houston, Mar. 18, 2011, 14 (copy in author's possession). On the rate of growth of opposition to the Moynihan Report, see Geary, "Tangled Ideologies." See also James T. Patterson, *Freedom Is Not Enough: The Moynihan Report and America's Struggle over Black Family Life from LBJ to Obama* (New York: Basic Books, 2010).

58. "The Negro Family: Visceral Reaction," *Newsweek,* Dec. 6, 1965, 40; Charles A. Valentine, *Culture and Poverty: Critique and Counter-Proposals* (Chicago: University of Chicago Press, 1968), 20, 29.

59. John W. Blassingame, *The Slave Community: Plantation Life in the Antebellum South* (New York: Oxford University Press, 1972); Herbert G. Gutman, *The Black Family in Slavery and Freedom, 1750–1925* (New York: Pantheon Books, 1976); Andrew Billingsley, *Black Families in White America* (Englewood Cliffs, NJ: Prentice-Hall, 1968); Joyce Ladner, *Tomorrow's Tomorrow: The Black Woman* (Garden City, NY: Doubleday, 1971); Carol B. Stack, *All Our Kin: Strategies for Survival in a Black Community* (New York: Harper & Row, 1974); Reginald Jones quoted in Scott, *Contempt and Pity,* 177; Scott, *Contempt and Pity,* 162.

60. Ralph Ellison, *Invisible Man* (New York: Random House, 1952). Murray's first published novel was *Train Whistle Guitar* (New York: McGraw-Hill, 1974). On Murray's life and career, see Henry Louis Gates Jr., "King of Cats," in *Thirteen Ways of Looking at a Black Man* (New York: Vintage, 1997), 21–46, quotation at xxiii.

61. Albert Murray, "Social Science Fiction in Harlem," *New Leader,* Jan. 17, 1966, 21–23.

62. Albert Murray, *The Omni-Americans: New Perspectives on Black Experience and American Culture* (New York: Outerbridge & Dienstfrey, 1970), 40–41, 180, 74–75.

63. Ibid., 40–41, 148–149.

64. Scott, *Contempt and Pity;* O'Connor, *Poverty Knowledge;* Murray, *Omni-Americans,* 40–41, 43.

65. Scott, *Contempt and Pity,* 156–157; Edward C. Banfield, *The Unheavenly City: The Nature and Future of Our Urban Crisis* (Boston: Little, Brown, 1970); Jennifer S. Light, *From Warfare to Welfare: Defense Intellectuals and Urban Problems in Cold War America* (Baltimore: Johns Hopkins University Press, 2003).

66. Murray, *Omni-Americans,* 41–42; Clark, *Dark Ghetto,* 74, xv.

67. Murray, *Omni-Americans,* 7 (emphasis added), 74, 76; Albert Murray, untitled manuscript, n.d., in envelope marked "Remarks on Some of the Limitations of Protest Writers (from Hemingway ms)," 4–5, box 1, Albert Murray Papers, Houghton Library, Harvard University, Cambridge, MA.

68. George M. Fredrickson, *The Black Image in the White Mind: The Debate on Afro-American Character and Destiny, 1817–1914* (1971; repr., Hanover, NH: Wesleyan University Press, 1987), 52, 123–124, 328–330. For "White Negro" primitivism, see Norman Mailer, "The White Negro" (1957), in *Protest,* ed. Gene Feldman and Max Gartenberg (London: Panther, 1960), 288–306. The relationship between Mailer's and Murray's depictions of black urban life is discussed in Chapter 3 of this book.

69. Kenneth B. Clark to Myron Kolatch, Jan. 27, 1966, box 26, folder 2, Clark Papers; Kenneth B. Clark, "Draft, Address Delivered at City College Ethnic Conference," 2–4, n.d., box 167, folder 2, Clark Papers.

70. Mailer, "White Negro"; Norman Mailer, "Theatre: The Blacks" (1961), in *The Presidential Papers* (1963; repr., St. Albans, UK: Panther Books, 1976), 219; Seymour Krim, "Ask for a White Cadillac" (1959), in *Missing a Beat: The Rants and Regrets of Seymour Krim,* ed. Mark Cohen (Syracuse, NY: Syracuse University Press, 2010), 115; Edward Kosner and Alfred T. Hicks, "Harlem and Beyond: The New Negro Middle Class," *New York Post,* May 4, 1962, 41.

71. Phyllis A. Wallace, "Interview with Dr. Kenneth B. Clark," Nov. 12, 1970, typescript, 26–29, 37, 32–33, box 192, folder 3, Clark Papers. On Columbia, see Joseph Rocco Mitchell and David L. Stebenne, *New City upon a Hill: A History of Columbia, Maryland* (Charleston, SC: History Press, 2007). On the cultural politics of "soul," see Richard Green, ed., *Soul: Black Power, Politics, and Pleasure* (New York: New York University Press, 2012). Phyllis Wallace was a colleague of Clark's at the Metropolitan Applied Research Center (see below).

72. Clark, *Dark Ghetto,* 204–205, 222, xxxii. For a persuasive argument that Clark anticipated the "interest-convergence" principle proposed by Derrick Bell and other critical race theorists, see Freeman, "Kenneth B. Clark and the Problem of Power," 429–431.

73. Murray, *Omni-Americans,* 41; Clark, *Dark Ghetto,* 14–15. For the argument that damage theorists viewed the black oppressed as "too afflicted to stand up for their own rights," see Scott, *Contempt and Pity,* 139.

74. Cross, *Shades of Black,* 3–38; John P. Jackson Jr., *Social Scientists for Social Justice: Making the Case against Segregation* (New York: New York University Press, 2001), 152, 154–155, 221; Scott, *Contempt and Pity,* 123–124.

75. Kenneth B. Clark, "Mid-Century White House Conference on Children and Youth: Paper, 'The Effects of Prejudice and Discrimination on Personality Development'" (1950), in *Toward Humanity and Justice: The Writings of Kenneth B. Clark, Scholar of the 1954* Brown v. Board of Education *Decision,* ed. Woody Klein (Westport, CT: Praeger, 2004), 206–210; "Text of the Supreme Court Opinions, May 17, 1954," reprinted in Kenneth B. Clark, *Prejudice and Your Child,* 2nd ed. (Boston: Beacon Press, 1963), 158–165. For Clark's account of these events, see ibid., 207–235, esp. 210. See also Keppel, *Work of Democracy,* 97–131.

76. Ruth E. Horowitz, "Racial Aspects of Self-Identification in Nursery School Children," *Journal of Psychology* 7 (1939): 91–99; Kenneth B. Clark and Mamie P. Clark, "Racial Identification and Preference in Negro Children" (1947), in *Black Scholars on the Line: Race, Social Science, and American Thought in the Twentieth Century,* ed. Jonathan Scott Holloway and Ben Keppel (Notre Dame, IN: Notre Dame University Press, 2007), 417, 424; Jackson, *Social Scientists for Social Justice,* 32, 34.

77. "The Effects of Segregation and the Consequences of Desegregation: A Social Science Statement," reprinted in Clark, *Prejudice and Your Child,* 2nd ed., 166–184; Scott, *Contempt and Pity,* 123–124; Jackson, *Social Scientists for Social Justice,* 153–154; Park quoted in Scott, *Contempt and Pity,* 22. For "marginal man" theory, see also Wirth, *Ghetto.* As Scott notes, the University of Chicago psychologist Allison Davis argued in 1943 that segregated schools were havens from exposure to racism. See Scott, *Contempt and Pity,* 124.

78. Kenneth B. Clark to William Delano, Feb. 19, 1952, quoted in Jackson, *Social Scientists for Social Justice,* 153.

79. Clark, *Prejudice and Your Child,* 45–46; Clark to Delano, quoted in Jackson, 153–154.

80. Cross, *Shades of Black,* 28; Scott, *Contempt and Pity,* 123–124.

81. O'Connor, *Poverty Knowledge,* 101, 103–104. As examples of this functionalist approach, O'Connor cites Kingsley Davis and Wilbert E. Moore, "Some Principles of Social Stratification," *American Sociological Review* 10 (1945): 242–249; R. J. Havinghurst et al., *Growing Up in River City* (New York: John Wiley and Sons, 1962).

82. Kenneth B. Clark, "Racial Prejudice in Relation to the Etiology of Mental Illness," paper delivered at the Symposium on the Etiology of Neuroses, Society of Medical Psychoanalysts, Mar. 17, 1962, typescript, 6, box 173, folder 6, Clark Papers.

83. Frederick S. Perls, Ralph F. Hefferline, and Paul Goodman, *Gestalt Therapy: Excitement and Growth in the Human Personality* (New York: Julian Press, 1951); Ellen Herman, *The Romance of Psychology: Political Culture in the Age of Experts* (Berkeley: University of California Press, 1995), 273–274; Abraham H. Maslow, *Toward a Psychology of Being* (Princeton, NJ: Van Nostrand, 1962), 7. See also J. F. T. Bugental, "Humanistic Psychology: A New Break-Through," *American Psychologist* 18 (1963): 563–567.

84. Kenneth B. Clark, "Speech at Annual Meeting, Boston, Nov. 18–23 [1968]," transcript dated Jan. 1969, 3–4, box 161, folder 4, Clark Papers. On

Maslow's often derisive attitudes toward 1960s protest movements, see Herman, *Romance of Psychology*, 273; Edward Hoffman, *The Right to Be Human: A Biography of Abraham Maslow* (Wellingborough, UK: Crucible, 1989), 293–294.

85. Clark, *Dark Ghetto*, 88; Clark, *Prejudice and Your Child*, 45–46.

86. Keppel, *Work of Democracy*, 154; Clark, *Dark Ghetto*, 15–16 (emphasis added).

87. Kenneth B. Clark and James Barker, "The Zoot Effect in Personality: A Race Riot Participant," *Journal of Abnormal and Social Psychology* 40 (1945): 147, 143; "*New York Herald Tribune* Luncheon," n.d. [June 1964], transcript, 28, box 190, folder 5, Clark Papers; "Six Thoughtful Men on the Summer Ahead," *New York Herald Tribune*, June 14, 1964, in *The Black Power Movement, Part I: Amiri Baraka from Black Arts to Black Radicalism*, ed. Komozi Woodard (microfilm, 9 reels) (Bethesda, MD: University Publications of America, 2000), reel 1, frames 10–13. Clark's connection of rioting to ego resilience had been somewhat anticipated by Ann Petry in her story "In Darkness and Confusion" (1947), which portrayed the 1943 Harlem riot as a moment of existential and social awakening. See George R. Adams, "Riot as Ritual: Ann Petry's 'In Darkness and Confusion,'" *African American Review* 6 (1972): 54–57, 60. I am grateful to an anonymous reader for this observation.

88. Clark, *Dark Ghetto*, 14–16, 28; Kenneth B. Clark, "The Wonder Is That There Have Been So Few Riots," *New York Times Magazine*, Sept. 5, 1965, 10.

89. Clark, *Dark Ghetto*, 16–19.

90. Herman, *Romance of Psychology*, 222, 225–229, 223, 231; Kenneth B. Clark, testimony before the National Advisory Commission on Civil Disorders, Sept. 13, 1967, transcript, 1231, enclosed in Alvin A. Spivak to Kenneth B. Clark, Sept. 26, 1967, box 201, folder 4, Clark Papers; Elliot Liebow, *Tally's Corner: A Study of Negro Streetcorner Men* (Boston: Little, Brown, 1967); Clark, *Dark Ghetto*, 88.

91. Clark, *Dark Ghetto*, 11; Kenneth B. Clark, "Some Aspects of Urban Tensions," address delivered to Urban Affairs Conference, Long Island University, Brooklyn Center, New York, n.d. [1964], transcript, 8, box 169, folder 4, Clark Papers; HARYOU, *Youth in the Ghetto*, 4–5, 21.

92. HARYOU, *Youth in the Ghetto*, 568, 387. In *Dark Ghetto*, Clark asserted that the "methods" of mainstream civil rights organizations had not been "as relevant or appropriate" in the urban North as in the South. See Clark, *Dark Ghetto*, 184. On Jesse Gray and the Harlem rent strikes, see Sugrue, *Sweet Land of Liberty*, 402–407. On the wider history of civil rights activism in New York City from the 1940s to the early 1960s, see Martha Biondi, *To Stand and Fight: The Struggle for Civil Rights in Postwar New York City* (Cambridge, MA: Harvard University Press, 2003).

93. HARYOU, *Youth in the Ghetto*, 407–415, 415–421, 443–448, 465–474, 479–490, 449–464, 388, 75; Keppel, *Work of Democracy*, 149; Kenneth B. Clark, "News from Harlem Youth Opportunities Unlimited, Inc. (HARYOU)," Oct. 8, 1963, press release, 5, box 50, folder 8, Clark Papers. Keppel argues that while HARYOU's "goal" was a conventional one, the rhetoric and analysis of power

and colonialism in *Youth in the Ghetto* constitute the novel aspects of Clark's vision. See Keppel, *Work of Democracy,* 149–150.

94. O'Connor, *Poverty Knowledge,* 124. On the origins of "community action," see O'Connor, 124–136; Peter Marris and Martin Rein, *Dilemmas of Social Reform: Poverty and Community Action in the United States* (London: Routledge and Kegan Paul, 1967), 7–32; Michael B. Katz, *The Undeserving Poor: From the War on Poverty to the War on Welfare* (New York: Pantheon Books, 1989), 95–101.

95. HARYOU, *Youth in the Ghetto,* 390–391, 36, 389, 402, 365.

96. Ibid., 397, 368; Kenneth B. Clark, "HARYOU: An Experiment," *Freedomways* 3 (1963): 441–442.

97. HARYOU, *Youth in the Ghetto,* 368–369, 88, 567–568, 581. In a study of early community action programs, Noel Cazenave emphasizes the technocratic nature of the HARYOU proposal and describes Clark's commitment to "social action" on the part of residents as largely a matter of "rhetoric." However, Cazenave substantially understates the importance that *Youth in the Ghetto* attaches to the neighborhood boards and HYU. He thus fails to acknowledge that the technocratic planning phase produced a design for the creation of an organizational infrastructure that was intended precisely to facilitate grassroots democratic participation. Cazenave views HARYOU through the lens of "elite competition" theory, which identifies social scientists and other professionals as "knowledge elites or experts, who monopolize power in the pursuit of their own professional interests." Accordingly, he sees Clark's "rhetoric" of grassroots social action and empowerment of the Harlem community primarily as a cover for an alternative motive, the empowerment of elite social science professionals. Yet Cazenave devotes scant attention to Clark's ideas as a psychologist. He therefore fails to recognize the therapeutics of rebellion that was evident in Clark's thought even in the early 1950s, and which ensured that the HARYOU proposal demanded the creation of institutions through which neighborhood residents could "challenge the powers that be." See Noel A. Cazenave, *Impossible Democracy: The Unlikely Success of the War on Poverty Community Action Programs* (Albany: State University of New York Press, 2007), 85–104 and 11–12, quotations at 98, 11.

98. Clark, "HARYOU: An Experiment," 440, 443. On the rise of "community psychiatry," see Herman, *Romance of American Psychology,* 223–224, 249–264. See also Leigh M. Roberts, Seymour L. Halleck, and Martin B. Loeb, eds., *Community Psychiatry* (Madison: University of Wisconsin Press, 1966).

99. Students for a Democratic Society, "The Port Huron Statement" (1962), reprinted as appendix to James Miller, *Democracy in the Streets: From Port Huron to the Siege of Chicago* (New York: Simon & Schuster, 1988), 336, 332–333; HARYOU, *Youth in the Ghetto,* 368. On the therapeutic ethos in postwar American politics, see Philip Rieff, *The Triumph of the Therapeutic: Uses of Faith after Freud* (1966; repr., Wilmington, DE: ISI Books, 2006); Alan Brinkley, *Liberalism and Its Discontents* (Cambridge, MA: Harvard University Press, 1998), 222–236; Halliwell, *Therapeutic Revolutions.*

100. Richard H. King, *Civil Rights and the Idea of Freedom* (New York: Oxford University Press, 1992), 6–7, 146, 150. Another revealing analysis of the political

ideals of the civil rights movement may be found in Marc Stears, *Demanding Democracy: American Radicals in Search of a New Politics* (Princeton, NJ: Princeton University Press, 2010), 145–164.

101. Paul Goodman, *Growing Up Absurd: Problems of Youth in the Organized System* (New York: Random House, 1960); Charles E. Silberman, *Crisis in Black and White* (1964; repr., London, Jonathan Cape, 1965), 323–325, 334–335. On Goodman's ideas and their reception, see Richard King, *The Party of Eros: Radical Social Thought and the Realm of Freedom* (Chapel Hill: University of North Carolina Press, 1972), 78–115, esp. 106, 113; King, *Civil Rights and the Idea of Freedom,* 150. On Alinsky's influence on 1960s radicalism, see Doug Rossinow, *Visions of Progress: The Left-Liberal Tradition in America* (Philadelphia: University of Pennsylvania Press, 2008), 207. See also John Hall Fish, *Black Power/White Control: The Struggle of The Woodlawn Organization in Chicago* (Princeton, NJ: Princeton University Press, 1973).

102. Clark, *Dark Ghetto,* 215–216; Kenneth B. Clark, "A Negro Looks at 'Black Power,'" *New York Post,* Nov. 11, 1967, 30; Clark Reminiscences, Feb. 4, 1976, transcript, 35.

103. Clark, "Negro Looks at 'Black Power,'" 30; Clark, *Prejudice and Your Child,* esp. 17–81. On the Nation of Islam's view of whites as "devils," see Edward E. Curtis, *Black Muslim Religion in the Nation of Islam, 1960–1975* (Chapel Hill: University of North Carolina Press, 2006), 40, 133. On the antiwhite pronouncements of LeRoi Jones/Amiri Baraka, see Chapter 2 of this book.

104. Clark, "Speech at Annual Meeting," 5; Clark, *Prejudice and Your Child,* 134, 87; Clark, *Dark Ghetto,* 117.

105. Clark, *Dark Ghetto,* 107. Clark's decision to support Baraka's voter registration and education campaign with up to $10,000 from the budget of the Metropolitan Applied Research Center, of which Clark was director, is recorded in Sol Markoff, "Memorandum: Notes re, Conference with Committee for a Unified Newark," May 12, 1969, box 367, folder 6, Clark Papers. On the Black Panther Party's bid to enhance community power in Oakland, see Robert Self, "'To Plan Our Liberation': Black Power and the Politics of Place in Oakland, California, 1965–1977," *Journal of Urban History* 26 (2000): 759–792. On the Committee for Unified Newark, see Chapter 2 of this book.

106. Kenneth B. Clark, "The Civil Rights Movement: Momentum and Organization," in *The Negro American,* ed. Kenneth B. Clark and Talcott Parsons (1966; repr., Boston: Beacon Press, 1967), 612, 603; Kenneth B. Clark, "Introduction: The Dilemma of Power," in ibid., xvii–xviii.

107. Kwame Ture (Stokely Carmichael) and Charles V. Hamilton, *Black Power: The Politics of Liberation in America* (1967; repr., New York: Vintage, 1992), 2, 18; Clark, *Dark Ghetto,* 11, 27–28. On the interwar "black belt thesis" as an articulation of internal colonialism and on Malcolm X's view of African Americans as a colonized people, see Stephen Howe, *Afrocentrism: Mythical Pasts and Imagined Homes* (London: Verso, 1998), 89, 93. For Harold Cruse's notions of internal colonialism, see Harold Cruse, "Revolutionary Nationalism and the Afro-American" (1962), in *Rebellion or Revolution?* (New York: William Morrow,

1968), 74–96. For a critique of the black power movement's ideas of internal co-lonialism, see King, *Civil Rights and the Idea of Freedom,* 153–155.

108. Scott, *Contempt and Pity,* 177; Ture (Carmichael) and Hamilton, *Black Power,* 29, quoting Clark, *Dark Ghetto,* 63–64; "Anti-Depression Program of the Republic of New Africa: To End Poverty, Dependence, Cultural Malnutrition, and Crime among Black People in the United States and Promote Inter-Racial Peace: Presented for Enactment to Both Houses of the United States Congress," Mar. 1972, 9, 14–16, 20–21, quotation at 15, box 1, Republic of New Africa (America) Records, Schomburg Center for Research in Black Culture, New York Public Library. On the Republic of New Africa, see William L. Van Deburg, *New Day in Babylon: The Black Power Movement and American Culture, 1965–1975* (Chicago: University of Chicago Press, 1992), 145. While Ben Keppel has noted Carmichael and Hamilton's endorsement of Clark's characterization of ghettos as colonies and Damon Freeman has pointed out Clark's willingness to postpone the pursuit of integration, the literature on Clark otherwise overlooks the points of convergence between his views and those of black power theorists, especially regarding psychological and social pathologies. See Keppel, *Work of Democracy,* 169–170; Freeman, "Kenneth B. Clark and the Problem of Power," 431–432.

109. Scott, *Contempt and Pity,* 172; Frantz Fanon, *The Wretched of the Earth,* trans. Constance Farrington (1963; repr., New York: Grove Press, 1966), 73; Clark, "HARYOU: An Experiment," 443. For studies that remark on the high regard for Fanon within the black power movement, see, for example, Simon Wendt, "The Roots of Black Power? Armed Resistance and the Radicalization of the Civil Rights Movement," in *The Black Power Movement: Rethinking the Civil Rights–Black Power Era,* ed. Peniel E. Joseph (New York: Routledge, 2006), 159–160; Peniel E. Joseph, *Waiting 'til the Midnight Hour: A Narrative History of Black Power in America* (New York: Henry Holt, 2006), 209. On Fanon's Adlerian orientation and his therapeutics of action and violence, see King, *Civil Rights and the Idea of Freedom,* 172–200. The exception to historians' failure to detect pathologism within the black power movement is King, *Race, Culture, and the Intellectuals,* 159. Clark did not, to the best of this author's knowledge, comment directly on Fanon's writings or acknowledge similarities between their ideas. In an interview in 1981 in which Clark was asked to make "free associations" with a series of names, he responded to Fanon's name as follows: "Don't know at all. The young people are certainly very impressed with him and his particular philosophy of rebellion or revolution." See "Dr. Kenneth B. Clark: Interpreter of Mankind," transcript, 42.

110. For Clark's accounts of HARYOU's influence on the War on Poverty, see Hentoff, "Profiles," 58–59; Clark Reminiscences, May 10, 1976, transcript, 173. For the text of the "community action" clauses of the Economic Opportunity Act, see Daniel P. Moynihan, *Maximum Feasible Misunderstanding: Community Action and the War on Poverty* (New York: Free Press, 1969), 88. On the planning of the federal antipoverty policies, see Lemann, *Promised Land,* 128; Katz, *Undeserving Poor,* 95–101. David Hackett's close involvement in the HARYOU planning phase is noted in HARYOU, *Youth in the Ghetto,* 24–25.

111. James T. Patterson, *America's Struggle against Poverty in the Twentieth Century* (Cambridge, MA: Harvard University Press, 2000), 141; Daniel Immerwahr, "Quests for Community: The United States, Community Development, and the World" (unpublished PhD dissertation, University of California, Berkeley, 2011), 117–145; Thomas F. Jackson, "The State, the Movement, and the Urban Poor: The War on Poverty and Political Mobilization in the 1960s," in *The "Underclass" Debate: Views from History,* ed. Michael B. Katz (Princeton, NJ: Princeton University Press, 1993), 415.

112. Clark Reminiscences, Mar. 19 and July 7, 1976, transcript, 124, 231; Silberman, *Crisis in Black and White,* 350.

113. Clark, "HARYOU: An Experiment," 443; Clark Reminiscences, Apr. 7, 1976, transcript, 163.

114. Clark Reminiscences, Apr. 7, 1976, transcript, 162–163; Jackson, "State, the Movement, and the Urban Poor," 420–421. See also Patterson, *America's Struggle against Poverty in the Twentieth Century,* 142–143.

115. Keppel, *Work of Democracy,* 150; Cazenave, *Impossible Democracy,* 111; Clark Reminiscences, May 10, 1976, transcript, 168.

116. Charles V. Hamilton, *Adam Clayton Powell, Jr.: The Political Biography of an American Dilemma* (New York: Atheneum, 1991), 376; Freeman, "Kenneth B. Clark and the Problem of Power," 424; Keppel, *Work of Democracy,* 150–151; Allen J. Matusow, *The Unraveling of America: A History of Liberalism in the 1960s* (1984; repr., Athens: University of Georgia Press, 2009), 257–258; Woody Klein, "Powell Turns on Pressure, Seeks to Boss $110 Million Harlem Project," *New York World Telegram and Sun,* June 5, 1964, 1; "New Battle of Harlem," *New York Post,* June 10, 1964, 46; Woody Klein, "People vs. Politicians: Defeat in Harlem," *Nation,* July 27, 1964, 28; Markowitz and Rosner, *Children, Race, and Power,* 198; Kenneth B. Clark to Arthur Logan, July 28, 1964, box 24, folder 8, Clark Papers; R. W. Apple Jr., "Clark Quits Post on HARYOU Board," *New York Times,* July 30, 1964, 1. For an account of the complex power struggles that determined Powell's defeat of Clark, which involved the White House, the President's Committee on Juvenile Delinquency, and Mayor Richard Wagner's New York administration, see Cazenave, *Impossible Democracy,* 109–111.

117. Clark, *Dark Ghetto,* 162–168, quotations at 163, 168. On Powell's misuse of public funds, see Hamilton, *Adam Clayton Powell,* 8–9. Hamilton's biography gives a more balanced view than *Dark Ghetto* of Powell's political achievements and shortcomings.

118. L. L. L. Golden, "Public Relations," *Saturday Review,* Jan. 13, 1968, 116. On MARC, see Freeman, "Kenneth B. Clark and the Problem of Power," 437.

119. Kenneth B. Clark, "*Dark Ghetto* Revisited," paper delivered at MARC colloquium, New York, Dec. 5, 1967, typescript, 2, 9–11, box 161, folder 1, Clark Papers.

120. Ibid., 9; Thomas W. Ottenad, "Armed Suppression rather than Solution to Riots Is Forecast by Negro Psychologist," *St. Louis Post-Dispatch,* July 30, 1967, box 221, folder 2, Clark Papers. On Ellison and Elkins, see King, *Race, Culture, and the Intellectuals,* 298–299. For a detailed treatment of comparisons between

African American suffering and the Holocaust, see Eric J. Sundquist, *Strangers in the Land: Blacks, Jews, Post-Holocaust America* (Cambridge, MA: Belknap Press of Harvard University Press, 2005), 170–238.

121. Clark, testimony before the National Advisory Commission on Civil Disorders, transcript, 1233, 1238, 1230, 1240; Clark, *Dark Ghetto*, 19, 11.

122. Drew Pearson, "Pessimism over Riots: Kenneth Clark's Testimony Had Biggest Impact on Commission on Disorders," *Washington Post*, Mar. 10, 1968, B7; *Report of the National Advisory Commission on Civil Disorders* (New York: Bantam Books, 1968), 2; Lemann, *Promised Land*, 191; Henry W. Pierce, "Psychologist Predicts Doom for Riot Panel's Proposals," *Pittsburgh Post-Gazette*, Apr. 4, 1968, box 221, folder 3, Clark Papers.

123. David Bird, "Dr. Clark Says Racial Violence Hints Terminal Decay of U.S.," *New York Times*, Mar. 4, 1968, 25; Kenneth B. Clark and Jeanette Hopkins, *A Relevant War against Poverty: A Study of Community Action Programs and Observable Social Change* (1968; repr., New York: Harper & Row, 1969), vi, 61, 225, 220–221; Jackson, "State, the Movement, and the Urban Poor"; Fred Powledge, "The Troubles of Haryou," *New York Times*, Oct. 13, 1965, 36.

124. Clark and Hopkins, *Relevant War against Poverty*, x, v–vi, 247–248, 128.

125. Ibid., x; Geoffrey Hodgson, *The Gentleman from New York: Daniel Patrick Moynihan: A Biography* (Boston: Houghton Mifflin, 2000), 158; Kenneth B. Clark to Daniel P. Moynihan, Nov. 20, 1974, box 199, folder 4, Clark Papers; Clark, *Pathos of Power*, 126–130. For a more favorable reading of the intentions behind Moynihan's memorandum, see Lemann, *Promised Land*, 209.

126. Clark Reminiscences, July 20 and Aug. 3, 1976, transcript, 304–305, 341.

127. Ibid., July 20, 1976, transcript, 306; "Board of Directors Hears Report: Clark Urges Social Responsibility," *APA Monitor*, Jan. 1971, 1. On the APA's 1969 convention, see Herman, *Romance of Psychology*, 289.

128. Clark Reminiscences, Aug. 3, 1976, transcript, 341 (emphasis added); "John Dewey Discussion," transcript, 41–42, box 192, folder 4, Clark Papers (emphasis added); Clark, "Pathos of Power," 1047–1048.

129. Clark, "Pathos of Power," 1048–1051.

130. Ibid., 1051–1052 (emphasis added).

131. Ibid., 1052–1055.

132. Ibid., 1055–1056. Clark later cited as grounds for optimism research into behavior modification through stimulation of specific brain regions by the neurophysiologist José Delgado of Yale University. See Clark Reminiscences, Aug. 3, 1976, transcript, 351; José M. R. Delgado, *Physical Control of the Mind: Toward a Psychocivilized Society* (New York: Harper & Row, 1969). Responding to Clark's address, an article in *American Druggist* highlighted research by the psychiatrist Heinz Lehmann of McGill University "in the field of personality-altering chemicals." In 1967, Lehmann had predicted that a "peace pill" or "anti-aggression" drug could be available within twenty years. The same article noted the similarity between Clark's argument and that of Arthur Koestler's philosophical work *The Ghost in the Machine* (1967), which had also called for a pharmaceutical solution to the threat of nuclear destruction. See Dan Kushner, "Will 'Peace Drugs'

Save Us from the Bomb?" *American Druggist,* Oct. 4, 1971, 13, 75, box 223, folder 1, Clark Papers; Arthur Koestler, *The Ghost in the Machine* (1967; repr., London: Pan Books, 1975). For an overview of research into biochemical behavior modification dating from this period, including Delgado's, see Edward A. Sullivan, "Bio-Chemical Behavior Control: Toward 1984 and the Brave New World," *Current,* June 1972, 49–56.

133. Clark Reminiscences, Sept. 9, 1976, transcript, 372; Clark, "Pathos of Power," 1056–1057.

134. Boyce Rensberger, "Kenneth Clark Asks New Drugs to Curb Hostility of Leaders," *New York Times,* Sept. 5, 1971, box 22, folder 8, Clark Papers; "Turn 'Em to Turnips," New York *Daily News,* Sept. 8, 1971, box 22, folder 8, Clark Papers; Boyce Rensberger, "Clark Disputed on Peace Drugs," *New York Times,* Sept. 7, 1971, box 22, folder 8, Clark Papers; "Tot Character Set in Classes, Agnew Charges," *St. Paul (MN) Pioneer Press,* Nov. 18, 1971, box 223, folder 2, Clark Papers; "Agnew Raps 'Drivel' in New Education," *Milwaukee Journal,* Nov. 18, 1971, box 223, folder 2, Clark Papers; "Drugs for Leaders?" *New York Times,* Sept. 8, 1971, box 22, folder 8, Clark Papers; Lee R. Steiner, "Psychology at the Barricades," *New York Herald Tribune,* Sept. 26, 1971, box 22, folder 8, Clark Papers. For further examples from a thick file of overwhelmingly hostile press cuttings, see box 22, folder 8, Clark Papers. The three academics who joined Herbert Kelman to denounced Clark's proposals were the neurophysiologist Karl Pribham of Stanford University, the animal behavior expert Ethel Tobach of the American Museum of Natural History, and the psychiatrist and pharmacologist Conan Kornetsky of the Boston University School of Medicine. See Rensberger, "Clark Disputed on Peace Drugs."

135. Clark, "Pathos of Power," 1056–1057. During the 1930s, progressively inclined American theorists such as George Soule and Stuart Chase had placed their hopes in the prospects of an enlightened scientific technocracy and had similarly failed to explain how such an enlightened leadership could come into being, and come to power, within a society and political system that these theorists viewed as self-interested and corrupt. See Stears, *Demanding Democracy,* 79–83.

136. Clark Reminiscences, Aug. 3, 1976, transcript, 343; Marvin H. Gerwitz to "Sponsor," Feb. 4, 1960, box 21, folder 1, Clark Papers; Robert Dallek, *Nixon and Kissinger: Partners in Power* (New York: HarperCollins, 2007), 285–324; Matthew Kroenig, *Exporting the Bomb: Technological Transfer and the Spread of Nuclear Weapons* (Ithaca, NY: Cornell University Press, 2010), 158.

137. Clark Reminiscences, Aug. 3, 1976, transcript, 341 (emphasis added).

138. Clark, *Dark Ghetto,* 15; Clark, "Pathos of Power," 1048; "John Dewey Discussion," transcript, 41; Clark Reminiscences, Feb. 4, 1976, transcript, 56.

139. Clark, "Kurt Lewin Memorial Award Address," 16, 10; M. Brewster Smith, "Kurt Lewin Memorial Award Address, 1965: Introduction," *Journal of Social Issues* 21 (1965): 2; Bertrand Russell, *Power: A New Social Analysis* (New York: W. W. Norton, 1938), quoted in Clark, "Kurt Lewin Memorial Award Address," 4. Clark had written to Russell in 1963 about "the Negro's struggle for

democracy in America" and referred to a meeting between them that had taken place "last summer." He did not make reference to Russell's well-known advocacy of nuclear disarmament, but did remark: "Your courage and clarity are needed in a world that is still groping toward the minimal decency necessary for survival." See Kenneth B. Clark to Lord Bertrand Russell, Dec. 30, 1963, box 24, folder 1, Clark Papers; Bertrand Russell, *Common Sense and Nuclear Warfare* (London: Allen & Unwin, 1959).

140. Clark, "Pathos of Power," 1050–1052, 1054, 1056 (emphasis added); "Useful for All Mankind?" *Chicago Sun-Times,* Sept. 5, 1971, box 222, folder 8, Clark Papers.

141. Clark, *Dark Ghetto,* xxxii; Kenneth B. Clark, "Equality and Opportunity," *Playboy,* Jan. 1, 1969, 273–275 (emphasis added); Bird, "Dr. Clark Says Racial Violence Hints Terminal Decay of U.S.," 25.

142. Clark, "Wonder Is There Have Been So Few Riots," 10; Clark, "Pathos of Power," 1049–1050.

143. Clark, "Equality and Opportunity," 275; Clark, "Pathos of Power," 1054, 1056, 1049; Clark and Hopkins, *Relevant War against Poverty,* vi.

144. Kenneth B. Clark, "20 Years after 'Brown'—the Unresolved Dilemma," *New York Times,* May 17, 1974, 39; Kenneth B. Clark, "The Role of Race," *New York Times Magazine,* Oct. 5, 1980, 25–28; Kenneth B. Clark, "In Cities, Who Is the Real Mugger?" *New York Times,* Jan. 14, 1985, A19; Clark, "Racial Progress and Retreat," 18. On Clark's service on the New York State Board of Regents between 1966 and 1986, see Jeffrey A. Raffel, "Kenneth Bancroft Clark," *Historical Dictionary of School Segregation and Desegregation: The American Experience* (Westport, CT: Greenwood Press, 1998), 55.

145. Clark Reminiscences, Sept. 9, 1976, transcript, 384–385 (emphasis added).

2. Be Even Blacker

1. On the *Negro Digest* poll, see Werner Sollors, *Amiri Baraka/LeRoi Jones: The Quest for a "Populist Modernism"* (New York: Columbia University Press, 1978), 264 n.6. For Rampersad's remark, see LeRoi Jones/Amiri Baraka, *The LeRoi Jones/Amiri Baraka Reader,* ed. William J. Harris (New York: Thunder's Mouth Press, 1991), back cover. The remaining seven writers named by Rampersad are Phillis Wheatley, Frederick Douglass, Paul Laurence Dunbar, Langston Hughes, Zora Neale Hurston, Richard Wright, and Ralph Ellison. James Baldwin's omission is the most glaring. Other major treatments of Baraka's life and work are Komozi Woodard, *A Nation within a Nation: Amiri Baraka (LeRoi Jones) and Black Power Politics* (Chapel Hill: University of North Carolina Press, 1999); Jerry Gafio Watts, *Amiri Baraka: The Politics and Art of a Black Intellectual* (New York: New York University Press, 2001); Kimberly W. Benston, *Baraka: The Renegade and the Mask* (New Haven, CT: Yale University Press, 1976); Kimberly W. Benston, ed., *Imamu Amiri Baraka (LeRoi Jones): A Collection of Critical Essays* (Englewood Cliffs, NJ: Prentice-Hall, 1978); Lloyd W. Brown, *Amiri Baraka* (Boston: Twayne Publishers, 1980); Harry J. Elam Jr., *Taking It to the Streets: The Social Protest Theater of Luis Valdez and Amiri Baraka* (Detroit: University of Michigan Press, 2001); James

B. Gwynne, ed., *Amiri Baraka: The Kaleidoscopic Torch* (New York: Steppingstone Press, 1985); William J. Harris, *The Poetry and Poetics of Amiri Baraka: The Jazz Aesthetic* (Columbia: University of Missouri Press, 1985); Alex Houen, *Powers of Possibility: Experimental American Writing since the 1960s* (Oxford: Oxford University Press, 2012), 62–102; Theodore R. Hudson, *From LeRoi Jones to Amiri Baraka: The Literary Works* (Durham, NC: Duke University Press, 1973); Henry C. Lacey, *To Raise, Destroy, and Create: The Poetry, Drama, and Fiction of Imamu Amiri Baraka* (Troy, NY: Whitson Publishing, 1981).

2. Dorothy Ross, "Grand Narrative in American Historical Writing: From Romance to Uncertainty," *American Historical Review* 100 (1995): 652–653; LeRoi Jones, "HOME" (1965), in *Home: Social Essays* (1966; repr., Hopewell, NJ: Ecco Press, 1998), 9–10. Ross adheres closely to the characterization of "romance" offered by Northrop Frye in his *Anatomy of Criticism: Four Essays* (Princeton, NJ: Princeton University Press, 1957) and *The Secular Scripture: A Study of the Structure of Romance* (Cambridge, MA: Harvard University Press, 1976).

3. Clyde Taylor, "Baraka as Poet," in Benston, *Imamu Amiri Baraka (LeRoi Jones)*, 114; Harold Cruse, *The Crisis of the Negro Intellectual: From Its Origins to the Present* (1967; repr., London, W. H. Allen, 1969).

4. Amiri Baraka, *The Autobiography of LeRoi Jones*, rev. ed. (Chicago: Lawrence Hill Books, 1997), 457; Austin Clarke, "An Interview with LeRoi Jones" (1968), in *Conversations with Amiri Baraka*, ed. Charlie Reilly (Jackson: University Press of Mississippi, 1994), 39. Baraka's autobiography was first published in 1984 by Freundlich Books, in an abbreviated form. The 1997 Lawrence Hill Books edition, to which all future citations will refer, includes "all the excised material." See Baraka, *Autobiography*, ix.

5. Michele Wallace, *Black Macho and the Myth of the Superwoman* (1978; repr., New York: Verso, 1999), 62; bell hooks, *Ain't I a Woman: Black Women and Feminism* (1981; repr., London: Pluto Press, 1982), 106.

6. Todd Gitlin, *The Sixties: Years of Hope, Days of Rage*, rev. ed. (New York: Bantam Books, 1993), 350; Paula Giddings, *When and Where I Enter: The Impact of Black Women on Race and Sex in America* (New York: William Morrow, 1984), 315; Kevin K. Gaines, *Uplifting the Race: Black Leadership, Politics, and Culture in the Twentieth Century* (Chapel Hill: University of North Carolina Press, 1996), quotation at xiv.

7. Gaines, *Uplifting the Race*, 255, 126. Evelyn Brooks Higginbotham has similarly argued that uplift's "preoccupation with respectability" entailed "an attack on the values and lifestyle of those blacks who transgressed white middle-class propriety," especially "poor blacks." See Evelyn Brooks Higginbotham, *Righteous Discontent: The Women's Movement in the Black Baptist Church, 1880–1920* (Cambridge, MA: Harvard University Press, 1993), 15.

8. LeRoi Jones, "BLACK DADA NIHILISMUS," in *The Dead Lecturer* (New York: Grove Press, 1964), 63; Eldridge Cleaver, *Soul on Ice* (1968; repr., London: 1969), 25.

9. Cleaver, *Soul on Ice*, 24–25; "'He Was a Symbol': Eldridge Cleaver Dies at 62," CNN, May 1, 1998, www.edition.cnn.com/US/9805/01/cleaver.late.obit/;

Malcolm X with the assistance of Alex Haley, *The Autobiography of Malcolm X* (New York: Grove Press, 1965); George Jackson, *Soledad Brother: The Prison Letters of George Jackson* (New York: Coward-McCann, 1970).

10. Garvey quoted in William L. Van Deburg, introduction to *Modern Black Nationalism: From Marcus Garvey to Louis Farrakhan,* ed. William L. Van Deburg (New York: New York University Press, 1997), 16.

11. Thomas L. Blair, *Retreat to the Ghetto* (London: Wildwood House, 1977); Ellen Herman, *The Romance of American Psychology: Political Culture in the Age of Experts* (Berkeley: University of California Press, 1995); Philip Rieff, *The Triumph of the Therapeutic: Uses of Faith after Freud* (1966; repr., Wilmington, DE: ISI Books, 2006). On the history of American efforts to combat urban poverty through moral reform, see Joel Schwartz, *Fighting Poverty with Virtue: Moral Reform and America's Urban Poor, 1825–2000* (Bloomington: Indiana University Press, 2000).

12. LeRoi Jones, "Speech at San Francisco State College," n.d. [1967], transcript, 6, box 8, "Speech at San Francisco State College" folder, Amiri Baraka Papers, Moorland-Spingarn Research Center, Howard University, Washington, DC (hereafter cited as Baraka Papers).

13. Langston Hughes, *Black Magic: A Pictorial History of the Negro in American Entertainment* (1967; repr., Englewood Cliffs, NJ: Prentice-Hall, 1971), quoted in Sollors, *Amiri Baraka/LeRoi Jones,* 281 n.10; Amiri Baraka interviewed by Komozi Woodard, Jan. 4, 1986, transcript, in *The Black Power Movement, Part I: Amiri Baraka from Black Arts to Black Radicalism,* ed. Komozi Woodard (microfilm, 9 reels) (Bethesda, MD: University Publications of America, 2000), reel 8, frames 585–586; LeRoi Jones, *Dutchman,* in *"Dutchman" and "The Slave": Two Plays by LeRoi Jones* (New York: Morrow Quill Paperbacks, 1964), 1–38.

14. Burroughs quoted in James Campbell, *This Is the Beat Generation: New York—San Francisco—Paris* (London: Secker & Warburg, 1999), 199; Baraka, *Autobiography,* 53, 1–7, 18–20, 63.

15. On Jones's period at Howard University, see Judy Stone, "If It's Anger . . . Maybe That's Good: An Interview with LeRoi Jones" (1964), in Reilly, *Conversations with Amiri Baraka,* 9; LeRoi Jones, "Philistinism and the Negro Writer," in *Anger, and Beyond: The Negro Writer in the United States,* ed. Herbert Hill (New York: Harper & Row, 1966), 51–52; Baraka, *Autobiography,* 95–135, quotation at 128. On his time in the air force, see Baraka, *Autobiography,* 137–178. A few years after his discharge, Jones dramatized his air force career in an unpublished three-act play. See LeRoi Jones, "A Recent Killing," n.d., typescript, box 2, Amiri Baraka Collection of Playscripts, Schomburg Center for Research in Black Culture, New York.

16. LeRoi Jones, "How You Sound??" (1959), in *The New American Poetry, 1945–1960,* ed. Donald M. Allen (New York: Grove Press, 1960), reprinted in Jones/Baraka, *LeRoi Jones/Amiri Baraka Reader,* 16–17; Baraka, *Autobiography,* 181–182, 191, 202–203, 215; Hettie Jones, *How I Became Hettie Jones* (New York: Grove Press, 1990), 22, 30, 61–63; James Baldwin, *Another Country* (1962; repr., London: Penguin, 2001). On black participation in Manhattan's downtown artistic

avant-garde, see Sally Banes, *Greenwich Village 1963: Avant-Garde Performance and the Effervescent Body* (Durham, NC: Duke University Press, 1993), 145–158.

17. David Ossman, "LeRoi Jones: An Interview on *Yugen*" (1960), in Reilly, *Conversations with Amiri Baraka,* 3–7; Baraka, *Autobiography,* 220; Hettie Jones, *How I Became Hettie Jones,* 46, 74; LeRoi Jones, "Everybody Believe in God Raise Your Hand," n.d., typescript, box 1, folder 1, Amiri Baraka Collection of Unpublished Poetry, Schomburg Center for Research in Black Culture, New York; LeRoi Jones, "Hymn for Lanie Poo," in *Preface to a Twenty Volume Suicide Note. . . .* (New York: Totem/Corinth, 1964), 10.

18. LeRoi Jones, "Cuba Libre," *Evergreen Review,* Nov.–Dec. 1960, reprinted in Jones, *Home,* 11–62, quotations at 20, 47, 44. Gilbert Sorrentino is identified as the source of the offending remark in Baraka, *Autobiography,* 236. On the Longview Award, see Hettie Jones, *How I Became Hettie Jones,* 113. For a critique of the Beats as "nonpolitical rebels," see Hazel E. Barnes, *An Existentialist Ethics* (1967; repr., Chicago: University of Chicago Press, 1978), 150–210, esp. 156.

19. Jones, "Cuba Libre," 61; LeRoi Jones, "An Organization of Young Men," leaflet, Apr. 18, 1961, in Woodard, *Black Power Movement, Part I,* reel 1, frame 6; Baraka, *Autobiography,* 248–249. On Jones's participation in the protests at the United Nations Headquarters over Lumumba's assassination, see Peniel E. Joseph, *Waiting 'til the Midnight Hour: A Narrative History of Black Power in America* (New York: Henry Holt, 2006), 38–44.

20. LeRoi Jones, "Correspondence: The Beat Generation," *Partisan Review* 25 (Summer 1958): 472–473; Norman Podhoretz, "The Know-Nothing Bohemians," *Partisan Review* 25 (Spring 1958): 305–318, quotation at 311–313; Hettie Jones, *How I Became Hettie Jones,* 28; E. Franklin Frazier, *Black Bourgeoisie: The Rise of a New Middle Class* (New York: Free Press, 1957), 24–26. During the early 1960s, Jones also addressed a poem to Frazier concerning his Newark childhood. See LeRoi Jones, "Letter to E. Franklin Frazier," in *Black Magic: Sabotage, Target Study, Black Art; Collected Poetry, 1961–1967* (Indianapolis: Bobbs-Merrill, 1969), 9.

21. LeRoi Jones, "City of Harlem" (1962), in *Home,* 87–88, 93.

22. LeRoi Jones, "Soul Food" (1962), in *Home,* 102; LeRoi Jones, "Cold, Hurt, and Sorrow (Streets of Despair)" (1962), in *Home,* 94–96; James Baldwin, "The Harlem Ghetto" (1948), in *Collected Essays,* ed. Toni Morrison (New York: Library of America, 1998), 42–53; Ralph Ellison, "Harlem Is Nowhere" (1948), in *The Collected Essays of Ralph Ellison,* ed. John F. Callahan (New York: Modern Library, 1995), 320–327; Kenneth B. Clark, *Dark Ghetto: Dilemmas of Social Power* (New York: Harper & Row, 1965), 195; Stone, "If It's Anger," 10; LeRoi Jones, "Street Protest" (1962), in *Home,* 98–99.

23. LeRoi Jones, "Tokenism: 300 Years for Five Cents" (1962), in *Home,* 73, 79; LeRoi Jones, " 'Black' Is a Country" (1962), in *Home,* 83, 85. "Tokenism" was originally published in *Kultur,* a Beat journal of which Jones was an editor.

24. LeRoi Jones (Amiri Baraka), *Blues People: Negro Music in White America* (1963; repr., New York: Perennial, 2002), 130–131, 236; Ralph Ellison, "Blues People" (1964), in *Collected Essays,* 283–284; Jack Kerouac, *On the Road* (1957; repr., London: Penguin Books, 1972). For Hughes's and Hentoff's endorsements,

see Jones (Baraka), *Blues People,* back cover. *Blues People* was originally published by William Morrow.

25. LeRoi Jones/Amiri Baraka, "The Screamers" (1963), in *The Fiction of LeRoi Jones/Amiri Baraka,* ed. Greg Tate (Chicago: Lawrence Hill Books, 2000), 181–186, quotations at 184–186; Kerouac quoted in Jones (Baraka), *Blues People,* 234. Jones had cited Olson as an influence in 1959. See Jones, "How You Sound??" 16–17; Charles Olson, "Projective Verse" (1950), in Charles Olson, *Human Universe and Other Essays,* ed. Donald Allen (New York: Grove Press, 1967), 51–61.

26. LeRoi Jones, "Betancourt," in *Preface to a Twenty Volume Suicide Note. . . . ,* 38. On Jones's encounter with the young revolutionary Rubi Betancourt, see Jones, "Cuba Libre," 42. For further analysis of the poem's imagery, see Sollors, *Amiri Baraka/LeRoi Jones,* 69.

27. LeRoi Jones/Amiri Baraka, "The System of Dante's Hell" (1965), in *Fiction of LeRoi Jones/Amiri Baraka,* 17, 101, 106, 114–115, 120–123; Baraka, *Autobiography,* 170. The prose poem was originally published by Grove Press as a freestanding work.

28. LeRoi Jones, *The Toilet,* in *"The Baptism" and "The Toilet"* (New York: Grove Press, 1967), 33–62; Baraka, *Autobiography,* 235; Hettie Jones, *How I Became Hettie Jones,* 86; Diane di Prima, *Recollections of My Life as a Woman: The New York Years* (New York: Viking, 2001), 220–221, 229–231, 267, 298; Peter Orlovsky to Allen Ginsberg, Sept. 23, 1963, quoted in Watts, *Amiri Baraka,* 530 n.16. The partial exception to the exclusively metaphorical reading of homosexuality in literary analyses of these works is in Werner Sollors's study, which quotes Jones's remark in 1964 that *The Toilet* came "out of my memory, so exact," though Sollors does not elaborate on this. See Sollors, *Amiri Baraka/LeRoi Jones,* 110. On Jones's sexuality, see also Ron Simmons, "Baraka's Dilemma: To Be or Not to Be?" in *Black Men on Race, Gender, and Sexuality: A Critical Reader,* ed. Devon Carbado (New York: New York University Press, 1999), 317–323.

29. Ross Posnock, *Color and Culture: Black Writers and the Making of the Modern Intellectual* (Cambridge, MA: Harvard University Press, 1998), 222.

30. LeRoi Jones, "SHORT SPEECH TO MY FRIENDS," in *Dead Lecturer,* 29; Jones, "BLACK DADA NIHILISMUS," 63; Hettie Jones, *How I Became Hettie Jones,* 226.

31. LeRoi Jones, "American Sexual Reference: Black Male" (1965), in *Home,* 228; Norman Mailer, "The White Negro" (1957), in *Protest,* ed. Gene Feldman and Max Gartenberg (London: Panther, 1960), 297; Frantz Fanon, *The Wretched of the Earth,* trans. Constance Farrington (1963; repr., New York: Grove Press, 1966), 73; Jones, "BLACK DADA NIHILISMUS," 61. On Fanon's ethics of violence, see Richard H. King, *Civil Rights and the Idea of Freedom* (New York: Oxford University Press, 1992), 176–197. On Jones's "rage" and his dependence on a "victim-status appeal" to white audiences, see also Watts, *Amiri Baraka,* 126–140, 467.

32. Jones quoted in "Six Thoughtful Men on the Summer Ahead," *New York Herald Tribune,* June 14, 1964, in Woodard, *Black Power Movement, Part I,* reel 1, frame 12; Sollors, *Amiri Baraka/LeRoi Jones,* 284 n.1; Jones, *Dutchman,* 3, 13, 31–35.

33. Wallace, *Black Macho,* 65–66; Jones, *Dutchman,* 35–37, 21, 31; Stanley Crouch, "On the Corner: The Sellout of Miles Davis" (1990), in *Considering Genius: Writings on Jazz* (New York: Basic Civitas Books, 2006), 240–257.

34. Watts, *Amiri Baraka,* 47; Mailer quoted in Sollors, *Amiri Baraka/LeRoi Jones,* 1; Howard Taubman, "The Theater: 'Dutchman'; Drama Opens on Triple Bill at Cherry Lane," *New York Times,* Mar. 25, 1964, 46; "Nation: The Root of the Negro Problem," *Time,* May 17, 1963, www.time.com/time/magazine/article /0,9171,830326,00.html; James Baldwin, *The Fire Next Time* (1963), repr. in Baldwin, *Collected Essays,* 287–347; Baraka, *Autobiography,* 276–277; *Playboy* quoted in Hudson, *From LeRoi Jones to Amiri Baraka,* 19.

35. "Six Thoughtful Men," frame 12; LeRoi Jones, "LeRoi Jones Talking" (1964), *Sunday Herald Tribune Magazine,* reprinted in *Home,* 183; Baraka, *Autobiography,* 283; Hettie Jones, *How I Became Hettie Jones,* 214.

36. LeRoi Jones, *The Slave* (1964), in *"Dutchman" and "The Slave,"* 52, 74, 59, 80, 86–88.

37. Ibid., 60, 73; Stewart Smith and Peter Thorn, "An Interview with LeRoi Jones" (1966), in Reilly, *Conversations with Amiri Baraka,* 14; LeRoi Jones, "The Revolutionary Theatre" (1964), in *Home,* 210–211, 213.

38. Hettie Jones, *How I Became Hettie Jones,* 219; Baraka, *Autobiography,* 287–288; Sollors, *Amiri Baraka/LeRoi Jones,* 289 n.29; Stanley Kauffmann, "LeRoi Jones and the Tradition of the Fake," *Dissent* 12 (1965): 207, 211; George Dennison, "The Demagogy of LeRoi Jones," *Commentary* 39 (Feb. 1965): 68. Baraka is probably referring to a cartoon by "Bloom/Leonard," "The Adventures of Superiorman," *Realist* no. 59 (1965): 16–17. The black "hero" of the cartoon is "Leroy Baldlose," who is married to a white woman and is transformed into "Superiorman" whenever he says the word "Muthafuckerrr!" See Sollors, *Amiri Baraka/LeRoi Jones,* 174.

39. Harry Gilroy, "Racial Debate Displaces Jazz Program," *New York Times,* Feb. 10, 1965, 47; Baraka, *Autobiography,* 293–294; Hettie Jones, *How I Became Hettie Jones,* 223, 227; Jones, *Home;* Jones, "HOME," 10. Theodore Hudson traces Jones's concrete plans to work in Harlem to late 1964. See Hudson, *From LeRoi Jones to Amiri Baraka,* 21.

40. On BARTS as an institutional model for the black arts movement, see James Edward Smethurst, *The Black Arts Movement: Literary Nationalism in the 1960s and 1970s* (Chapel Hill: University of North Carolina Press, 2005), 150.

41. LeRoi Jones, "The Legacy of Malcolm X, and the Coming of the Black Nation" (1965), in *Home,* 242, 244, 249; James Boggs with Grace Lee Boggs, "The City Is the Black Man's Land," *Monthly Review* (Apr. 1966), reprinted in James Boggs, *Racism and the Class Struggle: Further Pages from a Black Worker's Notebook* (New York: Monthly Review Press, 1970), 39–50. The mainstream press reported Jones's calls for "black sovereignty" in Harlem. See, for example, James Sullivan, "The Negro 'National Consciousness' of LeRoi Jones," *New York Herald Tribune,* n.d. [1965], in Woodard, *Black Power Movement, Part I,* reel 1, frame 4.

42. Larry Neal, "The Social Background of the Black Arts Movement," *Black Scholar* 18 (Jan./Feb. 1987): 11; LeRoi Jones/Amiri Baraka, "Words" (1965), in

Tales (New York: Grove Press, 1967), reprinted in *Fiction of LeRoi Jones/Amiri Baraka,* 193–194; David Llorens, "The *Fellah,* the Chosen Ones, the Guardian," in *Black Fire: An Anthology of Afro-American Writing,* ed. LeRoi Jones and Larry Neal (New York: William Morrow, 1968), 173–174; Haki Madhubuti quoted in C. W. E. Bigsby, *The Second Renaissance: Essays in Black Literature* (Westport, CT: Greenwood Press, 1980), 288; Lawrence P. Neal, "Development of LeRoi Jones [Part II]," *Liberator,* Feb. 1966, 19. "Baby shrew," in "Words," conceivably refers to Jones's lover during this period, Vashti (see below).

43. Bigsby, *Second Renaissance;* Carmichael quoted in Philip Brian Harper, *Are We Not Men? Masculine Anxiety and the Problem of African-American Identity* (New York: Oxford University Press, 1996), 51; H. Rap Brown, *Die Nigger Die!* (1969; repr., London: Allison and Busby, 1970), 91, 83; Larry Neal, "The Black Arts Movement" (1968), in *The Black Aesthetic,* ed. Addison Gayle Jr. (Garden City, NY: Doubleday, 1971), 272; Jones, "Legacy of Malcolm X," 248. Cruse, a close observer and participant in BARTS, believed that the organization had "an auspicious beginning" and represented a step in the direction of a viable black cultural nationalism, though he also offered a critique of Jones's leadership as a factor in the organization's demise. See Cruse, *Crisis of the Negro Intellectual,* 533–543, esp. 539. On debates within the black power movement over the revolutionary efficacy of the arts, see Brian Ward, "Jazz and Soul, Race and Class, Cultural Nationalists and Black Panthers: A Black Power Debate Revisited," in *Media, Culture, and the Modern African American Freedom Struggle,* ed. Brian Ward (Gainesville: University Press of Florida, 2001), 161–196.

44. Neal, "Black Arts Movement," 272, 286; Ed Bullins, "The So-Called Western Avant-Garde Drama," *Liberator,* Dec. 1967, 16–17; Harper, *Are We Not Men?* 51–52.

45. Jones, "Legacy of Malcolm X," 247–248; Neal, "Black Arts Movement," 278; Addison Gayle Jr., "Introduction" (1971), in Gayle, *Black Aesthetic,* xxiii.

46. W. E. B. Du Bois, "The Talented Tenth" (1903), in *Writings by W. E. B. Du Bois in Non-Periodical Literature Edited by Others,* ed. Herbert Aptheker (Millwood, NY: Kraus-Thomson, 1982), 29, 17; LeRoi Jones, "The Black Arts," leaflet, 1965, in Woodard, *Black Power Movement: Part I,* reel 1, frame 226. The phrase "Talented Tenth" was first used by Henry Morehouse of the white American Baptist Home Missionary Society. See Higginbotham, *Righteous Discontent,* 25. However, Du Bois's notion of a "Talented Tenth" was substantially an elaboration of the ideas of Alexander Crummell and the other founders of the American Negro Academy (1897). See Wilson Jeremiah Moses, *Creative Conflict in African American Thought: Frederick Douglass, Alexander Crummell, Booker T. Washington, W. E. B. Du Bois, and Marcus Garvey* (Cambridge: Cambridge University Press, 2004), 121–138. For a critique of the class and gender implications of the "Talented Tenth" concept, see Joy James, *Transcending the Talented Tenth: Black Leaders and American Intellectuals* (New York: Routledge, 1997).

47. Watts, *Amiri Baraka,* 164–165; Smethurst, *Black Arts Movement,* 58–59, 388 n.2. Smethurst acknowledges that his term "populist avant-garde" is influenced

by Sollors's interpretation of Jones's phrase of 1963, "a populist modernism." See Sollors, *Amiri Baraka/LeRoi Jones,* 77–78; LeRoi Jones, introduction to *The Moderns: An Anthology of New Writing in America,* ed. LeRoi Jones (1963; repr., London: MacGibbon & Kee, 1965), xvi. On uplift ideology's reliance on a politics of social differentiation, by which the "better class" emphasized their difference from the "mass" even as they proclaimed themselves to be the vanguard of progress for the whole race, see Gaines, *Uplifting the Race,* xiv. See also W. E. B. Du Bois, *The Philadelphia Negro: A Social Study* (1899; repr., Millwood, NY: Kraus-Thomson, 1973). Watts brands Baraka as a "crude and simple-minded political thinker." See Watts, *Amiri Baraka,* 470.

48. "The Black Arts Repertory Theatre/School [Summer Program]," n.d. [ca. May 1965], typescript, in Woodard, *Black Power Movement, Part I,* reel 1, frame 218; Jones, "Black Arts," frame 226; Gaines, *Uplifting the Race,* xiv; Baraka, *Autobiography,* 309–315; "LeRoi Jones Replies to Gertrude Wilson," New York *Amsterdam News,* Nov. 13, 1965, 3; LeRoi Jones, "State/ment" (1965), in *Home,* 251.

49. Watts, *Amiri Baraka,* 165; LeRoi Jones, Charles Patterson, and Steve Young to "Friends," n.d. [1965], in Woodard, *Black Power Movement: Part I,* reel 1, frame 222; Jones, "Black Arts," frame 226; "Black Arts Repertory Theatre/School [Summer Program]." Smethurst also overlooks the organization's broader efforts at educational and social provision in the frequent references to BARTS throughout his study. See Smethurst, *Black Arts Movement.*

50. "The Black Arts Proposal," June 25, 1965, typescript, box 12, 2nd folder, Baraka Papers; "Poverty: The War within the War," *Time,* May 13, 1966, www.time.com/time/magazine/article/0,9171,835478–8,00.html; Kenneth B. Clark and Jeanette Hopkins, *A Relevant War against Poverty: A Study of Community Action Programs and Observable Social Change* (1968; repr., New York: Harper & Row, 1969), 221; Alphonso Pinkney and Roger S. Woock, *Poverty and Politics in Harlem: Report on Project Uplift, 1965* (New Haven, CT: College and University Press Services, 1971). In his autobiography, Baraka sardonically refers to Project Uplift as "Operation Bootstrap," an indication of his later Marxist scorn for the rhetoric of self-help. See Baraka, *Autobiography,* 306.

51. "Poverty: The War within the War"; Baraka, *Autobiography,* 310, 329; Watts, *Amiri Baraka,* 159–160; Allen J. Matusow, *The Unraveling of America: A History of Liberalism in the 1960s* (1984; repr., Athens: University of Georgia Press, 2009), 259; Cruse, *Crisis of the Negro Intellectual,* 541; "The Black Arts Speaks Every Week Day," leaflet, n.d. [1965], box 16, "Black Arts" folder, Baraka Papers; "Harlem Terrorists Called 'Assassins,'" *New York World-Telegram and Sun,* Mar. 19, 1966, box 34, folder 7, Larry Neal Papers, Schomburg Center for Research in Black Culture, New York.

52. E. Spriggs, "haryou the pimp," n.d., typescript, in Woodard, *Black Power Movement, Part I,* reel 1, frame 243.

53. Amiri Baraka, *A Black Mass* (1965), in *Four Black Revolutionary Plays* (1969; repr., New York: Marion Boyars, 1998), 33–56, esp. 46, 48–49, 56. *A Black Mass* was "written at the Black Arts," according to Baraka, *Autobiography,* 338. On the play's popularity, see Benston, *Baraka,* 242. On the Nation of Islam's mythology,

see C. Eric Lincoln, *The Black Muslims in America,* rev. ed. (Boston: Beacon Press, 1973), 77–80.

54. Baraka, *Autobiography,* 329–334, 319.

55. Ibid., 339, 343; Watts, *Amiri Baraka,* 293. The date and venue of the Newark performance of *A Black Mass* are listed in Baraka, *Black Mass,* 35. Jones's anguish over Osafemi's death is evident in his writings from this period. See LeRoi Jones, "Bumi," in *Black Magic,* 196; LeRoi Jones/Amiri Baraka, "New Spirit," in *Fiction of LeRoi Jones/Amiri Baraka,* 205–207.

56. Malcolm X, *Autobiography of Malcolm X,* 403 (as the same passage also noted, Elijah Muhammad had not, apparently, exercised such forbearance himself); "The Outlook of LeRoi Jones," *Muhammad Speaks,* Dec. 2, 1966, 7; Marvin X and Faruk, "Islam and Black Art: An Interview with LeRoi Jones," in Reilly, *Conversations with Amiri Baraka,* 51–52. Though first published in *Negro Digest* in January 1969, the wide-ranging interview by Marvin X and Faruk would appear to have been conducted a year or two earlier on the basis of its exclusion of Kawaida (see below). Jones met Marvin X in San Francisco early in 1967, and this may have been the occasion of the interview. See Baraka, *Autobiography,* 352.

57. Hettie Jones, *How I Became Hettie Jones,* 167; Daniel Patrick Moynihan, *The Negro Family: The Case for National Action* (1965), in *The Moynihan Report and the Politics of Controversy: A Trans-Action Social Science and Public Policy Report,* ed. Lee Rainwater and William L. Yancey (Cambridge, MA: MIT Press, 1967), 41–124, esp. 51, 75, 90, 93–94; McKissick quoted in Lee Rainwater and William L. Yancey, "After Watts the Issue Is Joined," in Rainwater and Yancey, *Moynihan Report,* 200.

58. Wallace, *Black Macho,* 109–116; Bayard Rustin quoted in Lee Rainwater and William L. Yancey, "Confrontation at the Conference," in Rainwater and Yancey, *Moynihan Report,* 270; "The Role of the Black Woman in a White Society," *Liberator,* Aug. 1965, 4–5; Abdul Basit Naeem, "U.S. Booklet Admits Negro Plight Worse, Notes Muslim Enlistments," *Muhammad Speaks,* Apr. 8, 1966, 10; E. U. Essien-Udom, *Black Nationalism: A Search for an Identity in America* (Chicago: University of Illinois Press, 1962), 14–15.

59. *Atlantic Monthly* quoted in Kevin Mumford, *Newark: A History of Race, Rights, and Riots in America* (New York: New York University Press, 2007), 52; *Report of the National Advisory Commission on Civil Disorders* (New York: Bantam Books, 1968), 30–31; Mumford, *Newark,* 23, 102; Clark Taylor, "Newark: Parasitic Suburbs," *Society* 9–10 (Sept.–Oct. 1972): 39; Robert L. Allen, *Black Awakening in Capitalist America: An Analytic History* (Garden City, NY: Doubleday, 1969), 109–110.

60. Imamu Amiri Baraka (LeRoi Jones), "Newark Courthouse—'66 Wreck (Nigger Rec Room)" (1966), in *Raise, Race, Rays, Raze: Essays since 1965* (New York: Vintage, 1972), 4–7; Gaines, *Uplifting the Race,* 4.

61. Imamu Amiri Baraka (LeRoi Jones), "Work Notes—'66" (1966), in *Raise, Race, Rays, Raze,* 13; Baraka, *Autobiography,* 358, 334–353, 376–377.

62. Baraka, *Autobiography,* 350; Scot Brown, *Fighting for US: Maulana Karenga, the US Organization, and Black Cultural Nationalism* (New York: New York University

Press, 2003), 18–22, 47–48; Imamu Amiri Baraka (LeRoi Jones), "November 1966: One Year Eight Months Later" (1966), in *Raise, Race, Rays, Raze, 29.*

63. Brown, *Fighting for US,* 8–12, 34–35; Imamu Halisi, ed., *Kitabu: Beginning Concepts in Kawaida* (Los Angeles: US Organization, 1971).

64. Baraka, *Autobiography,* 350–351; Jones (Baraka), *Blues People;* Ron Karenga, "Black Cultural Nationalism" (1968), in Gayle, *Black Aesthetic,* 38; Imamu Amiri Baraka (LeRoi Jones), "Black Woman" (1970), in *Raise, Race, Rays, Raze,* 152. See also Christopher Funkhouser, "LeRoi Jones, Larry Neal, and 'The Cricket': Jazz and Poets' Black Fire," *African American Review* 37 (2003): 237–244.

65. Ron Karenga, "Overturning Ourselves: From Mystification to Meaningful Struggle," *Black Scholar* 4 (Oct. 1972): 8; Imamu Amiri Baraka, "7 Principles of US Maulana Karenga and the Need for a Black Value System" (1969), in *Raise, Race, Rays, Raze,* 138; Baraka, "Black Woman," 147; Imamu Amiri Baraka (LeRoi Jones), "From: The Book of Life" (1967), in *Raise, Race, Rays, Raze,* 51; Ameer Baraka, foreword to Jones and Neal, *Black Fire,* xvii–xviii. On Pan-Africanist narratives of civilization, see Wilson Jeremiah Moses, *Afrotopia: The Roots of African American Popular History* (Cambridge: Cambridge University Press, 1998); Tunde Adeleke, *UnAfrican Americans: Nineteenth-Century Black Nationalists and the Civilizing Mission* (Lexington: University Press of Kentucky, 1998).

66. Karenga quoted in Halisi, *Kitabu,* 6; Imamu Amiri Baraka, "The Art of Excellence in Black Life," address delivered at Columbia University Law School, New York, Feb. 28, 1973, transcript, 6, box 3, "Columbia University" folder, Baraka Papers.

67. Baraka, *Autobiography,* 355–357 (emphasis added); Baraka, "Black Woman," 147–153, quotation at 149; Baraka interviewed by Woodard, frames 587, 594; Jones, "LeRoi Jones Talking," 183; Imamu Amiri Baraka (LeRoi Jones), "Negro Theater Pimps Get Big off Nationalism" (1970), in *Raise, Race, Rays, Raze,* 115.

68. Karenga, "Black Cultural Nationalism," 33–34; Baraka, *Autobiography,* 376; Halisi, *Kitabu,* 8 n.4; Imamu Amiri Baraka, "All in the Street," in *Spirit Reach* (Newark, NJ: Jihad Publications, 1972), 11; Askia Muhammad Touré, "Jihad!" *Negro Digest,* July 1969, 12–13.

69. Jones (Baraka), *Blues People,* 29; Saul Gottlieb, "They Think You're an Airplane and You're Really a Bird" (1967), in Reilly, *Conversations with Amiri Baraka,* 30; Karenga quoted in Brown, *Fighting for US,* 35; Halisi, *Kitabu,* 6–7, 7 n.13. See also Baraka's statement "you are my 'house,' I live in you," in Baraka, "Black Woman," 148.

70. Baraka, "7 Principles," 136, 146 (emphasis added); Imamu Amiri Baraka, "Raise #3: Presidents" (1968), in *Raise, Race, Rays, Raze,* 89 (emphasis added). For his earlier hostility toward Christianity, see, for example, Jones, "Tokenism," 78. On black preachers as organic intellectuals, see Cornel West, "The Dilemma of the Black Intellectual," *Cultural Critique* no. 1 (1985): 114.

71. David L. Chappell, *A Stone of Hope: Prophetic Religion and the Death of Jim Crow* (Chapel Hill: University of North Carolina Press, 2004), 47; King quoted in David J. Garrow, *Bearing the Cross: Martin Luther King, Jr. and the Southern Christian Leadership Conference* (1986; repr., London: Vintage, 1993), 78; Baraka, "All in

the Street," 11; Baraka, "Raise #3," 89; LeRoi Jones, "What Does Nonviolence Mean?" (1963), in *Home,* 138–139; Amiri Baraka, "Soul Session," Nov. 9, 1969, typescript, box 26, "Notes for Speeches" folder, Baraka Papers.

72. William M. Banks, *Black Intellectuals: Race and Responsibility in American Life* (New York: W. W. Norton, 1996), 3–5; Amiri Baraka quoted in Sollors, *Amiri Baraka/LeRoi Jones,* 190–191. Despite quoting Baraka's "4 Reasons Why We Don't Allow Whites in Soul Session" [n.d.] ("space," "security," "soul," and "sincerity"), Sollors comments only on the "quasi-religious" character of these meetings and not on Baraka's medical imagery.

73. Amiri Baraka, *Madheart: A Morality Play* (1967), in *Four Black Revolutionary Plays,* 81, 94–95; Baraka, "Black Woman," 151; W. E. B. Du Bois, *The Souls of Black Folk: Essays and Sketches* (1903; repr., London: Archibald Constable & Co., 1905), 3; Imamu Amiri Baraka, [untitled address, Sept. 1970] in *African Congress: A Documentary of the First Modern Pan-African Congress,* ed. Imamu Amiri Baraka (New York: William Morrow, 1972). "The Black Arts" refers here to the Black Arts Alliance, San Francisco, an organization Baraka helped establish and to which he dedicated *Madheart.*

74. LeRoi Jones, "Part Two," n.d. [c. 1967], typescript, box 16, "Book of Life" folder, Baraka Papers; King, *Civil Rights and the Idea of Freedom,* 102; Vincent Harding, "Commentary," in *We Shall Overcome: Martin Luther King, Jr., and the Black Freedom Struggle,* ed. Peter J. Albert and Ronald Hoffman (New York: Pantheon, 1990), 165, quoted in King, *Civil Rights and the Idea of Freedom,* 124.

75. Scott, *Contempt and Pity,* 138, 148–149, 172, 176–177. While Scott acknowledges that previous generations of black nationalists had "used damage imagery as a foundation for their appeal to the masses," he asserts that the "black radical social scientists" of the 1960s "rejected" damage imagery. Moreover, he refers to social scientists as "Black Powerites" and "the Black Power generation" and claims that they "played no small part in shaping the nature of Black Power and New Left ideology." See Scott, *Contempt and Pity,* 163–165.

76. Richard H. King, *Race, Culture, and the Intellectuals, 1940–1970* (Washington, DC, and Baltimore: Woodrow Wilson Center Press and Johns Hopkins University Press, 2004), 159; Kwame Ture (Stokely Carmichael) and Charles V. Hamilton, *Black Power: The Politics of Liberation in America* (1967; repr., New York: Vintage, 1992), 29; Neal, "Black Arts Movement," 288.

77. Amiri Baraka, "Umoja," n.d. [c. 1970], typescript, box 22, "Black Newark Radio Program Editorials" folder, Baraka Papers; Baraka (Jones), "Work Notes—'66," 14.

78. John Ringgold, quoted in Ward, "Jazz and Soul," 181; Newton quoted in Robert Carr, *Black Nationalism in the New World: Reading the African-American and West Indian Experience* (Durham, NC: Duke University Press, 2002), 196.

79. "Rules of the Black Panther Party" (Oct. 1966), in *The Black Panthers Speak,* ed. Philip S. Foner (Philadelphia: Lippincott, 1970), 4–6; Eddie S. Glaude Jr., "Introduction: Black Power Revisited," in *Is It Nation Time? Contemporary Essays on Black Power and Black Nationalism,* ed. Eddie S. Glaude Jr. (Chicago: University of Chicago Press, 2002), 4; Robin D. G. Kelley, "Stormy Weather:

Reconstructing Black (Inter)Nationalism in the Cold War Era," in Glaude, *Is It Nation Time?* 83–85; Robert F. Williams, *Negroes with Guns* (New York: Marzani and Munsell, 1962).

80. William E. Cross Jr., "The Negro-to-Black Conversion Experience: Toward a Psychology of Black Liberation," *Black World,* July 1971, 13–27; Baraka, "Raise #3," 88; Imamu Amiri Baraka, "The Practice of the New Nationalism" (1970), in *Raise, Race, Rays, Raze,* 160.

81. Mumford, *Newark,* 98, 125–127; Allen, *Black Awakening,* 109–114; *Report of the National Advisory Commission on Civil Disorders,* 30–38.

82. Ron Porambo, *No Cause for Indictment: An Autopsy of Newark* (New York: Holt, Reinhart and Winston, 1971), 34–35; Baraka, *Autobiography,* 368–369, 381; LeRoi Jones, "Black People!" in *Black Magic,* 225; Watts, *Amiri Baraka,* 300–301; "Jones Is Acquitted of Weapon Charge in Newark Retrial," *New York Times,* July 3, 1969, 18. Theodore Hudson points out that the average sentence in similar riot-related weapons convictions was six months, often including probation. See Hudson, *From LeRoi Jones to Amiri Baraka,* 31.

83. Baraka, "From: The Book of Life," 49–55. On the provenance of this essay, see Baraka, *Autobiography,* 373.

84. Woodard, *Nation within a Nation,* 84–87; untitled FBI report, Mar. 21, 1968, box 9, 2nd FBI file, Baraka Papers; photograph contained in box 48, Baraka Papers; Baraka, *Autobiography,* 373. Baraka had given similar warnings against rioting to a student audience in Cincinnati on February 17, 1968. See SAC Cincinnati to FBI Director, Mar. 20, 1968, box 9, 2nd FBI file, Baraka Papers.

85. Askia Muhammad Touré quoted in "Lafayette Theatre: Reaction to *The Bombers,*" *Black Theatre* no. 4 (1970): 16–17; St. Clair Drake interviewed by Robert Martin, July 28, 1969, transcript, 165, Civil Rights Documentation Project, Moorland-Spingarn Research Center, Howard University, Washington, DC. Baraka quoted in Woodard, *Nation within a Nation,* 110; Baraka quoted in Allen, *Black Awakening,* 115.

86. Robert Self, " 'To Plan Our Liberation': Black Power and the Politics of Place in Oakland, California, 1965–1977," *Journal of Urban History* 26 (2000): 759–792, esp. 759–760, 769–770. Self's research on the Black Panther Party forms part of his larger study of the dynamics of race and urban geography in Oakland in the three decades following the Second World War. See Robert O. Self, *American Babylon: Race and the Struggle for Postwar Oakland* (Princeton, NJ: Princeton University Press, 2003).

87. Imamu Amiri Baraka, "Newark—before Black Men Conquered" (1967), in *Raise, Race, Rays, Raze,* 64–67; Clark, *Dark Ghetto,* 11; Kenneth B. Clark, "*Dark Ghetto* Revisited," paper delivered at MARC colloquium, New York, Dec. 5, 1967, typescript, 11, box 161, folder 1, Kenneth B. Clark Papers, Manuscript Division, Library of Congress, Washington, DC (hereafter cited as Clark Papers).

88. Baraka, "Newark," 71, 79; Woodard, *Nation within a Nation,* 88–89; Clyde Halisi and James Mtume, eds., *The Quotable Karenga* (Los Angeles: US Organiza-

tion, 1971), 19. An undated membership list suggests that four of the forty-five "United Brothers" were in fact women. See untitled document, n.d., box 17, "United Bros. Members" folder, Baraka Papers. See also Leonard M. Moore, *Carl B. Stokes and the Rise of Black Political Power* (Urbana: University of Illinois Press, 2003); David R. Colburn and Jeffrey S. Adler, eds., *African-American Mayors: Race, Politics, and the American City* (Urbana: University of Illinois Press, 2001).

89. Blair, *Retreat to the Ghetto,* 207. Baraka elaborated on his ideas for metropolitan fiscal reform in an essay of 1970; see Imamu Amiri Baraka, "Mwalimu Texts (from the Book of Life pt 2)" (1970), in *Raise, Race, Rays, Raze,* 163–164.

90. Self, " 'To Plan Our Liberation,' " 787; Woodard, *Nation within a Nation,* 143–154, 184–218.

91. Imamu Amiri Baraka (LeRoi Jones) and [photographs by] Fundi (Billy Abernathy), *In Our Terribleness: Some Elements and Meanings in Black Style* (Indianapolis: Bobbs-Merrill, 1970) [unpaginated]; Baraka, *Autobiography,* 371, 385; Baraka, "Newark," 78; Halisi and Mtume, *Quotable Karenga,* 2; Imamu Amiri Baraka (LeRoi Jones), "An Article/Story about Newark Policemen Using Their Real Names, &c." (1968), in *Raise, Race, Rays, Raze,* 94; Imamu Amiri Baraka (LeRoi Jones), "Need for a Cultural Base for Civil Rites & Bpower Mooments" (1967), in *Raise, Race, Rays, Raze,* 44.

92. Amiri Baraka interviewed by Ellis Haizlip, Nov. 5, 1972, for the television program *SOUL* (broadcast Nov. 8, 1972), Channel 13, CD sound recording, Hatch-Billops Archives, New York. In the absence of comprehensive membership lists, I am grateful to Professor Komozi Woodard of Sarah Lawrence College, Bronxville, NY, a former CFUN member, for estimating the organization's size and outlining its institutional development in a personal communication. Some details of CFUN's housing and employment arrangements can be found in an untitled draft CFUN brochure, 1971, box 21, "CFUN Brochure" folder, Baraka Papers. For the birth dates of the Barakas' children, see Baraka, *Autobiography,* 426.

93. Baraka, "Black Woman," 147–153; Halisi and Mtume, *Quotable Karenga,* 20–21.

94. Moynihan, *Negro Family,* 62, 29; E. Frances White, "Africa on My Mind: Gender, Counter Discourse, and African American Nationalism," in Glaude, *Is It Nation Time?* 130–155, quotations at 152; Baraka quoted in Gottlieb, "They Think You're an Airplane," 32; Baraka, "Mwalimu Texts," 166. On the gender ideology of the civil rights movement, see Sara Evans, *Personal Politics: The Roots of Women's Liberation in the Civil Rights Movement and the New Left* (New York: Vintage, 1980); Peter J. Ling and Sharon Monteith, eds., *Gender in the Civil Rights Movement* (New York: Garland, 1999); Bettye Collier-Thomas and V. P. Franklin, eds., *Sisters in the Struggle: African American Women in the Civil Rights–Black Power Movement* (New York: New York University Press, 2001).

95. Wallace, *Black Macho,* 62–66; hooks, *Ain't I a Woman,* 106; Baraka, *Madheart,* 99; see the sixteenth of Karenga's *kanuni,* reproduced in Brown, *Fighting for US,* 48.

96. LeRoi Jones, *Arm Yourself, or Harm Yourself! A Message of Self-Defense to Black Men!* (Newark, NJ: Jihad Publications, n.d.), 7, box 1, folder 1, Amiri Baraka Collection of Playscripts; LeRoi Jones, "Beautiful Black Women," in *Black Magic,* 148; Touré, "Jihad!" 12–13, 16; Wallace, *Black Macho,* 62; Lethonia Gee, "Black Music Man," in Jones and Neal, *Black Fire,* 222; Nikki Giovanni, "Poem for Black Boys," in *Black Judgement* (Detroit: Broadside Press, 1968), 5; Nikki Giovanni, "Of Liberation," in *Black Judgement,* 4. On black women's resistance to male chauvinism within the black power movement, see Benita Roth, "The Making of the Vanguard Center: Black Feminist Emergence in the 1960s and 1970s," in *Still Lifting, Still Climbing: African American Women's Contemporary Activism,* ed. Kimberly Springer (New York: New York University Press, 1999), 70–90; Trayce Matthews, " 'No One Ever Asks, What a Man's Role in the Revolution Is': Gender and the Politics of the Black Panther Party, 1966–1971," in *The Black Panther Party (Reconsidered),* ed. Charles E. Jones (Baltimore: Black Classic Press, 1998), 267–304; Angela D. LeBlanc-Ernest, " 'The Most Qualified Person to Handle the Job': Black Panther Party Women, 1966–1982," in Charles Jones, *Black Panther Party,* 305–334.

97. "Marriage Ceremony," n.d., typescript, in Woodard, *Black Power Movement, Part I,* reel 1, frame 824; Muminina Akiba, "African Wedding," *Black NewArk,* Sept. 1972, ibid., frames 821–823; "Ahadi ya Akika," n.d., typescript, ibid., frame 831; "Kuziliwa Karamu," n.d., typescript, ibid., frame 832.

98. Brown, *Fighting for US,* 62–65, 48; rules of the Republic of New Africa, reproduced in Ronald Walters, "The Re-Africanization of the Black American," in *Topics in Afro-American Studies,* ed. Henry J. Richards (Buffalo, NY: Black Academy Press, 1971), 113–114; Sandra Hollin Flowers, *African American Nationalist Literature of the 1960s: Pens of Fire* (New York: Garland, 1996), xv.

99. Brown, *Fighting for US,* 127; Baraka, *Autobiography,* 417, 341–343; Baraka interviewed by Haizlip.

100. Yablonsky's study cited in Arthur Marwick, *The Sixties: Cultural Revolution in Britain, France, Italy, and the United States, c. 1958–c. 1974* (Oxford: Oxford University Press, 1998), 485; Baraka, untitled address, Sept. 1970, reprinted in Baraka, *African Congress,* 95 (emphasis added); Imamu Amiri Baraka, *Junkies Are Full of (SHHH . . .)* (1971), in *Black Drama Anthology,* ed. Woodie King and Ron Milner (New York: Columbia University Press, 1972), 11–23; Daniel H. Watts, "Editorial: Let It Crawl," *Liberator,* Feb. 1970, 3. For a black nationalist critique of the hippies as middle-class, part-time rebels, see Clayton Riley, "Black Nationalists and the Hippies," *Liberator,* Dec. 1967, 4–7. For black nationalist condemnation of drug use, see also "The Drug Culture," *Liberator,* July 1970, 8–10, and Clayton Riley, "Drugs Are Real," *Liberator,* Sept. 1970, 10–11.

101. Baraka, untitled address, Sept. 1970, reprinted in Baraka, *African Congress,* 93–94; Booker T. Washington, "The Standard Printed Version of the Atlanta Exposition Address," Sept. 18, 1895, in *The Booker T. Washington Papers,* ed. Louis R. Harlan et al., vol. 3 (Urbana: University of Illinois Press, 1974), 583–587, quotation at 583.

102. Saidi Nguvu interviewed by Komozi Woodard, Nov. 15, 1985, transcript, in Woodard, *Black Power Movement, Part I,* reel 9, frames 193, 221, 224–225.

103. Taalamu (Tim Holiday) interviewed by Komozi Woodard, May 4, 1985, transcript, in Woodard, *Black Power Movement, Part I,* reel 9, frames 352, 360, 370; Salimu (Nettie Rogers) interviewed by Komozi Woodard, transcript dated 1986, ibid., frames 312–313, 330–331; Nguvu interviewed by Woodard, ibid., frames 235–236.

104. Mumininas of Committee for Unified NewArk, *Mwanamke Mwanamchi (The Nationalist Woman)* (Newark, NJ: Mumininas of CFUN, 1971), in Woodard, *Black Power Movement, Part I,* reel 1, frames 839, 841; "African Free School," *Black NewArk,* Sept. 1972, ibid., reel 7, frame 532.

105. Baba Ngola, "Super Simba News," *Black NewArk,* Jan. 1973, in Woodard, *Black Power Movement, Part I,* reel 7, frame 557; untitled draft CFUN brochure (see above). Nguvu recalls a "circle of elders" within CFUN, while *Black NewArk* defined *Wazee* as "elders." See Nguvu interviewed by Woodard, frame 245; "Kiswahili Lesson," *Black NewArk,* Mar. 1973, in Woodard, *Black Power Movement, Part I,* reel 7, frame 567.

106. Terence Ranger, "The Invention of Tradition in Colonial Africa," in *The Invention of Tradition,* ed. Eric Hobsbawm and Terence Ranger (Cambridge: Cambridge University Press, 1983), 211–262; Baraka, "Black Woman," 152; Gaines, *Uplifting the Race,* xix; Baraka, "7 Principles," 134. Kawaida's appropriation of "invented" African traditions is also noted in White, "Africa on My Mind," 146–148.

107. Imamu Ameer Baraka to "Committee and Circle Heads," Sept. 23, 1969, box 16, "Custom & Concept" folder, Baraka Papers; Brown, *Fighting for US,* 91, 94–96; Woodard, *Nation within a Nation,* 165–166; FBI Director to SAC Newark, Oct. 9, 1970, box 9, 3rd FBI file, Baraka Papers.

108. Thomas Collins, "From the Ghetto, the Cry of an Impassioned Poet," *Newsday,* Feb. 10, 1971, box 8, "Spirit House" folder, Baraka Papers; Michael Mok, "*Publishers Weekly* Interviews LeRoi Jones," *Publishers Weekly,* Sept. 11, 1972, 20–21, 94.

109. Baraka, "Practice of the New Nationalism," 163; Baraka, "Negro Theater Pimps," 115; Imamu Ameer Baraka, "The Book of Life," n.d., typescript, box 16, "Book of Life" folder, Baraka Papers. Clark's decision to support CFUN's voter education and registration efforts with up to $10,000 from the budget of the Metropolitan Applied Research Center is noted in Sol Markoff, "Memorandum: Notes re, Conference with Committee for a Unified Newark," May 12, 1969, box 367, folder 6, Clark Papers. On Puritan "New-Ark," see Mumford, *Newark,* 13, 17 (map).

110. Imamu Amiri Baraka (LeRoi Jones), "It's Nation Time," in *It's Nation Time* (Chicago: Third World Press, 1970), 22; Baraka, untitled address, Sept. 1970, reprinted in Baraka, *African Congress,* 101–103; Baraka and Fundi (Billy Abernathy), *In Our Terribleness* [unpaginated].

111. Jennifer Jordan, "Cultural Nationalism in the 1960s: Politics and Poetry," in *Race, Politics, and Culture: Critical Essays on the Radicalism of the 1960s,* ed. Adolph Reed Jr. (Westport, CT: Greenwood Press, 1986), 44–46; Baraka and Fundi (Billy Abernathy), *In Our Terribleness* [unpaginated]. Jordan is remarking on, rather than endorsing, Baraka's use of the term "niggers."

112. *Super Fly,* dir. Gordon Parks Jr. (Warner Bros., 1972); Imamu Amiri Baraka, "Raise!" *Black NewArk,* Oct. 1972, in Woodard, *Black Power Movement, Part I,* reel 7, frame 544; Amiri Baraka, "Europeans Have 'The Flies,' Afrikans Have 'SuperFlies,'" Nov. 1972, typescript, box 3, "New York Times" folder, Baraka Papers. See also Eithne Quinn, "'Tryin' to Get Over': *Super Fly,* Black Politics, and Post-Civil Rights Film Enterprise," *Cinema Journal* 49 (Winter 2010): 86–105.

113. Imamu Amiri Baraka (LeRoi Jones), "Nationalism vs PimpArt" (1969), in *Raise, Race, Rays, Raze,* 129.

114. "CAP Yajenga Nchi," n.d., typescript, box 16, "CAP-CFUN Documents" folder, Baraka Papers.

115. Ibid.; Kawaida Towers press release, Mar. 1, 1973, box 26, "Kawaida Towers" folder, Baraka Papers; Untitled CFUN newsletter, n.d., box 12, 3rd folder, Baraka Papers; Donald Tucker interviewed by Komozi Woodard, Jan. 31, 1986, transcript, in Woodard, *Black Power Movement: Part I,* reel 9, frame 413; James C. Hall, *Mercy, Mercy Me: African-American Culture and the American Sixties* (New York: Oxford University Press, 2001), 28, 6. Hall's use of "antimodernism" connotes not opposition to literary modernism but "a protest against or rejection of modernity" (vii–viii) and is informed by T. J. Jackson Lears, *No Place of Grace: Antimodernism and the Transformation of American Culture, 1880–1920* (New York: Pantheon, 1981).

116. Baraka, "Mwalimu Texts," 165–167 (emphasis added); Baraka, "Practice of the New Nationalism," 164.

117. Woodard, *Nation within a Nation,* 230, 233–244, 253; Mitchell Leon, "Imperiale Vows to Block Work: 300 in N. Ward Protest Kawaida Picket," *Newark Star-Ledger,* Nov. 9, 1972, box 26, "Kawaida Towers" folder, Baraka Papers.

118. Amiri Baraka, untitled typescript, n.d. [1974], 1, box 26, "Speech Notes" folder, Baraka Papers (hereafter cited as Baraka, Neocolonialism MS).

119. Baraka, *Autobiography,* 409, 430; Baraka, Neocolonialism MS, 1–2, 4. For Baraka's recollections of the African Liberation Support Committee and his engagement with the ideas of Nkrumah and Cabral, see Baraka, *Autobiography,* 417, 427, 433. See also Kwame Nkrumah, *Neo-Colonialism: The Last Stage of Imperialism* (London: Nelson, 1965), and Amilcar Cabral, *Revolution in Guinea: Selected Texts* (New York: Monthly Review Press, 1969). For a somewhat more sympathetic portrayal of Gibson's administration, see Mumford, *Newark,* 191–213.

120. "CFUN: On Conflicting Ideas of Social Organization & Our Understanding of Revolutionary Kawaida," n.d., typescript, 1–2, 5, box 16, "CAP-CFUN Documents" folder, Baraka Papers; Baraka, *Autobiography,* 419, 424, 444; Imamu Amiri Baraka, "Comments of Chairman on Resignations of Haki Madhubuti and Jitu Weusi," May 21, 1974, memorandum, in Woodard, *Black Power Move-*

ment, Part I, reel 2, frames 807–808. Some of Baraka's early Marxist writings are collected in Amiri Baraka, *Daggers and Javelins: Essays, 1974–1979* (New York: William Morrow, 1984).

121. Baraka, *Autobiography,* 342–343. The immediate context for these remarks is Baraka's reflection on his failed experiment with polygamy at Spirit House in 1966, but his reference here to "claiming a 'blackness' that in many ways was bogus" is indicative of his Marxist renunciation of "my naive cultural nationalist delusion" in general (443).

122. Amiri Baraka, "Confessions of a Former Anti-Semite," *Village Voice,* Dec. 17–23, 1980, 1, 21–23; Charlie Reilly, "The Former LeRoi Jones: An Interview with Amiri Baraka" (1976), in Reilly, *Conversations with Amiri Baraka,* 99, 104.

3. Harlem without Walls

1. While many commentators have assumed that the original collages were displayed alongside the enlarged prints, Ruth Fine, the curator of a major retrospective on Romare Bearden in 2003–2004 at the National Gallery of Art in Washington, D.C., notes that there is no documentary evidence of this, and that many of the reviews of the Cordier & Ekstrom exhibition imply that only the prints were displayed. She allows, however, that the collages "may have been at the gallery and available for private viewing." See Ruth Fine, "The Spaces Between: Romare Bearden," in *The Art of Romare Bearden,* ex. cat., ed. Ruth Fine (New York: Harry N. Abrams, 2003), 40 and 257 n.122. Whether or not they were displayed in the initial exhibition, the collages immediately became sought-after works in their own right: Joseph H. Hirshhorn acquired three of them from Cordier & Ekstrom on November 19, 1964, and donated them to the Hirshhorn Museum in 1966. Thanks to Aimee Soubier of the Hirshhorn Museum and Sculpture Garden, Washington, D.C., for details of these acquisitions.

2. "Art in New York: Uptown; Romare Bearden," *Time,* Oct. 23, 1964, NY5; "Tormented Faces," *Newsweek,* Oct. 19, 1964, 105; Dore Ashton, "Romare Bearden: Projections," *Quadrum* 17 (1965): 100; Stuart Preston, "Bonnard Retrospective at Modern Museum," *New York Times,* Oct. 10, 1964, microfilm N68-87, Romare Bearden Papers, Archives of American Art, Smithsonian Institution, Washington, DC, frame 381 (hereafter cited as Bearden Papers).

3. Romare Bearden, "Rectangular Structure in My Montage Paintings," *Leonardo* 2, no. 1 (1969): 18.

4. Robert Hughes, "Visual Jazz from a Sharp Eye," *Time,* June 10, 1991, 72; Michael Kimmerman, "Life's Abundance, Captured in a Collage," *New York Times,* Oct. 15, 2004, E32; Mary Schmidt Campbell, "Tradition and Conflict: Images of a Turbulent Decade, 1962–1973," in *Tradition and Conflict: Images of a Turbulent Decade, 1962–1973,* ex. cat., ed. Mary Schmidt Campbell (New York: The Studio Museum in Harlem, 1985), 48; Myron Schwartzman, *Romare Bearden: His Life and Art* (New York: Harry N. Abrams, 1990); Myron Schwartzman, "Of Mecklenburg, Memory, and the Blues: Romare Bearden's Collaboration with Albert Murray," *Bulletin of Research in the Humanities* 86 (Summer 1983): 140–161; Henry Louis Gates Jr., "King of Cats," in *Thirteen Ways of Looking at a Black Man*

(New York: Vintage, 1997), 37. On the persistent tendency for Bearden and other African American artists to be overlooked in accounts of "mainstream" American art, see Ruth Fine, "Expanding the Mainstream: Romare Bearden Revisited," *Proceedings of the American Philosophical Society* 149 (2005): 40–55.

5. Albert Murray, *The Omni-Americans: New Perspectives on Black Experience and American Culture* (New York: Outerbridge & Dienstfrey, 1970), 7; Bearden quoted in Charles Childs, "Bearden: Identification and Identity," *ARTnews,* Oct. 1964, 62.

6. Passing references to the Harlem riot are found in Mary Schmidt Campbell, "History and the Art of Romare Bearden," in *Memory and Metaphor: The Art of Romare Bearden, 1940–1987,* ex. cat., ed. Kinshasha Holman Conwill (New York: The Studio Museum in Harlem and Oxford University Press, 1991), 15–16; Louis Kaplan, "Community in Fragments: Romare Bearden's Projections and the Interruption of Myth," *American Exposures: Photography and Community in the Twentieth Century* (Minneapolis: University of Minnesota Press, 2005), 122.

7. Oral history interview with Romare Bearden [by Henri Ghent], June 29, 1968, transcript, Archives of American Art, Smithsonian Institution, Washington, DC (hereafter cited as Bearden Oral History), http://www.aaa.si.edu/collections /interviews/oral-history-interview-romare-bearden-11481; Childs, "Bearden," 25.

8. Albert Murray, "The Visual Equivalent of the Blues," in *Romare Bearden: 1970–1980,* ex. cat., ed. Jerald L. Melberg and Milton J. Bloch (Charlotte, NC: The Mint Museum, 1980), 26; W. E. B. Du Bois, *The Souls of Black Folk: Essays and Sketches* (1903; repr., London: Archibald Constable & Co., 1905), 109; Ralph Ellison, "The Art of Romare Bearden" (1968), in *The Collected Essays of Ralph Ellison,* ed. John F. Callahan (New York: Modern Library, 1995), 693; André Malraux, *Voices of Silence,* trans. Stuart Gilbert (Garden City, NY: Doubleday, 1953). On Bearden's admiration for Malraux and the "Museum without Walls," see Sarah Kennel, "Bearden's Musée Imaginaire," in Fine, *Art of Romare Bearden,* 138–155.

9. Childs, "Bearden," 25; Bearden Oral History; Romare Bearden, "The Negro Artist's Dilemma," *Critique: A Review of Contemporary Art* 1 (Nov. 1946): 16–22.

10. For early biographical information see Schwartzman, *Romare Bearden,* 10–17; Glenda Elizabeth Gilmore, "Romare Bearden's Mecklenburg Memories," in Carla M. Hanzal et al., *Romare Bearden: Southern Recollections,* ex. cat. (Charlotte, NC: The Mint Museum, 2011), 40–42. Detailed information covering the duration of Bearden's life can also be found in Rocío Aranda-Alvarado and Sarah Kennel with Carmenita Higginbotham, "Romare Bearden: A Chronology," in Fine, *Art of Romare Bearden,* 212–247. For an impressive analysis of visual, literary, and musical representations of the Great Migration (though one that curiously omits Bearden's work), see Farah Jasmine Griffin, *"Who Set You Flowin'?" The African-American Migration Narrative* (New York: Oxford University Press, 1995).

11. Bessye Bearden, untitled curriculum vitae, n.d., folder 1, Bessye B. Bearden Papers, Schomburg Center for Research in Black Culture, New York; Schwartzman, *Romare Bearden,* 68–69; Mary Schmidt Campbell, "Romare Bearden: A Creative Mythology" (unpublished PhD dissertation, Syracuse University, 1982).

12. Gilmore, "Romare Bearden's Mecklenburg Memories," 44, 56; Calvin Tomkins, "Profiles: Putting Something over Something Else," *New Yorker,* Nov. 28, 1977, 55.

13. Fine, "Spaces Between," 7; Tomkins, "Profiles," 55; Aranda-Alvarado et al., "Romare Bearden: A Chronology," 215; Schwartzman, *Romare Bearden,* 73–74.

14. Romare Bearden, "His Master's Voice," *Baltimore Afro-American,* June 6, 1936, reproduced in Aranda-Alvarado et al., "Romare Bearden: A Chronology," 215; Schwartzman, *Romare Bearden,* 76; Romare Bearden, "His Master's Voice," *Baltimore Afro-American,* Nov. 2, 1935, 6; Bearden, "Rectangular Structure," 11.

15. Schwartzman, *Romare Bearden,* 82; Aranda-Alvarado et al., "Romare Bearden: A Chronology," 215; Ellison, "Art of Romare Bearden," 688. See also Anna Indych-López, *Muralism without Walls: Rivera, Orozco, and Siqueiros in the United States, 1927–1940* (Pittsburgh: University of Pittsburgh Press, 2009).

16. Bearden, "Rectangular Structure," 11; Bearden Oral History. See also the essays in Frank Whitford, ed., *The Berlin of George Grosz: Drawings, Watercolors and Prints,* ex. cat. (New Haven, CT: Yale University Press, 1997).

17. Stacy I. Morgan, *Rethinking Social Realism: African American Art and Literature, 1930–1953* (Athens: University of Georgia Press, 2006), 29–31; "The Negro's War," *Fortune,* June 1942, microfilm N68-87, Bearden Papers, frame 247. For details of the 1939 group exhibition, see Aranda-Alvarado et al., "Romare Bearden: A Chronology," 216.

18. Alston quoted in Tomkins, "Profiles," 58, 56; Edward Ellis, "Welfare Worker Arrives in Art: Romare Bearden's Job Provides Him with Inspiration," *New York World-Telegram,* Oct. 21, 1949, 31.

19. Gilmore, "Romare Bearden's Mecklenburg Memories," 42; Campbell, "Romare Bearden," 69–70; Bearden Oral History.

20. Gilmore, "Romare Bearden's Mecklenburg Memories," 40–42; Schwartzman, *Romare Bearden,* 70–71; Henry Louis Gates Jr., "The Passing of Anatole Broyard," in Gates, *Thirteen Ways of Looking at a Black Man,* 180–214; Ellison, "Art of Romare Bearden," 689.

21. Isaac Julien and Kobena Mercer, "De Margin and De Centre" (1988), in *Black British Cultural Studies: A Reader,* ed. Houston A. Baker, Manthia Diawara, and Ruth H. Lindeborg (Chicago: University of Chicago Press, 1996), 197; Romare Bearden to Walter Quirt, Jan. 20, 1942, microfilm 570, Walter Quirt Papers, Archives of American Art, Smithsonian Institution, Washington, DC, frame 605; Romare Bearden, untitled proposal, n.d., incorporated as an appendix to Campbell, "Romare Bearden," 513.

22. James W. Lane, "Afro-American Art on Both Continents," *ARTnews,* Oct. 15–31, 1941, 25, microfilm N68-87, Bearden Papers, frame 499; *New Yorker,* Dec. 27, 1941, microfilm N68-87, Bearden Papers, frame 503. Bearden later quoted Lane's review in disgust. See Bearden, "Negro Artist's Dilemma," 20.

23. Schwartzman, *Romare Bearden,* 121–124; Ann Eden Gibson, *Abstract Expressionism: Other Politics* (New Haven, CT: Yale University Press, 1997), 43–57; Edward Alden Jewell, "Landscape in a Rich Panorama," *New York Times,* Nov. 11,

1945, 51; Richard J. Powell, "What Becomes a Legend Most? Reflections on Romare Bearden," *Transition* 55 (Spring 1992): 69; Martin Duberman, *Paul Robeson* (1968; repr., London: Bodley Head, 1989), 381–428. The group exhibition in question was *The Negro Artist Comes of Age: A National Survey of Contemporary Artists*, held at the Albany Institute of History and Art from January 3 to February 11, 1945. On the universalist attitudes that dominated the postwar moment, see Richard H. King, *Race, Culture, and the Intellectuals, 1940–1970* (Washington, DC: Woodrow Wilson Center Press, and Baltimore: Johns Hopkins University Press, 2004), 2–12.

24. Bearden, "Negro Artist's Dilemma," 19–20. On the Harmon Foundation, see Gary A. Reynolds and Beryl J. Wright, eds., *Against the Odds: African-American Artists and the Harmon Foundation* (Newark, NJ: Newark Museum, 1989).

25. Romare Bearden, "The Negro Artist and Modern Art," *Opportunity: A Journal of Negro Life* 12 (Dec. 1934): 371–372; Bearden, "Negro Artist's Dilemma," 21–22.

26. Romare Bearden, [introduction to] *Romare Bearden: First New York Exhibition: The Passion of Christ*, ex. cat. (1945), microfilm N68-87, Bearden Papers, frame 171; Ben Wolf, "Bearden—He Wrestles with Angels," *Art Digest,* Oct. 1, 1945, microfilm N68-87, Bearden Papers, frame 506; [author and title unclear,] *Art Digest,* Oct. 14, 1945, microfilm N68-87, Bearden Papers, frame 513; Matthew S. Witkovsky, "Experience vs. Theory: Romare Bearden and Abstract Expressionism," *Black American Literature Forum* 23 (1989): 260; Schwartzman, *Romare Bearden,* 132–133, 152.

27. Witkovsky, "Experience vs. Theory," 266; Bearden quoted in Schwartzman, *Romare Bearden,* 146; Romare Bearden interviewed by Avis Berman, Long Island City, NY, July 31, 1980, transcript, 4–5, "Restricted 1 of 1" box, Bearden Papers; Romare Bearden to Carl Holty, n.d. [1950], microfilm 670, Holty Papers, frame 554.

28. Romare Bearden interviewed by Esther G. Rolick, Mercy College, n.d. [c. 1970/1971], cassette recording, Esther G. Rolick Papers, Archives of American Art, Smithsonian Institution, Washington, DC; Tomkins, "Profiles," 64; Romare Bearden to Carl Holty, n.d. ["Tuesday"], microfilm 670, Holty Papers, frame 425; Aranda-Alvarado et al., "Romare Bearden: A Chronology," 221–222; Richard Kostelanetz, *SoHo: The Rise and Fall of an Artists' Colony* (New York: Routledge, 2003); Bearden quoted in Schwartzman, *Romare Bearden,* 182.

29. Romare Bearden and Carl Holty, *The Painter's Mind: A Study in the Relations of Structure and Space in Painting* (New York: Crown Publishers, 1969), 10; Romare Bearden to Carl Holty, n.d. ["Sunday"], microfilm 670, Holty Papers, frame 436; Romare Bearden to Carl Holty, n.d., microfilm 670, Holty Papers, frames 441–443; Romare Bearden to Carl Holty, n.d., microfilm 670, Holty Papers, frame 464.

30. Tomkins, "Profiles," 64; Bearden and Holty, *Painter's Mind,* 215; Fine, "Spaces Between," 22; Bearden, "Negro Artist's Dilemma," 17.

31. Carlyle Burrows, "Bearden's Return," *New York Herald Tribune,* Jan. 24, 1960, section 4, p. 6.

32. Bearden quoted in Childs, "Bearden," 61.

33. Bearden, "Negro Artist and Modern Art," 371.

34. Gates, "King of Cats," 31; David Remnick, "Visible Man" (1994), in *The Devil Problem: And Other True Stories* (London: Picador, 2000), 239; Ralph Ellison, *Invisible Man* (1952; repr., London: Penguin, 2001), 581. On Murray's career, see also Stanley Crouch, "Chitlins at the Waldorf: The Work of Albert Murray" (1980), in *Notes of a Hanging Judge: Essays and Reviews, 1979–1989* (New York: Oxford University Press, 1990), 42–48; Sanford Pinsker, "Albert Murray: The Black Intellectuals' Maverick Patriarch," *Virginia Quarterly Review* 72 (Autumn 1996): 678–684.

35. Albert Murray interviewed by Robert O'Meally, New York, July 1, 1994, Smithsonian Institution Jazz Oral History Program, transcript, 149–151, 160 (hereafter cited as Murray Oral History), box 1, Albert Murray Papers, Houghton Library, Harvard University, Cambridge, MA (hereafter cited as Murray Papers); Schwartzman, *Romare Bearden,* 216.

36. Murray Oral History, July 1 and Aug. 8, 1994, transcript, 159–161; Bearden interviewed by Berman, transcript, 18; Schwartzman, *Romare Bearden,* 194; Bearden, "Rectangular Structure," 14–15; Bearden Oral History.

37. Henry Louis Gates Jr., introduction to *Thirteen Ways of Looking at a Black Man,* xxiii; Gates, "King of Cats," 37.

38. Gates, "King of Cats"; Houston A. Baker Jr., *Blues, Ideology, and Afro-American Literature: A Vernacular Theory* (Chicago: University of Chicago Press, 1984), 12, 112, 202; Crouch, "Chitlins at the Waldorf."

39. Bearden Oral History; *First Group Showing: Works in Black & White,* ex. cat. (1965), microfilm N68-87, Bearden Papers, frame 225; Romare Bearden to Guggenheim Memorial Foundation, n.d. [received Oct. 15, 1963], box 6, Archive of the Romare Bearden Foundation, New York (hereafter cited as Bearden Foundation Archive).

40. Murray Oral History, Aug. 8, 1994, transcript, 163–165.

41. Ibid., 165, 161, 167 (emphasis added).

42. Romare Bearden to Mary Schmidt Campbell, Sept. 22, 1973, incorporated as an appendix to Campbell, "Romare Bearden," 561; Emma Amos interviewed by Camille Billops, Dec. 6, 1974, transcript, www.negroartists.com /writings/EMMA%20AMOS/Interview%20of%20Emma%20Amos%20by %20Camille%20Billops.htm. Murray's presence at the first Spiral meeting is reported in Romare Bearden and Harry Henderson, *A History of African-American Artists: From 1792 to the Present* (New York: Pantheon, 1993), 511 n.16. This book was completed by Henderson after Bearden's death. Other members of Spiral included Richard Mayhew, William Majors, and Reginald Gammon. For biographical information on Spiral's members, see *First Group Showing,* frames 228–229.

43. Jeanne Siegel, "Why Spiral?" *ARTnews,* Sept. 1966, 48–51; Grace Glueck, "Art Notes: A Brueghel from Harlem," *New York Times,* Feb. 22, 1969, section 2, p. 29. Bearden's comments to Siegel refute Floyd Coleman's blanket assertions that "the Spiralists believed that art should not be burdened with political and

social concerns," and that "they strove to achieve an art that was neither ethnic nor racial but universal." See Floyd Coleman, "The Changing Same: Spiral, the Sixties, and African American Art," in *A Shared Heritage: Art by Four African Americans,* ex. cat., ed. William E. Taylor and Harriet G. Warkel (Indianapolis: Indianapolis Museum of Art with Indiana University Press, 1996), 152.

44. Albert Murray, *South to a Very Old Place* (New York: McGraw-Hill, 1971), 219–227, quotation at 223.

45. Murray, *Omni-Americans,* 17–18.

46. Albert Murray, untitled manuscript, n.d., in envelope marked "Remarks on Some of the Limitations of Protest Writers (from Hemingway ms)," 4–5, box 1, Murray Papers; Murray, *South to a Very Old Place,* 218.

47. Murray, *South to a Very Old Place,* 19. On Ellison's attitude toward the New Deal, see Arnold Rampersad, *Ralph Ellison: A Biography* (New York: Alfred A. Knopf, 2007), 533.

48. Albert Murray, *Train Whistle Guitar* (1974; repr., New York: Vintage, 1998), quotations at 124–125; Murray, *Omni-Americans,* 6–7.

49. Ralph Ellison, "'A Very Stern Discipline'" (1967), in *Collected Essays,* 730; Norman Mailer, "The White Negro" (1957), in *Protest,* ed. Gene Feldman and Max Gartenberg (London: Panther, 1960), 291; George M. Fredrickson, *The Black Image in the White Mind: The Debate on Afro-American Character and Destiny, 1817–1914* (1971; repr., Hanover, NH: Wesleyan University Press, 1987), 328.

50. Ralph Ellison, "What Are These Children Like?" (1963), in *Collected Essays,* 548; Ellison, "Art of Romare Bearden," 691–692; Rampersad, *Ralph Ellison,* 379.

51. Bearden Oral History; Amos interviewed by Billops.

52. Bearden to Holty, n.d., frame 436; Bearden to Holty, n.d., frame 442; Bearden, "Rectangular Structure," 11.

53. Murray, "Visual Equivalent of the Blues," 17, 27–28; Albert Murray, *Stomping the Blues* (1976; repr., London: Quartet Books, 1978), 87. On Murray's notion of "heroism," see Daniel Matlin, "Blues under Siege: Ralph Ellison, Albert Murray, and the Idea of America," in *Uncertain Empire: American History and the Idea of the Cold War,* ed. Joel Isaac and Duncan Bell (New York: Oxford University Press, 2012), 195–222.

54. Murray, "Visual Equivalent of the Blues," 26; Murray Oral History, July 1, 1994, transcript, 101; Murray, *South to a Very Old Place,* 223.

55. Campbell, "History and the Art of Romare Bearden," 9 (emphasis added); Bearden quoted in Childs, "Bearden," 25.

56. Bearden, "Rectangular Structure," 18; Robert Delevoy, *Breugel,* trans. Stuart Gilbert (New York: Rizzoli, 1990), 60.

57. Bearden Oral History (emphasis added); Linda Nochlin, *Gustave Courbet: A Study of Style and Society* (New York: Garland, 1976), 63, 153, 4; Courbet quoted in Michael Fried, *Courbet's Realism* (Chicago: University of Chicago Press, 1990), 99–100; Petra Ten Doesschate Chu, *French Realism and the Dutch Masters* (Utrecht: Haentjens Dekker & Gumbert, 1974), 48.

58. Murray, *Omni-Americans,* 7; Bearden quoted in Childs, "Bearden," 62; Ellison quoted in Rampersad, *Ralph Ellison,* 218 (emphasis added). On the relationship between Bearden's and Ellison's modernist visions, see also Kobena Mercer, "Romare Bearden: African-American Modernism at Mid-Century," in *Art History, Aesthetics, and Visual Studies,* ed. Michael Ann Holly and Keith Moxon (Williamstown, MA: Sterling and Francine Clark Art Institute, 2002), 29–46.

59. Romare Bearden, untitled typescript, n.d. [1976], 3, box 3, folder 1, Bearden Papers, available as image 12 at www.aaa.si.edu/collectionsonline/bear roma/container191315.htm.

60. Ellison, "Art of Romare Bearden," 697; Hilton Kramer, "Bearden's Patchwork Cubism," *New York Times,* Dec. 3, 1978, section 2, p. 36; Clement Greenberg, "The Decline of Cubism" (1948), in *The Collected Essays and Criticism,* vol. 2, ed. John O'Brian (Chicago: University of Chicago Press, 1986), 214. On the antecedents of modernist collage, see Diane Waldman, *Collage, Assemblage, and the Found Object* (London: Phaidon, 1992), 8–9; Norman Laliberté, *Collage, Montage, Assemblage: History and Contemporary Techniques* (New York: Van Nostrand Reinhold, 1971), 7. Kobena Mercer argues that Bearden's collages "disclose an understanding of African American identity as something that has itself been 'collaged' by the vicissitudes of modern history." See Kobena Mercer, "Romare Bearden, 1964: Collage as Kunstwollen," in *Cosmopolitan Modernisms,* ed. Kobena Mercer (Cambridge, MA: MIT Press, 2005), 125.

61. Bearden's first collages used material from magazines including *Life, Vogue, Harper's Bazaar, McCall's,* and *Ebony.* See Tomkins, "Profiles," 71–72.

62. Bearden quoted in Childs, "Bearden," 25, 62 (emphasis added); Bearden, "Rectangular Structure," 18; Bearden quoted in Tomkins, "Profiles," 72. "You Are There" was the title of a historical documentary series aired on CBS Television between 1952 and 1957, hosted by Walter Cronkite.

63. Bearden to Quirt, Jan. 20, 1942, frame 605; Bearden Oral History; Ashton, "Romare Bearden," 100.

64. Childs, "Bearden," 53–54; Gail Gelburd, "Romare Bearden in Black-and-White: The Photomontage Projections of 1964," in Gail Gelburd and Thelma Golden, *Romare Bearden in Black-and-White: Photomontage Projections 1964,* ex. cat. (New York: Whitney Museum of American Art, 1997), 25, 29. Childs reproduced Bearden's collage alongside de Hooch's painting, but mistakenly titled the latter *The Spinner and the Housemaid.* See Lee Stephens Glazer, "Signifying Identity: Art and Race in Romare Bearden's Projections," *Art Bulletin* 76 (1994): 419 n.51.

65. W. E. B. Du Bois, *The Philadelphia Negro: A Social Study* (1899; repr., Millwood, NY: Kraus-Thomson, 1973), 193. Bearden's invocation of Cézanne and Velázquez is noted in Glazer, "Signifying Identity," 417, 419. On the importance of ritual in Bearden's art, see Campbell, "History and the Art of Romare Bearden."

66. Glazer, "Signifying Identity," 417; Bearden quoted in Childs, "Bearden," 62; Frantz Fanon, *The Wretched of the Earth,* trans. Constance Farrington (1963; repr., New York: Grove Press, 1966), 252; "Touching at the Core," *Time,* Oct. 27,

320 Notes to Pages 237–242

1967, 64. Bearden's library is housed in the offices of the Romare Bearden Foundation, New York. On the anticolonial critique of Western notions of universality, see King, *Race, Culture, and the Intellectuals,* 239–265.

67. Ellison, *Invisible Man,* 200–202; Murray, *Omni-Americans,* 74, 22. Kobena Mercer points out that Bearden's collage figurations of African American subjects also recall Alain Locke's remark of 1942 that "To be Negro . . . is to be distinctively composite." See Mercer, "Romare Bearden: African American Modernism at Mid-Century," 34.

68. Murray, *Omni-Americans,* 74; "The Artist's Inner Vision," discussion moderated by Alvin C. Hollingsworth, Nov. 21, 1970, cassette recording, Bearden Papers.

69. Thomas Crow, *The Rise of the Sixties: American and European Art in the Era of Dissent, 1955–69* (London: Weidenfeld & Nicolson, 1996), 19. See also Waldman, *Collage, Assemblage, and the Found Object;* Jed Perl, *New Art City: Manhattan at Mid-Century* (New York: Alfred A. Knopf, 2005), 433–463.

70. James Baldwin, *The Fire Next Time* (1963), reprinted in James Baldwin, *Collected Essays,* ed. Toni Morrison (New York: Library of America, 1998), 340; Bearden quoted in Siegel, "Why Spiral?" 49; Romare Bearden, untitled seminar, Oct. 22, 1975, transcript, Bearden Foundation Archive. On the CORE benefit, see Fine, "Spaces Between," 29. On the "devalued status for the human body" and the focus on objects within the "new realism," see Crow, *Rise of the Sixties,* 105.

71. Bearden Oral History; Bearden, "Rectangular Structure," 15. Bearden's ambivalence about the train is in contrast to the celebratory treatment of the train in Murray, *Train Whistle Guitar.* On the gender politics of the train as a liberatory symbol, see Hazel V. Carby, "It Jus Be's Dat Way Sometime: The Sexual Politics of Women's Blues" (1986), in *The Jazz Cadence of American Culture,* ed. Robert G. O'Meally (New York: Columbia University Press, 1998), 476–477.

72. Bearden, "Rectangular Structure," 17; Bearden quoted in Ashton, "Romare Bearden," 109.

73. Bearden Oral History; Bearden quoted in Tomkins, "Profiles," 65. Bearden's recollections of the practices and customs he had encountered among Gypsies—from insurance frauds to the proceedings of Gypsy courts—accord strikingly with an anthropological study of New York's Gypsies by Rena Gropper, a former student of Ruth Benedict. See Bearden Oral History; Bearden quoted in Schwartzman, *Romare Bearden,* 178–179; Rena C. Gropper, *Gypsies in the City: Culture Patterns and Survival* (Princeton, NJ: Darwin Press, 1975), 15, 86–89. On "Foolish-Jack" stories, see Gropper, *Gypsies in the City,* 180.

74. Bearden Oral History; Oscar Lewis, *Five Families: Mexican Case Studies in the Culture of Poverty* (New York: Basic Books, 1959); Albert Murray to Bayard Hooper, n.d. [1965], box 1, folder 2.2b, Murray Papers. On Bearden's retirement from social work, see Aranda-Alvarado et al., "Romare Bearden: A Chronology," 226.

75. Bearden Oral History; Bearden quoted in Childs, "Bearden," 25; Bearden, "Rectangular Structure," 18; Bearden quoted in Siegel, "Why Spiral?" 49; Nnamdi Elleh, "Bearden's Dialogue with Africa and the Avant-Garde," in Fine,

Art of Romare Bearden, 158–161, 171; Campbell, "Romare Bearden," 216. On the tradition of African American identification with the biblical Jews, and the contrary tendency to identify with the civilization of the pharaohs, see Wilson Jeremiah Moses, *Afrotopia: The Roots of African American Popular History* (Cambridge: Cambridge University Press, 1998), 44.

76. Murray quoted in Gates, "King of Cats," 32. For Murray's recollections about the title of *Sermons: In That Number,* see Gail Gelburd, "Bearden in Theory and Ritual: A Conversation with Albert Murray," in Gelburd and Golden, *Romare Bearden in Black-and-White,* 58.

77. Murray, *Omni-American,* 153, 47; Murray Oral History, transcript, Sept. 23, 1994, 245, 241–242; Romare Bearden, untitled typescript, n.d., folder 2, Romare H. Bearden Papers, Schomburg Center for Research in Black Culture, New York.

78. Paul Mocsanyi, untitled foreword in *Protest and Hope: An Exhibition of Contemporary American Art,* ex. cat. (New York: New School for Social Research, 1967), microfilm N68-87, Bearden Papers, frame 239; Bearden quoted in Siegel, "Why Spiral?" 49. On Murray's air force career, see Gates, "King of Cats," 32. On Murray and Ellison's support for American intervention in Vietnam, see Rampersad, *Ralph Ellison,* 438–439; Douglas Brinkley, "Bookend: The Other Vietnam Generation," *New York Times,* Feb. 28, 1999, http://www.nytimes.com/books/99/02/28/bookend/bookend.html. On Murray and Ellison's Cold War liberalism, see Matlin, "Blues under Siege."

79. Bearden Oral History.

80. Ibid.

81. Ibid.; Grace Glueck, "Negro Art from 1800 to 1950 Is on Display at City College," *New York Times,* Oct. 16, 1967, 47–48; Romare Bearden to Mr. Ryder, n.d. [c. 1968], microfilm N68-87, Bearden Papers, frame 27; Robin M. Bennefield, "The Studio Museum Celebrated 30 Years of Uplifting Black Art," *Crisis* (Feb.–Mar. 1998), 43; Grace Glueck, "Minority Artists Find a Welcome at New Showcase," *New York Times,* Dec. 23, 1969, 22.

82. Faith Ringgold, *We Flew over the Bridge* (Durham, NC: Duke University Press, 2005), 167–168; Grace Glueck, "1930's Show at Whitney Picketed by Negro Artists Who Call It Incomplete," *New York Times,* Nov. 18, 1968, 31.

83. Henry Louis Gates Jr., foreword (1995) to *Harlem on My Mind: Cultural Capital of Black America, 1900–1968,* ed. Allon Schoener, rev. ed. (New York: New Press, 1995) [unpaginated]; Allon Schoener, "Introduction to the New Edition" (1995), in Schoener, *Harlem on My Mind* [unpaginated]; John Henrik Clarke to Romare Bearden, Aug. 28, 1968, microfilm N68-87, Bearden Papers, frame 155.

84. Romare Bearden to Allon [Schoener], June 6, 1968, microfilm N68-87, Bearden Papers, frame 8; "'Harlem on My Mind' Exhibition," leaflet, n.d., microfilm N68-87, Bearden Papers, frame 16; Jeffrey Magee, *Irving Berlin's American Musical Theater* (New York: Oxford University Press, 2012), 185–186.

85. Bearden to Schoener, June 6, 1968, frame 8; Schoener, "Introduction to the New Edition" [unpaginated]; Candice Van Ellison, introduction (1968) to Schoener, *Harlem on My Mind* [unpaginated]; Benny Andrews, "Benny Andrews'

Journal: A Black Artist's View of Artistic and Political Activism, 1963–1973," in Campbell, *Tradition and Conflict,* 69; Bearden quoted in Tomkins, "Profiles," 76. On the exhibition, see also Steven C. Dubin, *Displays of Power: Controversy in the American Museum from the Enola Gay to Sensation* (New York: New York University Press, 2001), 18–63.

86. Romare Bearden to Ralph Ellison, n.d. [1969], box 37, folder 6, Ralph Ellison Papers, Manuscript Division, Library of Congress, Washington, DC; "The Black Artist in America: A Symposium," *Metropolitan Museum of Art Bulletin* 27 (Jan. 1969): 248, 251–252; Bearden, "Rectangular Structure," 11; Romare Bearden to Reginald Gammon, Mar. 13, 1971, Reginald Gammon Papers (unprocessed), Archives of American Art, Smithsonian Institution, Washington, DC (hereafter cited as Gammon Papers); Ellison, "Art of Romare Bearden," 693.

87. John Canaday, "Romare Bearden Focuses on the Negro," *New York Times,* Oct. 14, 1967, 23; Bearden Oral History; Fine, "Spaces Between," 44; Bearden quoted in Tomkins, "Profiles," 72.

88. "Touching at the Core," 64; Cathy Aldridge, "Bearden's Collages Sold though Exhibit Goes On," New York *Amsterdam News,* Nov. 4, 1967, 23; *Time,* Nov. 1, 1968; Vincent Cannato, *The Ungovernable City: John Lindsay and the Struggle to Save New York* (New York: Basic Books, 2002); Artinomis, "In the Galleries: Romare Bearden at Cordier & Eckstrom," *Arts Magazine,* Mar. 1970, 57.

89. Ringgold, *We Flew over the Bridge,* 171; Aranda-Alvarado et al., "Romare Bearden: A Chronology," 230–231.

90. Douglas Davis, "Putting Things Together," *Newsweek,* Apr. 5, 1971, 52–53; Romare Bearden to Reginald Gammon, Oct. 26, 1970, Gammon Papers (unprocessed); Charles Allen, "Have the Walls Come Tumbling Down?" *New York Times,* Apr. 11, 1971, D28.

91. Henderson quoted in Tomkins, "Profiles," 53. Bearden and Henderson coauthored two books of art history: Romare Bearden and Harry Henderson, *Six Black Masters of American Art* (New York: Zenith Books, 1972), for juveniles; and *History of African-American Artists,* for adults, published five years after Bearden's death.

92. Murray, *Stomping the Blues,* 20; David Bourdon, "Music to the Eyes," *Village Voice,* Mar. 10, 1975, 34; Kramer, "Bearden's 'Patchwork Cubism,'" 36; "Interviews: Romare Bearden" (Dec. 9, 1984), in *Since the Harlem Renaissance: 50 Years of Afro-American Art,* ex. cat (Lewisburg, PA: Center Gallery of Bucknell University, 1985), 13; Bearden quoted in Carlyle C. Douglas, "Romare Bearden," *Ebony,* Nov. 1975, 122. On Bearden's time on St. Martin, see Romare Bearden, "An Artist's Renewal in the Sun," *New York Times Magazine,* Oct. 2, 1983, 46–52. Madhu Dubey has argued that a similar nostalgia for southern black folk life in much African American literature since the 1970s has served as a mode of "escape" from the ongoing urban crisis. See Madhu Dubey, *Signs and Cities: Black Literary Postmodernism* (Chicago: University of Chicago Press, 2003), 144–185.

93. Preston, "Bonnard Retrospective," frame 381; Allen, "Have the Walls Come Tumbling Down?" D28; Ashton, "Romare Bearden," 100; Bearden, "Rectangular Structure," 18.

94. Bearden Oral History; "What's News, What's Coming: Romare Bearden," *Vogue,* Feb. 1981, 38. On the decline of urban rioting after 1968 and the corresponding demotion of the urban crisis within the national agenda, see Thomas F. Pettigrew, "Black Unrest in the 1960s," in *Social Policy and Public Policy: Inequality and Justice,* ed. Lee Rainwater (1974; repr., New Brunswick, NJ: Transaction Publishers, 2009), 223–224; Carlo Rotella, *October Cities: The Redevelopment of Urban Literature* (Berkeley: University of California Press, 1998), 216.

95. "Object: Diversity," *Time,* Apr. 6, 1970; Michael D. Harris, "Urban Totems: The Communal Spirit of Black Murals," in *Walls of Heritage, Walls of Pride: African American Murals,* ed. James Prigoff and Robin J. Dunitz (San Francisco: Pomegranate, 2000), 24–43; Grace Glueck, "Negroes' Art Is What's In Just Now," *New York Times,* Feb. 27, 1969, 34; Campbell, "Tradition and Conflict," 56.

96. Kimmerman, "Life's Abundance," E32; Murray Oral History, July 1, 1994, transcript, 161; Bearden quoted in Joy Hakanson Colby, "Getting Back on an Upward Spiral," *Detroit News,* June 28, 1989, 3D.

Epilogue

1. Kenneth B. Clark, *Dark Ghetto: Dilemmas of Social Power* (New York: Harper & Row, 1965), xxiii, xvii, 11; Reminiscences of Kenneth B. Clark, Sept. 9, 1976, transcript, 384, Oral History Collection of Columbia University in the City of New York.

2. LeRoi Jones, "BLACK DADA NIHILISMUS," in *The Dead Lecturer* (New York: Grove Press, 1964), 61–64; LeRoi Jones, *"Dutchman" and "The Slave": Two Plays by LeRoi Jones* (New York: Morrow Quill Paperbacks, 1964), quotation at 31; Amiri Baraka interviewed by Komozi Woodard, Jan. 4, 1986, transcript, in *The Black Power Movement, Part I: Amiri Baraka from Black Arts to Black Radicalism,* ed. Komozi Woodard (microfilm, 9 reels) (Bethesda, MD: University Publications of America, 2000), reel 8, frames 585–586; LeRoi Jones, "HOME" (1965), in *Home: Social Essays* (1966; Hopewell, NJ: Ecco Press, 1998), 9–10.

3. Oral history interview with Romare Bearden [by Henri Ghent], June 29, 1968, transcript, Archives of American Art, Smithsonian Institution, Washington, DC, http://www.aaa.si.edu/collections/interviews/oral-history-interview-romare-bearden-11481; Charles Childs, "Bearden: Identification and Identity," *ARTnews,* Oct. 1964, 62; Calvin Tomkins, "Profiles: Putting Something over Something Else," *New Yorker,* Nov. 28, 1977, 72; Romare Bearden, "Rectangular Structure in My Montage Paintings," *Leonardo* 2, no. 1 (1969): 18; Stuart Preston, "Bonnard Retrospective at Modern Museum," *New York Times,* Oct. 10, 1964, microfilm N68–87, Romare Bearden Papers, Archives of American Art, Smithsonian Institution, Washington, DC, frame 381.

4. "John Dewey Discussion," transcript, 42, box 192, folder 4, Kenneth B. Clark Papers, Manuscript Division, Library of Congress, Washington, DC; Jerry Gafio Watts, *Heroism and the Black Intellectual: Ralph Ellison, Politics, and Afro-American Intellectual Life* (Chapel Hill: University of North Carolina Press, 1994), 119–120; Jeanne Siegel, "Why Spiral?" *ARTnews,* Sept. 1966, 51; Childs, "Bearden," 62.

5. Ross Posnock, *Color and Culture: Black Writers and the Making of the Modern Intellectal* (Cambridge, MA: Harvard University Press, 1998), 5; W. E. B. Du Bois, *The Souls of Black Folk: Essays and Sketches* (1903; repr., London: Archibald Constable & Co., 1905), 4.

6. John Hannigan, *Fantasy City: Pleasure and Profit in the Postmodern Metropolis* (London: Routledge, 1998); Monique M. Taylor, *Harlem between Heaven and Hell* (Minneapolis: University of Minnesota Press, 2002); Ange-Marie Hancock, *The Politics of Disgust: The Public Identity of the Welfare Queen* (New York: New York University Press, 2004); Katheryn Russell-Brown, *The Color of Crime,* 2nd ed. (New York: New York University Press, 2009); Tricia Rose, *The Hip Hop Wars: What We Talk about When We Talk about Hip Hop—and Why It Matters* (New York: Basic Books, 2008); Nathan D. Abrams, "Antonio's B-Boys: Rap, Rappers, and Gramsci's Intellectuals," *Popular Music and Society* 19 (Winter 1995): 1–19; Henry Louis Gates Jr., "2 Live Crew, Decoded," *New York Times,* June 19, 1990, A23. On the suburban majority in the United States, see James T. Patterson, *Restless Giant: The United States from Watergate to* Bush v. Gore (New York: Oxford University Press, 2005), 322.

7. Michael Bérubé, "Public Academy," *New Yorker,* Jan. 9, 1995, 73–80; Robert Boynton, "The New Intellectuals," *Atlantic Monthly,* Mar. 1995, 53–70; Henry Louis Gates Jr. and Cornel West, *The Future of the Race* (New York: Alfred A. Knopf, 1996), xv–xvi; Jonathan Scott Holloway, "The Black Intellectual and the 'Crisis Canon' in the Twentieth Century," *Black Scholar* 31 (Spring 2001): 9–10; bell hooks, *Salvation: Black People and Love* (New York: William Morrow, 2001); Michael Eric Dyson, *Debating Race with Michael Eric Dyson* (New York: Basic Civitas Books, 2007); Martha Biondi, *The Black Revolution on Campus* (Berkeley: University of California Press, 2012); Fabio Rojas, *From Black Power to Black Studies: How a Radical Social Movement Became an Academic Discipline* (Baltimore: Johns Hopkins University Press, 2007). See also Ethan Goffman, "The (Not So) New Black Public Intellectuals, from the Nineties to the Oughts," in *The New York Public Intellectuals and Beyond: Exploring Liberal Humanism, Jewish Identity, and the American Protestant Tradition,* ed. Ethan Goffman and Daniel Morris (West Lafayette, IN: Purdue University Press, 2009), 194–212.

8. William M. Banks and Joseph Jewell, "Intellectuals and the Persisting Significance of Race," *Journal of Negro Education* 64 (1995): 75–86; Jonathan Scott Holloway, "The Black Scholar, the Humanities, and the Politics of Racial Knowledge since 1945," in *The Humanities and the Dynamics of Social Inclusion since World War II,* ed. David A. Hollinger (Baltimore: Johns Hopkins University Press, 2006), 239, 241; Michael L. Ondaatje, *Black Conservative Intellectuals in Modern America* (Philadelphia: University of Pennsylvania Press, 2009); Thomas Sowell, *Civil Rights: Rhetoric or Reality?* (New York: William Morrow, 1984); Shelby Steele, *The Content of Our Character: A New Vision of Race in America* (New York: HarperPerennial, 1991); Charles M. Blow, "Black in the Age of Obama," *New York Times,* Dec. 4, 2009, www.nytimes.com/2009/12/05/opinion/05blow.html.

9. Warren J. Carson, untitled review of Roberta S. Maguire, ed., *Conversations with Albert Murray* (Jackson: University Press of Mississippi, 1997), *African Ameri-*

can Review 34 (2000): 547; publisher's description of Michael Eric Dyson, *Between God and Gangsta Rap: Bearing Witness to Black Culture* (New York: Oxford University Press, 1996), http://www.oup.com/us/catalog/general/subject/Literature English/AmericanLiterature/AfricanAmerican/?view=usa&ci=9780195115697; Percival Everett, *Erasure: A Novel* (New York: Hyperion, 2001); Sharifa Rhodes-Pitts, *Harlem Is Nowhere: A Journey to the Mecca of Black America* (New York: Little, Brown, 2011), 118; Albert Murray, *The Omni-Americans: New Perspectives on Black Experience and American Culture* (New York: Outerbridge & Dienstfrey, 1970), 69. On African American novelists' responses to the problems of racial representation intensified by widening class divisions, see Madhu Dubey, *Signs and Cities: Black Literary Postmodernism* (Chicago: University of Chicago Press, 2003).

10. Carlo Rotella, *October Cities: The Redevelopment of Urban Literature* (Berkeley: University of California Press, 1998), 216; Michael B. Katz, "The Urban 'Underclass' as a Metaphor of Social Transformation," in *The "Underclass" Debate: Views from History,* ed. Michael B. Katz (Princeton, NJ: Princeton University Press, 1993), 3–23, esp. 17; Gunnar Myrdal, *Challenge to Affluence* (New York: Pantheon Books, 1963), 34; Dinesh D'Souza, *The End of Racism: Principles for a Multiracial Society* (New York: Free Press, 1995); Loïc Wacquant, " 'A Black City within the White': Revisiting America's Dark Ghetto," *Black Renaissance—Renaissance Noire* 2 (1998): 141–151.

11. Daryl Michael Scott, *Contempt and Pity: Social Policy and the Image of the Damaged Black Psyche, 1880–1996* (Chapel Hill: University of North Carolina Press, 1997), 187–202; Toni Morrison, *Beloved: A Novel* (New York: Alfred A. Knopf, 1987); James Berger, "Ghosts of Liberalism: Morrison's *Beloved* and the Moynihan Report," *PMLA* 111 (1996): 408–420; Cornel West, "Black Sexuality" (1993), in *Race Matters,* rev. ed. (Boston: Beacon Press, 2001), 85; Cornel West, "Preface 2001: Democracy Matters in Race Matters," in *Race Matters,* xiii; bell books, *Rock My Soul: Black People and Self-Esteem* (New York: Atria Books), 161–172.

12. Haki Madhubuti and Maulana Karenga, eds., *Million Man March/Day of Absence: A Commemorative Anthology* (Chicago: Third World Press, 1996); Theodore M. Shaw, "Beyond What Bill Cosby Said," *Washington Post,* May 27, 2004, A31.

13. William Julius Wilson, *The Truly Disadvantaged: The Inner City, the Underclass, and Public Policy* (Chicago: University of Chicago Press, 1987), 21; Adolph Reed Jr., "The Liberal Technocrat," *Nation,* Feb. 6, 1988, 167–170; *Precious: Based on the Novel "Push" by Sapphire,* dir. Lee Daniels (Lionsgate, 2009); Sapphire, *Push* (New York: Alfred A. Knopf, 1996); Armond White, "Pride & Precious," *New York Press,* Nov. 4, 2009, www.nypress.com/pride-precious/.

14. Michael B. Katz, "The Existential Problem of Urban Studies," *Dissent* 57 (Fall 2010): 65, 68. For a sample of the wider scholarly debate about "structure" and "agency," see Gabrielle M. Spiegel, ed., *Practicing History: New Directions in Historical Writing after the Linguistic Turn* (New York: Routledge, 2005); James C. Scott, *Domination and the Arts of Resistance: Hidden Transcripts* (New Haven, CT:

Yale University Press, 1990); Walter Johnson, "On Agency," *Journal of Social History* 37 (Fall 2003): 113–124.

15. Robin D. G. Kelley, *Yo' Mama's Disfunktional! Fighting the Culture Wars in Urban America* (Boston: Beacon Press, 1997), 2, 4, 73.

16. Hazel Carby, "The Politics of Fiction, Anthropology, and the Folk: Zora Neale Hurston," in *History and Memory in African-American Culture,* ed. Geneviève Fabre and Robert O'Meally (New York: Oxford University Press, 1994), 41, quoted in Holloway, "Black Scholar," 239; Murray, *Omni-Americans,* 7; Zora Neale Hurston, *Their Eyes Were Watching God: A Novel* (Philadelphia: J. B. Lippincott, 1937). For a collection of essays arguing for the importance of pleasure in African American experience, see Monique Guillory and Richard C. Green, eds., *Soul: Black Power, Politics, and Pleasure* (New York: New York University Press, 2008).

17. Scott, *Contempt and Pity,* 168; Ralph Ellison, "The Charlie Christian Story" (1958), in *The Collected Essays of Ralph Ellison,* ed. John F. Callahan (New York: Modern Library, 1995), 270.

Acknowledgments

On the Corner bears the imprints of countless people and institutions whose help I've benefited from in innumerable ways. Crossing the Atlantic to conduct research is an expensive habit, and I've been extremely fortunate to receive generous funding from the Arts and Humanities Research Council, the Glenfield Trust, and the Master and Fellows of Christ's College, Cambridge. Reproducing fine art images has also involved daunting outlays and would not have been possible without assistance from the Master and Fellows of Christ's College, Cambridge, and the Department of History and the School of Arts and Humanities at King's College London.

Some sections of Chapter 2 of this book expand on ideas previously explored in my article " 'Lift Up Yr Self!' Reinterpreting Amiri Baraka (LeRoi Jones), Black Power, and the Uplift Tradition," *Journal of American History* 93 (June 2006): 91–116. Portions of the Introduction, Chapters 1 and 3, and the Epilogue were previously published in "Who Speaks for Harlem? Kenneth B. Clark, Albert Murray, and the Controversies of Black Urban Life," *Journal of American Studies* 46 (Nov. 2012): 875–894, and are used by permission.

This book's dedication is a small, all-too-belated expression of thanks to someone whose impact on my life, and many other people's, would require a book-length acknowledgment in itself. As far as my own education goes, before there was American history, there was jazz and there was Fergus Read. His unbounded talent, energy, and enthusiasm for music, teaching, and friendship elude my efforts at description. Thanks, too, to Ulfet Read, whose continuing friendship I greatly value.

That my musical interests developed into a fascination with American history and culture more broadly conceived is thanks in large measure to Michael O'Brien. From my undergraduate work on jazz, race, and identity to my doctoral research, Michael offered far more by way of intellectual insight, encouragement, reassurance, patience, and commitment than any student could reasonably hope for. As a generous and tireless supporter of my research and career, Tony Badger also has my very deep gratitude.

Many other teachers, friends, and colleagues during my ten years of studying and teaching in Cambridge contributed in one way or another to my ability to undertake this project and see it through. I'm extremely thankful to all those in the following, inevitably truncated list: Susan Bayly, Duncan Bell, William Dusinberre, Patrick Flack, Nancy Hewitt, Joel Isaac, Sam James, Max Jones, James Kloppenberg, Steven Lawson, Mike Lewis, Elizabeth Lundeen, Catherine Maddison, Rachel Malkin, William O'Reilly, Andrew Preston, David Reynolds, John Thompson, Sebastiaan Verweij, and Brittany Wellner James. I owe huge thanks to Robin Vandome and Andrew Fearnley, whose friendship and constant generosity with their ideas—together with the example of their own scholarship—have been a tremendous source of support and inspiration.

Christ's College, Cambridge, where I was an undergraduate and graduate student and held the A. H. Lloyd Research Fellowship, was a wonderful place to live, learn, and teach. I'm grateful to all those whom I studied under or worked alongside at Christ's, at Cambridge's American History Seminar, and at the Centre for History and Economics at Magdalene College and King's College, Cambridge. I'm very lucky to have spent two years as a Leverhulme Early Career Fellow in the School of History at Queen Mary, University of London. More recently, I've been privileged to join the hugely dynamic, collegial, and supportive Department of History at King's College London, and I'm grateful to my colleagues and students there, and in the Institute of North American Studies at King's, for making me so welcome as I was bringing this project to completion.

Further afield, in the course of researching and writing this book I've accrued a large debt of thanks to many people who have answered queries, read work-in-progress, discussed my ideas, and shaped my thinking about my project, including Phil Dray, Daniel Geary, Kate Clark Harris, Jonathan Scott Holloway, Ashley Howard, Daniel Immerwahr, E. Ethelbert Miller, Selina Mills, Leah Mullen, Matthew Mullen, Craig Schiffert, Daryl Michael Scott, Stephanie Steiker, Michele Wallace, Ronald Walters, and Komozi Woodard. Richard King first introduced me to the work of Romare Bearden, and has read and commented on virtually everything I've written since I was a graduate student—I'm immensely grateful for the generous and insightful attention he's given my work.

Among the many librarians, archivists, and curators who went out of their way to assist me are Joellen El Bashir of the Moorland-Spingarn Research Center at Howard University, Alice Lotvin Birney of the Library of Congress, all the staff in the Manuscript Division of the Schomburg Center for Research in Black Culture, Elizabeth Botten of the Smithsonian Institution's

Archives of American Art, Aimee Soubier of the Hirshhorn Museum and Sculpture Garden, Mary Lee Corlett of the National Gallery of Art, and James Hatch and Camille Billops, who have subsequently donated their extraordinary archive of materials on the history of African American visual and performing arts to Emory University. A special word of thanks is due to Ruth Fine, formerly Curator of Special Projects in Modern Art at the National Gallery of Art, for her many helpful responses to my questions about Bearden. The tireless support of Diedra Harris-Kelley and her colleagues at the Romare Bearden Foundation has been immensely important in enabling me to complete this project. I was fortunate in 2006 to spend several months, with the support of the Arts and Humanities Research Council, as a British Research Council Fellow at the John W. Kluge Center at the Library of Congress. I thank Carolyn Brown, Mary Lou Reker, and my colleagues at the Kluge Center for providing such a stimulating place to work at a crucial point in the development of my ideas.

For their extraordinary hospitality and friendship during my visits to New York City and Washington, D.C., and for all their valuable questions and comments about my research, I'm enormously grateful to Emily Vargas-Barón, Inga Adams Pizarro, Fernando Pizarro, Roman and Halina Frydman, and Helena Hessel. Their generosity and companionship made my visits to the United States hugely enjoyable and contributed in a multitude of ways to my ability to finish this book. I'm deeply grateful. Those in London, Cambridge, and elsewhere whose friendship saw me through the various highs and lows of the years I've spent on this project are too numerous to mention here, but I hope they realize how important they've been to me.

I'm grateful to Kathleen McDermott, my editor at Harvard University Press, for her confidence in this book and her patience and guidance in seeing me through the publication process. Thanks are also due to Andrew Kinney and others at HUP who have worked on the book, and to the two anonymous readers for the Press whose detailed and insightful reports on the manuscript have enabled me to clarify and develop my arguments in a number of ways.

My parents, Irena and Stephen, have given me so much, in so many ways, that it's difficult to know what to thank them for. During long car journeys on family holidays many years ago, I demanded a running commentary on the *1812 Overture* ("the French soldiers are retreating . . .") and they have been aiding and abetting my interest in the past ever since. More recently, my mother's knowledge of and passion for art and our visits to museums and galleries helped to make one part of this project possible. My father and my sister, Arianne, both know the ins and outs of academic life and provided sage advice and reassurance when these were needed. A final, enormous thank you to Heather Goldstein, without whose love, kindness, patience, and humor this book would never have been completed.

Index

Brown, Edmund, 72
Brown, Elaine, 10, 174
Brown, H. Rap, 150, 172, 173
Brown, James, 131–132
Brown, Marion, 153–154
Brown, Sterling, 133
Browne, George Byron, 210
Brown v. Board of Education, 4, 36, 39, 43, 47,
    54–56, 79–81, 110, 122
Broyard, Anatole, 207
Brueghel the Elder, Pieter, 199, 204–205,
    213, 227, 228, 231
Bullins, Ed, 151
Bunche, Ralph, 53, 54
Burroughs, William, 132
"Business and the Urban Crisis" *(Time),* 7

Cabral, Amilcar, 192
Calder, Alexander, 210
Campbell, Elmer Simms, 202–203
Campbell, Mary Schmidt, 198, 206,
    226–227, 241, 242, 254
Canaday, John, 249
Caravaggio, 235
Carby, Hazel, 266
The Card Players (Cézanne), 235
The Cardsharps (Caravaggio), 235
Caribbean immigrants. *See* West Indian
    immigrants
Carmichael, Stokely, 98–99, 148, 150, 168
Carson, Rachel, 31
Castro, Fidel, 21, 135
Cayton, Horace, 22, 59
the celebratory: in Bearden's work, 198–199,
    226, 251–253, 254, 255; in Murray's work,
    17–18, 73, 199, 221–222, 266
Central Harlem, 19, 20
Cézanne, Paul, 235
Challenge to Affluence (Myrdal), 264
Chandler, Dana, 254
Chappell, David, 165
Cheever, John, 23
Cherry Lane Theater, 5–6, 143
Chicago riot (1919), 107
Childs, Charles, 200–201, 232–233, 234
China, 117
Chomsky, Noam, 26
Christian, Charlie, 266–267
Chu, Petra Ten Doesschate, 229
Cinque Gallery, 245
Circus (Circus: The Artist's Center Ring)
    (Bearden), *figure 8,* 213

"The City Is the Black Man's Land" (Boggs
    & Boggs), 149
"City of Harlem" (Baraka), 137
Civil Rights Act, 4, 41, 46
civil rights movement: and American
    political culture, 94–95; Baraka's criticism
    of, 136, 138; Bearden's response to, 34,
    217–220, 224–225, 227; black artists,
    responsibilities/obligations, 220, 224–225,
    227; black power movement's critique of,
    98; Clark in relation to, 94–95, 98, 121;
    fractures in, 132; gender ideologies, 178;
    HARYOU's role in preparing youth for,
    89–90; pathologism of, 168; pop art
    depictions of, 238; reinvigoration of, 33,
    135; violence increasing in, 40–41;
    women's role in, 10
Clark, Arthur, 25, 51, 52
Clark, Beulah, 51
Clark, Hilton, 50
Clark, Kate, 50
Clark, Kenneth B.: Adlerian psychology,
    48–49, 100, 112–113; background, 25–26,
    42–43, 50–56, 77–78; Baldwin and, 4, 12,
    16, 25, 41–42, 57, 59–60; Baraka and, 5–6,
    12, 39, 132, 145, 154, 159, 174, 186;
    Bearden and, 12, 25–26, 200, 210, 237,
    254; as a black intellectual, 9–10, 32–34,
    40, 56–57, 111–112, 117–118, 121–122,
    256–257, 259–260; black power movement
    and, 5, 39, 96–100, 186; civil rights
    movement, relationship with, 94–95, 98,
    121; community action, ideas concerning,
    38–39, 90–94, 97, 100, 106, 108–109;
    conservative politics, response to, 110,
    254; damage thesis, 13, 15–16, 17, 39,
    47–49, 62–63, 79–83, 86, 259; disillusion-
    ment, 38, 39, 40, 106–110, 117, 121;
    Ellison and, 14, 25, 58, 69; on ghetto, use
    of term, 23, 24, 48; Harlem riot (1964)
    and, 1–2, 3, 7–8, 85–88; influences on,
    48–49, 53, 54, 56, 58–60, 112, 118;
    integration, commitment to, 35, 36–37,
    39, 50, 54, 76–77, 82, 96–97; Kennedy
    meeting, 40–42; liberal political
    leadership, view of, 38, 39–40, 102, 106,
    108, 120; mental health, radical concep-
    tion of, 16, 38, 79, 80–86, 93–94, 99–100;
    Murray and, 14, 17–18, 25, 29, 69–75, 237,
    265; pathologism of, 13–16, 39, 60–73,
    78–79; photograph of, *figure 1;* Powell and,
    103–106, 118; racial equality/justice,
    pursuit of, 36, 39–40, 47, 50, 53–56,

respect for, 217, 262; on social sciences, 240–241; on Spiral group, 218–219; on "U.S. Negro culture," 221

Murray, Albert, Bearden and: artistic alliance, 198, 216; on collage (photomontage) aesthetic of, 218, 225–226, 252; divergence, areas of, 18, 198–200, 216–221, 227, 229, 237, 240–244; endorsement of, 14, 222; friendship, 18, 73, 198, 215–216; intellectual relationship, 214, 215–216; *Projections,* concerns over, 218–219, 222; similarities, 14, 198, 200, 216; on works of, 218, 225–226

Murray, Albert, works: the celebratory in, 17–18, 73, 199, 221–222, 266; *The Omni-Americans,* 69–75, 223, 236–237, 243; romanticization of black urban life, 17–18, 73–75, 199, 222, 229, 265–267; "Social Science Fiction in Harlem," 70, 74; *Stomping the Blues,* 226, 252; *Train Whistle Guitar,* 222–223

Museum without Walls concept, 200, 213, 214, 228, 236, 237, 260

Muste, A. J., 147

Myrdal, Gunnar, 45, 56, 58, 59, 264

National Advisory Commission on Civil Disorders. *See* Kerner Commission (National Advisory Commission on Civil Disorders)

National Association for the Advancement of Colored People (NAACP), 54, 79, 98, 136, 138, 203

National Committee for a Sane Nuclear Policy, 116

National Institute of Arts and Letters, 250

National Urban League, 98, 105, 136, 209

Nation of Islam, 4, 21, 96, 138, 149, 155, 157, 158, 159, 160, 170, 264. *See also* Black Muslims

Native Son (Wright), 59

The Nature of Prejudice (Allport), 47

Nazism, 24, 106–107. *See also* concentration camps; Holocaust

Neal, Larry, 148, 149, 150–151, 152, 154–155, 168

Négritude, 218, 220–221

The Negro American (Clark & Parsons, eds.), 98

"The Negro Artist and Modern Art" (Bearden), 209–210

"The Negro Artist's Dilemma" (Bearden), 201, 209, 213, 224, 232

Negroes with Guns (Williams), 170

The Negro Family (Moynihan). *See* Moynihan Report

The Negro Ghetto (Weaver), 23

"A Negro Looks at 'Black Power'" (Clark), 5

"The Negro's War" *(Fortune),* 205

"Negro-to-Black Conversion Experience," 170

Newark, New Jersey: Black Power Conference, 172–173; police violence, 171–172; riots, 3, 6, 88, 107, 171–173; urban crisis, 158, 171, 174–175

Newark, New Jersey, Baraka and: birthplace of, 6, 26, 123; *A Black Mass* production, 156; black power leader in, 16, 186; black self-government goal, 173, 175–176; childhood, 26, 133, 136; continued residence, 193; firearms possession conviction, 172; Kawaida Towers project, 190–191; nationalist urban redevelopment, 189–191; political mobilization, 98, 169, 173, 175–176; portrayal of black community in, 21, 158–159, 187–188, 191–192; "Raise!" (monthly column in *Black NewArk*), 131, 188; return to, 6, 26, 124, 125, 126, 156; riots, 171–173; in "The Screamers," 139–140; self-identity, 125–126; urban crisis analysis, 174–175, 192–193; vision of regeneration, 161, 175–176, 184, 186. *See also* Committee for Unified Newark (CFUN); Spirit House

New Deal, 25, 222

New Left activists, 39, 94–95, 185

Newman, Barnett, 211

"New Negro," 20, 208

"new Negro" concept of King, 165, 170

new realism, 238

Newton, Huey, 148, 169

New York School, 210

New York State Board of Regents, 121

New York subway, 5–6, 18, 132, 143–144, 145, 153

"New York: The Breakdown of a City" *(Time),* 7

New York University, 202–203, 214, 219

Nguvu, Saidi, 182–183, 184

Niebuhr, Reinhold, 145

The 1930's: Painting and Sculpture in America (exhibition), 246

Nixon, Richard, administration, 109–110

Nkrumah, Kwame, 192